D1557214

That May Know Him

That May Know Him

A life in Christ is a life of restfulness. There may be no ecstasy of feeling, but there should be an abiding, peaceful trust. Your hope is not in yourself; it is in Christ. Your weakness is united to His strength, your ignorance to His wisdom, your frailty to His enduring might. So you are not to look to yourself, not to let the mind dwell upon self, but look to Christ. Let the mind dwell upon His love, upon the beauty, the perfection, of His character. Christ in His self-denial, Christ in His humiliation, Christ in His purity and holiness, Christ in His matchless love—this is the subject for the soul's contemplation. It is by loving Him, copying Him, depending wholly upon Him, that you are to be transformed into His likeness.—Steps to Christ, pp. 70, 71.

Ellen G. White

REVIEW AND HERALD® PUBLISHING ASSOCIATION
HAGERSTOWN, MD 21740

Copyright © 1964, renewed 1992 by
THE ELLEN G. WHITE PUBLICATIONS
PRINTED IN THE U.S.A.

Cover design copyright © 2003 by Review and Herald® Publishing
Association

Cover illlustration: *Road to Emmaus* ©Greg Olsen. By arrangement with
Mill Pond Press, Inc. Venice, Florida, 34292. For information on the art
prints by Greg Olsen, please contact Mill Pond Press at 1-800--535-0331.

Library of Congress Catalog Card No. 64-17650

ISBN 0-8280-1789-1

To order, call **1-800-765-6955**
Visit us at www.reviewandherald.org for more information on
Review and Herald® products.

FOREWORD

Those who are familiar with the Ellen G. White writings and who have treasured devotional books from her inspired pen in the past will welcome this volume from the same rich source. More than half of the book is drawn from the wealth of inspired material in the articles from her pen that appeared during her long lifetime in such periodicals as the *Review and Herald, Youth's Instructor, and Signs of the Times*. About one third is drawn from previously unpublished manuscripts and letters in the custody of the trustees of the Ellen G. White writings, under whose direction the volume has been prepared. Many of these items are from personal heart-to-heart messages sent to individuals—messages that come to us today with the same earnest appeal, the same tender admonition and encouragement, as when they were written. Of special interest are several pages that contain extracts from early morning entries in Ellen White's diary, and give the reader significant glimpses into her personal prayer life.

In order to bring each reading into the compass of a single page, frequent deletions have been necessary, and these are indicated in the usual way. Great care has been exercised to preserve without distortion the thought and intent of the writer. It should be noted that when lines from a hymn or a poem appear they were quoted by Ellen White herself. The daily Bible verses have been chosen to harmonize with the message of each day.

That I May Know Him goes forth with our prayer that it may truly help each reader to become better acquainted with Jesus, our Lord and Savior. It is our hope that each may gain a deeper appreciation of His amazing sacrifice for the lost human race, gain clearer views of the beauty and perfection of His character, and understand better the heights we may reach in our own character development as clothed in the garments of His righteousness, we strive to become "complete in Him."

THE TRUSTEES OF THE ELLEN G. WHITE® ESTATE
Silver Spring, MD

"THAT I MAY KNOW *HIM*"

"But what things were gain to me, those I counted loss for Christ. Yea doubtless, and I count all things but loss for the excellency of the knowledge of Christ Jesus my Lord. . . . That I may know him, and the power of his resurrection, and the fellowship of his sufferings, being made conformable unto his death; if by any means I might attain unto the resurrection of the dead." Philippians 3:7-11.

"And this is life eternal, that they might know thee the only true God, and Jesus Christ, whom thou hast sent." John 17:3.

"Acquaint now thyself with him, and be at peace." Job 22:21.

"It would be well for us to spend a thoughtful hour each day in contemplation of the life of Christ. We should take it point by point, and let the imagination grasp each scene, especially the closing ones. As we thus dwell upon His great sacrifice for us, our confidence in Him will be more constant, our love will be quickened, and we shall be more deeply imbued with His spirit."—The Desire of Ages, *p. 83.*

UNLOCK THE STOREHOUSE!

Unto me, who am less than the least of all saints, is this grace given, that I should preach among the Gentiles the unsearchable riches of Christ. Eph. 3:8.

In the Word of God there are rich mines of truth that we may spend our whole lifetime in exploring, and yet we shall find that we have only begun to view their precious stores. . . . There are unsearchable riches for us. It will take us all eternity to comprehend the riches of the glory of God and of Jesus Christ. . . .

Christ has said: "If any man thirst, let him come unto me, and drink" (John 7:37). Have you exhausted the fountain? No, for it is inexhaustible. Just as soon as you feel your need, you may drink, and drink again. The fountain is always full. And when you have once drunk of that fountain you will not be seeking to quench your thirst from the broken cisterns of this world; you will not be studying how you can find the most pleasure, amusement, fun, and frolic. No, because you have been drinking from the stream which makes glad the city of God. Then your joy will be full, for Christ will be in you.[1]

Jehovah Immanuel—He "in whom are hid all the treasures of wisdom and knowledge," in whom dwells "all the fulness of the Godhead bodily" (Col. 2:3, 9)—to be brought into sympathy with Him, to know Him, to possess Him, as the heart opens more and more to receive His attributes; to know His love and power, to possess the unsearchable riches of Christ, to comprehend more and more "what is the breadth, and length, and depth, and height; and to know the love of Christ, which passeth knowledge, that ye might be filled with all the fulness of God" (Eph. 3:18, 19)—"this is the heritage of the servants of the Lord, and their righteousness is of me, saith the Lord" (Isa. 54:17).[2]

There is no need for us to hunger, there is no need for us to thirst, while the storehouse of heaven is open for us and the key is given into our possession. What is the key? Faith, which is the gift of God. Unlock the storehouse; take of its rich treasures.[3]

WHERE WISDOM BEGINS

The fear of the Lord is the beginning of wisdom: and the knowledge of the holy is understanding. Prov. 9:10.

There is a wide difference between what God has given men capacity to become, and the degree of excellence to which they actually attain.[4]

The Word of God presents the most potent means of education, as well as the most valuable source of knowledge, within the reach of man. The understanding adapts itself to the dimensions of the subjects with which it is required to deal. If occupied with trivial, commonplace matters only, never summoned to earnest effort to comprehend great and eternal truths, it becomes dwarfed and enfeebled. Hence the value of the Scriptures, as a means of intellectual culture. . . . They lead directly to the contemplation of the most exalted, the most ennobling, and the most stupendous truths that are presented to the mind of man. They direct our thoughts to the infinite Author of all things. We see revealed the character of the Eternal, and listen to His voice as He communes with patriarchs and prophets. We see explained the mysteries of His providence, the great problems which have engaged the attention of every thoughtful mind, but which, without the aid of revelation, human intellect seeks in vain to solve. They open to our understanding a simple yet sublime system of theology, presenting truths which a child may grasp, but which are yet so far reaching as to baffle the powers of the strongest mind.

The more closely God's Word is searched, and the better understood, the more vividly will the student realize that there is, beyond, infinite wisdom, knowledge, and power. . . .

If the youth will but learn of the heavenly Teacher, as did Daniel, they will know that the fear of the Lord is the beginning of wisdom. . . . Those who consecrate themselves to God, and who have the protection of His grace and the quickening influence of His Spirit, will manifest keener intellectual power than the mere worldling. They will be able to reach the highest, noblest exercise of every faculty.[5]

8

WHO MAY KNOW GOD?

Canst thou by searching find out God? canst thou find out the Almighty unto perfection? Job 11:7.

We cannot by searching find out God, but He has revealed Himself in His Son, who is the brightness of the Father's glory and the express image of His person. If we desire a knowledge of God we must be Christlike. . . . Living a pure life through faith in Christ as a personal Saviour will bring to the believer a clearer, higher conception of God. . . .

Eternal life is the reward that will be given to all who obey the two great principles of God's law—love to God and love to man. The first four commandments define and enjoin love to God; the last six, love to our fellow men. Obedience to these commands is the only evidence man can give that he possesses a genuine, saving knowledge of God. Love for God is demonstrated by love for those for whom Christ has died. While enshrouded in the pillar of cloud, Christ gave directions regarding this love. Distinctly and clearly He laid down the principles of heaven as rules that His chosen people were to observe in their dealings one with another. These principles Christ lived out in His life of humanity. In His teaching He presented the motives that should govern the lives of His followers. . . .

Those who partake of God's love through a reception of the truth will give evidence of this by making earnest, self-sacrificing efforts to give the message of God's love to others. Thus they become laborers together with Christ. Love for God and for one another unites them to Christ by golden links. Their life is bound up with His life in sanctified, elevated union. . . . This union causes rich currents of Christ's love to flow continually into the heart, and then flow forth again in love for others.

The qualities that it is essential for all to possess in order to know God are those that mark the completeness of Christ's character—His love, His patience, His unselfishness. These attributes are cultivated by doing kind actions with a kindly heart.[6]

SUPERFICIAL KNOWLEDGE NOT ENOUGH

To whom God would make known what is the riches of the glory of this mystery among the Gentiles; which is Christ in you, the hope of glory. Col. 1:27.

There are many mysteries in the Word of God that we do not comprehend, and many of us are content to stop our investigation when we have just begun to receive a little knowledge concerning Christ. When there begins to be a little unfolding of the divine purposes to the mind, and we begin to obtain a slight knowledge of the character of God, we become satisfied and think that we have received about all the light that there is for us in the Word of God. But the truth of God is infinite. With painstaking effort we should work in the mines of truth, discovering the precious jewels that have been hidden. . . . Jesus meant just what He said when He directed His disciples to *"search* the Scriptures" (John 5:39). Searching means to compare scripture with scripture, and spiritual things with spiritual. We should not be satisfied with a superficial knowledge.[7]

We do not half realize what the Lord is willing to do for His people. . . . Our petitions, mingled with faith and contrition, should go up to God for an understanding of the mysteries that God would make known to His saints. . . . An angel's pen could not portray all the glory of the revealed plan of redemption. The Bible tells how Christ bore our sins and carried our sorrows. Here is revealed how mercy and truth have met together at the cross of Calvary, how righteousness and peace have kissed each other, how the righteousness of Christ may be imparted to fallen man. There infinite wisdom, infinite justice, infinite mercy, and infinite love were displayed. Depths, heights, lengths, and breadths of love and wisdom, all passing knowledge, are made known in the plan of salvation.[8]

He who desires the truth in his heart, who longs for the working of its power upon the life and character, will be sure to have it. Says the Saviour, "Blessed are they which do hunger and thirst after righteousness: for they shall be filled" (Matt. 5:6).[9]

CHRIST THE ETERNAL WORD

In the beginning was the Word, and the Word was with God, and the Word was God. The same was in the beginning with God. All things were made by him; and without him was not any thing made that was made. John 1:1-3.

Christ, the Word, the only begotten of God, was one with the eternal Father—one in nature, in character, in purpose—the only being that could enter into all the counsels and purposes of God. "His name shall be called Wonderful, Counsellor, The mighty God, The everlasting Father, The Prince of Peace." His "goings forth have been from of old, from everlasting." And the Son of God declares concerning Himself: "The Lord possessed me in the beginning of his way, before his works of old. I was set up from everlasting. . . . When he appointed the foundations of the earth: then I was by him, as one brought up with him" (Isa. 9:6; Micah 5:2; Prov. 8:22-30).

The Father wrought by His Son in the creation of all heavenly beings. By him were all things created, . . . whether they be thrones, or dominions, or principalities, or powers: all things were created by him, and for him (Col. 1:16). Angels are God's ministers, radiant with the light ever flowing from His presence, and speeding on rapid wing to execute His will. But the Son, the anointed of God, the "express image of his person," "the brightness of his glory," "upholding all things by the word of his power," holds supremacy over them all (Heb. 1:3).[10]

Christ was God essentially, and in the highest sense. . . . The Lord Jesus Christ, the divine Son of God, existed from eternity, a distinct person, yet one with the Father. He was the surpassing glory of heaven. He was the commander of the heavenly intelligences, and the adoring homage of the angels was received by Him as His right. . . .

There are light and glory in the truth that Christ was one with the Father before the foundation of the world was laid. This is the light shining in a dark place, making it resplendent with divine, original glory.[11]

11

THE GREAT I AM

Jesus said unto them, Verily, verily, I say unto you, Before Abraham was, I am. John 8:58.

I AM means an eternal presence; the past, present, and future are alike with God. He sees the most remote events of past history and the far distant future with as clear a vision as we do those things which are transpiring daily. We know not what is before us, and if we did, it would not contribute to our eternal welfare. God gives us an opportunity to exercise faith and trust in the great I AM. . . . Our Saviour says, "Your father Abraham rejoiced to see my day: and he saw it, and was glad" (John 8:56). Fifteen hundred years before Christ laid off His royal robe, His kingly crown, and left His position of honor in the heavenly courts, assumed humanity, and walked a man among the children of men, Abraham saw His day, and was glad. "Then said the Jews unto him, Thou art not yet fifty years old, and hast thou seen Abraham? Jesus said unto them, Verily, verily, I say unto you, Before Abraham was, I am" (verses 57, 58). . . .

Christ was using the great name of God that was given to Moses to express the idea of the eternal presence. [See Ex. 3:14.] Isaiah also saw Christ, and his prophetic words are full of significance. He says, "For unto us a child is born, unto us a son is given: and the government shall be upon his shoulder: and his name shall be called Wonderful, Counsellor, The mighty God, The everlasting Father, The Prince of Peace" (Isa. 9:6). Speaking through him, the Lord says, "I am the Lord thy God, the Holy One of Israel, thy Saviour. . . . Fear not: for I *am* with thee. . . . I, even I, am the Lord; and beside me there is no saviour. . . . Ye are my witnesses, saith the Lord, that I am God. Yea, before the day was I am he. . . . I am the Lord, your Holy One, the creator of Israel, your King" (Isa. 43:3-15). . . . When Jesus came to our world, He proclaimed Himself, "I am the way, the truth, and the life: no man cometh unto the Father, but by me" (John 14:6). . . .

The Lord must be believed and served as the great "I AM," and we must trust implicitly in Him.[12]

12

COWORKERS IN CREATION

And God said, Let us make man in our image, after our likeness. . . . So God created man in his own image, in the image of God created he him; male and female created he them. Gen. 1:26, 27.

After the earth was created, and the beasts upon it, the Father and Son carried out their purpose, which was designed before the fall of Satan, to make man in their own image. They had wrought together in the creation of the earth and every living thing upon it. And now God said to His Son, "Let us make man in our image."[13]

Adam and Eve came forth from the hand of their Creator in the perfection of every physical, mental, and spiritual endowment. God planted for them a garden and surrounded them with everything lovely and attractive to the eye, and that which their physical necessities required. . . .

The holy pair looked upon nature as a picture of unsurpassed loveliness. The brown earth was clothed with a carpet of living green, diversified with an endless variety of self-propagating, self-perpetuating flowers. Shrubs, flowers, and trailing vines regaled the senses with their beauty and fragrance. The many varieties of lofty trees were laden with fruit of every kind and of delicious flavor. . . .

Adam and Eve could trace the skill and glory of God in every spire of grass and in every shrub and flower. The natural loveliness which surrounded them, like a mirror reflected the wisdom, excellence, and love of their heavenly Father. And their songs of affection and praise rose sweetly and reverentially to heaven, harmonizing with the songs of the exalted angels, and with the happy birds who were caroling forth their music without a care. There was no disease, decay, nor death anywhere. Life, life was in everything the eye rested upon. The atmosphere was impregnated with life. . . .

Adam could reflect that he was created in the image of God, to be like Him in righteousness and holiness. His mind was capable of continual cultivation, expansion, refinement and noble elevation, for God was his teacher, and angels were his companions.[14]

A SAD DAY FOR THE UNIVERSE

Wherefore, as by one man sin entered into the world, and death by sin; and so death passed upon all men, for that all have sinned. Rom. 5:12.

When our first parents were placed in the beautiful garden of Eden, they were tested in regard to their loyalty to God. They were free to choose the service of God, or by disobedience to ally themselves with the enemy of God and man. . . . If they disregarded God's commands, and listened to the voice of Satan, as he spoke through the serpent, they would not only forfeit their claim to Eden, but to life itself.[15]

The first great moral lesson given Adam was that of self-denial. The reins of self-government were placed in his hands. Judgment, reason, and conscience were to bear sway. . . .

Adam and Eve were permitted to partake of every tree in the Garden save one. There was only a single prohibition. The forbidden tree was as attractive and lovely as any of the trees in the Garden. It was called the tree of knowledge, because in partaking of that tree, of which God had said, "Thou shalt not eat of it" (Gen. 2:17), they would have a knowledge of sin, an experience in disobedience.[16]

With what intense interest the whole universe watched the conflict that was to decide the position of Adam and Eve. How attentively the angels listened to the words of Satan, the originator of sin, as he . . . sought to make of none effect the law of God through his deceptive reasoning! How anxiously they waited to see if the holy pair would be deluded by the tempter, and yield to his arts! They asked themselves, Will the holy pair transfer their faith and love from the Father and Son to Satan? Will they accept his falsehoods as truth?[17]

Adam and Eve persuaded themselves that in so small a matter as eating of the forbidden fruit, there could not result such terrible consequences as God had declared. But this small matter was sin, the transgression of God's immutable and holy law, and it opened the floodgates of death and untold woe upon our world. . . . Let us not esteem sin as a trivial thing.[18]

14

THE MYSTERY OF SIN

Thou art the anointed cherub that covereth; and I have set thee so. Thou wast perfect in thy ways from the day that thou wast created, till iniquity was found in thee. Eze. 28:14, 15.

It is impossible to explain the origin of sin so as to give a reason for its existence. Yet enough may be understood concerning both the origin and the final disposition of sin, to make fully manifest the justice and benevolence of God in all His dealings with evil. Nothing is more plainly taught in Scripture than that God was in no wise responsible for the entrance of sin. . . . Sin is an intruder, for whose presence no reason can be given. It is mysterious, unaccountable; to excuse it, is to defend it. Could excuse for it be found, or cause be shown for its existence, it would cease to be sin. Our only definition of sin is that given in the word of God; it is the "transgression of the law" (1 John 3:4), it is the outworking of a principle at war with the great law of love which is the foundation of the divine government.[19]

Sin originated in self-seeking. Lucifer, the covering cherub, desired to be first in heaven. He sought to gain control of heavenly beings, to draw them away from their Creator, and to win their homage to himself. . . . Thus he deceived angels. Thus he deceived men. He led them to doubt the word of God, and to distrust His goodness. . . . Thus he drew men to join him in rebellion against God, and the night of woe settled down upon the world.[20]

Sin appeared in a perfect universe. . . . The reason of its inception or development was never explained and never can be, even at the last great day when the judgment shall sit and the books be opened. . . . At that day it will be evident to all that there is not, and never was, any cause for sin. At the final condemnation of Satan and his angels and of all men who have finally identified themselves with him as transgressors of God's law, every mouth will be stopped. When the hosts of rebellion, from the first great rebel to the last transgressor, are asked why they have broken the law of God, they will be speechless. There will be no answer to give.[21]

DIVINE ENMITY IN THE SOUL

And I will put enmity between thee and the woman, and between thy seed and her seed; it shall bruise thy head, and thou shalt bruise his heel. Gen. 3:15.

Adam and Eve stood as criminals before their God, awaiting the sentence which transgression had incurred. But before they hear of the thorn and the thistle, the sorrow and anguish which should be their portion, and the dust to which they should return, they listen to words which must have inspired them with hope. Though they must suffer . . . , they might look forward to ultimate victory.

God declares, "I will put enmity." This enmity is supernaturally put, and not naturally entertained. When man sinned, his nature became evil, and he was in harmony, and not at variance, with Satan. The lofty usurper, having succeeded in seducing our first parents as he had seduced angels, counted on securing their allegiance and cooperation in all his enterprises against the government of Heaven. . . . But when Satan heard that the seed of the woman should bruise the serpent's head, he knew that though he had succeeded in depraving human nature . . . , yet by some mysterious process God would restore to man his lost power, and enable him to resist and overcome his conqueror.

It is the grace that Christ implants in the soul that creates the enmity against Satan. Without this grace, man would continue the captive of Satan, a servant ever ready to do his bidding. The new principle in the soul creates conflict where hitherto had been peace. The power which Christ imparts, enables man to resist the tyrant and usurper. Whenever a man is seen to abhor sin instead of loving it, when he resists and conquers those passions that have held sway within, there is seen the operation of a principle wholly from above. The Holy Spirit must be constantly imparted to man, or he has no disposition to contend against the powers of darkness.[22]

Shall we not accept the enmity which Christ has placed between man and the serpent? . . . We have a right to say, In the strength of Jesus Christ I will be a conqueror.[23]

A STAR OF HOPE

Behold the Lamb of God, which taketh away the sin of the world.
John 1:29.

To fallen man was revealed the plan of infinite sacrifice through which salvation was to be provided. Nothing but the death of God's dear Son could expiate man's sin, and Adam marveled at the goodness of God in providing such a ransom for the sinner. Through the love of God, a star of hope illumined the terrible future that spreads before the transgressor. Through the institution of the typical system of sacrifice and offering, the death of Christ was ever to be kept before guilty man, that he might better comprehend the nature of sin, the results of transgression, and the merit of the divine offering. Had there been no sin, man would never have known death. But in the innocent offering slain by his own hand he beheld the fruits of sin— the death of the Son of God in his behalf. He sees the immutable character of the law he has transgressed, and confesses his sin; he relies upon the merits of the Lamb of God. . . .

In becoming man's substitute, in bearing the curse which should fall upon man, Christ has pledged Himself in behalf of the race to maintain the sacred and exalted honor of His Father's law. . . . God has given the world into the hands of Christ, that He may completely vindicate the binding claims of the law and make manifest the holiness of every principle.[24]

The sacrifice of beasts shadowed forth the sinless offering of God's dear Son, and pointed forward to His death upon the cross. But at the crucifixion type met antitype, and the typical system there ceased. . . .

The Son of God is the center of the great plan of redemption which covers all dispensations. He is the "Lamb slain from the foundation of the world" (Rev. 13:8). He is the Redeemer of the fallen sons and daughters of Adam in all ages of human probation. "Neither is there salvation in any other: for there is none other name under heaven given among men, whereby we must be saved" (Acts 4:12).[25]

17

GOD'S CHARACTER REVEALED

But God commendeth his love toward us, in that, while we were yet sinners, Christ died for us. Rom. 5:8.

The fall of man, with all its consequences, was not hidden from the Omnipotent. Redemption was not an afterthought, a plan formulated after the fall of Adam, but an eternal purpose, suffered to be wrought out for the blessing not only of this atom of a world, but for the good of all the worlds that God had created. . . .

When man sinned, all heaven was filled with sorrow. . . . Out of harmony with the nature of God, unyielding to the claims of His law, naught but destruction was before the human race. Since the divine law is as changeless as the character of God, there could be no hope for man unless some way could be devised whereby his transgression might be pardoned, his nature renewed, and his spirit restored to reflect the image of God. Divine love had conceived such a plan. . . .

In the work of creation Christ was with God. He was one with God, equal with Him. . . . He alone, the Creator of man, could be his Saviour. No angel of heaven could reveal the Father to the sinner, and win him back to allegiance to God. But Christ could manifest the Father's love, for God was in Christ, reconciling the world unto Himself. Christ could be the "daysman" between a holy God and lost humanity, one who could "lay his hand upon us both" (Job 9:33). . . . He proposed to take upon Himself the guilt and shame of sin—sin so offensive in the sight of God that it would necessitate separation from His Father. Christ proposed to reach to the depths of man's degradation and woe, and restore the repenting, believing soul to harmony with God. Christ, the Lamb slain from the foundation of the world, offered Himself as a sacrifice and substitute for the fallen sons of Adam.[26]

Through creation and redemption, through nature and through Christ, the glories of the divine character are revealed. By the marvelous display of His love in giving "his only begotten Son," . . . the character of God is revealed to the intelligences of the universe.[27]

LOVE SO AMAZING!

For God so loved the world, that he gave his only begotten Son, that whosoever believeth in him should not perish, but have everlasting life. John 3:16.

Having undertaken the work of man's redemption, the Father would spare nothing, however dear, which was essential for the completion of His work. He would make opportunities for men; He would pour upon them His blessings; He would heap favor upon favor, gift upon gift, until the whole treasury of heaven was open to those whom He came to save. Having collected all the riches of the universe, and laid open all the resources of His divine nature, God gave them all for the use of man. They were His free gift. What an ocean of love is circulating, like a divine atmosphere, around the world! What manner of love is this, that the eternal God should adopt human nature in the person of His Son, and carry the same into the highest heaven!

All the heavenly intelligences were watching with intense interest the warfare that was going on upon the earth—the earth that Satan claimed as his dominion. Every moment was big with eternal realities. How would the conflict end? The angels looked for the justice of God to be revealed, His anger to be aroused against the prince of darkness and his sympathizers. But lo, mercy prevailed. When the Son of God might have come to the world to condemn, He came as righteousness and peace, to save not merely the descendants of Abraham, Isaac, and Jacob, but all the world—every son and daughter of Adam who would believe on Him, the Way, the Truth, and the Life. What an exhibition of the love of Jehovah! This is love without a parallel.[28]

Our Redeemer determined on nothing less than that through His merits the love of God should be transfused through the soul that believes in Him. As our life, the vitality of God's love is to circulate through every part of our nature, that it may abide in us as it dwells in Christ Jesus. United with Christ by living faith, the Father loves us as the members of Christ's mystical body, of which Christ is the glorified head.[29]

ISAAC A FIGURE OF CHRIST

By faith Abraham, when he was tried, offered up Isaac: and he that had received the promises offered up his only begotten son, of whom it was said, That in Isaac shall thy seed be called. Heb. 11:17, 18.

The offering of Isaac was designed by God to prefigure the sacrifice of His Son. Isaac was a figure of the Son of God, who was offered a sacrifice for the sins of the world. God desired to impress upon Abraham the gospel of salvation to men. . . . He was made to understand in his own experience how great was the self-denial of the infinite God in giving His Son to rescue man from ruin.

To Abraham no mental torture could be equal to that which he endured in obeying the command to sacrifice his son. . . . With a breaking heart and unnerved hand, he takes the fire, while Isaac inquires, "Behold the fire and the wood: but where is the lamb for the burnt offering?" (Gen. 22:7). But oh, Abraham cannot tell him now! Father and son build the altar, and the terrible moment comes for Abraham to make known to Isaac that which has agonized his soul during all that long journey—that Isaac himself is the victim. . . . The son submits to the sacrifice because he believes in the integrity of his father. But when everything is ready, when the faith of the father and the submission of the son are fully tested, the angel of God stays the uplifted hand of Abraham, and tells him that it is enough. "Now I know that thou fearest God, seeing thou hast not withheld thy son, thine only son from me" (verse 12).[30]

Our heavenly Father surrendered His beloved Son to the agonies of the crucifixion. Legions of angels witnessed the humiliation and soul anguish of the Son of God, but were not permitted to interpose as in the case of Isaac. No voice was heard to stay the sacrifice. God's dear Son, the world's Redeemer, was insulted, mocked at, derided, and tortured, until He bowed His head in death. What greater proof can the Infinite One give us of His divine love and pity? "He that spared not his own Son, but delivered him up for us all, how shall he not with him also freely give us all things?" (Rom. 8:32).[31]

CHRIST THE MYSTIC LADDER

And he dreamed, and behold a ladder set up on the earth, and the top of it reached to heaven: and behold the angels of God ascending and descending on it. Gen. 28:12.

Jacob's experience as a wanderer from his home, when he was shown the mystic ladder, . . . was designed to teach a great truth in regard to the plan of salvation. . . .

The ladder represented Christ. He is the channel of communication between heaven and earth, and angels go to and fro in continual intercourse with the fallen race. The words of Christ to Nathanael were in harmony with the figure of the ladder, when He said, "Verily, verily, I say unto you, Hereafter ye shall see heaven open, and the angels of God ascending and descending upon the Son of man" (John 1:51). Here the Redeemer identifies Himself as the mystic ladder that makes communication possible between heaven and earth. . . .

In assuming humanity, Christ planted the ladder firmly upon the earth. The ladder reaches unto the highest heaven, and God's glory shines from its summit and illuminates its whole length, while the angels pass to and fro with messages from God to man, with petition and praise from man to God. . . . In the vision of Jacob was represented the union of the human and the divine in Christ. As the angels pass to and fro on the ladder, God is represented as looking down with favor upon the children of men because of the merit of His Son. . . .

The gaining of eternal life is no easy thing. By living faith we are to keep on reaching forward, ascending the ladder round by round, seeing and taking the necessary steps; and yet we must understand that not one holy thought, not one unselfish act, can be originated in self. It is only through Christ that there can be any virtue in humanity. . . . But while we can do nothing without Him, we have something to do in connection with Him. At no time must we relax our spiritual vigilance, for we are hanging, as it were, between heaven and earth. We must cling to Christ, climb up by Christ, become laborers together with Him in the saving of our souls.[32]

21

CHRIST'S FIRST ADVENT PREFIGURED

By faith Moses, when he was come to years, refused to be called the son of Pharaoh's daughter; choosing rather to suffer affliction with the people of God, than to enjoy the pleasures of sin for a season. Heb. 11:24, 25.

While he [Moses] was sitting under the very shadow of the throne, the Spirit of the Lord stirred his heart to lift the crushing weight that was pressing his brethren into the lowest degradation and slavery. His heart ached with sorrow, as if he himself were in slavery, laboring in the brick kiln, and sharing their degradation. They were slaves, suffering under the cruel lash. They were a reproach and a hissing to all the Egyptians, from Pharaoh down to the lowest serf.

But the Lord had singled out Moses as the one to deliver the oppressed race, and by forty years of exile, under the discipline of God, he was prepared for the work. Understanding the evil disposition of his own countrymen, knowing how many would be perverse and unreasonable, understanding that they might betray him, he was yet considering ways and means to accomplish their deliverance, though supposing that he himself had forfeited all right to be the instrument. But God, in the bush which though burning was yet unconsumed by the fire, presented Himself, and selected Moses as His agent. . . .

Moses was accepted as a coworker with God. He knew that scorn, hatred, persecution, and maybe death would be his portion if he should act any part in espousing the cause of the Hebrew captives. . . . He had stood in great popularity as the general of Pharaoh's armies, and he knew that now his name would be bandied round and falsified, but he esteemed "the reproach of Christ greater riches than the treasures in Egypt" (Heb. 11:26). He laid down the prospect of a kingly crown, and took up the burdens of his oppressed and afflicted people.[33]

Moses was chosen of God to break the yoke of bondage upon the children of Israel, and . . . in his work he prefigured Christ's first advent to break Satan's power over the human family and deliver those who were made captives by his power.[34]

THE SMITTEN ROCK

Behold, I will stand before thee there upon the rock in Horeb; and thou shalt smite the rock, and there shall come water out of it, that the people may drink. And Moses did so in the sight of the elders of Israel. Ex. 17:6.

From the smitten rock in Horeb first flowed the living stream that refreshed Israel in the desert. During all their wanderings, wherever the need existed, they were supplied with water by a miracle of God's mercy. . . .

It was Christ, by the power of His word, that caused the refreshing stream to flow for Israel. "They drank of that spiritual Rock that followed them: and that Rock was Christ" (1 Cor. 10:4). He was the source of all temporal as well as spiritual blessings. Christ, the true Rock, was with them in all their wanderings. "They thirsted not when he led them through the deserts: he caused the waters to flow out of the rock for them." "They ran in the dry places like a river" (Isa. 48:21; Ps. 105:41).

The smitten rock was a figure of Christ, and through this symbol the most precious spiritual truths are taught. As the life-giving waters flowed from the smitten rock, so from Christ, "smitten of God," "wounded for our transgressions," "bruised for our iniquities" (Isa. 53:4, 5), the stream of salvation flows for a lost race. As the rock had been once smitten, so Christ was to be "once offered to bear the sins of many" (Heb. 9:28). Our Saviour was not to be sacrificed a second time; and it is only necessary for those who seek the blessings of His grace to ask in the name of Jesus, pouring forth the heart's desire in penitential prayer. Such prayer will bring before the Lord of hosts the wounds of Jesus, and then will flow forth afresh the life-giving blood, symbolized by the flowing of the living water for Israel. . . .

The refreshing water, welling up in a parched and barren land, . . . is an emblem of the divine grace which Christ alone can bestow, and which is as the living water purifying, refreshing, and invigorating the soul. He in whom Christ is abiding has within him a never-failing fountain of grace and strength.[35]

THE LIVING WATER

And did all drink the same spiritual drink: for they drank of that spiritual Rock that followed them: and that Rock was Christ. 1 Cor. 10:4.

Christ combines the two types. He is the rock, He is the living water.

The same beautiful and expressive figures are carried throughout the Bible. Centuries before the advent of Christ, Moses pointed to Him as the rock of Israel's salvation; the psalmist sung of Him as "my redeemer," "the rock of my strength," "the rock that is higher than I," "a rock of habitation," "rock of my heart," "rock of my refuge." In David's song His grace is pictured also as the cool, "still waters," amid green pastures, beside which the heavenly Shepherd leads His flock. Again, "Thou shalt make them," he says, "drink of the river of thy pleasures. For with thee is the fountain of life." And the wise man declares, "The wellspring of wisdom [is] as a flowing brook." To Jeremiah, Christ is "the fountain of living waters"; to Zechariah, "a fountain opened . . . for sin and for uncleanness."

Isaiah describes Him as the "rock of ages," and "the shadow of a great rock in a weary land." And he records the precious promise, bringing vividly to mind the living stream that flowed for Israel: "When the poor and needy seek water, and there is none, and their tongue faileth for thirst, I the Lord will hear them, I the God of Israel will not forsake them." "I will pour water upon him that is thirsty, and floods upon the dry ground"; "in the wilderness shall waters break out, and streams in the desert." The invitation is given, "Ho, every one that thirsteth, come ye to the waters." And in the closing pages of the sacred word this invitation is echoed. The river of the water of life, clear as crystal, proceeds from the throne of God and the Lamb; and the gracious call is ringing down through the ages, "Whosoever will, let him take the water of life freely." [36]

REFERENCES: Deut. 32:15; Ps. 19:14; 62:7; 61:2; 71:3 (margin); 73:26 (margin); 94:22; 23:2; 36:8, 9; Prov. 18:4; Jer. 2:13; Zech. 13:1; Isa. 26:4 (margin); 32:2; 41:17; 44:3; 35:6; 55:1; Rev. 22:1, 17.

GOD IN HUMAN FLESH

And the Word was made flesh, and dwelt among us, (and we beheld his glory, the glory as of the only begotten of the Father,) full of grace and truth. John 1:14.

When we want a deep problem to study, let us fix our minds on the most marvelous thing that ever took place in earth or heaven— the incarnation of the Son of God.[37]

Christ alone was able to represent the Deity. . . . God Himself must be revealed to humanity. In order to do this, our Saviour clothed His divinity with humanity. He employed the human faculties, for only by adopting these could He be comprehended by humanity. Only humanity could reach humanity. He lived out the character of God through the human body which God had prepared for Him.[38]

Had Christ come in His divine form, humanity could not have endured the sight. The contrast would have been too painful, the glory too overwhelming. Humanity could not have endured the presence of one of the pure, bright angels from glory; therefore Christ took not on Him the nature of angels; He came in the likeness of men.[39]

Looking upon Him, we behold the invisible God, who clothed His divinity with humanity in order that through humanity He might shed forth a subdued and softened glory, so that our eyes might be enabled to rest upon Him, and our souls not be extinguished by His undimmed splendor. We behold God through Christ, our Creator and Redeemer. It is our privilege to contemplate Jesus by faith, and see Him standing between humanity and the eternal throne. He is our Advocate, presenting our prayers and offerings as spiritual sacrifices to God. Jesus is the great sinless propitiation, and through His merit God and man may hold converse together.

Christ has carried His humanity into eternity. He stands before God as the representative of our race. When we are clothed with the wedding garment of His righteousness, we become one with Him, and He says of us, "They shall walk with me in white: for they are worthy" (Rev. 3:4). His saints will behold Him in His glory, with no dimming veil between.[40]

THE BABE OF BETHLEHEM

Unto you is born this day in the city of David a Saviour, which is Christ the Lord. And this shall be a sign unto you; Ye shall find the babe wrapped in swaddling clothes, lying in a manger. Luke 2:11, 12.

We cannot understand how Christ became a little, helpless babe. He could have come to earth in such beauty that He would have been unlike the sons of men. His face could have been bright with light, and His form could have been tall and beautiful. He could have come in such a way as to charm those who looked upon Him, but this was not the way that God planned He should come among the sons of men. He was to be like those who belonged to the human family and to the Jewish race. His features were to be like those of other human beings and He was not to have such beauty of person as to make people point Him out as different from others. He was to come as one of the human family, and to stand as a man before heaven and earth. He had come to take man's place, to pledge Himself in man's behalf, to pay the debt that sinners owed. He was to live a pure life on the earth, and show that Satan had told a falsehood when he claimed that the human family belonged to him forever, and that God could not take men out of his hands.

Men first beheld Christ as a babe, as a child. His parents were very poor, and He had nothing in this earth save that which the poor have. He passed through all the trials that the poor and lowly pass through from babyhood to childhood, from youth to manhood. . . .

The more we think about Christ's becoming a babe here on earth, the more wonderful it appears. How can it be that the helpless babe in Bethlehem's manger is still the divine Son of God? Though we cannot understand it, we can believe that He who made the worlds, for our sakes became a helpless babe. Though higher than any of the angels, though as great as the Father on the throne of heaven, He became one with us. In Him God and man became one, and it is in this fact that we find the hope of our fallen race. Looking upon Christ in the flesh, we look upon God in humanity and see in Him the brightness of divine glory, the express image of God the Father.[41]

A LIGHT TO THE YOUNG

And the child grew, and waxed strong in spirit, filled with wisdom: and the grace of God was upon him. Luke 2:40.

The example of Jesus is a light to the young as well as to those of mature years, for His was a representative childhood and youth. From His earliest years His example was perfect. In both His physical and His spiritual nature He followed the divine order of growth illustrated by the plant, as He wishes all youth to do. Although He was the Majesty of heaven, the King of glory, He became a babe in Bethlehem, and for a time represented the helpless infant in its mother's care. In childhood He did the works of an obedient child. He spoke and acted with the wisdom of a child and not of a man, honoring His parents, and carrying out their wishes in helpful ways, according to the ability of a child. But at each stage of His development He was perfect, with the simple, natural grace of a sinless life.[42]

Joseph, and especially Mary, kept before them the remembrance of their child's divine Fatherhood. Jesus was instructed in accordance with the sacred character of His mission. His inclination to right was a constant gratification to His parents. The questions He asked them led them to study most earnestly the great elements of truth. His soul-stirring words about nature and the God of nature opened and enlightened their minds.

On the rocks and knolls about His home the eye of the Son of God often rested. He was familiar with the things of nature. He saw the sun in the heavens, the moon and the stars fulfilling their mission. With the voice of singing He welcomed the morning light. He listened to the lark caroling forth music to its God, and joined His voice with the voice of praise and thanksgiving.[43]

Quiet and gentle, He seemed as one who was set apart. Whenever He could He went out alone into the fields and on the mountainsides to commune with the God of nature. When His work was done He wandered by the lakeside, among the trees of the forest, and in the green valleys, where He could think about God and lift His soul to heaven in prayer.[44]

A CHILD IN THE TEMPLE

Wist ye not that I must be about my Father's business? Luke 2:49.

When Christ was twelve years old He went with His parents to Jerusalem to attend the feast of the Passover, and on their return He was lost in the multitude. After Joseph and Mary had searched for Him for three days, they found Him in the court of the Temple, "sitting in the midst of the doctors, both hearing them, and asking them questions. And all that heard him were astonished at his understanding and answers" (Luke 2:46, 47).[45]

His parents listened in amazement as they heard His searching inquiries. . . . Though taking the attitude of a learner, Christ imparted light in every word He uttered. He interpreted the Scripture to the darkened mind of the rabbis, and gave them clear light in regard to the Lamb of God that taketh away the sins of the world. The sharp, clear questions of the child learner brought a flood of light to their darkened understanding. The truth shone out as the clear shining of a light in a darkened place, as He received and imparted the knowledge of the plan of salvation.

It is plainly stated that Christ grew in knowledge. What a lesson is found in this incident in the life of Christ for all youth! If they shall diligently search the Word of God, and through the Holy Spirit receive divine guidance, they will be able to impart light to others. . . .

Mary, the mother of Jesus, . . . asked, "son, why hast thou thus dealt with us? behold, thy father and I have sought thee sorrowing." Divine light shone through humanity as Jesus lifted His right hand and asked, "How is it that ye sought me? wist ye not that I must be about my Father's business? And they understood not the saying which he spake unto them" (verses 48-50). They did not comprehend the true meaning of His words. But, though He was the Son of God, He went down with His parents and came unto Nazareth, and was subject unto them. . . . At the age of twelve the Holy Spirit was abiding upon Jesus and He felt something of the burden of the mission for which He had come to our world.[46]

KEEP THE SAVIOUR WITH YOU!

And when they had fulfilled the days, as they returned, the child Jesus tarried behind in Jerusalem; and Joseph and his mother knew not of it. Luke 2:43.

Not one act in the life of Christ was unimportant. Every event of His life was for the benefit of His followers in future time. This circumstance of the tarry of Christ in Jerusalem teaches an important lesson. . . .

Jesus was acquainted with hearts. He knew that, as the crowd returned in company from Jerusalem, there would be much talking and visiting which would not be seasoned with humility and grace, and the Messiah and His mission would be nearly forgotten. It was His choice to return from Jerusalem with His parents alone; for in being retired, His father and mother would have more time for reflection, and for meditation upon the prophecies which referred to His future sufferings and death. He did not wish the painful events which they were to experience in His offering up His life for the sins of the world, to be new and unexpected to them. He was separated from them in their return to Jerusalem. After the celebration of the Passover, they sought Him sorrowing three days. . . .

Here is a lesson of instruction to all the followers of Christ. . . . There is necessity of carefulness of words and actions when Christians are associated together, lest Jesus be forgotten of them, and they pass along careless of the fact that Jesus is not among them. When they are aroused to their condition, they discover that they have journeyed without the presence of Him who could give peace and joy to their hearts, and days are occupied in returning, and searching for Him whom they should have retained with them every moment. Jesus will not be found in the company of those who are careless of His presence, and who engage in conversation having no reference to their Redeemer. . . . It is the privilege of all to retain Jesus with them. If they do this, their words must he select, seasoned with grace. The thoughts of their hearts must be disciplined to meditate upon heavenly and divine things.[47]

THE IDEAL FOR ALL HUMANITY

And Jesus increased in wisdom and stature, and in favour with God and man. Luke 2:52.

Christ lived the life of a toiler from His earliest years. In His youth He worked with His father at the carpenter's trade, and thus honored all labor. Though He was the King of glory, yet by His practice of following a humble employment He rebuked idleness in every member of the human family, and dignified all labor as noble and Christlike. . . . From childhood He was a pattern of obedience and industry. He was as a pleasant sunbeam in the home circle. . . .

Though His wisdom had astonished the doctors, yet He meekly subjected Himself to His human guardians. . . . The knowledge He was daily obtaining of His wonderful mission did not disqualify Him for performing the most humble duties. He cheerfully took up the work that devolves upon youth who dwell in humble households pressed by poverty. He understood the temptations of children, for He bore their sorrows and trials. Firm and steadfast was His purpose to do the right. Though enticed to evil, He refused to depart in a single instance from the strictest truth and rectitude.[48]

Christ is the ideal for all humanity. He has left a perfect example for childhood, youth, and manhood. He came to this earth, and passed through the different phases of human life. He talked and acted like other children and youth, except that He did no wrong. Sin found no place in His life. Ever He lived in an atmosphere of heavenly purity. . . .

In the sanctuary of the home, Jesus received His education, not merely from His parents, but from His heavenly Father. As He grew older, God opened to Him more and more of the great work before Him. But notwithstanding His knowledge of this, He assumed no airs of superiority. Never did He by disrespect cause His parents pain or anxiety. He delighted to honor and obey them. Although He was not ignorant of His great mission, He consulted their wishes, and submitted to their authority.[49]

THE MEANING OF CHRIST'S BAPTISM

Then cometh Jesus from Galilee to Jordan unto John, to be baptized of him. Matt. 3:13.

Many had come to him [John] to receive the baptism of repentance, confessing their sins. . . . Christ came not confessing His own sins, but guilt was imputed to Him as the sinner's substitute. He came not to repent on His own account, but in behalf of the sinner. . . . Christ honored the ordinance of baptism by submitting to this rite. In this act He identified Himself with His people as their representative and head. As their substitute He takes upon Him their sins, numbering Himself with the transgressors, taking the steps the sinner is required to take, and doing the work the sinner must do. . . .

After Christ rose up from the water . . . He walked out to the bank of Jordan and bowed in the attitude of prayer. . . . As the believer's example, His sinless humanity supplicated support and strength from His heavenly Father, as He was about to commence His public labor as the Messiah. . . .

Never before had angels listened to such a prayer as Christ offered at His baptism, and they were solicitous to be the bearers of the message from the Father to His Son. But, no! Direct from the Father issues the light of His glory. The heavens were opened and beams of glory rested upon the Son of God and assumed the form of a dove, in appearance like burnished gold. The dovelike form was emblematical of the meekness and gentleness of Christ. . . . From the opening heavens came these words: "This is my beloved Son, in whom I am well pleased." . . . Notwithstanding the Son of God was clothed with humanity, yet Jehovah, with His own voice, assures Him of His sonship with the Eternal. In this manifestation to His Son, God accepts humanity as exalted through the excellence of His beloved Son.[50]

Christ's prayer on the banks of the Jordan includes everyone who will believe in Him. The promise that you are accepted in the Beloved comes to you. God said, "This is my beloved Son, in whom I am well pleased." . . . Christ has cleaved the way for you to the throne of the infinite God.[51]

31

THE WILDERNESS TEMPTATION

Then was Jesus led up of the spirit into the wilderness to be tempted of the devil. Matt. 4:1.

Why was it that at the beginning of His public ministry Christ was led into the wilderness to be tempted? . . . He went, not in His own behalf, but in our behalf; to overcome for us. . . . He was to be tried and tested as a representative of the race. He was to meet the foe in personal encounter, to overthrow him who claimed to be the head of the kingdoms of the world.[52]

Satan met Him and tempted Him on the very points where man will be tempted. Our Substitute and Surety passed over the ground where Adam stumbled and fell. And the question was, Will He stumble and fall as Adam did over God's commandments? He met Satan's attacks again and again with "It is written," and Satan left the field of conflict a conquered foe. Christ has redeemed Adam's disgraceful fall, and has perfected a character of perfect obedience, and left an example for the human family. . . . Had He failed on one point in reference to the law of God, He would not have been a perfect offering, for it was on one point only that Adam failed. . . .

Our Saviour withstood on every point the test of temptation, and in this way He has made it possible for man to overcome. Now, there is enough in this idea, in this thought, to fill our hearts with gratitude every day of our lives. As Jesus was accepted as our substitute and surety, every one of us will be accepted if we stand the test and trial for ourselves. He took our nature that He might become acquainted with the trials wherewith man should be beset, and He is our mediator and intercessor before the Father.[53]

Those who would overcome must put to the tax every power of their being. They must agonize on their knees before God for divine power. . . . Men may have a power to resist evil—a power that neither earth, nor death, nor hell can master; a power that will place them where they may overcome as Christ overcame. Divinity and humanity may be combined in them.[54]

A LIFE WITHOUT SIN

We have not an high priest which cannot be touched with the feeling of our infirmities; but was in all points tempted like us we are, yet without sin. Heb. 4:15.

Let us consider how much it cost our Saviour in the wilderness of temptation to carry on in our behalf the conflict with the wily, malignant foe. Satan knew that everything depended upon his success or failure in his attempt to overcome Christ with his manifold temptations. Satan knew that the plan of salvation would be carried out to its fulfillment, that his power would be taken away, that his destruction would be certain, if Christ bore the test that Adam failed to endure. The temptations of Satan were most effective in degrading human nature, for man could not stand against their powerful influence; but Christ in man's behalf, as man's representative, resting wholly upon the power of God, endured the severe conflict, in order that He might be a perfect example to us. There is hope for man. . . . The work before us is to overcome as Christ overcame. He fasted forty days, and suffered the keenest pangs of hunger. Christ suffered on our account beyond our comprehension, and we should welcome trial and suffering on our own account for Christ's sake, that we may overcome as Christ also overcame, and be exalted to the throne of our Redeemer. . . .

We have everything to gain in the conflict with our mighty foe, and we dare not for a moment yield to his temptations. We know that in our own strength it is not possible for us to succeed; but as Christ humbled Himself, and took upon Himself our nature, He is acquainted with our necessities, and has Himself borne the heaviest temptations that man will have to bear, has conquered the enemy in resisting his suggestions, in order that man may learn how to be conqueror. He was clothed with a body like ours, and in every respect suffered what man will suffer, and very much more. We shall never be called upon to suffer as Christ suffered, for the sins not of one, but the sins of the whole world were laid upon Christ. He endured humiliation, reproach, suffering, and death, that we by following His example might inherit all things.[55]

CHRIST SUFFERED, BEING TEMPTED

For verily he took not on him the nature of angels; but he took on him the seed of Abraham. Heb. 2:16.

We need not place the obedience of Christ by itself, as something for which He was particularly adapted, by His particular divine nature, for He stood before God as man's representative and was tempted as man's substitute and surety. If Christ had a special power which it is not the privilege of man to have, Satan would have made capital of this matter. The work of Christ was to take from the claims of Satan his control of man, and He could do this only in the way that He came—a man, tempted as a man, rendering the obedience of a man.[56]

Would that we could comprehend the significance of the words, Christ "suffered being tempted" (Heb. 2:18). While He was free from the taint of sin, the refined sensibilities of His holy nature rendered contact with evil unspeakably painful to Him. Yet with human nature upon Him, He met the arch apostate face to face, and single-handed withstood the foe of His throne. Not even by a thought could Christ be brought to yield to the power of temptation.

Satan finds in human hearts some point where he can gain a foothold; some sinful desire is cherished, by means of which his temptations assert their power. But Christ declared of Himself, "The prince of this world cometh, and hath nothing in me" (John 14:30). The storms of temptation burst upon Him, but they could not cause Him to swerve from His allegiance to God.

All the followers of Christ have to meet the same malignant foe that assailed their Master. With marvelous skill he adapts his temptations to their circumstances, their temperament, their mental and moral bias, their strong passions. He is ever whispering in the ears of the children of men, as he points to worldly pleasures, gains, or honors, "All this will I give you, if you will do my bidding." We must look to Christ; we must resist as He resisted; we must pray as He prayed; we must agonize as He agonized, if we would conquer as He conquered.[57]

OUR DIVINE REDEEMER

Who, being in the form of God, thought it not robbery to be equal with God. Phil. 2.6.

Jesus Christ "counted it not a thing to be grasped to be equal with God." Because divinity alone could be efficacious in the restoration of man from the poisonous bruise of the serpent, God Himself, in His only begotten Son, assumed human nature, and in the weakness of human nature sustained the character of God, vindicated His holy law in every particular, and accepted the sentence of wrath and death for the sons of men. What a thought is this! He who was one with the Father before the world was made had such compassion for a world lost and ruined by transgression that He gave His life a ransom for it. He who was the brightness of the Father's glory, the express image of His person, bore our sins in His own body on the tree, suffering the penalty of man's transgression until justice was satisfied and required no more. How great is the redemption that has been worked out for us! So great that the Son of God died the cruel death of the cross to bring to us life and immortality through faith in Him.

This wonderful problem—how God could be just and yet the justifier of sinners—is beyond human ken. As we attempt to fathom it, it broadens and deepens beyond our comprehension. When we look with the eye of faith upon the cross of Calvary, and see our sins laid upon the victim hanging in weakness and ignominy there—when we grasp the fact that this is God, the everlasting Father, the Prince of Peace—we are led to exclaim, "Behold, what manner of love the Father hath bestowed upon us" (1 John 3:1)! . . .

When man can measure the exalted character of the Lord of hosts, and distinguish between the eternal God and finite humanity, he will know how great has been the sacrifice of Heaven to bring man from where he has fallen through disobedience to become part of the family of God. . . . The divinity of Christ is our assurance of eternal life. . . . He, the Sin Bearer of the world, is our only medium of reconciliation with a holy God.[58]

MARVEL OF THE HEAVENLY HOSTS

But made himself of no reputation, and took upon him the form of a servant, and was made in the likeness of men. Phil. 2:7.

It is important that we each study to know the reason of the life of Christ in humanity, and what it means to us—why the Son of God left the courts of heaven—why He stepped down from His position as commander of the heavenly angels who came and went at His bidding—why He clothed His divinity with humanity, and in lowliness and humility came to the world as our Redeemer.

It was the marvel of the heavenly hosts that Christ should come to earth and do as He did—that His life here should be one of poverty, in such incomparable contrast with His glory in the heavenly courts. He might have come attended by the angelic throng. . . .

Before the universe of heaven, Christ condescended to take upon Him the form of humanity, and stand among the lowly ones of earth, that He might reach them where they were, and by precept and example teach them, that though among the poor and oppressed they might be pure, and true, and noble. He came to reveal to the world that the life and character need not become contaminated amid poverty and lowliness. The lily that rests upon the bosom of the lake may be surrounded with weeds and unsightly debris, yet, unsullied, it opens its fragrant white blossom to the sunlight. It strikes its channeled stem down through the mass of rubbish to the pure sands beneath. Refusing everything that would defile, it gathers to itself only those properties that will develop into the spotless, fragrant flower.

The lily is a representation of Christ among men. He came to a world all seared and marred with the curse, but He was not polluted by His surroundings. He was the Light, the Life, and the Way. He voluntarily became an inhabitant of earth, that He might grasp the whole world in His merciful arms and lay it in the arms of His heavenly Father. What love is manifested in this sacrifice, that the Lord Himself should come to the help of the fallen sons and daughters of Adams![59]

THE GREATNESS OF HUMILITY

And being found in fashion as a man, lie humbled himself, and became obedient unto death, even the death of the cross. Phil. 2:8.

Christ came to this world for no other purpose than to manifest the glory of God, that man might be uplifted by its restoring power. All power and grace were given to Him. His heart was a wellspring of living water, a never-failing fountain, ever ready to flow forth in a rich, clear stream to those around Him. His whole life was spent in pure disinterested benevolence. His purposes were full of love and sympathy. He rejoiced that He could do more for His followers than they could ask or think. His constant prayer for them was that they might be sanctified through the truth, and He prayed with assurance, knowing that an almighty decree had been given before the world was made. He knew that the gospel of the kingdom would be preached in all the world; that truth, armed with the omnipotence of the Holy Spirit, would conquer in the contest with evil; and that the bloodstained banner would one day wave triumphantly over His followers.

Yet Christ came in great humility. When He was here He pleased not Himself, but "humbled himself, and became obedient unto death, even the death of the cross." To His followers He says, "Take my yoke upon you, and learn of me; for I am meek and lowly in heart: and ye shall find rest unto your souls" (Matt. 11:29). . . .

From the root of true humility springs the most precious greatness of mind—greatness which leads men to conform to the image of Christ. Those who possess this greatness gain patience and trust in God. Their faith is invincible. Their true consecration and devotion keep self hidden. The words that fall from their lips are molded into expressions of Christlike tenderness and love. Having a sense of their own weakness, they appreciate the help which the Lord gives them, and they crave His grace that they may do that which is right and true. By their manner, their attitude, and their spirit, they carry with them the credentials of learners in the school of Christ.[60]

CHRIST THE REVELATION OF GOD

No man hath seen God at any time; the only begotten Son, which is in the bosom of the Father, he hath declared him. John 1:18.

Christ came to the world to reveal the character of the Father and to redeem the fallen race. The world's Redeemer was equal with God. His authority was as the authority of God. He declared that He had no existence separate from the Father. The authority by which He spoke and wrought miracles was expressly His own, yet He assures us that He and the Father are one. . . .

Jesus had imparted a knowledge of God to patriarchs, prophets, and apostles. The revelations of the Old Testament were emphatically the unfoldings of the gospel, the unveiling of the purpose and will of the infinite Father. Through the holy men of old, Christ labored for the salvation of fallen humanity. And when He came to the world it was with the same message of redemption from sin, and restoration to the favor of God.[1]

What speech is to thought, so is Christ to the invisible Father. He is the manifestation of the Father, and is called the Word of God. God sent His Son into the world, His divinity clothed with humanity, that man might bear the image of the invisible God. He made known in His words, His character, His power and majesty, the nature and attributes of God.[2]

As legislator, Jesus exercised the authority of God; His commands and decisions were supported by the sovereignty of the eternal throne. The glory of the Father was revealed in the Son; Christ made manifest the character of the Father. He was so perfectly connected with God, so completely embraced in His encircling light, that he who had seen the Son had seen the Father. His voice was as the voice of God. . . . He says, "I am in the Father, and the Father in me." "No man knoweth the Son, but the Father; neither knoweth any man the Father, save the Son, and he to whomsoever the Son will reveal him." "He that hath seen me hath seen the Father" (John 14:11; Matt. 11:27; John 14:9).[3]

CHRIST IN THE HOME

And the third day there was a marriage in Cana of Galilee; and the mother of Jesus was there. and both Jesus was called, and his disciples, to the marriage. John 2:1, 2.

On the occasion of the marriage feast He [Christ] desired to express His sympathy with, and approval of, those at the wedding. Christ did not come to this world to forbid marriage or to break down or destroy the relationship and influence which exist in the domestic circle. He came to restore, elevate, purify, and ennoble every current of pure affection, that the family on earth might become a symbol of the family in heaven. . . .

Mothers are under the tender care of heavenly angels. How interestedly the Lord Jesus knocks at the door of families where there are little children to be educated and trained! How gently He watches over the mothers' interest, and how sad He feels to see children neglected. . . . In the home characters are formed; human beings are molded and fashioned to be either a blessing or a curse. To the mother the Lord has committed the younger members of the family as they come into our world weak and helpless. Infinite wisdom and infinite love does not commit this gentle office, so pregnant with eternal results, to the fathers, full of business plans and cares. Woman's heart is full of patience and love if that woman has surrendered her heart to God. She must cooperate with God and her husband in training the precious souls entrusted to her, to grow up into Christ Jesus. And the father, relying upon the grace of God, should bear the sacred responsibility that rests upon him as the husband, which means house-band.

In babyhood and childhood, when the nature is pliable, God would have the firmest impressions made for right. A battle is constantly going on between the Prince of life and the prince of this world. The question to be settled is, Whom will the mother choose as her coworker to mold and fashion the characters of her children? If she will learn that love is the key to the souls of her children, Christ will preside in the home, filling it with heavenly sunshine. This is His work in every home that will admit Him.[4]

LOVER OF LITTLE CHILDREN

Then were there brought unto him little children, that he should put his hands on them, and pray: and the disciples rebuked them. But Jesus said, Suffer little children, and forbid them not, to come unto me: for of such is the kingdom of heaven. And he laid his hands on them. Matt. 19:13-15.

Children are the Lord's heritage. The soul of the little child that believes in Christ is as precious in His sight as are the angels about His throne. They are to be brought to Christ, and trained for Christ. They are to be guided in the path of obedience, not indulged in appetite or vanity.

When the disciples sought to send away the mothers who were bringing their little ones to Christ, He rebuked their narrow faith, saying, "Suffer little children, and forbid them not, to come unto me: for of such is the kingdom of heaven." He was grieved that the disciples should rebuke the mothers for bringing their children to Him; that His followers should say, by word or action, that His grace was limited, and that children should be kept away from Him. . . .

A great responsibility rests upon parents, for the education and training which shape the eternal destiny of children and youth are received in their early childhood. The parents' work is to sow the good seed diligently and untiringly in the hearts of their children, occupying their hearts with seed which will bring forth a harvest of right habits, of truthfulness and willing obedience. Correct, virtuous habits formed in youth will generally mark the course of the individual through life. In most cases those who reverence God and honor the right will be found to have learned this lesson before the world could stamp its image of sin upon the soul. . . .

O that parents were truly the sons and daughters of God! Their lives would then be fragrant with good works. A holy atmosphere would surround their souls. Their earnest supplications for grace and for the guidance of the Holy Spirit would ascend to heaven, and religion would be diffused through their homes as the bright, warming rays of the sun are diffused through the earth.[5]

A MESSAGE FOR BOYS AND GIRLS

Come, ye children, hearken unto me: I will teach you the fear of the Lord. Ps. 34:11.

Every child and every youth should bear in mind, "I am of value in the sight of God; I am bought with a price, and I am the property of Jesus Christ. As a follower of Christ I am to practice His virtues, that I may represent my Saviour."

Pray much. While at your work let your heart be uplifted to God. When you have committed to God the keeping of your soul, do not go away and act directly contrary to the prayer you have made. Watch as well as pray, lest you be overcome with temptation. Resist the first inclination to do wrong. Pray in your heart, "Jesus, help me; preserve me from evil," and then do what you know Christ would be pleased to have you do. . . .

You may ask, as many others have done, How may I know that Jesus receives me and loves me? Shall I know by my feelings? No; by obedience to His Holy Word. Appropriate to yourself the rich promises of God. Believe His word that Jesus is abiding in your heart by faith. Through faith and trust in God you may have His peace, and you can then say, "I know in whom I have believed. I will listen to every whisper of His Holy Spirit."

There is but one way to be victorious. Serve God with all your heart because you love Him. Seek Him daily because you love Him and know what He is to you. Be faithful in the little things, although no eye but the Lord's may review your work. Remember that you are doing service for Christ. You may now be obtaining a precious experience every day in serving God. Plant the principles of truth in your own soul, and reveal Christ in your character. Do not be satisfied with a common, low level. You can . . . resemble Christ in character. . . .

Look unto Jesus constantly if you would advance step by step in the narrow path cast up for the chosen of the Lord to walk in, saying in your heart, "Thee will I seek, O God; Thee will I follow; Thee will I serve; under Thy guidance I can and will go forward."[6]

ARMIES OF MISSIONARY CHILDREN

Even a child is known by his doings, whether his work be pure, and whether it be right. Prov. 20:11.

God wants the children and youth to join the Lord's army. . . . The children have as strong temptations to meet, on the right hand and on the left, as do the older soldiers. Satan and his legions will work every device to ensnare the young. It is the privilege of the children to enlist in the army of the Lord and seek to persuade others to join their ranks. Children must be educated and trained for Jesus Christ. They must be trained to resist temptation and to fight the good fight of faith. Direct their minds to Jesus as soon as they can comprehend your lessons in simple words, easy to be understood. Teach them self-control. Teach them to begin the work of overcoming when young, and they will receive the precious help that Jesus can and will give, connected with prayerful efforts of parents. Cheer them with encouraging words for the battles they fight in resisting temptation and coming off conquerors through grace given them of Jesus Christ. . . .

Parents should hang in memory's hall the precious sayings of Christ. The children will repeat the words they hear often on the parents' lips—of Christ, and faith, and truth. Precious truth may be spoken by children. Whole armies of children may come under Christ's banner as missionaries, even in their childhood years. Never repulse the desire of children to do something for Jesus. Never quench their ardor for working in some way for the Master. Children rightly educated will learn to love Jesus and to grieve if they think they have grieved the Saviour by any sin committed by them. Keep their hearts tender and sensitive by your own words and example.[7]

The angels of God are ever near your little ones. . . . Let love and tenderness, patience and self-control, be at all times the law of your speech. Winning love is to be like deep waters, ever flowing forth in the management of your children. All through His life, Christ performed acts of love and tenderness for the children.[8]

MISSIONARY TO THE POOR

The Spirit of the Lord is upon me, because he hath anointed me to preach the gospel to the poor; he hath sent me to heal the brokenhearted, to preach deliverance to the captives, and recovering of sight to the blind, to set at liberty them that are bruised. Luke 4:18.

The sufferings of humanity ever touched the heart and called forth the sympathy and love of Christ. He exercised pity and compassion toward those who were afflicted in soul or body. His example in the matter of treating the suffering and afflicted should teach us how to have compassion and pity for the sufferings of His creatures.

Christ suffered in the flesh. . . . He knew what it was to suffer keen pangs of hunger, and He has given special lessons in regard to feeding the hungry and caring for the needy poor, and has declared that in ministering to the needy we are ministering to Himself in the person of His saints. He says, "I was an hungred, and ye gave me meat" (Matt. 25:35). He knew the discomfort and suffering of thirst, and He declared that a cup of cold water given in His name to any of His disciples should not lose its reward.[9]

Christ was an active, constant worker. He found the domain of religion fenced in by high, steep walls of seclusion as too sacred a matter for everyday life. He threw down the walls of partition, and exercised His helping power in behalf of every one who needed Him. He brought cheerfulness and hope to the desponding. . . . He did not ask, What is your creed? To what church do you belong? Active, earnest, loving interest marked His life. . . .

The Lord Jesus knows what poverty means. He is the great missionary to the poor, the sick, the suffering. The King of heaven, He could have led a life of wealth and have lived among the wealthiest; but He chose poverty. And He has honored the poor who believe in Him, for He blessed them forever. Poverty with Christ is riches of the highest value. This poverty is sanctified and blessed. . . .

In the humanity of Christ there are golden threads that bind the believing, trusting poor man to His own soul of infinite love.[10]

THE PATTERN MAN

For ye know the grace of our Lord Jesus Christ, that, though he was rich, yet for your sakes he became poor, that ye through his poverty might be rich. 2 Cor. 8:9.

This world has been visited by the Majesty of heaven, the Son of God. . . . Christ came to this world as the expression of the very heart and mind and nature and character of God. . . . But He laid aside His royal robe and kingly crown, and stepped down from His high command to take the place of a servant. He was rich, but for our sake, that we might have eternal riches, He became poor. He made the world, but so completely did He empty Himself that during His ministry He declared, ". . . the Son of man hath not where to lay his head." . . .

Christ stood at the head of humanity in the garb of humanity. So full of sympathy and love was His attitude that the poorest was not afraid to come to Him. He was kind to all; easily approached by the most lowly. He went from house to house, healing the sick, feeding the hungry, comforting the mourners, soothing the afflicted, speaking peace to the distressed. He took the little children in His arms and blessed them, and spoke words of hope and comfort to the weary mothers. With unfailing tenderness and gentleness He met every form of human woe and affliction. Not for Himself, but for others did He labor. He was willing to humble Himself, to deny Himself. He did not seek to distinguish Himself. He was the servant of all. It was His meat and drink to be a comfort and a consolation to others, to gladden the sad and heavy-laden ones with whom He daily came in contact.

Christ stands before us as the pattern Man, the great Medical Missionary—an example for all who should come after. His love, pure and holy, blessed all who came within the sphere of its influence. His character was absolutely perfect, free from the slightest stain of sin. He came as an expression of the perfect love of God, not to crush, not to judge and condemn, but to heal every weak, defective character, to save men and women from Satan's power. He is the Creator, Redeemer, and Sustainer of the human race.[11]

TENDER, LOVING, COMPASSIONATE

But thou, O Lord, art a God full of compassion, and gracious, long-suffering, and plenteous in mercy and truth. Ps. 86:15.

God has ordained according to the law of ministry that we should comfort one another in tenderness and love when great sorrows come upon us. No man liveth unto himself. No one dieth unto himself. Life and death both mean something to every human being. . . . God has enjoined the duty upon His human agents to communicate the character of God, testifying to His grace, His wisdom, and His benevolence, by manifesting His refined, tender, merciful love. . . . Jesus . . . was ever touched with human woe, and our hearts should be softened and subdued by His Holy Spirit, that we may be like Him. . . .

Our work is to restore the moral image of God in man through the abundant grace given us of God by Jesus Christ. Everywhere we shall find souls ready to die, and how essential it is that the compassion of Christ shall be given us of Him, in order that we may never place one soul in defiance by not manifesting long forbearance and pitying tenderness. . . . I inquire, Will we ever learn the gentleness of Christ? Oh, how much we need to know Jesus and our heavenly Father that we may represent Him in character! . . .

Jesus calls us to Himself not simply to refresh us with His grace and presence for a few hours, and then to send us forth from His light to walk apart from Him in sadness and gloom. No, no. He tells us that we must abide with Him and He with us. Wherever His work is to be done He is present—tender, loving, and compassionate. He has prepared for you and me an abiding dwelling place in Himself. He is our refuge. Our experience should broaden and deepen. Jesus has opened up all the divine fullness of His inexpressible love, and He declares to you, Ye are labourers together with God (1 Cor. 3:9). O what meaning these words have—"Abide in me" (John 15:4), "Take my yoke upon you" (Matt. 11:29). Will we take it? for the promise is, "Ye shall find rest unto your souls." There is rest, complete rest in abiding in Christ.[12]

45

AN ATTRIBUTE WE MAY SHARE

Be ye therefore merciful, as your Father also is merciful. Luke 6:36.

Mercy is an attribute that the human agent may share with God, thus cooperating with Him. Mercy is kind, pitiful. Mercy and the love of God purify the soul and beautify the heart, cleansing the life from selfishness. . . .

God's love for the angelic host is as a part of Himself, direct and positive in its divinity. God's love for the human race is a peculiar form—a love born of mercy, for the human subject is all-undeserving. . . .

Mercy implies the imperfection of the object upon which it is bestowed. Because of man's imperfection, mercy was brought into active existence. Sin is not the object of God's love, but of His hatred. Yet He pities the sinner, because the guilty one bears the Creator's image and has received from Him the capabilities that make it possible for him to become a son of God, not through his own merits, but through the imputed merits of Jesus Christ, through the great sacrifice the Saviour has made in his behalf. . . .

In the church militant the children of men will be ever in need of restoration from the results of sin. . . . We are all dependent on one another. Almost invariably a man who is superior to another man in some respect is inferior to him in other respects. Every human being on earth is subject to temptation. And all are in need of human influence and sympathy. . . . He who cooperates with God by showing mercy brings himself into a position where God will extend mercy to him, for he is in harmony with the divine attributes.

God's love and mercy are ever extended toward sinners. Shall men who themselves have sinned against God, refuse to forgive and accept a repentant sinner? . . . God loved us while we were yet sinners. How clear and unmistakable the line of duty is made by the words, "As ye would that men should do to you, do ye also to them likewise" (Luke 6:31). . . . Only those who walk with Christ can be truly merciful.[13]

THE COMPASSIONATE HEALER

And Jesus went forth, and saw a great multitude, and was moved with compassion toward them, and he healed their sick. Matt. 14:14.

Jesus, precious Saviour, never seemed to become weary of the importunities of the sin-sick souls and the sick with all kinds of diseases. And Jesus, when he came out, saw much people, and was moved with compassion toward them (Mark 6:34). This means a great deal to the suffering ones. He identified His interest with theirs. He shared their burdens. He felt their fears. He had yearning pity that was pain to the heart of Christ.

O what love, what matchless love! He has become one with us that He might share with humanity in all their experience. He was tempted in all points like as we are, yet was without sin. Humanity is not to be demerited as a cheap and common thing. Christ clothed His divinity with humanity that humanity might be clothed with the righteousness of Christ. Man is the object of His solicitude and great love.

Redemption—O how much is comprehended in the word! All who will consent to be redeemed are uplifted and sanctified, redeemed through Jesus Christ from all commonness and earthliness, and enabled to cooperate with God in the great work of salvation. Jesus accepted humanity and revealed in His own life and character what man may be even when, in the providence of God, he is placed in the poorest circumstances of life. He had not even a penny wherewith to pay the tax money exacted, and wrought a miracle to obtain the little sum.

Jesus, precious Saviour, was homeless and often hungry. He had not where to lay His head. He was wearied oft. Humanity is honored because Jesus assumed humanity to reveal to the world what humanity may become. He came to bring life and immortality to light, to fill the commonplace, homeliest pursuits of life with brightness. Jesus is bending over us, searching into our characters to see if His own character is reflected in us.[14]

BEARER OF OUR AFFLICTIONS

That it might be fulfilled which was spoken by Esaias the prophet, saying, Himself took our infirmities, and bare our sicknesses. Matt. 8:17.

Christ alone was able to bear the afflictions of the many. "In all their affliction he was afflicted" (Isa. 63:9). He never bore disease in His own flesh, but He carried the sickness of others. With tenderest sympathy He looked upon the suffering ones who pressed about Him. He groaned in spirit as He saw the work of Satan revealed in all their woe, and He made every case of need and of sorrow His own. No multiplicity of numbers distracted Him. No anguish overwhelmed Him. With a power that never quailed He cast out the evil spirits that possessed mind and body, while the pain of the sufferers thrilled through His whole being. The power of love was in all His healing. He identified His interests with suffering humanity.

Christ was health and strength in Himself, and when sufferers were in His immediate presence, disease was always rebuked. It was for this reason that He did not go at once to Lazarus. He could not witness his suffering and not bring him relief. He could not witness disease or death without combating the power of Satan. The death of Lazarus was permitted that through his resurrection the last and crowning evidence might be given to the Jews that Jesus was the Son of God.

And in all this conflict with the power of evil there was ever before Christ the darkened shadow into which He Himself must enter. Ever before Him was the means by which He must pay the ransom for these souls. . . . When He raised Lazarus from the dead He knew that for that life He must pay the ransom on the cross of Calvary. Every rescue made was to cause Him the deepest humiliation. He was to taste death for every man. . . . Of the suffering multitudes brought to Christ it is said, "He healed them all" (Matt. 12:15). Thus He expressed His love for the children of men. His miracles were part of His mission. . . . He knows how to speak the word "Be whole," and when He has healed the sufferer He says, "Go and sin no more."[15]

SHARING HEAVEN'S TREASURES

Freely ye have received, freely give. Matt. 10:8.

The blessed Redeemer has set us an example in living out the precepts of the law. He says to His followers, "Freely ye have received, freely give." We are to have an open heart to receive the rich treasures of heaven, and our hearts are to be opened to let those rich treasures out to others. Oh, we need to abide in Christ, then we will be a constant channel through which God will communicate to our brethren and to the world His own gracious Spirit. . . .

When we have an assurance which is bright and clear of our own salvation, we shall exhibit cheerfulness and joyfulness, which becomes every follower of Jesus Christ. The softening, subduing influence of the love of God, brought into practical life, will make impressions upon minds that will be a savor of life unto life. But a harsh, denunciatory spirit, if manifested, will turn many souls away from the truth into the ranks of the enemy. Solemn thought! To deal patiently with the tempted requires us to battle with self. But God has given Jesus to us, and believing on Him as our personal Saviour, all heaven is at our command. The purchased possession of Christ is around us on every hand. There is want, there is wretchedness and sin on every side. "Freely ye have received, freely give."

> "Oh, hearts are bruised, dead,
> And homes are bare and cold,
> And lambs for whom the Shepherd bled,
> Are straying from the fold.
>
> .   .   .   .   .
>
> "The captives to release,
> To God the lost to bring,
> To teach the way of life and peace,
> It is a Christlike thing."[16]

49

THE GREATEST TEACHER

And we know that the Son of God is come, and hath given us an understanding, that we may know him that is true, and we are in him that is true, even in his Son Jesus Christ. This is the true God, and eternal life. 1 John 5:20.

The world's Redeemer did not come with outward display, or a show of worldly wisdom. Men could not see beneath the disguise of humility the glory of the Son of God. . . .

Christ reached the people where they were. He presented the plain truth to their minds in the most forcible and simple language. The humble poor, the most unlearned, could comprehend, through faith in Him, the most exalted truths of God. No one needed to consult the learned doctors as to His meaning. He did not perplex the ignorant with mysterious inferences, or use unaccustomed and learned words of which they had no knowledge. The greatest Teacher the world has ever known was the most definite, simple, and practical in His instruction. . . .

He attracted attention to purity of life, to humility of spirit, and to devotion to God and His cause without hope of worldly honor or reward. He must divest religion of the narrow, conceited formalism which made it a burden and a reproach. He must present a complete, harmonious salvation to all. The narrow bounds of national exclusiveness must be overthrown, for His salvation was to reach the ends of the earth. He rejoiced in spirit as He beheld the poor of this world eagerly accepting the precious message which He brought. He looked up to heaven and said, "I thank thee, O Father, Lord of heaven and earth, because thou hast hid these things from the wise and prudent, and hast revealed them unto babes" (Matt. 11:25). . . .

Men of the highest education and accomplishments have learned the most precious lessons from the precept and example of the humble follower of Christ, who is designated as "unlearned" by the world. But could men look with deeper insight they would see that these humble men had obtained an education in the highest of all schools, even in the school of the divine Teacher, who spake as never man spake.[17]

TEACHING IN DEPTH

The officers answered, Never man spake like this man. John 7:46.

Of Christ's teaching it is said, "The common people heard him gladly" (Mark 12:37). Never man spake like this man, declared the officers who were sent to take Him. His words comforted, strengthened, and blessed those who were hungering for that peace which He alone could give. O how tender and forbearing was Christ! how filled with pity and tenderness were His lessons to the poor, the afflicted, and the oppressed! . . . His illustrations were taken from the things of daily life, and . . . had in them a wonderful depth of meaning. The fowls of the air, the lilies of the field, the seed, the shepherd and the sheep—with these objects Christ illustrated immortal truth, and ever afterward, when His hearers chanced to see these things of nature, they recalled His words. . . .

Christ's words, so comforting and cheering to those that listened to them, are for us today. As a faithful shepherd knows and cares for his sheep, so Christ cares for His children. He knows the trials and difficulties surrounding each one. "He shall feed his flock like a shepherd," declares Isaiah: "he shall gather the lambs with his arms, and carry them in his bosom." Christ knows His sheep intimately, and the suffering and helpless are objects of His special care. . . .

Christ has weighed every human affliction, every human sorrow. He bears the weight of the yoke for every soul that yokes up with Him. He knows the sorrows which we feel to the depth of our being, and which we cannot express. If no human heart is aroused to sympathy for us, we need not feel that we are without sympathy. Christ knows; and He says, Look unto Me, and live. "Come unto me, all ye that labour and are heavy laden, and I will give you rest" (Matt. 11:28). I have borne your griefs and carried your sorrows. You have the deepest, richest sympathy in the tender, pitying love of your Shepherd. . . . His humanity is not lost in the exalted character of His Omnipotence. He is ever longing to pour out His sympathy and love upon those whom He has chosen, and who will respond to His invitation.[18]

51

CHRIST THE GOOD SHEPHERD

I am the good shepherd, and know my sheep, and am known of mine. As the Father knoweth me, even so know I the Father: and I lay down my life for the sheep. John 10:14, 15.

Jesus says, "I know my sheep." Let us consider this statement. We are known by God before we receive Him. "I know my sheep." How do souls become Christ's sheep? By choosing to receive Him. But Christ had first chosen them. He knew everyone who would respond to His drawing, and He knew everyone who would be inclined to receive Him but who, through popular opposing influences, would turn from Him. John says to all, "Behold the Lamb of God, which taketh away the sin of the world" (John 1:29). Those who heard the voice and did behold Jesus as the Lamb of God believed in Him and became His property from their own choice. But . . . their choosing of Christ was in response to His drawing. The love of Jesus was expressed to us before we loved Him. . . .

To Jesus the whole human family is entrusted, as the flocks of sheep are entrusted to a shepherd. These sheep and lambs are to be tended with pastoral care. They will be guarded by the faithful Chief Shepherd, under the care of faithful under shepherds, and if they will obey the voice of the Chief Shepherd they will not be left to be devoured by wolves. . . .

Jesus says, "My sheep hear my voice, . . . and they follow me" (John 10:27). The Shepherd of Israel does not drive His flock, but He leads them. His attitude is wholly one of invitation. "My sheep hear my voice." If we are indeed sons and daughters of God we not only hear, but recognize the voice above all others. We appreciate the words of Christ, we distinguish the truth as it is in Jesus from all error, and the truth refreshes the soul, and fills it with gladness. . . .

The beautiful illustration in Revelation 7 is a pastoral symbol. ". . . They shall hunger no more, neither thirst any more; neither shall the sun light on them, nor any heat. For the Lamb which is in the midst of the throne shall feed them, and shall lead them unto living fountains of waters . . ." (Rev. 7:16, 17).[19]

IN THE BOSOM OF THE SHEPHERD

He shall feed his flock like a shepherd: he shall gather the lambs with his arms, and carry them in his bosom, and shall gently lead those that are with young. Isa. 40:11.

A true shepherd knows and pities and helps the sheep that most need his help—those that are bruised and lame and feeble. "He shall feed his flock like a shepherd."

Far more intimately than the patriarch Jacob knew the weak, the suffering, and the lame among his sheep, does the Chief Shepherd know His flock. He knows what no one else knows. He has Himself weighed every burden. No one knows the weight like Himself, for He has borne all our griefs, and carried all our sorrows. It was this that made Him a man of sorrows and acquainted with grief. . . .

If there is not another soul in the universe that regards you, the Lord God of Israel is looking upon you with thoughts of compassion, tenderness, and sympathy. He sees you with your strong impulses when fainthearted and discouraged. . . . You have the deepest, the richest, the most refreshing sympathy in the bosom of the great Shepherd. We have not an high priest who cannot sympathize with us, but One who was in all points tempted like as we are, yet without sin. . . .

Not only has every provision been made that when tried and tempted you should find help and strength and grace, but also that your influence upon other minds should be fragrant. Not only does Christ know every soul, and the temptations and trials of that soul, but He knows all the circumstances that irritate and chafe the spirit. Your great danger is in being self-sufficient. This will not do for a Christian. Christ will give you His patience if you ask for it. . . .

God's abounding love and presence will give you the power of self-control. He will mold and fashion your mind and character. He will direct your aims and purposes and capabilities in a channel that will give you moral and spiritual power which you will not have to leave here in this world but can carry with you and retain through eternal ages.[20]

THE SONS OF GOD

But as many as received him, to them gave he power to become the sons o f God, even to them that believe on his name. John 1:12.

How did men treat Christ when He came? . . . "He came unto his own, and his own received him not" (John 1:11). Thus it is today. This history is being repeated, and will be repeated again and again before the Lord shall come in the clouds of heaven. The deceptions of Satan will be upon those who dwell on the earth. . . .

"But as many as received him, to them gave he power to become the sons of God." . . . After fitting up this world as the dwelling place of man, God looked upon it, and rejoiced in it, pronouncing it very good. So He will accept of and rejoice in the reformation wrought out by those who, receiving Christ as their Saviour, have obtained power to become the sons of God. . . .

The first chapter of Colossians shows us the heights to which it is our privilege to attain. We may be "filled with the knowledge of his will in all wisdom and spiritual understanding," walking "worthy of the Lord," "being fruitful in every good work, and increasing in the knowledge of God; strengthened with all might, according to his glorious power, unto all patience and longsuffering with joyfulness; giving thanks unto the Father, which hath made us meet to be partakers of the inheritance of the saints in light: who hath delivered us from the power of darkness, and hath translated us into the kingdom of his dear Son: in whom we have redemption through his blood, even the forgiveness of sins" (Col. 1:9-14).

Is there not woe enough in this sin-stricken, sin-cursed earth to lead us to consecrate ourselves to the work of proclaiming the message that "God so loved the world, that he gave his only begotten Son, that whosoever believeth in him should not perish, but have everlasting life" (John 3:16)? This earth has been trodden by the Son of God. He came to bring men light and life, to set them free from the bondage of sin. He is coming again in power and great glory to receive to Himself those who during this life have followed in His footsteps.[21]

WHEN MAN COOPERATES

For it is God which worketh in you both to will and to do of his good pleasure. Phil. 2:13.

"Behold, I stand at the door, and knock: if any man hear my voice, and open the door, I will come in to him, and will sup with him, and he with me" (Rev. 3:20). Thus the world's Redeemer illustrates the work of the Holy Spirit upon the human heart. The living agent, by an act of faith of his own, places himself in the hands of the Lord for Him to work in him His good pleasure in His time. There must be a continual exercise of faith to be in Christ and keep in Christ, abiding by faith in Him.

This is a training process, a constant discipline of the mind and heart, that Christ shall work His great work in human hearts. Self, the old natural self, dies, and Christ's will is our will, His way is our way, and the human agent becomes, with heart, mind, and intellect, an instrument in the hands of God to work no more wickedness but the righteousness of Christ. . . .

In the divine arrangement God does nothing without the cooperation of man. He compels no man's will. That must be given to the Lord completely, else the Lord is not able to accomplish His divine work that He would do through the human agency. Jesus declared that in a certain place He could not do many mighty works among the people because of their unbelief. He wanted to do for them in that place just what He knew that they needed to have done, but He could not because unbelief barred the way. The potter cannot mold and fashion unto honor that which has never been placed in his hands. The Christian life is one of daily surrender, submission, and continual overcoming, gaining fresh victories every day. This is the growing up into Christ, fashioning the life into the divine Model. . . .

Devotion, piety, and sanctification of the entire man come through Jesus Christ our righteousness. The love of God needs to be constantly cultivated. O how my heart cries out to the living God for the mind of Jesus Christ! I want to lose sight of self.[22]

WILL YOU LET HIM IN?

The Lord hath appeared of old unto me, saying, Yea, I have loved thee with an everlasting love: therefore with lovingkindness have I drawn thee. Jer. 31:3.

The work dearest to the heart of Christ is that of drawing souls to Him. . . . Look at Jesus, the Majesty of heaven.* What do you behold in His life history? His divinity clothed with humanity, a whole life of continual humility, the doing of one act of condescension after another, a line of continual descent from the heavenly courts to a world all seared and marred with the curse, and in a world unworthy of His presence, descending lower and still lower, taking the form of a servant, to be despised and rejected of men, obliged to flee from place to place to save His life, and at last betrayed, rejected, crucified. Then, as sinners for whom Jesus suffered more than the power of mortal can portray, shall we refuse to humble our proud will?

Study day and night the character of Christ. It was His tender compassion, His inexpressible, unparalleled love for your soul, that led Him to endure all the shame, the revilings, the abuse, the misapprehensions of earth. Approach nearer Him, behold His hands and His feet, bruised and wounded for our transgressions. "The chastisement of our peace was upon him; and with his stripes we are healed."

Lose no time, let not another day pass into eternity, but just as you are, whatever your weakness, your unworthiness, your neglect, delay not to come now. . . . The call of Jesus to come to Him, the presentation of a crown of glory that fadeth not away, the life, the eternal life that measures with the life of God, has not been of sufficient inducement to lead you to serve Him with your undivided affections. . . .

Be no longer on Satan's side of the question. Make decided, radical changes through the grace given you of God. No longer insult His grace. He is saying with tears, "Ye will not come to me, that ye might have life" (John 5:40). Now Jesus is inviting you, knocking at the door of your heart for entrance. Will you let Him come in?[23]

---

*From a personal letter of appeal.

THE HOLY SPIRIT OUR HELPER

For as many as are led by the Spirit of God, they are the sons of God. Rom. 8:14.

Through the ministry of the angels the Holy Spirit is enabled to work upon the mind and heart of the human agent and draw him to Christ. . . . But the Spirit of God does not interfere with the freedom of the human agent. The Holy Spirit is given to be a helper, so that man may cooperate with the Divine, and it is given to Him to draw the soul but never to force obedience.

Christ is ready to impart all heavenly influences. He knows every temptation that comes to man, and the capabilities of each. He weighs his strength. He sees the present and the future, and presents before the mind the obligations that should be met, and urges that common, earthly things shall not be permitted to be so absorbing that eternal things shall be lost out of the reckoning. The Lord has fullness of grace to bestow on every one that will receive of the heavenly gift. The Holy Spirit will bring the God-entrusted capabilities into Christ's service, and will mold and fashion the human agent according to the divine Pattern.[24]

The Holy Spirit is our efficiency in the work of character building, in forming characters after the divine similitude. When we think ourselves capable of molding our own experience, we make a great mistake. We can never of ourselves obtain the victory over temptation. But those who have genuine faith in Christ will be worked by the Holy Spirit. The soul in whose heart faith abides will grow into a beautiful temple for the Lord. He is directed by the grace of Christ. Just in proportion as he depends on the Holy Spirit's teaching he will grow.[25]

The influence of the Holy Spirit is the life of Christ in the soul. We do not now see Christ and speak to Him, but His Holy Spirit is just as near us in one place as another. It works in and through everyone who receives Christ. Those who know the indwelling of the Spirit reveal the fruit of the Spirit—love, joy, peace, long-suffering, gentleness, goodness, faith.[26]

A HIDDEN TREASURE

Again, the kingdom of heaven is like unto treasure hid in a field; the which when a man hath found, he hideth, and for joy thereof goeth and selleth all that he hath, and buyeth that field. Matt. 13:44.

Without the kingdom of God we are lost . . . and are without hope in the world, but salvation has been provided for us through faith in Jesus Christ. He is the treasure, and when the rubbish of the world is swept away, we are enabled to discern His infinite value. . . .

The divinity of Christ was as a hidden treasure. At times when He was upon earth divinity flashed through humanity, and His true character was revealed. The God of heaven testified to His oneness with His Son. At His baptism the heavens were opened and the glory of God in the similitude of a dove like burnished gold hovered over the Saviour, and a voice came from heaven, saying, "This is my beloved Son, in whom I am well pleased" (Matt. 3:17). But the nation to whom Christ came, though professing to be the peculiar people of God, did not recognize the heavenly treasure in the person of Jesus Christ. . . .

The Majesty of heaven was not discerned in the disguise of humanity. He was the divine Teacher sent from God, the glorious Treasure given to humanity. He was fairer than the sons of men, but His matchless glory was hidden under a cover of poverty and suffering. He veiled His glory in order that divinity might touch humanity, and the treasure of immense value was not discerned by the human race. . . .

"The Word was made flesh, and dwelt among us" (John 1:14). The treasure indeed is hidden under the garb of humanity. Christ is the unsearchable riches, and he who finds Christ finds heaven. The human agent who looks upon Jesus, who dwells by faith on His matchless charms, finds the eternal treasure.[27]

Christ does not use this parable to commend the man who hides the treasure until he can buy the field, but His object in using this illustration is to convey to our mind the value of spiritual things. To obtain worldly treasure, the man would make a sacrifice of his all, and how much more should we give for the priceless, heavenly treasure![28]

HAVE YOU ENROLLED?

My son, give me thine heart, and let thine eyes observe my ways. Prov. 23:26.

Dear youth, the very best thing you can do is to enlist freely and decidedly in the army of the Lord. Surrender yourself into the hands of God, that your will and ways may be guided by the One who is unerring in wisdom and infinite in goodness. To withhold yourself from God is to rob God of that which is His own. The Lord hath need of you, and you have need of the Lord. It is not safe for you to put off the decisive step, or delay the matter of making a complete surrender of yourself to God. If you have not already given yourself to God, I beseech you to do it now. Let your name be enrolled in the heavenly records as one of the chosen and elect of God. . . .

"God so loved the world, that he gave his only begotten Son, that whosoever believeth in him should not perish, but have everlasting life" (John 3:16). . . . It is through the inestimable gift of Christ that all our blessings come. Life, health, friends, reason, happiness, are ours through the merit of Christ. O that the young and the old might realize that all comes to them through the virtue of Christ's life and death, and acknowledge the ownership of God. . . .

Even when we were under the control of a cruel master, even when the prince of darkness ruled our spirits, the Lord Jesus Christ paid the ransom price of His own blood for us. You have been bought with a price, even with the precious blood of Christ; you are His property, therefore glorify God in your body, and in your spirit, which are God's. . . .

Were it not for the love freely given us of Christ, we should now be in hopeless despair, in spiritual midnight. Thank God every day that He gave us Jesus. Will you not accept His gift? Will you not be His witness? Time is short, and it becomes you to work while the day lasts, living an imperishable life, hiding your life with Christ in God. Then "when Christ, who is our life, shall appear, then shall ye also appear with him in glory" (Col. 3:4).[29]

"WHAT MANNER OF LOVE"!

Behold, what manner of love the Father hath bestowed upon us, that we should be called the sons of God: therefore the world knoweth us not, because it knew him not. 1 John 3:1.

"But as many as received him, to them gave he power to become the sons of God" (John 1:12). . . . "For as many as are led by the Spirit of God, they are the sons of God. For ye have not received the spirit of bondage again to fear; but ye have received the spirit of adoption, whereby we cry, Abba, Father. The Spirit itself beareth witness with our spirit, that we are the children of God: and if children, then heirs; heirs of God, and joint-heirs with Christ; if so be that we suffer with him, that we may be also glorified together. For I reckon that the sufferings of this present time are not worthy to be compared with the glory which shall be revealed in us" (Rom. 8:14-18).

John cannot find adequate words wherein to describe the amazing love of God to sinful man, but he calls upon all to behold the love of God revealed in the gift of His only begotten Son. Through the perfection of the sacrifice given for the guilty race, those who believe in Christ . . . may be saved from eternal ruin. Christ was one with the Father, yet when sin entered our world through Adam's transgression, He was willing to step down from the exaltation of One who was equal with God, who dwelt in light unapproachable by humanity, so full of glory that no man could behold His face and live, and submit to insult, mockery, suffering, pain, and death, in order to answer the claims of the immutable law of God, and make a way of escape for the transgressor by His death and righteousness. This was the work which His Father gave Him to do, and those who accept Christ, relying wholly upon His merits, are made the adopted sons and daughters of God—are heirs of God, and joint heirs with Jesus Christ. . . .

Let no one . . . think that it is a condescension for any man, however talented or learned or honored, to accept Christ. Every human being should look to heaven with reverence and gratitude, and exclaim with amazement, "Behold, what manner of love the Father hath bestowed upon us."[30]

"WE SHALL BE LIKE HIM"

Beloved, now are we the sons of God, and it doth not yet appear what we shall be: but we know that, when he shall appear, we shall be like him; for we shall see him as he is. 1 John 3:2.

Jesus, the world's Redeemer, knows all His children by name, and on those who believe shall come the glory of God. . . . Those who behold Jesus become changed to His image, become assimilated to His nature, and the glory of God that shines in the face of Jesus, is reflected in the lives of His followers. More and more the Christian is changed from glory to glory. . . . The more he looks on Christ, the more he loves and longs to look again, and the more light and love and glory he sees in Christ, the more his light increases. . . .

It is by faith that the spiritual eye beholds the glory of Jesus. This glory is hidden until the Lord imparts the light of spiritual truth, for the eye of reason cannot see it. The glory and mystery of Christ remains incomprehensible, clouded by its excessive brightness, until the Lord flashes its meaning before the soul. . . . By faith the soul catches divine light from Jesus. We see matchless charms in His purity and humility, His self-denial, His wonderful sacrifice to save fallen man. Contemplation of Christ leads man to place a proper estimate upon himself. . . . The possibility of being like Jesus, whom he loves and adores, inspires within him that faith which works by love and purifies the heart. . . .

Jesus is more precious to the soul that beholds Him by the eye of faith than is anything else beside, and the believing soul is more precious to Jesus than fine gold of Ophir. Christ looks upon His hands—the marks of the crucifixion are there—and He says, "I have graven thee upon the palms of my hands; thy walls are continually before me" (Isa. 49:16). The Christian is walled in by the rich full promises of an infinite God.

The Lord is coming with power and great glory. All who have made Christ their refuge will reflect His image, and they will be like Him, for they shall see Him as He is. They are to be presented to Him without "spot, or wrinkle, or any such thing" (Eph. 5:27).[31]

UNDER THE GREAT TEACHER

Therefore if any man be in Christ, he is a new creature: old things are passed away; behold, all things are become new. 2 Cor. 5:17.

When true conversion takes place in the heart, it is made manifest in a transformation of character, for those who are converted become Christlike. Pride no longer lives in the heart, sin seems abominable. The converted soul hates the thing that depraves his moral sensibilities. He hates that which crucified the Lord of life and glory. Those who are truly converted grow in the knowledge of the Lord and Saviour Jesus Christ, and as knowledge of Christ increases, they see more clearly where their own weakness lies; they realize the deep depravity of their natures. They understand the strength of sin, and know the power of their old habits. . . . They have daily a sense of their entire inability to do anything without the help of Jesus Christ, therefore they say to Him, "I cast my helpless soul upon Thee. 'In my hand no price I bring, Simply to Thy cross I cling.'"

As the sinner beholds the Lamb of God, he sees more clearly what provision God has made to take away the sins of the world. He sees the sufficiency and adaptation of the Spirit of grace for every conflict. The mysterious provision for the taking away of sin is Jesus Christ. . . . "He is the propitiation for our sins: and not for our's only, but also for the sins of the whole world" (1 John 2:2). . . .

The true Christian will not refuse to practice self-denial for Christ's sake. Those who are children of God are earnest workers; they are not slothful servants. There are no drones in the household of God. Every member of the household of faith has his work appointed to him. . . . If he is a learner in the school of Christ, he will learn how to give a testimony, how to pray, how to be a living witness for the Master. . . .

The true Christian will be a diligent and constant student. He will realize that he lacks wisdom, strength, and experience, and he will place his will and all his interests in the care of the great Teacher.[32]

REDEEMED BY CHRIST'S BLOOD

Forasmuch as ye know that ye were not redeemed with corruptible things, as silver and gold, from your vain conversation received by tradition from your fathers; but with the precious blood of Christ, as of a lamb without blemish and without spot. 1 Peter 1:18, 19.

"Ye are not your own. . . . Ye are bought with a price: therefore glorify God in your body, and in your spirit, which are God's" (1 Cor. 6:19, 20). Will you give back to God that which He has ransomed with the price of His own blood? Will you give Him your reasoning powers; will you set them apart for His glory? They are His; He has bought them with a price. Will you place yourselves in the school of Christ, that your conscience may be enlightened, that it may be a good conscience, a faithful sentinel to guard the highest interests of the soul? Christ has purchased the affections; will you trifle with them, will you pervert them? Will you place them upon unworthy objects, center them upon human beings and make the creature instead of the Creator your god to worship? Or shall your affections be purified, ennobled, refined, and made to twine about your Creator and Redeemer? . . .

God will not occupy a divided heart or reign from a divided throne. Every rival that holds the affections and diverts them from the God of love must be dethroned. The Lord demands all that there is of us, and there must be no reserve. Christ has purchased us, we are His heritage, and we are to be honored by being co-laborers with Jesus Christ. Wear the yoke with Christ, and daily walk with God. How shall we do this? By laying hold upon the help which God has provided. The Lord has said, "Ask, and it shall be given you; seek, and ye shall find; knock, and it shall be opened unto you" (Matt. 7:7).[33]

God has bought us, and He claims a throne in each heart. Our minds and bodies must be subordinated to Him, and the natural habits and appetites must be made subservient to the higher wants of the soul. But we can place no dependence upon ourselves in this work. We cannot with safety follow our own guidance. The Holy Spirit must renew and sanctify us. In God's service there must be no halfway work.[34]

THE WEIGHT OF GOD'S WRATH

All we like sheep have gone astray; we have turned every one to his own way; and the Lord hath laid on him the iniquity of us all. Isa. 53:6.

In the Garden of Gethsemane Christ suffered in man's stead, and the human nature of the Son of God staggered under the terrible horror of the guilt of sin, until from His pale and quivering lips was forced the agonizing cry, "O my Father, if it be possible, let this cup pass from me"; but if there is no other way by which the salvation of fallen man may be accomplished, then "not as I will, but as thou wilt" (Matt. 26:39).

The power that inflicted retributive justice upon man's substitute and surety, was the power that sustained and upheld the suffering One under the tremendous weight of wrath that would have fallen upon a sinful world. Christ was suffering the death that was pronounced upon the transgressors of God's law. It is a fearful thing for the unrepenting sinner to fall into the hands of the living God. This is proved by the history of the destruction of the old world by a flood, by the record of the fire which fell from heaven and destroyed the inhabitants of Sodom. But never was this proved to so great an extent as in the agony of Christ, . . . when He bore the wrath of God for a sinful world. . . .

Man has not been made a sin-bearer, and he will never know the horror of the curse of sin which the Saviour bore. No sorrow can bear any comparison with the sorrow of Him upon whom the wrath of God fell with overwhelming force. Human nature can endure but a limited amount of test and trial. The finite can only endure the finite measure, and human nature succumbs; but the nature of Christ had a greater capacity for suffering; for the human existed in the divine nature, and created a capacity for suffering to endure that which resulted from the sins of a lost world. The agony which Christ endured, broadens, deepens, and gives a more extended conception of the character of sin, and the character of the retribution which God will bring upon those who continue in sin. The wages of sin is death, but the gift of God is eternal life through Jesus Christ.[35]

THE CROSS OF CALVARY

And when they were come to the place, which is called Calvary, there they crucified him, and the malefactors, one on the right hand, and the other on the left. Luke 23:33.

The cross of Calvary appeals in power, affording a reason why we should love Christ now, and why we should consider Him first, and best, and last, in everything. We should take our fitting place in humble penitence at the foot of the cross. We may learn the lessons of meekness and lowliness of mind as we go up to Mount Calvary, and, looking upon the cross, see our Saviour in agony, the Son of God dying, the Just for the unjust. Behold Him who could summon legions of angels to His assistance with one word, a subject of jest and merriment, of reviling and hatred. He gives Himself a sacrifice for sin. When reviled, He threatened not; when falsely accused, He opened not His mouth. He prays on the cross for His murderers. He is dying for them. He is paying an infinite price for every one of them. He would not lose one whom He has purchased at so great cost. He gives Himself to be smitten and scourged without a murmur. And this uncomplaining victim is the Son of God. His throne is from everlasting, and His kingdom shall have no end. . . . Look, O look upon the cross of Calvary; behold the royal victim suffering on your account. . . .

The Son of God was rejected and despised for our sakes. Can you, in full view of the cross, beholding by the eye of faith the sufferings of Christ, tell your tale of woe, your trials? Can you nurse revenge of your enemies in your heart while the prayer of Christ comes from His pale and quivering lips for His revilers, His murderers—"Father, forgive them; for they know not what they do" (Luke 23:34)? . . .

We must not shrink from the depths of humiliation to which the Son of God submitted in order to raise us from the degradation and bondage of sin to a seat at His right hand. . . . It is high time we devoted the few remaining precious hours of our probation to washing our robes of character and making them white in the blood of the Lamb, that we may be of that white-robed company who shall stand about the great white throne.[36]

"DESPISED AND REJECTED"

He is despised and rejected of men; a man of sorrows, and acquainted with grief: and we hid as it were our faces from him; he was despised, and we esteemed him not. Isa. 53:3.

How few have any conception of the anguish which rent the heart of the Son of God during His thirty years of life upon earth. The path from the manger to Calvary was shadowed by sorrow and grief. He was the Man of Sorrows, and endured such heartache as no human language can portray. He could have said in truth, "Behold, and see if there be any sorrow like unto my sorrow" (Lam. 1:12). His suffering was the deepest anguish of the soul; and what man could have sympathy with the soul anguish of the Son of the infinite God? Hating sin with a perfect hatred, He yet gathered to His soul the sins of the whole world, as He trod the path to Calvary, suffering the penalty of the transgressor. Guiltless, He bore the punishment of the guilty; innocent, yet offering Himself to bear the penalty of the transgression of the law of God. The punishment of the sins of every soul was borne by the Son of the infinite God. The guilt of every sin pressed its weight upon the divine soul of the world's Redeemer. He who knew no sin became sin for us that we might be made the righteousness of God in Him. In assuming the nature of man, He placed Himself where He was wounded for our transgressions, bruised for our iniquities, that by His stripes we might be healed.

In His humanity Christ was tried with as much greater temptation, with as much more persevering energy than man is tried by the evil one, as His nature was greater than man's. This is a deep mysterious truth, that Christ is bound to humanity by the most sensitive sympathies. The evil works, the evil thoughts, the evil words of every son and daughter of Adam press upon His divine soul. The sins of men called for retribution upon Himself, for He had become man's substitute, and took upon Him the sins of the world. He bore the sins of every sinner, for all transgressions were imputed unto Him. . . . "How shall we escape, if we neglect so great salvation?" (Heb. 2:3).[1]

"WOUNDED FOR OUR TRANSGRESSIONS"

Surely he hath borne our griefs, and carried our sorrows: yet we did esteem him stricken, smitten of God, and afflicted. But he was wounded for our transgressions, he was bruised for our iniquities: the chastisement of our peace was upon him; and with his stripes we are healed. Isa. 53:4, 5.

The sincere Christian may indeed grieve as he sees the havoc sin has wrought, but only in a limited sense can the human agent comprehend the sadness of Christ as He looks upon sin as it exists in the human heart. . . .

From the light of His exalted purity the world's Redeemer could see that the maladies from which the human family were suffering were brought upon them by transgression of the law of God. Every case of suffering He could trace back to its cause. He read the sad and awful history of the final end of unrepenting sinners. He knew that He alone could rescue them from the pit into which they had fallen. He alone could place their feet in the right path. His perfection alone could avail for their imperfection. He alone could cover their nakedness with His own spotless robe of righteousness.

Christ wanted all. He could not endure that one should be lost. O if the human family could only see the results of sin in the transgression and violence and crime that exist in the world! If they could see the transformation of men from the image of God to the similitude of Satan! Man was created pure and holy, but through transgression he came to possess the attributes of Satan. . . .

In coming to the world in human form, in becoming subject to the law, in revealing to men that He bore their sickness, their sorrow, their guilt, Christ did not become a sinner. He was pure and uncontaminated by any disease. Not one stain of sin was found upon Him. . . . He stood before the world the spotless Lamb of God. When suffering humanity pressed about Him, He who was in the health of perfect manhood was as one afflicted with them. This was essential, that He might express His perfect love in behalf of humanity. . . . Christ was strong to save the whole world.[2]

DEPTHS OF HUMILIATION

Forasmuch then as the children are partakers of flesh and blood, he also himself likewise took part of the same; that through death he might destroy him that had the power of death, that is, the devil. Heb. 2:14.

Wondrous combination of man and God . . . He [Christ] humbled Himself to man's nature. He did this that the Scripture might be fulfilled; and the plan was entered into by the Son of God, knowing all the steps in His humiliation, that He must descend to make an expiation for the sins of a condemned, groaning world. What humility was this! It amazed angels. The tongue can never describe it; the imagination cannot take it in. The eternal Word consented to be made flesh! God became man! It was a wonderful humility.

But He stepped still lower; the Man must humble Himself as a man to bear insult, reproach, shameful accusations, and abuse. There seemed to be no safe place for Him in His own territory. He had to flee from place to place for His life. He was betrayed by one of His disciples; He was denied by one of His most zealous followers. He was mocked. He was crowned with a crown of thorns. He was scourged. He was forced to bear the burden of the cross.

He was not insensible to this contempt and ignominy. He submitted, but, oh! He felt the bitterness as no other being could feel it. He was pure, holy, and undefiled, yet arraigned as a criminal! The adorable Redeemer stepped down from the highest exaltation. Step by step He humbled Himself to die—but what a death! It was the most shameful, the most cruel—the death upon the cross as a malefactor. He did not die as a hero in the eyes of the world, loaded with honors, as men in battle. He died as a condemned criminal, suspended between the heavens and the earth—died a lingering death of shame, exposed to the tauntings and revilings of a debased, crime-loaded, profligate multitude! . . .

All this humiliation of the Majesty of heaven was for guilty, condemned man. He went lower and lower in His humiliation, until there were no lower depths that He could reach, in order to lift man up from his moral defilement. All this was for you.[3]

CALVARY—GOD'S CROWNING WORK

Herein is love, not that we loved God, but that he loved us, and sent his Son to be the propitiation for our sins. 1 John 4:10.

The love of God was Christ's theme when speaking of His mission and His work. "Therefore doth my Father love me," He says, "because I lay down my life, that I might take it again" (John 10:17). My Father loves you with a love so unbounded that He loves Me the more because I have given My life to redeem you. He loves you, and He loves Me more because I love you, and give My life for you. . . . Well did the disciples understand this love as they saw their Saviour enduring shame, reproach, doubt, and betrayal, as they saw His agony in the Garden, and His death on Calvary's cross. This is a love the depth of which no sounding can ever fathom. As the disciples comprehended it, as their perception took hold of God's divine compassion, they realized that there is a sense in which the sufferings of the Son were the sufferings of the Father. . . .

When our Redeemer consented to take the cup of suffering in order to save sinners, His capacity for suffering was the only limitation to His suffering. . . . By dying in our behalf, He gave an equivalent for our debt. Thus He removed from God all charge of lessening the guilt of sin. By virtue of My oneness with the Father, He says, My suffering and death enable Me to pay the penalty of sin. By My death a restraint is removed from His love. His grace can act with unbounded efficiency.[4]

Christ is our Redeemer. He is the Word that became flesh and dwelt among us. He is the fountain in which we may be washed and cleansed from all impurity. He is the costly sacrifice that has been given for the reconciliation of man. The universe of heaven, the worlds unfallen, the fallen world, and the confederacy of evil cannot say that God could do more for the salvation of man than He has done. Never can His gift be surpassed, never can He display a richer depth of love. Calvary represents His crowning work. It is man's part to respond to His great love by appropriating the great salvation the blessing of the Lord has made it possible for man to obtain.[5]

CHRIST OUR DIVINE RANSOM

Blessed be the God and Father of our Lord Jesus Christ, which according to his abundant mercy hath begotten us again unto a lively hope by the resurrection of Jesus Christ from the dead, to an inheritance incorruptible, and undefiled, and that fadeth not away, reserved in heaven for you. 1 Peter 1:3, 4.

"In him dwelleth all the fulness of the Godhead bodily" (Col. 2:9). Men need to understand that Deity suffered and sank under the agonies of Calvary. Yet Jesus Christ, whom God gave for the ransom of the world, purchased the church with His own blood. The Majesty of heaven was made to suffer at the hands of religious zealots, who claimed to be the most enlightened people upon the face of the earth.

Men whom God had created, and who were dependent upon Him for every moment of their lives, who claimed to be the children of Abraham, worked out the wrath of Satan upon the innocent Son of the infinite God. While Christ was bearing the heavy guilt incurred by transgression of the law, while in the very act of bearing our sins, of carrying our sorrows, He was mocked . . . by the chief priests and rulers. . . . It was there [on the cross] that mercy and truth met together, righteousness and peace embraced each other. Here is a theme which all need to understand. Here are lengths and breadths, depths and heights, that pass any computation. . . .

The character of Christ is an infinitely perfect character. The Word declares Him. He is lifted up and proclaimed as the One who gave His life for the life of the world. . . . Christ gave His own life, that all the disloyal and disobedient might realize the truth of the promise given in the first chapter of John: "As many as received him, to them gave he power to become the sons of God, even to them that believe on his name" (John 1:12) . Tell it over and over again. We may become the sons of God, members of the royal family, children of the heavenly King. All who accept Jesus Christ and hold the beginning of their confidence firm unto the end will be heirs of God and joint heirs with Christ to "an inheritance incorruptible, and undefiled, and that fadeth not away."[6]

RESURRECTION TO NEW LIFE

Therefore we are buried with him by baptism into death: that like as Christ was raised up from the dead by the glory of the Father, even so we also should walk in newness of life. Rom. 6:4.

The repentant believer, who takes the steps required in conversion, commemorates in his baptism the death, burial, and resurrection of Christ. He goes down into the water in the likeness of Christ's death and burial, and he is raised out of the water in the likeness of His resurrection—not to take up the old life of sin, but to live a new life in Christ Jesus.[7]

He who had said, "I lay down my life, that I might take it again" (John 10:17), came forth from the grave to life that was in Himself. Humanity died; divinity did not die. In His divinity Christ possessed the power to break the bonds of death. He declares that He has life in Himself to quicken whom He will.

All created beings live by the will and power of God. They are recipients of the life of the Son of God. However able and talented, however large their capacities, they are replenished with life from the Source of all life. He is the spring, the fountain, of life. Only He who alone hath immortality, dwelling in light and life, should say, "I have power to lay it [my life] down, and I have power to take it again" (verse 18). . . . Christ was invested with the right to give immortality. The life which He had laid down in humanity, He again took up and gave to humanity. . . .

Christ became one with humanity that humanity might become one in spirit and life with Him. By virtue of this union in obedience to the Word of God, His life becomes their life. He says to the penitent, "I am the resurrection, and the life" (John 11:25). Death is looked upon by Christ as sleep—silence, darkness, sleep. He speaks of it as if it were of little moment. "Whosoever liveth and believeth in me," He says, "shall never die" (verse 26). . . . "He shall never see death" (John 8:51). And to the believing one, death is but a small matter. With him to die is but to sleep. "Them also which sleep in Jesus will God bring with him" (1 Thess. 4:14).[8]

THE GLORIOUS REUNION IN HEAVEN

Lift up your heads, O ye gates; and be ye lift up, ye everlasting doors; and the King of glory shall come in. Who is this King of glory? The Lord strong and mighty, the Lord mighty in battle. . . . He is the King of glory. Ps. 24:7-10.

Christ came to earth as God in the guise of humanity. He ascended to heaven as the King of saints. His ascension was worthy of His exalted character. He went as one mighty in battle, a conqueror, leading captivity captive. He was attended by the heavenly host, amid shouts and acclamations of praise and celestial song. . . . All heaven united in His reception.[9]

The most precious fact to the disciples in the ascension of Jesus was that He went from them into heaven in the tangible form of their divine Teacher. . . . The last remembrance that the disciples were to have of their Lord was as the sympathizing Friend, the glorified Redeemer. . . . The brightness of the heavenly escort and the opening of the glorious gates of God to welcome Him were not to be discerned by mortal eyes.

Had the track of Christ to heaven been revealed to the disciples in all its inexpressible glory, they could not have endured the sight. Had they beheld the myriads of angels, and heard the bursts of triumph from the battlements of heaven, as the everlasting doors were lifted up, the contrast between that glory and their own lives in a world of trial, would have been so great that they would hardly have been able to again take up the burden of their earthly lives. . . .

Their senses were not to become so infatuated with the glories of heaven that they would lose sight of the character of Christ on earth, which they were to copy in themselves. They were to keep distinctly before their minds the beauty and majesty of His life, the perfect harmony of all His attributes, and the mysterious union of the divine and human in His nature. It was better that the earthly acquaintance of the disciples with their Saviour should end in the solemn, quiet, and sublime manner in which it did. His visible ascent from the world was in harmony with the meekness and quiet of His life.[10]

A PERFECT ATONEMENT

And not only so, but we also joy in God through our Lord Jesus Christ, by whom we have now received the atonement. Rom. 5:11.

Our great High Priest completed the sacrificial offering of Himself when He suffered without the gate. Then a perfect atonement was made for the sins of the people. Jesus is our Advocate, our High Priest, our Intercessor. Our present position therefore is like that of the Israelites, standing in the outer court, waiting and looking for that blessed hope, the glorious appearing of our Lord and Saviour Jesus Christ. . . .

When the high priest entered the holy place, representing the place where our High Priest is now pleading, and offered sacrifice on the altar, no propitiatory sacrifices were offered without. While the high priest was interceding within, every heart was to be bowed in contrition before God, pleading for the pardon of transgression. Type met antitype in the death of Christ, the Lamb slain for the sins of the world. The great High Priest has made the only sacrifice that will be of any value. . . .

In His intercession as our Advocate, Christ needs no man's virtue, no man's intercession. Christ is the only sin bearer, the only sin offering. Prayer and confession are to be offered only to Him who has entered once for all into the holy place. . . .

Christ represented His Father to the world, and He represents before God the chosen ones in whom He has restored the moral image of God. They are His heritage. . . . No priest, no religionist, can reveal the Father to any son or daughter of Adam. Men have only one Advocate, one Intercessor, who is able to pardon transgression. Shall not our hearts swell with gratitude to Him who gave Jesus to be the propitiation for our sins? Think deeply upon the love the Father has manifested in our behalf, the love that He has expressed for us. We cannot measure this love. Measurement there is none. We can only point to Calvary, to the Lamb slain from the foundation of the world. It is an infinite sacrifice. Can we comprehend and measure infinity?[11]

A CONQUEROR CLAIMING HIS VICTORY

Wherefore in all things it behoved him to be made like unto his brethren, that he might be a merciful and faithful high priest in things pertaining to God, to make reconciliation for the sins of the people. Heb. 2:17.

Of the high priest of Israel we read, "Aaron shall bear the names of the children of Israel in the breastplate of judgment upon his heart, when he goeth in unto the holy place, for a memorial before the Lord continually" (Ex. 28:29). What a beautiful and expressive figure this is of the unchanging love of Christ for His church! Our great High Priest, of whom Aaron was a type, bears His people upon His heart. . . . Christ as the great high priest, making a perfect atonement for sin, stands alone in divine majesty and glory. Other high priests were only types, and when He appeared, the need of their services vanished. . . . Let human beings, subject to temptation, remember that in the heavenly courts they have a high priest who is touched with the feeling of their infirmities, because He Himself was tempted, even as they are.[12]

Christ is the minister of the true tabernacle, the high priest of all who believe in Him as a personal Saviour, and His office no other can take. He is the high priest of the church. . . .

Christ offered up His broken body to purchase back God's heritage, to give man another trial. "Wherefore he is able also to save them to the uttermost that come unto God by him, seeing he ever liveth to make intercession for them" (Heb. 7:25). By His spotless life, His obedience, His death on the cross of Calvary, Christ interceded for the lost race. And now, not as a mere petitioner does the Captain of our salvation intercede for us, but as a conqueror claiming His victory. His offering is complete, and as our intercessor He executes His self-appointed work, holding before God the censer containing His own spotless merits and the prayers, confessions, and thanksgiving of His people. Perfumed with the fragrance of His righteousness, these ascend to God as a sweet savor. The offering is wholly acceptable, and pardon covers all transgression.[13]

MOMENTARILY OFFERING SACRIFICE

Who is he that condemneth? It is Christ that died, yea rather, that is risen again, who is even at the right hand of God, who also maketh intercession for us. Rom. 8:34.

Christ Jesus is represented as continually standing at the altar, momentarily offering up the sacrifice for the sins of the world. He is a minister of the true tabernacle which the Lord pitched and not man. . . . A daily and yearly typical atonement is no longer to be made, but the atoning sacrifice through a mediator is essential because of the constant commission of sin. Jesus is officiating in the presence of God, offering up His shed blood, as it had been a lamb slain. . . .

Christ, our Mediator, and the Holy Spirit are constantly interceding in man's behalf, but the Spirit pleads not for us as does Christ who presents His blood, shed from the foundation of the world; the Spirit works upon our hearts, drawing out prayers and penitence, praise and thanksgiving. . . .

The religious services, the prayers, the praise, the penitent confession of sin ascend from true believers as incense to the heavenly sanctuary; but passing through the corrupt channels of humanity, they are so defiled that unless purified by blood, they can never be of value with God. They ascend not in spotless purity, and unless the Intercessor who is at God's right hand presents and purifies all by His righteousness, it is not acceptable to God. All incense from earthly tabernacles must be moist with the cleansing drops of the blood of Christ. He holds before the Father the censer of His own merits, in which there is no taint of earthly corruption. He gathers into this censer the prayers, the praise, and the confessions of His people, and with these He puts His own spotless righteousness. Then, perfumed with the merits of Christ's propitiation, the incense comes up before God wholly and entirely acceptable. . . .

O, that all may see that everything in obedience, in penitence, in praise and thanksgiving must be placed upon the glowing fire of the righteousness of Christ. The fragrance of this righteousness ascends like a cloud around the mercy seat.[14]

AN ADVOCATE CLOTHED IN OUR NATURE

My little children, these things write I unto you, that ye sin not. And if any man sin, we have an advocate with the Father, Jesus Christ the righteous. 1 John 2:1.

God's appointments and grants in our behalf are without limit. The throne of grace itself is occupied by One who permits us to call Him Father. . . . He has placed at His altar an Advocate clothed in our nature. As our Intercessor, Christ's office work is to introduce us to God as His sons and daughters. He intercedes in behalf of those who receive Him. With His own blood He has paid their ransom. By virtue of His merits He gives them power to become members of the royal family, children of the heavenly King. And the Father demonstrates His infinite love for Christ by receiving and welcoming Christ's friends as His friends. He is satisfied with the atonement made. He is glorified by the incarnation, the life, death, and mediation of His Son.

In Christ's name our petitions ascend to the Father. He intercedes in our behalf, and the Father lays open all the treasures of His grace for our appropriation, for us to enjoy and impart to others. . . .

Christ is the connecting link between God and man. . . . He places the whole virtue of His righteousness on the side of the suppliant. He pleads for man, and man, in need of divine help, pleads for himself in the presence of God, using the influence of the One who gave His life for the life of the world. As we acknowledge before God our appreciation of Christ's merits, fragrance is given to our intercessions. As we approach God through the virtue of the Redeemer's merits, Christ places us close by His side, encircling us with His human arm, while with His divine arm He grasps the throne of the Infinite. He puts His merits, as sweet incense, in the censer in our hands, in order to encourage our petitions. . . .

Yes, Christ has become the medium of prayer between man and God. He has also become the medium of blessing between God and man.[15]

WHEN JESUS INTERPOSES

For Christ is not entered into the holy places made with hands, which are the figures of the true; but into heaven itself, now to appear in the presence of God for us. Heb. 9:24.

Our precious Redeemer is standing before the Father as our intercessor. . . . Let those who would meet the divine standard search the Scriptures for themselves, that they may have a knowledge of the life of Christ and understand His mission and work. Let them behold Him as their Advocate, standing within the vail, having in His hand the golden censer from which the holy incense of the merits of His righteousness ascends to God in behalf of those who pray to Him. Could they thus behold Him they would feel an assurance that they have a powerful, influential Advocate in the heavenly courts, and that their suit is gained at the throne of God.

What an experience may be attained at the footstool of mercy; which is the only place of sure refuge! You may discern the fact that God is back of His promises, and not dread the issue of your prayers or doubt that Jesus is standing as your surety and substitute. As you confess your sins, as you repent of your iniquity, Christ takes your guilt upon Himself and imputes to you His own righteousness and power. To those who are contrite in spirit He gives the golden oil of love and the rich treasures of His grace. It is then that you may see that the sacrifice of self to God through the merits of Christ makes you of infinite value, for clothed in the robe of Christ's righteousness you become the sons and daughters of God. Those who . . . ask forgiveness in the name of Jesus will receive their request. At the very first expression of penitence Christ presents the humble suppliant's petition before the throne as His own desire in the sinner's behalf. He says, "I will pray the Father for you" (John 16:26).

Jesus, our precious Saviour, could not see us exposed to the fatal snares of Satan and forbear making an infinite sacrifice on our behalf. He interposes Himself between Satan and the tempted soul and says, "'Get thee behind me, Satan.' Let me come close to this tempted soul." He pities and loves every humble, trembling suppliant.[16]

SALVATION TO THE UTTERMOST

Wherefore he is able also to save them to the uttermost that come unto God by him, seeing he ever liveth to make intercession for them. Heb. 7:25.

What does intercession comprehend? It is the golden chain which binds finite man to the throne of the infinite God. The human agent whom Christ has died to save importunes the throne of God, and his petition is taken up by Jesus who has purchased him with His own blood. Our great High Priest places His righteousness on the side of the sincere suppliant, and the prayer of Christ blends with that of the human petitioner.

Christ has urged that His people pray without ceasing. This does not mean that we should always be upon our knees, but that prayer is to be as the breath of the soul. Our silent requests, wherever we may be, are to be ascending unto God, and Jesus our Advocate pleads in our behalf, bearing up with the incense of His righteousness our requests to the Father.

The Lord Jesus loves His people, and when they put their trust in Him, depending wholly upon Him, He strengthens them. He will live through them, giving them the inspiration of His sanctifying Spirit, imparting to the soul a vital transfusion of Himself. He acts through their faculties and causes them to choose His will and to act out His character. With the apostle Paul they then may say, "I am crucified with Christ: nevertheless I live; yet not I, but Christ liveth in me: and the life which I now live in the flesh I live by the faith of the Son of God, who loved me, and gave himself for me" (Gal. 2:20). . . .

The Lord will not leave His afflicted, tried children to be the sport of Satan's temptations. It is your privilege to trust in Jesus. The heavens are full of rich blessings. . . . We have not because we ask not, or because we do not pray in faith, believing that we shall be blessed with the special influence of the Holy Spirit. To the true seeker through the mediation of Christ the gracious influences of the Holy Spirit are imparted.[17]

SAFE IN EVERY STORM

Which hope we have as an anchor of the soul, both sure and stedfast, and which entereth into that within the veil; whither the forerunner is for us entered, even Jesus, made an high priest for ever after the order of Melchisedec. Heb. 6:19, 20.

Hope has been set before us, even the hope of eternal life. Nothing short of this blessing for us will satisfy our Redeemer, but it is our part to lay hold upon this hope by faith in Him who has promised. We may expect to suffer, for it is those who are partakers with Him in His sufferings who shall be partakers with Him in His glory. He has purchased forgiveness and immortality for the sinful, perishing souls of men, but it is our part to receive these gifts by faith. Believing in Him, we have this hope as an anchor of the soul, sure and steadfast. We are to understand that we may confidently expect God's favor not only in this world but in the heavenly world, since He paid such a price for our salvation. Faith in the atonement and intercession of Christ will keep us steadfast and immovable amid the temptations that press upon us in the church militant. Let us contemplate the glorious hope that is set before us, and by faith lay hold upon it. . . .

We gain heaven not through our own merits but through the merits of Jesus Christ. . . . Let your hope not be centered in yourself, but in Him who has entered within the vail. Talk of the blessed hope and the glorious appearing of our Lord Jesus Christ.

It is true that we are exposed to great moral peril; it is true that we are in danger of being corrupted. But this danger threatens us only as we trust in self and look no higher than our own human efforts. In doing this we shall make shipwreck of faith.[18]

In Christ our hope of eternal life is centered. . . . Our hope is an anchor to the soul both sure and steadfast when it entereth into that within the vail, for the tempest-tossed soul becomes a partaker of the divine nature. He is anchored in Christ. Amid the raging elements of temptation he will not be driven upon the rocks or drawn into the whirlpool. His ship will outride the storm.[19]

JESUS HOLDS US FAST!

My sheep hear my voice, and I know them, and they follow me: and I give unto them eternal life; and they shall never perish, neither shall any man pluck them out of my hand. John 10:27, 28.

In the courts above, Christ is pleading for His church—pleading for those for whom He has paid the redemption price of His blood. Centuries, ages, can never lessen the efficacy of His atoning sacrifice. Neither life nor death, height nor depth, can separate us from the love of God which is in Christ Jesus; not because we hold Him so firmly, but because He holds us so fast. If our salvation depended on our own efforts, we could not be saved; but it depends on the One who is behind all the promises. Our grasp on Him may seem feeble, but His love is that of an elder brother; so long as we maintain our union with Him, no one can pluck us out of His hand.[20]

Jesus, precious Jesus, "merciful and gracious, longsuffering, and abundant in goodness and truth, keeping mercy for thousands, forgiving iniquity and transgression and sin, and that will by no means clear the guilty" (Ex. 34:6, 7). O how privileged we are that we may come to Jesus just as we are and cast ourselves upon His love! We have no hope but in Jesus. He alone can reach us with His hand to lift us up out of the depths of discouragement and hopelessness and place our feet upon the Rock. Although the human soul may cling to Jesus with all the desperate sense of his great need, Jesus will cling to the souls bought by His own blood with a firmer grasp than the sinner clings to Him.

I read this over and over again, for it is so full of assurance: "Seeing then that we have a great high priest, that is passed into the heavens, Jesus the Son of God, let us hold fast our profession. For we have not an high priest which cannot be touched with the feeling of our infirmities; but was in all points tempted like as we are, yet without sin. Let us therefore come boldly unto the throne of grace, that we may obtain mercy, and find grace to help in time of need" (Heb. 4:14-16). . . . What a Saviour we have—a risen Saviour, One who can save all who come unto Him![21]

THE MYSTERY OF GODLINESS

He that spared not his own Son, but delivered him up for us all, how, shall he not with him also freely give us all things? Rom. 8:32.

Before this wonderful, priceless gift was bestowed, the whole heavenly universe was mightily stirred in an effort to understand God's unfathomable love, stirred to awaken in human hearts a gratitude proportionate to the value of the gift. Shall we for whom Christ has given His life, halt between two opinions? Shall we give God only a mite of the powers of our nature? Shall we return only a part of the capabilities and powers lent us by God? Can we do this while we know that He who was Commander of all heaven . . . , realizing the helplessness of the human race, came to this earth in human nature to make it possible for us to unite our humanity to His divinity?

He became poor that we might come into possession of the heavenly treasure, a far more exceeding and eternal weight of glory. To rescue the fallen race, He descended from one humiliation to another, until He, the divine-human suffering Christ, was uplifted on the cross, to draw all men unto Him. The Son of God could not have shown greater condescension than He did; He could not have stooped lower.

This is the mystery of godliness, the mystery which has inspired heavenly agencies so to minister through fallen humanity that in the world an interest will be aroused in the plan of salvation. This is the mystery that has stirred all heaven to unite with man in carrying out God's great plan for the salvation of a ruined world, that men and women may be led, by the signs in the heavens and in the earth, to prepare for the second coming of our Lord. . . .

As the Head of the church Christ is authoritatively calling upon every person who claims to believe on Him to follow His example of self-denial and self-sacrifice. . . . They are called upon to rally without delay under the blood-stained banner of Christ Jesus. Withholding nothing, they are to make an entire offering for the attainment of eternal, measureless results—the salvation of souls.[22]

A BRIDGE FOR THE GULF

Jesus saith unto him, I am the way, the truth, and the life: no man cometh unto the Father, but by me. John 14:6.

When Jesus said, "I am the way, the truth, and the life," He uttered a truth of wonderful significance. The transgression of man had separated earth from heaven, and finite man from the infinite God. As an island is separated from a continent, so earth was cut off from heaven, and a wide channel intervened between man and God. Jesus bridged this gulf, and made a way for man to come to God. He who has no spiritual light sees no way, has no hope, and men have originated theories of their own regarding the way to life. . . . But the only name given among men whereby they can be saved is Jesus. Across the gulf that sin has made come His words, "I am the way, the truth, and the life." . . .

Man can be justified alone through the imputation of Christ's righteousness. Man is justified freely by God's grace through faith, and not by works, lest any man should boast. Salvation is the gift of God through Jesus Christ our Lord. . . .

After the enemy had betrayed Adam and Eve into sin, the connection between heaven and earth was severed, and had it not been for Christ, the way to heaven would never have been known by the fallen race. . . . Christ is the mystic ladder, the base of which rests upon the earth, and whose topmost round reaches to the throne of the Infinite. The children of Adam are not left desolate and alienated from God, for through Christ's righteousness we have access unto the Father.

"By me," said Christ, "if any man enter in, he shall be saved, and shall go in and out, and find pasture" (John 10:9). Let earth be glad, let the inhabitants of the world rejoice, that Christ has bridged the gulf which sin had made, and has bound earth and heaven together. A highway has been cast up for the ransomed of the Lord. The weary and heavy laden may come unto Him and find rest to their souls. The pilgrim may journey toward the mansions that He has gone to prepare for those who love Him.[23]

THE PRICELESS PEARL

Again, the kingdom of heaven is like unto a merchant man, seeking goodly pearls: who, when he had found one pearl of great price, went and sold all that he had, and bought it. Matt. 13:45, 46.

This goodly pearl represents the priceless treasure of Christ, as does the gold hid in the field. In Christ we have everything that is needful for us in this life, and that which will make up the joy of the world to come. All the money in the world will not buy the gift of peace and rest and love. These gifts are provided for us through faith in Christ. We cannot purchase these gifts from God; we have nothing with which to buy them. We are the property of God, for mind, soul, and body have been purchased by the ransom of the life of the Son of God. . . .

Then what is it to buy the eternal treasure? It is simply to give back to Jesus His own, to receive Him into the heart by faith. It is cooperation with God; it is bearing the yoke with Christ; it is lifting His burdens. . . . The Lord Jesus laid aside His royal crown, He left His high command, He clothed His divinity with humanity, in order that through humanity He might uplift the human race. He so appreciated the possibility of the human race that He became man's substitute and surety. He places upon man His own merit, and thus elevates him in the scale of moral value with God.

Christ is the atoning sacrifice. He left the glory of heaven, He parted with His riches, He laid aside His honor, not in order to create love and interest for man in the heart of God, but to be an exponent of the love that existed in the heart of the Father. . . . Jesus paid the price of all His riches, He assumed humanity, He condescended to a life of poverty and humiliation, in order that He might seek and save that which was lost.

Through the grace of Christ we may be strengthened and matured, so that though now imperfect we may become complete in Him. We have mortgaged ourselves to Satan, but Christ came to ransom and redeem us. We cannot purchase anything from God. It is only by grace, the free gift of God in Christ, that we are saved.[24]

CHRIST'S PRECIOUS JEWELS

And they shall be mine, saith the Lord of hosts, in that day when I make up my jewels; and I will spare them, as a man spareth his own son that serveth him. Mal. 3:17.

The kingdom of heaven is represented as being like unto a merchantman "seeking goodly pearls: who, when he had found one pearl of great price, went and sold all that he had, and bought it."

This parable has a double significance, and applies not only to man seeking the kingdom of heaven, but to Christ seeking His lost inheritance. Through transgression man lost his holy innocence, and mortgaged himself to Satan. Christ, the only begotten Son of God, pledged Himself for the redemption of man, and paid the price of his ransom on the cross of Calvary. He left the worlds unfallen, the society of holy angels in the universe of heaven, for He could not be satisfied while humanity was alienated from Him. The heavenly Merchantman lays aside His royal robe and crown. Though the Prince and Commander of all heaven, He takes upon Him the garb of humanity, and comes to a world that is marred and seared with the curse, to seek for the one lost pearl, to seek for man fallen through disobedience. . . .

He finds His pearl buried in rubbish. Selfishness encrusts the human heart, and it is bound by the tyranny of Satan. But He lifts the soul out of its darkness to show forth the praises of Him who hath called us out of darkness into His marvelous light. We are brought into covenant relationship with God, and receive pardon and find peace. Jesus finds the pearl of lost humanity, and resets it in His own diadem. . . .

He would inspire the most sinful, the most debased, with hope. He says, "Him that cometh to me I will in no wise cast out" (John 6:37). When a soul finds the Saviour, the Saviour rejoices as a merchantman that has found his goodly pearl. By His grace He will work upon the soul until it will be like a jewel polished for the heavenly kingdom. "For God so loved the world, that he gave his only begotten Son, that whosoever believeth in him should not perish, but have everlasting life." [25]

LIFE'S BEST THINGS

I am come that they might have life, and that they might have it more abundantly. John 10:10.

Every moment of our life is intensely real. Life is no play; it is charged with awful importance, fraught with eternal responsibilities. When we look upon life from this point of view, we realize our need of divine help. The conviction will be forced upon us that a life without Christ will be a life of utter failure, but if Jesus abides with us, we shall live for a purpose. We shall then realize that without the power of God's grace and Spirit we cannot reach the high standard He has placed before us. There is a divine excellence of character to which we are to attain, and in striving to meet the standard of heaven, divine incentives will urge us on, the mind will become balanced, and the restlessness of the soul will be banished in repose in Christ.

How often do we come in contact with people who are never happy. They fail of enjoying the contentment and peace that Jesus can give. They profess to be Christians but they do not comply with the conditions upon which the promise of God is fulfilled. Jesus has said, "Come unto me. . . . Take my yoke upon you, and learn of me; for I am meek and lowly in heart: and ye shall find rest unto your souls. For my yoke is easy, and my burden is light" (Matt. 11:28-30). The reason why many are in a state of unrest is that they are not learning in the school of the Master. The submissive, self-sacrificing child of God understands by experience what it is to have the peace of Christ.[26]

Life's best things—simplicity, honesty, truthfulness, purity, unsullied integrity—are not to be bought or sold. They are free to the illiterate as to the educated, to the white man as to the black man, to the poor man as to the king upon his throne. . . .

In the field of life we are all sowing seeds. As we sow, so shall we reap. Those who sow self-love, bitterness, jealousy, will reap a like harvest. Those who sow unselfish love, kindness, tender thoughtfulness for the feelings of others, will reap a precious harvest.[27]

THE MOST PROFITABLE INVESTMENT

I will praise thee; for I am fearfully and wonderfully made: marvellous are thy works; and that my soul knoweth right well. Ps. 139:14.

Only one lease of life is granted us here, and the inquiry with everyone should be, How can I invest my life that it may yield the greatest profit? Life is valuable only as we improve it for the benefit of our fellow creatures and the glory of God. Careful cultivation of the abilities with which the Creator has endowed us will fit us for usefulness here and eternal life in the world to come.

That time is well spent which is directed to the establishment and preservation of sound physical and mental health. . . . It is easy to lose health, but it is difficult to regain it. . . .

We can ill afford to dwarf or cripple a single function of mind or body by overwork or by abuse of any part of the living machinery. So sure as we do this, we must suffer the consequences. It is our first duty to God and our fellow beings to develop all our powers. Every faculty with which the Creator has endowed us should be cultivated to the highest degree of perfection, that we may be able to do the greatest amount of good of which we are capable. The grace of Christ is needed to refine and purify the mind; this will enable us to see and correct our deficiencies, and to improve that which is excellent in our characters. This work, wrought for ourselves in the strength and name of Jesus, will be of more benefit to society than any sermon we might preach. The influence of a well-balanced, well-ordered life is of inestimable value. . . .

There are few as yet who are aroused sufficiently to understand how much their habits of diet have to do with their health, their characters, their usefulness in this world, and their eternal destiny. The appetite should ever be in subjection to the moral and intellectual organs. The body should be servant to the mind, and not the mind to the body. All should understand in regard to their own physical frames, that with the psalmist they may be able to exclaim, "I will praise thee; for I am fearfully and wonderfully made."[28]

ENTRUSTED CAPITAL

Then Jesus said unto them, Yet a little while is the light with you. Walk while ye have the light, lest darkness come upon you: for he that walketh in darkness knoweth not whither he goeth. John 12:35.

This is the warning we would give to you who claim to believe the truth. Yet a little while is the light with you. We would ask you to consider the shortness of human life, how swiftly time is passing. Golden opportunities and privileges are within our reach. The plenteous, abundant mercy of God is waiting your demand upon its richest treasures. The Saviour is waiting to dispense His blessings freely, and the only question is, Will you accept them? The rich provisions have been made, and light is shining in a variety of ways; but this light will lose its preciousness to those who do not appreciate it, who do not accept and respond to it, or, having received it, do not pass the light along to others.

Your life, your soul, your strength, your capabilities, your powers of mind and body, are to be regarded by you as entrusted capital to be improved for your Lord during the period of your life. You are to stand in your allotted order in God's great army, to work out His plan in saving your own soul and the souls of others. This you may do by living a consistent Christian life, by putting forth earnest efforts, by learning in the school of Christ His ways, His purposes, and subordinating your will and way to the will and way of Christ. . . .

The Christian is to live a life distinctly different from that of the worldling. The worldling lives a cheap quality of life. He consents not to spiritual life. It is he who has the love of God that has life; it is he whose hope is centered, not in this world, but in Christ, the great center. . . .

"He that hath the Son hath life; and he that hath not the Son of God hath not life" (1 John 5:12). Those who believe in Christ derive their motive power and the texture of their characters from Him in whom they believe. "Examine yourselves, whether ye be in the faith; prove your own selves" (2 Cor. 13:5).[29]

THE LIFE GOD USES

Even every one that is called by my name: for I have created him for my glory, I have formed him; yea, I have made him. Isa. 43:7.

Our life is the Lord's, and is invested with a responsibility that we do not fully comprehend. The threads of self have become woven into the fabric, and this has dishonored God.

Nehemiah, after gaining so great an influence over the monarch in whose court he lived and over his people in Jerusalem, instead of ascribing praise to his own excellent traits of character, his remarkable aptness and energy, stated the matter just as it was. He declared that his success was due to the good hand of God that was upon him. He cherished the truth that God was his safeguard in every position of influence. For every trait of character by which he obtained favor he praised the working power of God. . . .

We need to sense deeply that all influence is a precious talent to be used for God. . . . We need to appreciate every capability we possess, because it is lent capital, to be improved to God's glory. . . . There is constant temptation for human beings to consider that any influence they have gained is the result of something valuable in themselves. The Lord does not work with these, for He will not give to any human being the glory that belongs to His own name. . . . He makes the humble, trustful servant His representative—the one who will not lift himself up and think of himself more highly than He ought to think. The life of such a one will be dedicated to God as a living sacrifice, and that life He will accept and use and sustain. He longs to make men wise with His own wisdom, that that wisdom may be exercised in His own behalf. He manifests Himself through the consecrated humble worker. . . .

Carry every entrusted capability as a sacred treasure, to be used in imparting to others the knowledge and grace received. In this you will answer the purpose for which God gave them. The Lord requires us to sink self in Jesus Christ, and let the glory be all of God.[30]

MONITOR AND FRIEND

Remember the days of old, consider the years of many generations: ask thy father, and he will shew thee; thy elders, and they will tell thee. Deut. 32:7.

Life is like a voyage. We have storm and sunshine, but we bear in mind that we are nearing the desired haven. We shall soon be beyond the storms and tempests. Our present duty is to hearken to the voice that says, "Learn of me; for I am meek and lowly in heart" (Matt. 11:29). We must accept this invitation daily. The past is contained in the book where all things are written down. We cannot blot out the record, but we can learn many things if we choose. The past should teach us its lessons. As we make the past our monitor, we may also make it our friend. As we call to mind that in the past which has been disagreeable, let it teach us not to repeat it. In the future let nothing be traced which will cause regret in the by-and-by. We may now avoid a bad showing. Every day we live we are making our history. Today is ours, yesterday is beyond our amendment or control. Then let us not grieve the Spirit of God today, for tomorrow we shall not be able to recall this day; it will be yesterday to us. . . .

Jesus Christ has plentiful help and grace for all who will appreciate it. The Lord is our helper; with Him is forgiveness. He alone can blot out the sins of the past. He can strengthen the mind. If we regard the past as no longer our enemy but as a friend to warn us off the ground we should not approach, it will prove a true friend. . . .

Will we grasp and appreciate the good, and refuse the evil? Will we walk humbly with God? . . . We must not fail nor be discouraged; then the present work, now passing beyond our control, will be our paymaster. . . . We have only a little period in which to work. We are not to educate ourselves to worry. Keep the eye upward, fixed upon the mark of our high calling in Christ Jesus. We have a work to do; let us do it as in the sight of the whole universe of heaven. We are not to faint, to stumble on in unbelief. God desires us to look to Him as our sufficiency and strive to be complete in Him.[31]

FULFILLING LIFE'S OBLIGATIONS

For none of us liveth to himself, and no man dieth to himself.
Rom. 14:7.

Ask yourselves the question, "What is my life toward God and toward my fellowmen?" There is no one that liveth to himself. No life is lived on neutral ground. Our conceptions of life may be influenced by the enemy of all righteousness so that we do not realize its vast importance, but . . . we cannot cast off our responsibility and live without reference to the future, immortal life, and still do our duty to God and to our fellowmen. Each one is a part of the great web of humanity, and each one has a far-reaching influence. We cannot fulfill the obligations that rest upon us in our own strength alone. We must have divine aid in meeting our responsibilities, that our influence may . . . gather with Christ.

All our talents of time, ability, and influence were bestowed by God, and are to be given back to Him in willing service. The great object of the life which God has given is not the securing of temporal advantages, but the securing of eternal privileges in the kingdom of heaven. The Lord has bought all that there is of us by the precious blood of Christ, and it is the worst kind of robbery that could be practiced to withhold from Him His own.[32]

Our life is not our own, never was, and never can be. The question of importance to us is, Is our life interwoven with that of Jesus? . . . We shall come into judgment for the very atmosphere that surrounds the soul, for it is vital and is influencing souls for good or evil. . . .

If you connect with God, fearing Him, loving Him, obeying Him, and giving to the world a living example of what the Christian's life should be, you will fulfill your obligation to God and to your fellow men. You are to show forth in your life what it means to love God with all your heart, and your neighbor as yourself. Connected with the God of wisdom and love, you will demonstrate to the world the fact that you are not living for this world, but for that which is not temporal but eternal.[33]

THE HIGHEST OBJECTS OF AMBITION

Labour not for the meat which perisheth, but for that meat which endureth unto everlasting life, which the Son of man shall give unto you: for him hath God the Father sealed. John 6:27.

We cannot tell the ambitious man that he must cease to be ambitious if he would become a Christian. God places before him the highest objects of ambition—a spotless white robe, a crown studded with jewels, a scepter, a throne of glory, and honor that is as enduring as the throne of Jehovah. All the elements of character which help to make him successful and honored in the world—the irrepressible desire for some greater good, the indomitable will, the strenuous exertion, the untiring perseverance—are not to be crushed out. These are to remain, and through the grace of God received into the heart to be turned into another channel. These valuable traits of character may be exercised on objects as much higher and nobler than worldly pursuits as the heavens are higher than the earth.

Jesus presents a white robe, a crown of glory richer than any that ever decked the brow of a monarch, and titles above those of honored princes. The recompense for a life devoted to the service of Christ exceeds anything that the human imagination can grasp. Christ does not call upon men to lay aside their zeal, their desires for excellence and elevation, but He would have them seek, not for perishable treasure or fleeting honor, but for that which is enduring. . . .

God is well pleased if those striving for eternal life aim high. There will be strong temptations to indulge the natural traits of character by becoming worldly wise, scheming, and selfishly ambitious, gathering wealth to the neglect of the salvation which is of so much higher value. But every temptation resisted is a priceless victory gained in subduing self; it bends the powers to the service of Jesus, and increases faith, hope, patience, and forbearance. . . . Let us aim in the strength of Jesus for the crown heavy with stars. "They that be wise shall shine as . . . the firmament; and they that turn many to righteousness as the stars for ever and ever" (Dan. 12:3).[34]

SOWING AND REAPING

Be not deceived; God is not mocked: for whatsoever a man soweth, that shall he also reap. For he that soweth to his flesh shall of the flesh reap corruption; but he that soweth to the Spirit shall of the Spirit reap life everlasting. Gal. 6:7, 8.

What is it to sow to the flesh? It is to follow the desires and inclinations of our own natural hearts. Whatever may be our profession, if we are serving self instead of God we are sowing to the flesh. The Christian life is a life of self-denial and cross bearing. We are to endure hardness as good soldiers of Jesus Christ. . . . We cannot inquire, What is for our convenience? but only, What are our orders? No one looks upon the life of a soldier as a life of self-pleasing and gratification. We are on the battlefield today, and two great forces are ever contending for the mastery. . . .

What are you sowing in your daily life? Are you sowing to your flesh? Are you thinking only of your pleasure, your convenience? sowing to pride and vanity and ambition? . . . I entreat you to sow to the Spirit. Every temptation resisted will give you power to sow to the Spirit in another time of trial.[35]

If you are sowing faith, rendering obedience to Christ, you will reap faith and power for future obedience. If you are seeking to be a blessing to others, God will bless you. . . . The joy we give to others will be reflected upon us again, for as we sow, we shall reap. . . .

Abundant provision has been made that all who desire to live a godly life may have grace and strength through Jesus our divine Redeemer. The Christian's life is not to be one of burdens and cares, although the cross must be lifted and the burdens borne; for the servants of God are to draw peace and strength from the Source of their strength, and in so doing they will find life full of happiness and peace. . . . The whole being must be consecrated to God, for our precious Saviour never shares a divided heart. Our inclinations and desires must be under the control of the Spirit of God, and then we shall be strengthened to fight the good fight of faith. We should daily ask, What are the Captain's orders?[36]

LIFE NOT TO BE TRIFLED WITH

So then every one of us shall give account of himself to God. Rom. 14:12.

All of us, as beings blessed of God with reasoning powers, with intellect and judgment, should acknowledge our accountability to God. The life He has given us is a sacred responsibility, and no moment of it is to be trifled with, for we shall have to meet it again in the record of the judgment. In the books of heaven our lives are as accurately traced as in the picture on the plate of the photographer. Not only are we held accountable for what we have done, but for what we have left undone. We are held to account for our undeveloped characters, our unimproved opportunities. . . .

It is love of selfish ease, love of pleasure, your self-esteem, self-exaltation, that prevents you from learning the precious life lessons in the school of Christ. It is the Christian's duty not to permit surroundings and circumstances to mold him, but to live above surroundings, fashioning his character according to the divine Model. He is to be faithful in whatever place he is found. He is to do his duty with fidelity, improving the opportunities given him of God, making the most of his capabilities. . . .

If you are abiding in Christ, learning in His school, you will not be rude, dishonest, or unfaithful. The cross of Christ cuts to the root of all unholy passions and practices. Whatever the nature of your work, you will carry the principles of Christ into your labor and identify yourself with the task given into your hands. Your interest will be one with that of your employer. If you are paid for your time, you will realize that the time for work is not your own, but belongs to the one who pays you for it. If you are careless and extravagant, wasting material, squandering time, failing to be painstaking and diligent, you are registered in the books of heaven as an unfaithful servant. . . . Faithfulness, economy, caretaking, thoroughness, should characterize all our work. . . . "He that is faithful in that which is least is faithful also in much" (Luke 16:10).[37]

MOLDED AFTER HIS CHARACTER

But we all, with open face beholding as in a glass the glory of the Lord, are changed into the same image from glory to glory even as by the Spirit of the Lord. 2 Cor. 3:18.

When a man turns away from human imperfections and beholds Jesus, a divine transformation takes place in his character. He fixes his eye upon Christ as on a mirror which reflects the glory of God, and by beholding he becomes changed into the same image, from glory to glory, even as by the Spirit of the Lord. . . .

Turn your eyes from the imperfections of others and fix them steadfastly on Christ. With a contrite heart, study His life and character. You need not only to be more enlightened, but quickened, that you may see the banquet that is before you, and eat and drink the flesh and blood of the Son of God, which is *His Word*. By tasting the good Word of Life, by feeding on the Bread of Life, you may see the power of a world to come, and be created anew in Christ Jesus. If you receive His gifts you will be renewed unto holiness, and His grace will bring forth in you fruit unto the glory of God.

The Holy Spirit reveals Christ to the mind, and faith takes hold of Him. If you accept Christ as your personal Saviour, you will know by experience the value of the great sacrifice made in your behalf upon the cross of Calvary. The Spirit of Christ working upon the heart conforms it to His image, for Christ is the model upon which the Spirit works. By the ministry of His Word, by His providences, by His inward working, God stamps the likeness of Christ upon the soul.

To possess Christ is your first work, and to reveal Him as One who is able to save to the uttermost all who come to Him is your next work. To serve the Lord with full purpose of heart is to honor and glorify His name by dwelling upon holy things, by having a mind filled with the vital truths revealed in His Holy Word. . . .

Goodness, meekness, gentleness, patience, and love are the attributes of Christ's character. If you have the spirit of Christ, your character will be molded after His character.[38]

HOW TO ENJOY HEAVEN

Whereby are given unto us exceeding great and precious promises: that by these ye might be partakers of the divine nature, having escaped the corruption that is in the world through lust. 2 Peter 1:4.

The design of God in giving us rich promises is stated by the apostle Peter—that we might be partakers of the divine nature. We must have earthly, worldly tastes transformed to the divine and heavenly. Heaven would be no heaven to you or to me if our tastes and our meditations and our temper were not Christlike. The pure and heavenly mansions which Christ has gone to prepare for His children are such as the redeemed alone can value by being made meet for them by the inward work of grace in their hearts.

I might picture to you the blessedness of heaven, the crowns laid up for the conquerors, the white linen which is the righteousness—of Christ, the palm branches of victory, and the harps of gold. But all these alone will not make heaven a place of bliss for any one of us. Without any of these, if we have pure and holy characters, we would be happy, for we would have Jesus and His love. Purity and innocence and conformity to Christ's character will make heaven enjoyable. All the faculties will be strengthened, all in harmony. Perfect bliss can only dwell in the heart where Christ reigns supreme.

Christ came to our world to die, the Just for the unjust, . . . that He might elevate and ennoble men and women and stamp His divine image upon them. For this His Spirit strives with us that there may be an ever advancing vigor and perfection of spiritual life.[39]

We need not retain one sinful propensity. . . . As we partake of the divine nature, hereditary and cultivated tendencies to wrong are cut away from the character, and we are made a living power for good. Ever learning of the divine Teacher, daily partaking of His nature, we cooperate with God in overcoming Satan's temptations. God works, and man works, that man may be one with Christ as Christ is one with God. Then we sit together with Christ in heavenly places. The mind rests with peace and assurance in Jesus.[40]

PROVISION FOR EVERY EMERGENCY

How shall we escape, if we neglect so great salvation; which at the first began to be spoken by the Lord, and was confirmed unto us by them that heard him. Heb. 2:3.

The divine Author of salvation left nothing incomplete in the plan; every phase of it is perfect. The sin of the whole world was laid upon Jesus, and divinity gave its highest value to the suffering of humanity in Jesus that the whole world might be pardoned through faith in the Substitute. The most guilty need have no fear but that God will pardon, for because of the efficacy of the divine sacrifice the penalty of the law will be remitted. Through Christ the sinner may return to allegiance to God.

How wonderful is the plan of redemption in its simplicity and fullness. It not only provides for the full pardon of the sinner but also for the restoration of the transgressor, making a way whereby he may be accepted as a son of God. Through obedience he may be the possessor of love and peace and joy. His faith may unite him in his weakness to Christ, the source of divine strength, and through the merits of Christ he may find the approval of God, because Christ has satisfied the demands of the law, and He imputes His righteousness to the penitent, believing soul. . . .

What love, what wonderful love, was displayed by the Son of God. . . . Christ takes the sinner from the lowest degradation, and purifies, refines, and ennobles him. By beholding Jesus as He is, the sinner is transformed and elevated to the very summit of dignity, even to a seat with Christ upon His throne. . . .

The plan of redemption provides for every emergency and for every want of the soul. If it were deficient in any way, the sinner might find some excuse to plead for neglect of its terms, but the infinite God had a knowledge of every human necessity, and ample provision has been made to supply every need. . . . What, then, can the sinner say in the great day of final judgment as to why he refused to give attention, the most thorough and earnest, to the salvation proffered him?[41]

SOURCE OF ALL LIGHT

Then spoke Jesus again unto them, saying, I am the light of the world: he that followeth me shall not walk in darkness, but shall have the light of life. John 8:12.

Jesus of Nazareth declared Himself the Light of the world. What think ye of Him? What position does He occupy among the world's religious teachers? Hundreds, yes thousands, of men are recognized as having been great thinkers, men who speculated, who published their theories, and charmed the minds of many with their intellectual and moral attainments. These so-called great men who have left to the world the productions of their life of thought have been ranked as the wisest men the world has ever known. But these cannot compare with Christ. There was a revelation before man's productions were brought forth. His finite knowledge is but the result of beholding the wondrous things that have been shining in our world contained in the teachings of Christ, the greatest of all teachers. Whatever great ideas man may have evolved have come through Christ. Every precious gem of thought, every flash of the intellect, is revealed by the Light of the world. . . .

Christ makes no apology when He declares, "I am the light of the world." He was, in life and teaching, the gospel, the foundation of all pure doctrine. Just as the sun compares with the lesser lights in the heavens, so did Christ, the Source of all light, compare with the teachers of His day. He was before them all, and shining with the brightness of the sun, He diffused His penetrating, gladdening rays throughout the world. . . .

Measured by finite minds, men are called learned and great, but with all their boasted wisdom, their science and learning, they cannot thus know God, and Jesus Christ whom He has sent. . . . No man who has ever lived, or who ever will live, can claim to be the infallible guide, the supreme revealer of truth. Men may seek to reach the highest standard in learning, but there is One, "a teacher sent from God," who still stands higher than they. No human teacher can equal Him.[1]

CHRIST'S BLESSINGS UNIVERSAL

That was the true Light, which lighteth every man that cometh into the world. John 1:9.

The grace of Christ is not confined to a few. The message of mercy and forgiveness brought from heaven by Christ was to be heard by all. Our Saviour says, "I am the light of the world" (John 8:12). His blessings are universal, reaching to all nations, kindreds, tongues, and peoples. Christ came to break down every wall of partition . . . that every soul, whether Jew or Gentile, might be a free worshiper and have access to God. . . .

Through varied channels the heavenly messengers are in active communication with every part of the world, and when man calls upon the Lord with a true and earnest heart, God is represented as bending from His throne above. He listens to every yearning cry, and answers, "Here am I." He raises up the distressed and oppressed. He bestows His blessings on the evil as well as on the good.

In every precept that Christ taught, He was expounding His own life. God's holy law was magnified in this living representative. He was the revealer of the infinite mind. He uttered no uncertain sentiments or opinions, but pure and holy truth. . . . He invites men to take a close view of God in Himself, in the infinite love therein expressed.[2]

To know God is the most wonderful knowledge that men can have. There is much wisdom with worldly men, but with all their wisdom they behold not the beauty and majesty, the justice and wisdom, the goodness and holiness, of the Creator of all worlds. The Lord walks among men by His providences, but His stately steppings are not heard, His presence is not discerned, His hand is not recognized. The work of Christ's disciples is to shine as lights, making manifest to the world the character of God. They are to catch the increasing rays of light from the Word of God and reflect them to men enshrouded in the darkness of misapprehension of God. The servants of Christ must rightly represent the character of God and Christ to men.[3]

EQUALITY OF BELIEVERS IN CHRIST

For ye are all the children of God by faith in Christ Jesus. . . . There is neither Jew nor Greek, there is neither bond nor free, there is neither male nor female: for ye are all one in Christ Jesus. Gal. 3:26-28.

The secret of unity is found in the equality of believers in Christ. The reason for all division, discord, and difference is found in separation from Christ. Christ is the center to which all should be attracted; for the nearer we approach the center, the closer we shall come together in feeling, in sympathy, in love, growing into the character and image of Jesus. With God there is no respect of persons.

Jesus knew the worthlessness of earthly pomp, and He gave no attention to its display. In His dignity of soul, His elevation of character, His nobility of principle, He was far above the vain fashions of the world. . . . He desired not the applause of men. . . . Wealth, position, worldly rank in all its varieties and distinctions of human greatness, were all but so many degrees of littleness to Him who had left the honor and glory of heaven, and who possessed no earthly splendor, indulged in no luxury, and displayed no adornment but humility.

The lowly, those bound with poverty, pressed with care, burdened with toil, could find no reason in His life and example which would lead them to think that Jesus was not acquainted with their trials, knew not the pressure of their circumstances, and could not sympathize with them in their want and sorrow. The lowliness of His humble, daily life was in harmony with His lowly birth and circumstances. The Son of the infinite God, the Lord of life and glory, descended in humiliation to the life of the lowliest, that no one might feel himself excluded from His presence. He made Himself accessible to all. He did not select a favored few with whom to associate and ignore all others.[4]

All men are of one family by creation, and all are one through redemption. Christ came to demolish every wall of partition, . . . that every soul may have free access to God. His love is so broad, so deep, so full, that it penetrates everywhere.[5]

LINKED IN A COMMON BROTHERHOOD

But in every nation he that feareth him, and worketh righteousness, is accepted with him. Acts 10:35.

Jesus taught that the religion of the Bible does not consist in selfish exclusiveness, in personal enjoyment, but in the doing of loving deeds, in bringing the greatest good to others, in genuine goodness. . . . His life was free from all pride and ostentation. . . . Although He was the Creator of all worlds He yet testified of Himself while on earth that "the foxes have holes, and the birds of the air have nests; but the Son of man hath not where to lay his head" (Matt. 8:20). . . .

Jesus was the Majesty of heaven, the King of glory, and yet in His human life He was patient, kind, courteous, benevolent, full of love for little children, and full of pity and compassion for the tempted, the tried, and the oppressed. Of Himself He said, "The Spirit of the Lord is upon me, because he hath anointed me to preach the gospel to the poor; he hath sent me to heal the brokenhearted, to preach deliverance to the captives, and recovering of sight to the blind, to set at liberty them that are bruised, . . ." (Luke 4:18, 19).

Coming to earth to fulfill so gracious a mission, He was yet homeless, and often hungry and athirst. The men of His own nation hunted Him with craft and intrigue, with jealousy and hatred. . . .

He died a most shameful death, and made a full and complete sacrifice, in order that no one might perish, but that all might come to repentance. He made an atonement for every repenting, believing soul, in order that all might find in Him a sin bearer. If those who believe in Him will but practice His words, which are spirit and life; if they will follow His example, and become a precious light to the world, they will do that for the world which no human philosophy can accomplish. The lessons of Christ lay a foundation for a religion in which there is no caste—where Jew and Gentile, free and bond, are linked in a common brotherhood, equal before God, because they are all branches of the living Vine. They believe in Christ as their personal Saviour.[6]

ONE PLAN FOR ALL TIME

But we believe that through the grace of the Lord Jesus Christ we shall be saved, even as they. Acts 15:11.

God's truth is the same in all ages, although differently developed to meet the wants of His people in various periods. Under the Old Testament dispensation every important work was closely connected with the sanctuary. In the holy of holies the great I AM took up His abode. . . . There, above the mercy seat, overshadowed by the wings of the cherubim, dwelt the Shekinah of His glory, the perpetual token of His presence, while the breastplate of the high priest, set with precious stones, made known from the sacred precincts of the sanctuary the solemn message of Jehovah to the people. Wonderful dispensation, when the Holy One, the Creator of the heavens and the earth, thus manifested His glory, and revealed His will to the children of men!

The typical sacrifices and offerings of that dispensation represented Christ, who was to become the perfect offering for sinful man. Besides these mystic symbols and shadowy types pointing to a Saviour to come, there was a present Saviour to the Israelites. He it was, who, enshrouded in a pillar of cloud by day and a pillar of fire by night, led them in their travels, and He it was who gave direct words to Moses to be repeated to the people. . . . He who was equal with the Father in the creation of man was commander, lawgiver, and guide to His ancient people.[7]

Many look upon the days of Israel as a time of darkness, when men were without Christ, without repentance and faith. Many hold the erroneous doctrine that the religion of the children of Israel consisted in forms and ceremonies in which faith in Christ had no part. But men in that age were saved by Christ as verily as men are saved by Him today. . . . Christ was shadowed forth in the sacrifices and symbols, which were to last till type should reach antitype in His coming to our world. The Hebrews rejoiced in a Saviour to come. We rejoice in a Saviour who has come, and who is coming again. . . . Christ's blood avails for us, as it did for ancient Israel.[8]

THROUGH CHRIST TO GOD

God was in Christ, reconciling the world unto himself, not imputing their trespasses unto them; and hath committed unto us the word of reconciliation. 2 Cor. 5:19.

All through the pages of sacred history, where the dealings of God with His chosen people are recorded, there are burning traces of the great I AM. . . . In all these revelations of the divine presence, the glory of God was manifested through Christ. Not alone at the Saviour's advent, but through all the ages after the fall and the promise of redemption, God was in Christ, reconciling the world unto himself. Christ was the foundation and center of the sacrificial system in both the patriarchal and the Jewish age. Since the sin of our first parents, there has been no direct communication between God and man. The Father has given the world into the hands of Christ, that through His mediatorial work He may redeem man, and vindicate the authority and holiness of the law of God. All the communion between heaven and the fallen race has been through Christ. It was the Son of God that gave to our first parents the promise of redemption. It was He who revealed Himself to the patriarchs. Adam, Noah, Abraham, Isaac, Jacob, and Moses understood the gospel. They looked for salvation through man's Substitute and Surety. . . .

The solemn service of the sanctuary typified the grand truths that were to be revealed through successive generations. The cloud of incense ascending with the prayers of Israel represents His righteousness that alone can make the sinner's prayer acceptable to God; the bleeding victim on the altar of sacrifice testified of a Redeemer to come; and from the holy of holies the visible token of the divine presence shone forth. Thus through age after age of darkness and apostasy, faith was kept alive in the hearts of men until the time came for the advent of the promised Messiah. Jesus was the light of His people—the light of the world—before He came to earth in the form of humanity. . . . From Him has come every ray of heaven's brightness that has fallen upon the inhabitants of the earth. In the plan of redemption, Christ is the Alpha and the Omega—the First and the Last.[9]

ONE FAMILY IN CHRIST

For this cause I bow my knees unto the Father of our Lord Jesus Christ, of whom the whole family in heaven and earth is named. Eph. 3:14, 15.

Through faith in Christ we become members of the royal family, heirs of God, and joint heirs with Jesus Christ. In Christ we are one. As we come in sight of Calvary, and view the royal Sufferer who in man's nature bore the curse of the law in his behalf, all national distinctions, all sectarian differences, are obliterated; all honor of rank, all pride of caste is lost. The light shining from the throne of God upon the cross of Calvary forever puts an end to man-made separations between class and race. Men of every class become members of one family, children of the heavenly King, not through earthly power, but through the love of God who gave Jesus to a life of poverty, affliction, and humiliation, to a death of shame and agony, that He might bring many sons and daughters unto glory.

It is not the position, not the finite wisdom, not the qualifications, not the endowments of any person that makes him rank high in the esteem of God. The intellect, the reason, the talents of men, are the gifts of God to be employed to His glory, for the upbuilding of His eternal kingdom. It is the spiritual and moral character that is of value in the sight of Heaven, and that will survive the grave. . . .

All who are found worthy to be counted as the members of the family of God in heaven, will recognize one another as sons and daughters of God. They will realize that they all receive their strength and pardon from the same source, even from Jesus Christ who was crucified for their sins. They know that they are to wash their robes of character in His blood, to find acceptance with the Father in His name, if they would be in the bright assembly of the saints, clothed in the white robes of righteousness.[10]

The family is named after the Father. Those who enter the heavenly mansions will have the name of the Father and the name of the city of God written in their foreheads. They will bear the divine superscription and be partakers of the divine nature.[11]

THE SUM AND SUBSTANCE

And this is life eternal, that they might know thee the only true God and Jesus Christ, whom thou hast sent. John 17:3.

The sum and substance of the whole matter of Christian grace and experience is contained in believing on Christ, in knowing God and His Son whom He hath sent. But here is where many fail, for they lack faith in God. Instead of desiring to be brought into fellowship with Christ in His self-denial and humiliation, they are ever seeking for the supremacy of self. . . . O if we did but appreciate the love of God, how our hearts would be expanded, our limited sympathies would be enlarged, and break away from the icy barriers of selfishness, and our comprehension would be deeper than it now is. . . .

It is because we do not know God, we do not have faith in Christ, that we are not deeply impressed with the humiliation He endured in our behalf, that His abasement does not lead us to the humbling of self, to the exalting of Jesus. . . . O if you loved Him as He has loved you, you would not shun an experience in the dark chapters of the suffering of the Son of God!

In order to be partakers with Christ in His sufferings, we must behold the Lamb of God which taketh away the sin of the world. When we contemplate the humiliation of Christ, beholding His self-denial and self-sacrifice, we are filled with amazement at the manifestation of divine love for guilty man. When for Christ's sake we are called to pass through trials that are of a humiliating nature, if we have the mind of Christ we shall suffer them with meekness, not resenting injury, or resisting evil. We shall manifest the spirit that dwelt in Christ. . . . We are to understand what the sacrifice, the labors, and the sufferings of Christ are, in order that we may cooperate with Him in working out the great scheme of redemption.[12]

The knowledge of God and of Jesus Christ expressed in character is the very highest education. It is the key that opens the portals of the heavenly city. This knowledge it is God's purpose that all who put on Christ shall possess.[13]

WATER FOR THE THIRSTY

In the last day, that great day of the feast, Jesus stood and cried, saying, If any man thirst, let him come unto me, and drink. John 7:37.

Once a year, at the Feast of Tabernacles, the children of Israel called to mind the time when their fathers dwelt in tents in the wilderness, as they journeyed from Egypt to the land of Canaan. The services of the last day of this feast were of peculiar solemnity, but the greatest interest centered in the ceremony that commemorated the bringing of water from the rock. When in a golden vessel the waters of Siloam were borne by the priests into the temple, and, after being mingled with wine, were poured over the sacrifice on the altar, there was great rejoicing. . . . On this occasion, above all the confusion of the crowd and the sounds of rejoicing, a voice is heard: "If any man thirst, let him come unto me, and drink." The attention of the people is arrested. Outwardly all is joy, but the eye of Jesus, beholding the throng with the tenderest compassion, sees the soul parched and thirsting for the waters of life. . . .

The gracious invitation, "Come unto me, and drink," comes down through all the ages to our time. And we may stand in a position similar to that of the Jews in the time of Christ, rejoicing because the fountain of truth has been opened to us, while its living waters are not permitted to refresh our thirsty souls. We must drink. . . .

As the children of Israel celebrated the deliverance that God wrought for their fathers, and His miraculous preservation of them during their journeyings from Egypt to the Promised Land, so should the people of God at the present time gratefully call to mind the various ways He has devised to bring them out from the world, out from the darkness of error, into the precious light of truth. . . . We should gratefully regard the old waymarks, and refresh our souls with memories of the loving-kindness of our gracious Benefactor. . . .

As we journey onward, what a blessed privilege is ours to accept the invitation of Christ, "If any man thirst, let him come unto me, and drink."[14]

BREAD FOR THE HUNGRY

Jesus said unto them, I am the bread of life: he that cometh to me shall never hunger; and he that believeth on me shall never thirst. John 6:35.

Many are starved and strengthless because, instead of eating of the Bread which came down from heaven, they fill their minds with things of minor importance. But if the sinner will partake of the Bread of Life, he will, regenerated and restored, become a living soul. The Bread sent down from heaven will infuse new life into his weakened energies. The Holy Spirit will take of the things of God and show them to him, and if he will receive them his character will be cleansed from all selfishness, and refined and purified for heaven.

To the careless, the indifferent, the unconcerned, those standing on the precipice of ruin, Christ says: Open the door of your heart; give Me entrance, and I will make you a child of God. I will transform your weak, sinful nature into the divine image, giving it beauty and perfection. . . .

Not only does Christ give us the Bread of Life, but the Water of Life, which He gives, is as a well of water, springing up into everlasting life. It possesses life-giving properties and purifying efficacy for it proceeds from the throne of God.

Those who will permit God to work in them will grow up unto the full stature of men and women in Christ Jesus. Every power of the mind and body will be used in the service of God. . . . He has wonderful blessings to give to those who will receive Him. He is mighty in strength and wonderful in counsel. By the ministration of the Holy Spirit, He seeks to impress His image upon our characters. If we will feed upon Him we shall become new creatures in Christ Jesus. The virtues of a true Christian character, the excellences that are revealed in the character of Christ, will be seen in the life born of the Spirit. Man, with his human nature, will become a partaker of divinity. The power of Christ will work to sanctify every part of the being, diffusing life, activity, and soundness through the whole, and developing spiritual efficiency.[15]

PARTAKERS OF CHRIST

I am the living bread which came down from heaven: if any man eat of this bread, he shall live for ever: and the bread that I will give is my flesh, which I will give for the life of the world. John 6:51.

Bread cannot benefit us unless we eat it, unless it becomes a part of our being. A knowledge of Christ will avail nothing unless we become like Him in character, bearing the same likeness, and representing His spirit to the world. Christ is of no value to us unless He is formed within, the hope of glory. If we do not know Him as our personal Saviour, a theoretical knowledge will do us no good. Water will not quench thirst unless we drink it. Bread will not satisfy hunger unless we eat it. If we are feeding spiritually upon Christ we are partakers of His nature, we are eating of His flesh. . . .

When Christ uttered these words many of His disciples were in doubt as to what He meant, and He explained His words, saying: "It is the spirit that quickeneth; the flesh profiteth nothing: the words that I speak unto you, they are spirit, and they are life" (John 6:63).

If Christ is to you as a valuable treasure, if you find in Him your greatest satisfaction, if He is prized and cherished above all others, if you regard everything else as loss that you may win Him, you are eating of His flesh and drinking of His blood and are becoming conformed to His image. Those who hunger and thirst after righteousness will be filled. The invitation is: "Ho, every one that thirsteth, come ye to the waters, and he that hath no money; come ye, buy, and eat; yea, come, buy wine and milk without money and without price. Wherefore do ye spend money for that which is not bread? and your labour for that which satisfieth not? . . . eat ye that which is good, and let your soul delight itself in fatness" (Isa. 55:1, 2). . . .

All heaven rejoices at the redemption of the lost race. Christ rejoiced in the secret consciousness of what He purposed to do for man. He desires to do far more abundantly than we are able to ask or think. The fountain of His inexpressible love is inexhaustible, and it flows toward all those who believe in Him.[16]

A CHANGE OF RAIMENT

I will greatly rejoice in the Lord, my soul shall be joyful in my God; for he hath clothed me with the garments of salvation, he hath covered me with the robe of righteousness, as a bridegroom decketh himself with ornaments, and as a bride adorneth herself with her jewels. Isa. 61:10.

"And he shewed me Joshua the high priest"—a representative of the people who keep the commandments of God—"standing before the angel of the Lord, and Satan standing at his right hand to resist him" (Zech. 3:1).

Christ is our High Priest. Satan stands before Him night and day as an accuser of the brethren. With his masterly power he presents every objectionable feature of character as sufficient reason for the withdrawal of Christ's protecting power, thus allowing Satan to discourage and destroy those whom he has caused to sin. But Christ has made atonement for every sinner. Can we by faith hear our Advocate saying, "The Lord rebuke thee, O Satan; . . . is not this a brand plucked out of the fire?" (verse 2).

"Now Joshua was clothed with filthy garments" (verse 3). Thus sinners appear before the enemy who by his masterly, deceptive power has led them away from allegiance to God. With garments of sin and shame the enemy clothes those who have been overpowered by his temptations, and then he declares that it is unfair for Christ to be their Light, their Defender. . . . Hear the words of Jesus: . . . I will blot out his transgressions. I will cover his sins. . . .

The filthy garments are removed; for Christ says, "I have caused thine iniquity to pass from thee" (verse 4). The iniquity is transferred to the innocent, the pure, the holy Son of God; and man, all undeserving, stands before the Lord cleansed from all unrighteousness, and clothed with the imputed righteousness of Christ. Oh, what a change of raiment is this![17]

He takes every sin away, and puts on us His robe of righteousness woven in the loom of heaven. . . . We are adopted into the heavenly family, and we shall inherit the mansions prepared for those who are obedient.[18]

CHRIST OUR PEACE AND RIGHTEOUSNESS

Him hath God exalted with His right hand to be a Prince and a Saviour, for to give repentance to Israel, and forgiveness of sins. Acts 5:31.

He who has the spotless robe of righteousness, woven in the loom of heaven, in which is not a thread that sinful humanity can claim, is at the right hand of God, to clothe His believing children in the perfect garment of His righteousness. Those who are saved in the kingdom of God will have nothing of which to boast in themselves; the praise and the glory will all flow back to God. . . .

It is not now the work of the sinner to make peace with God, but to accept Christ as his peace and righteousness. Thus man becomes one with Christ and one with God. There is no way by which the heart may be made holy, save through faith in Christ. Yet many think that repentance is a kind of preparation which men must originate themselves before they can come to Christ. They must take steps themselves in order to find Christ a mediator in their behalf. It is true that there must be repentance before there is pardon, but the sinner must come to Christ before he can find repentance. It is the virtue of Christ that strengthens and enlightens the soul, so that repentance may be godly and acceptable. . . . Repentance is as certainly a gift of Jesus Christ as is forgiveness of sins. Repentance cannot be experienced without Christ, for it is the repentance of which He is the author that is the ground upon which we may apply for pardon. It is through the work of the Holy Spirit that men are led to repentance. It is from Christ that the grace of contrition comes, as well as the gift of pardon, and repentance as well as forgiveness of sins is procured only through the atoning blood of Christ. Those whom God pardons He first makes penitent.[19]

When the sinner accepts Christ and lives in Him, Jesus takes his sins and weaknesses and then grafts the repentant soul into Himself, so that he sustains the relation to Christ that the branch does to the vine. We have nothing, we are nothing, unless we receive virtue from Jesus Christ.[20]

JUSTIFIED BY FAITH

Therefore being justified by faith, we have peace with God through our Lord Jesus Christ: by whom also we have access by faith into this grace wherein we stand, and rejoice in hope of the glory of God. Rom. 5:1, 2.

When God pardons the sinner, remits the punishment he deserves, and treats him as though he had not sinned, He receives him into divine favor, and justifies him through the merits of Christ's righteousness. The sinner can be justified only through faith in the atonement made through God's dear Son, who became a sacrifice for the sins of the guilty world. No one can be justified by any works of his own. He can be delivered from the guilt of sin, from the condemnation of the law, from the penalty of transgression, only by virtue of the suffering, death, and resurrection of Christ. Faith is the only condition upon which justification can be obtained, and faith includes not only belief but trust. . . .

The sinner is represented as a lost sheep, and a lost sheep never returns to the fold unless he is sought after and brought back to the fold by the shepherd. No man of himself can repent, and make himself worthy of the blessing of justification. The Lord Jesus is constantly seeking to impress the sinner's mind and attract him to behold Himself, the Lamb of God. . . . We cannot take a step toward spiritual life save as Jesus draws and strengthens the soul, and leads us to experience that repentance which needeth not to be repented of. . . .

The faith that is unto salvation is not a casual faith, it is not the mere consent of the intellect, it is belief rooted in the heart, that embraces Christ as a personal Saviour. . . . When the soul lays hold upon Christ as the only hope of salvation, then genuine faith is manifested. This faith leads its possessor to place all the affections of the soul upon Christ; his understanding is under the control of the Holy Spirit, and his character is molded after the divine likeness. His faith is not a dead faith, but a faith that works by love, and leads him to behold the beauty of Christ, and to become assimilated to the divine character.[21]

OUR PERFECT PATTERN

He saith unto them, But whom say ye that I am? And Simon Peter answered and said, Thou art the Christ, the Son of the living God. Matt. 16:15, 16.

To human eyes Christ was only a man, yet He was a perfect man. In His humanity He was the impersonation of the divine character. God embodied His own attributes in His Son—His power, His wisdom, His goodness, His purity, His truthfulness, His spirituality, and His benevolence. In Him, though human, all perfection of character, all divine excellence, dwelt. And to the request of His disciple, "Shew us the Father, and it sufficeth us," He could reply, "Have I been so long time with you, and yet hast thou not known me, Philip? he that hath seen me hath seen the Father; and how sayest thou then, Shew us the Father?" "I and my Father are one" (John 14:8, 9; 10:30). . . .

The strong denunciation of the Pharisees against Jesus was, "Thou, being a man, makest thyself God" (John 10:33), and for this reason they sought to stone Him. Christ did not apologize for this supposed assumption on His part. He did not say to His accusers, "You misunderstand me; I am not God." He was manifesting God in humanity. Yet He was the humblest of all the prophets, and He exemplified in His life the truth that the more perfect the character of human beings, the more simple and humble they will be. He has given to men a pattern of what they may be in their humanity, through becoming partakers of the divine nature. . . .

The centuries that have passed since Christ was among men have not lessened the confidence of our testimony that Christ is all that He claimed to be. Today the question may be repeated, "What think ye of Christ?" (Matt. 22:42), and without a moment's hesitation the answer may be given, "He is the light of the world, the greatest religious thinker and teacher the world has ever known." All who hear His voice today, all who study the principles set forth in His teaching, must say, in truthfulness, as did the Jews of His day, "Never man spake like this man." "Is not this the Christ?" (John 7:46; 4:29).[22]

111

AN ALL-SUFFICIENT SAVIOUR

Look unto me, and be ye saved, all the ends of the earth: for I am God, and there is none else. Isa. 45:22.

Many are making laborious work of walking in the narrow way of holiness. To many the peace and rest of this blessed way seems no nearer today than it did years in the past. They look afar off for that which is nigh; they make intricate that which Jesus made very plain. He is "the way, the truth, and the life" (John 14:6). The plan of salvation has been plainly revealed in the Word of God, but the wisdom of the world has been sought too much, and the wisdom of Christ's righteousness too little. And souls that might have rested in the love of Jesus have been doubting and troubled about many things. . . .

We are wounded, polluted with sin. What shall we do to be healed from its leprosy? . . . In the wilderness, when the Lord permitted poisonous serpents to sting the rebellious Israelites, Moses was directed to lift up a brazen serpent and bid all the wounded look to it and live. But many saw no help in this Heaven-appointed remedy. . . .

If you are conscious of your wants, do not devote all your powers to representing them and mourning over them, but look and live. Jesus is our only Saviour, and notwithstanding millions who need to be healed will reject His offered mercy, not one who trusts in His merits will be left to perish. . . . Satan suggests that you are helpless and cannot bless yourself. It is true; you are helpless. But lift up Jesus before him: "I have a Saviour. In Him I trust, and He will never suffer me to be confounded. In His name I triumph. He is my righteousness, and my crown of rejoicing." . . .

It may seem to you that you are sinful and undone, but it is just on this account that you need a Saviour. If you have sins to confess, lose no time. These moments are golden. . . . Those who hunger and thirst after righteousness will be filled, for Jesus has promised it. Precious Saviour His arms are open to receive us, and His great heart of love is waiting to bless us.[23]

PROFESSION NOT ENOUGH

Not every one that saith unto me, Lord, Lord, shall enter into the kingdom of heaven; but he that doeth the will of my Father which is in heaven. Matt. 7:21.

A profession of religion is of no value unless good works testify to the sincerity and reality of its claim. . . . Those who make great professions and do not bear the fruits of godliness make it manifest that they are not abiding in the True Vine, for "by their fruits ye shall know them." They are dead branches. . . .

Conversion has become a matter of perplexity to many because of the confusing doctrines that are taught in regard to what is religion. Coming to Christ means something more than belonging to the church. There are many whose names are registered on the leaves of the church record but whose names are not written, in the Lamb's book of life. Coming to Christ does not require a severe mental effort and agony. It is simply accepting the terms of salvation that God has made plain in His Word.[24]

God desires the willing service of our hearts. He has endowed us with reasoning faculties, with talents of ability, and with means and influence, to be exercised for the good of mankind, that we may manifest His spirit before the world. Precious opportunities and privileges are placed within our reach, and if we neglect them we rob others, we defraud our own souls, and dishonor our Maker. We shall not want to meet these slighted opportunities and neglected privileges in the day of judgment. Our eternal interests for the future depend on the present diligent performance of duty in improving the talents that God has given into our trust for the salvation of souls. . . .

True religion works out the principles of God's law—love to God and love to man. Those who will be accepted of Heaven will have put their talents out to the exchangers for the glory of God and the good of humanity. They will have become laborers together with God, and will receive the approval of the Master when He comes in the clouds of heaven. Religion is something more than a profession, something deeper than an impulsive feeling. It is doing the will of God.[25]

THE RIGHTEOUSNESS THAT GOD REQUIRES

For I say unto you, That except your righteousness shall exceed the righteousness of the scribes and Pharisees, ye shall in no case enter into the kingdom of heaven. Matt. 5:20.

The righteousness of the scribes and Pharisees was of a selfish character, consisting of external forms. The righteousness which God requires is internal as well as external. The heart must be purified, else Christ cannot be enthroned there. The life must be conformed to the will of God.[26]

External forms cannot take the place of inward piety. The Jewish teachers exalted themselves as righteous; they called all those who differed from them accursed, and closed the gates of heaven to them, declaring that those who had not learned in their schools were not righteous. But with all their criticisms and exactions, with all their forms and ceremonies, they were an offense to God. They looked down upon and despised the very ones precious in the sight of the Lord. . . .

Human devices, human plans, and human counsels will be without power. Only in Christ Jesus will the church near the period of Christ's coming be able to stand. She is required of her Redeemer to advance in piety, to have increasing zeal, understanding better as she nears the end that her own "high calling" is "of God in Christ Jesus."

There are glorious truths to come before the people of God. Privileges and duties which they do not even suspect to be in the Bible will be laid open before the followers of Christ. As they follow on in the path of humble obedience, doing God's will, they will know more and more of the oracles of God, and be established in right doctrines.

The baptism of the Holy Spirit will dispel human imaginings, will break down self-erected barriers, and will cause to cease the feeling that I am holier than thou. There will be a humble spirit with all, more faith and love; self will not be exalted. . . . Christ's spirit, Christ's example, will be exemplified in His people. We shall follow more closely the ways and works of Jesus. . . . The love of Jesus will pervade our hearts.[27]

A FAITH THAT PURIFIES THE LIFE

But thou, O man of God, flee these things; and follow after righteousness, godliness, faith, love, patience, meekness. Fight the good fight of faith, lay hold on eternal life, whereunto thou art also called, and hast professed a good profession before many witnesses. 1 Tim. 6:11, 12.

Many teach that all that is necessary to salvation is to believe in Jesus, but what saith the word of truth?—"Faith without works is dead" (James 2:26). We are to "fight the good fight of faith, lay hold on eternal life," take up the cross, deny self, war against the flesh, and follow daily in the footsteps of the Redeemer. . . .

It is a fatal mistake to think that there is nothing for you to do in obtaining salvation. You are to cooperate with the agencies of heaven. . . . There is a cross to be lifted in the pathway, a wall to be scaled before you enter the eternal city, a ladder to be climbed before the gate of pearl is reached, and as you realize your inability and weakness and cry for help, a divine voice will come to you from the battlements of heaven saying, "Take hold of my strength" (Isa. 27:5) . . . .

The controversy that was waged between Christ and Satan is renewed over every soul that leaves the black banner of the prince of darkness to march under the blood-stained banner of Prince Emmanuel. The evil one will present the most subtle allurements to draw those away from their allegiance who would be true to Heaven, but we must yield all the powers of our being into the service of God, and then we shall be kept from falling into the snares of the enemy. . . .

Any course of action that weakens your physical or mental power unfits you for the service of your Creator. We are to love God with all our hearts, and if we have an eye single to His glory we shall eat, drink, and clothe ourselves with reference to His divine will. Every one who has a realizing sense of what it means to be a Christian will purify himself from everything that weakens and defiles. All the habits of his life will be brought into harmony with the requirements of the Word of truth, and he will not only believe, but will work out his own salvation with fear and trembling, while submitting to the molding of the Holy Spirit.[28]

115

SIMPLE FAITH AND UNQUESTIONING OBEDIENCE

And every one that hath forsaken houses, or brethren, or sisters, or father, or mother, or wife, or children, or lands, for my name's sake, shall receive an hundredfold, and shall inherit everlasting life. Matt. 19:29.

Many are strongly convinced of the truth, but either husband or wife prevents their stepping out. How can one who is in fellowship with Christ's sufferings refuse to obey His will and do His work? . . . It is by following in the path of obedience in simple faith that the character attains perfection. . . .

Christ has promised us sufficient power to reach this high standard. He says, "Whatsoever ye shall ask in my name, that will I do, that the Father may be glorified in the Son. If ye shall ask any thing in my name, I will do it. If ye love me, keep my commandments. And I will pray the Father, and he shall give you another Comforter, that he may abide with you for ever; even the Spirit of truth, whom the world cannot receive" (John 14:13-17).

Consider this statement a moment. Why "cannot" the world receive the truth? "Because it seeth him not, neither knoweth him" (verse 17). The world is leagued against the truth, because it does not desire to obey the truth. Shall I, who perceive the truth, close my eyes and heart to its saving power because the world chooses darkness rather than light? Shall I bind myself up with the bundles of tares because my neighbors refuse to be bound up with the wheat? Shall I refuse light, the evidence of truth which leads to obedience, because my relatives and friends choose to follow in the paths of disobedience which lead away from God? Shall I close my mind against the knowledge of truth because my neighbors and friends will not open their understanding to discern the truth as it is in Jesus? Shall I refuse to grow in the grace and knowledge of my Lord and Saviour Jesus Christ because my neighbors consent to remain dwarfs? . . .

We cannot overestimate the value of simple faith and unquestioning obedience.[29]

116

THE MEASURE OF CHARACTER

Charity suffereth long, and is kind; charity envieth not; charity vaunteth not itself, is not puffed up, doth not behave itself unseemly, seeketh not her own, is not easily provoked, thinketh no evil; rejoiceth not in iniquity, but rejoiceth in the truth; beareth all things, believeth all things, hopeth all things, endureth all things. 1 Cor. 13:4-7.

Through His inspired apostle Christ has presented to us the measure of the character that is imbued with the love of Christ. We are to bear the marks of Christ, we are to have His likeness. This example is given us that we may know the possibilities, the heights we may reach in and through Christ. The standard He presents is perfection in Him, and through His merits we may attain to it. We come short because we are content to look at earthly things rather than at heavenly. It is by beholding Christ that we are changed from glory to glory. The eye that views common things needs to be elevated. . . .

No man has yet measured the nature of God or the character of His Son. We must have a knowledge of God by living experience.[30]

This life is our time of probation. We are placed under the discipline and government of God to form characters and acquire habits for the higher life. . . . We shall be subject to heavy trials, opposition, bereavement, affliction, but we know that Jesus passed through all these. These experiences are valuable to us; the advantages are not by any means confined to this short life; they reach into eternal ages. . . . All the scenes of this life in which we must act a part are to be carefully studied, for they are a part of our education. We should bring solid timbers into our character building, for we are working both for this life and eternal life. And as we near the close of this earth's history we advance more and more rapidly in Christian growth, or we retrograde just as decidedly. . . .

Mercy and truth have met together in Christ, and righteousness and peace have embraced each other. It is when you are looking to His throne, offering up your penitence and praise and thanksgiving to God, that you perfect Christian character, and represent Christ to the world. You abide in Christ and Christ abides in you.[31]

117

CHILDREN, NOT SLAVES

Wherefore we receiving a kingdom which cannot be moved, let us have grace, whereby we may serve God acceptably with reverence and godly fear. Heb. 12:28.

There are many who profess to be Christ's followers and yet are not doers of His Word. They do not relish this Word because it presents service which is not agreeable to them. They do not relish the wholesome reproofs and close, earnest appeals. They do not love righteousness, but are mastered and tyrannized over by their own erratic, human impulses.

It makes every difference how we do service for God. The boy who drudges through his lessons because he must learn will never become a real student. The man who claims to keep the commandments of God because he thinks he must do it will never enter into the enjoyment of obedience.

The essence and flavor of all obedience is the outworking of a principle within—the love of righteousness, the love of the law of God. The essence of all righteousness is loyalty to our Redeemer, doing right because it is right. When the Word of God is a burden because it cuts directly across human inclinations, then the religious life is not a Christian life, but a tug and a strain, an enforced obedience. All the purity and godliness of religion are set aside.

But adoption into the family of God makes us children, not slaves. When the love of Christ enters the heart we strive to imitate the character of Christ. . . . The more we study the life of Christ with a heart to learn, the more Christlike we become. Into the heart of every true doer of the Word the Holy Spirit infuses clear understanding. The more we crucify selfish practices by imparting our blessings to others and by exercising our God-given ability, the more the heavenly graces will be strengthened and increased in us. We will grow in spirituality, in patience, in fortitude, in meekness, in gentleness. . . . A train of cars is not merely attached to the engine; they follow on the same track as the engine. Whom are we following?[32]

THE LOVELINESS OF CHRISTIAN CHARACTER

In that day shall the Lord of hosts be for a crown of glory, and for a diadem of beauty, unto the residue of his people. Isa. 28:5.

Many seem to think only of the outward adorning, and they make it evident that they are not in Christ by the apparel in which they deck themselves.[33]

We are to cultivate the loveliness of Christian character, and to seek the inward adorning. . . . The religion of Christ never degrades the receiver; it ennobles and elevates. Upon certain conditions we are assured that we may become members of the royal family, children of the heavenly King. Is not this exaltation something worth seeking for? Through faith in Christ and obedience to the requirements of His law we are offered a life that shall run parallel with the life of God. And in that immortal life there shall be no sorrow, no sighing, no pain, no sin, no death. O that we might be more heavenly-minded and bring more of heaven into our life and conversation!

But with all the rich promises of God, how many seem wholly absorbed in the things of earth. They are all taken up with the thought of what shall we eat, what shall we drink, and wherewithal shall we be clothed? God would not have us center our minds upon the things of this world. We are not to seek for our selfish gratification, but to center the mind upon Christ. Are you separating yourself from everything that will separate you from God? If you are in close connection with God you will talk of Him, you will have an abundance in your heart of the things of heaven. . . .

The Lord is waiting to do great things for His children who trust in Him. Do we expect to dwell with Christ in the eternal world? Then we must dwell with Him here, that He may help us in every time of trial and temptation and make us ready for His coming in the clouds of heaven. . . . The beauty and grace of Christ must be woven into our characters. We cannot keep Christ so apart from our lives as we do, and yet be fitted for His companionship in heaven. He is to be the all in all of heaven, and must be our all in all upon earth.[34]

THE REST CHRIST OFFERS

Come unto me, all ye that labour and are heavy laden, and I will give you rest. Matt. 11:28.

There is a condition to the rest and peace here offered us by Christ. It is that of yoking up with Him. All who will accept the condition will find that the yoke of Christ will help them to bear every burden needful for them to carry. Without Christ at our side to bear the heaviest part of the load, we must indeed say that it is heavy. But yoked with Him to our car of duty, the burdens of life may all be lightly carried. And just in proportion as man acts in willing obedience to the requirements of God will come rest of spirit. . . .

Meekness and humility will characterize all who are obedient to the law of God, all who will wear the yoke of Christ with submission. These graces will bring the desirable result of peace in the service of God. . . .

God knows that if we were left to follow our own inclinations, to go just where our will would lead us, we would fall into Satan's lines and become possessors of his attributes. Therefore the law of God confines us to the will of One who is high and noble and elevating. He desires that we shall patiently and wisely take up the duties of service. . . . A sullen submission to the will of the Father will develop the character of a rebel. The service is looked upon by such a one in the light of drudgery. It is not rendered cheerfully and in the love of God. It is a mere mechanical performance. . . . Such service brings no peace or quietude to the soul.

God presents to the world two classes. For the one—the wicked—He says, "There is no peace" (Isa. 48:22). Of the other, "Great peace have they which love thy law: and nothing shall offend them" (Ps. 119:165). . . .

The Lord calls His yoke easy and His burden light. Yet that yoke will not give us a life of ease and freedom and selfish indulgence. The life of Christ was one of self-denial and self-sacrifice at every step. And His true follower, with consistent, Christlike tenderness and love, will follow in the footsteps of his Master.[35]

UNDER CHRIST'S YOKE

Take my yoke upon you, and learn of me; for I am meek and lowly in heart: and ye shall find rest unto your souls. For my yoke is easy, and my burden is light. Matt. 11:29, 30.

The tempter often whispers that the Christian life is one of exaction, of rigorous duties, that it is hard to be on the watch continually, and there is no need of being so particular. It was thus that he deceived and overthrew Eve in Eden, telling her that God's commands were arbitrary and unjust. . . . Satan's object is the same now as then. He desires to deceive and ruin us. We should study the life of Christ and seek to cherish His spirit and copy His example, and the more we become like Him, the more clearly shall we discern the temptation of Satan, and the more successfully resist his power. . . .

True happiness is to be found, not in self-indulgence and self-pleasing, but in learning of Christ, taking His yoke, and bearing His burden. Those who trust to their own wisdom and follow their own ways, go complaining at every step, because the burden which selfishness binds upon them is so heavy and its yoke so galling. They might change all this if they would but come to Jesus and by His grace put off the yoke that links them to Satan, . . . take the burden which Christ gives them, and let His yoke bind them to Him in willing, happy service.

Jesus loves the young, and He longs to have them possess that peace which He alone can impart. . . . If we have become the disciples of Christ we shall be learning of Him—every day learning how to overcome some unlovely trait of character, every day copying His example and coming a little nearer the Pattern. If we are ever to inherit those mansions that He has gone to prepare for us we must here be forming such characters as the dwellers there are to possess.[36]

The requirements of God are made in wisdom and goodness. In obeying them, the mind enlarges, the character improves, and the soul finds a peace and rest that the world can neither give nor take away. When the heart is fully surrendered to Jesus, His ways will be found to be ways of pleasantness and peace.[37]

THE GRACE OF HUMILITY

Thus saith the high and lofty One that inhabiteth eternity, whose name is Holy; I dwell in the high and holy place, with him also that is of a contrite and humble spirit, to revive the spirit of the humble, and to revive the heart of the contrite ones. Isa. 57:15.

The grace of humility should be cherished by every one who names the name of Christ, for self-exaltation can find no place in the work of God. Those who would cooperate with the Lord of hosts must daily crucify self, placing worldly ambition in the background. They must be long-suffering and kind, full of mercy and tenderness to those around them. . . .

True humility is the evidence that we behold God and that we are in union with Jesus Christ. Unless we are meek and lowly we cannot claim that we have any true conception of the character of God. Men may think that they are serving God faithfully; their talents, learning, eloquence, or zeal may dazzle the eye, delight the fancy, and awaken the admiration of those who cannot see beneath the surface, but unless these qualifications are humbly consecrated to God, . . . they are regarded by God as unprofitable servants.[38]

God has been waiting long for His followers to manifest true humility that He may impart rich blessings to them. Those who offer Him the sacrifice of a broken and contrite spirit will be hidden in the cleft of the rock and will behold the Lamb of God, who taketh away the sins of the world. As Jesus, the Sin Bearer, the all-sufficient Sacrifice, is seen more distinctly, their lips are tuned to the loftiest praise. The more they see of the character of Christ the more humble they become, and the lower their estimate of themselves. . . . Self is lost sight of in their consciousness of their own unworthiness and of God's wonderful glory. . . .

Those who value a holy and happy walk with God, who prize the strength that a knowledge of Him brings; will leave nothing undone if only they may behold God. They will cherish the spirit that trembles at His word, and in every place and under every circumstance they will pray that they may be allowed to see His glory.[39]

A HEAVENLY PARTNERSHIP

Humble yourselves therefore under the mighty hand of God, that he may exalt you in due time. 1 Peter 5:6.

All heaven enters into copartnership with those who come to Christ for eternal life, submitting themselves to Him as those who have made a surrender of all to God. God requires His servants to stand under the blood-stained banner of Prince Emmanuel, striving in His power to keep the principles of truth pure and uncorrupted. They must never step aside from the path of self-denial and humility which every true Christian must travel. As they thus cooperate with God, Christ is formed within, "the hope of glory" (Col. 1:27). Clad in His meekness and lowliness they find their highest joy in doing His service. Earthly ambition gives way to a desire to serve the Master.

"Though the Lord be high, yet hath he respect unto the lowly: but the proud he knoweth afar off." "The sacrifices of God are a broken spirit: a broken and a contrite heart, O God, thou wilt not despise" (Ps. 138:6; 51:17). Those who reveal the meek and lowly spirit of Christ are tenderly regarded by God. Nothing is unnoticed by Him. He marks their self-denial, their effort to uplift Christ before the world. Though these humble workers may be looked upon with scorn by the world, they are of great value in the sight of God. Not only the wise, the great, the beneficent, will gain a passport into the heavenly courts—not only the busy worker, full of zeal and restless activity. No; the pure in heart, in whose lips there is found no guile; the poor in spirit, who are actuated by the Spirit of an abiding Christ; the peace-maker, whose highest ambition is to do God's will—these will gain an abundant entrance. They are God's jewels, and will be among that number of whom John writes, "I heard as it were the voice of a great multitude, . . . saying, Alleluia: for the Lord God omnipotent reigneth" (Rev. 19:6). They have washed their robes, and made them white in the blood of the Lamb. "Therefore are they before the throne of God, and serve him day and night in his temple: and he that sitteth on the throne shall dwell among them" (Rev. 7:15).[40]

LIGHT FOR THE HUMBLE

The meek will he guide in judgment: and the meek will he teach his way. Ps. 25:9.

Anything like pride in learning and dependence upon scientific knowledge which you place between your soul and the word of the Bible will most effectually close the door of your heart to the sweet, humble religion of the meek and lowly Jesus. . . .

It is the humble in heart that receive the enlightenment of Heaven that is more precious than the boasted wisdom of the world. . . . He [the repenting sinner] . . . becomes spiritual, and discerns spiritual things. The wisdom of God enlightens his mind, and he beholds wondrous things out of God's law. This salvation which offers pardon to the transgressor, presents to him the righteousness that will bear the scrutiny of the Omniscient One, gives victory over the powerful enemy of God and man, provides eternal life and joy for its receiver. . . .

It is the completeness of salvation that gives it its greatness. No man can measure or understand it by worldly wisdom. It may be contemplated with the most profound and concentrated study, but the mind loses itself in the untraceable majesty of its Author. But the soul united with God in meditation of His unfathomable riches is expanded, and becomes more capable of comprehending to a greater depth and height the glories of the plan of salvation. . . . His abilities develop and strengthen to comprehend and to do with increased skill and wisdom the requirements of God. The mind devoted unreservedly to God, under the guidance of the divine Spirit develops generally and harmoniously. The weak, vacillating character becomes changed through the power of God to one of strength and steadfastness. Continual devotion and piety establish so close a relation between Jesus and His disciple that the Christian becomes like Him in mind and character. After association with the Son of God the humble follower of Christ is found to be a person of sound principle, clear perception, and reliable judgment. He has a connection with God, the Source of light and understanding.[41]

THE MERITS OF JESUS' BLOOD

My soul shall make her boast in the Lord: the humble shall hear thereof, and be glad. Ps. 34:2.

He [the true Christian] realizes that an infinite sacrifice has been made for him, and that his life is of inestimable value through the merits of Jesus' blood, intercession, and righteousness. But while he comprehends the exalted privileges of the sons of God, his soul is filled with humility. There is no boasting of holiness from the lips of those who walk in the shadow of Calvary's cross. They feel that it was their sin which caused the agony that broke the heart of the Son of God. . . . Those who live nearest to Jesus feel most deeply their own unworthiness, and their only hope is in the merits of a crucified and risen Saviour. Like Moses, they have had a view of the awful majesty of holiness and they see their own insufficiency in contrast with the purity and exalted loveliness of Jesus.

Is there not occasion for humility? Is there not need of feeling our utter dependence upon Christ every day and hour? . . . He took on Him our nature, and became sin for us, that we might have "remission of sins that are past" (Rom. 3:25), and through His divine strength and grace might fulfill the righteous requirements of the law. Whoever takes the position that it makes no difference whether or not we keep the commandments of God is not acquainted with Christ. Jesus says, "I have kept my Father's commandments, and abide in his love" (John 15:10), and those who follow Jesus will do as He has done. . . .

Satan will seek to entice you to enter into the paths of sin, promising that some wonderful good will result from the transgression of God's law, but he is a deceiver. He would only work your ruin. . . . Christ came to break the rule of the evil one. . . . Man was so weakened through transgression that he did not possess sufficient moral power to turn from the service of Satan to the service of the only true God; but Jesus, the Prince of life, to whom is committed "all power in heaven and earth," will impart to every soul who desires salvation the strength necessary to overcome the enemy of all righteousness.[42]

125

TO GOD BE THE GLORY

Thus saith the Lord, Let not the wise man glory in his wisdom, neither let the mighty man glory in his might, let not the rich man glory in his riches: but let him that glorieth glory in this, that he understandeth and knoweth me, that I am the Lord which exercise lovingkindness, judgment, and righteousness, in the earth: for in these things I delight, saith the Lord. Jer. 9:23, 24.

This is the most precious reproof and encouragement, the most important lesson for every soul that is trying to serve God. Here is expressed in plain words that in which the Lord delights. All who understand and know God will know Him as One that exercises lovingkindness, judgment, and righteousness. If they walk humbly with God they will be enabled to keep the way of the Lord, to do His will in all kindness, compassion, mercy, tenderness, and love, for God has said, "In these things I delight." Then how careful should we be in regard to the fruit of the lips, that we dishonor not God by dealing unkindly with the purchase of His blood. If we express the character of God, we shall be Christian gentlemen and gentlewomen. . . .

Our prosperity as a people depends wholly upon our dependence upon God for our sufficiency, grace, and perfection of character in and through our Saviour, who has paid the ransom for us with His own glorious merits.[43]

Those who know Jesus Christ as their personal Saviour have the privilege of being educated and trained in a higher school than that of men, and of being tutored under higher wisdom than that of finite beings. They may come under the tutorship of the greatest Teacher the world ever knew, and partake of the same knowledge that He gave to Daniel. Those who are humble in heart, those who feel their need of higher wisdom and do not rely upon their own finite judgment, but search earnestly to know the will of God, may draw from the Source of all knowledge, and obtain grace, prudence, discretion, and judgment. They will realize the fulfillment of the assurance of God's Word: "The entrance of thy words giveth light; it giveth understanding unto the simple" (Ps. 119:130).[44]

"THE SPOT OF HIS CHILDREN"

Happy is that people, that is in such a case: yea, happy is that people, whose God is the Lord. Ps. 144:15.

I will thank the Lord my God for His great goodness and mercy and love expressed to the human family. I am impressed we should cultivate cheerfulness; and what does this do? It reveals to the world the peace and comfort that it is our privilege to claim. It is not honoring our Lord and Saviour to carry a shade of gloom. Many do this. . . .

"Give ear, O ye heavens, and I will speak; and hear, O earth, the words of my mouth. My doctrine shall drop as the rain, my speech shall distil as the dew, as the small rain upon the tender herb, and as the showers upon the grass: because I will publish the name of the Lord: ascribe ye greatness unto our God. He is the Rock, his work is perfect: for all his ways are judgment: a God of truth and without iniquity, just and right is he. They have corrupted themselves, their spot is not the spot of his children" (Deut. 32:1-5).

"Not the spot of his children." They do not possess the character of the sons and daughters of God; do not in spirit, in words, in actions, appear as the people who love God and keep His commandments. "Do ye thus requite the Lord, O foolish people and unwise? is not he thy father that hath bought thee? hath he not made thee, and established thee?" "For the Lord's portion is his people; Jacob is the lot of his inheritance. He found him in a desert land, and in the waste howling wilderness; he led him about, he instructed him, he kept him as the apple of his eye" (verses 6, 9, 10).

The tenderness of God to His people, His unceasing care for them, the riches of the wisdom of the methods He has taken to lead them to Himself, demand our gratitude offerings expressed in most earnest devotion to serve Him with all humility of mind and contrition of soul. The Lord is gracious, and He would have His people represent His loving-kindness by acknowledgment in cheerful thanksgiving to God. All who appreciate the favors of God will be a happy people.[1]

LIVE UP TO YOUR PROFESSION

I therefore, the prisoner of the Lord, beseech you that ye walk worthy of the vocation wherewith ye are called. Eph. 4:1.

Christ demands that those who take His name honor that name in spirit and word and deportment. In thought, word, and deed they are to be Christlike. Those who claim to be Christians and yet do not reveal in the life the virtues of Christ's character bear witness against the Saviour. They dishonor Him, putting Him to open shame. . . .

The revelation of His grace in humanity is an evidence of the power of the truth. Those who profess to follow Christ and yet do not reveal this grace . . . must know that their profession is a fraud. . . . A professing Christian cannot descend to the world's level without dishonoring the religion of Christ and making himself disloyal. Such a one is offensive to God. The Lord cannot own him as His disciple.

The Christian is to stand on vantage ground as a laborer together with God. But he is never to exalt himself. He is firmly to refuse the inducements presented by those who have no love for truth and righteousness, but his refusal is to be made in a Christlike spirit, not Pharisaically, with an attitude which says, "Stand aside; I am holier than thou." He must show that he cannot enter into sin because he is pledged by a most holy profession to honor the Lord Jesus Christ. By precept and example he is to discountenance all departure from Bible principles. But at the same time, by the manifestation of Christlike love, he is to make the religion of Christ attractive. He is to allow no bigotry to be seen in his life, but is to reveal tender compassion for those who have wandered away from Christ. . . .

Walk and work in the spirit of Christ. Stand ever on guard, for temptations will come, and the Lord's disciples are to be as true as steel to principle. . . .

Be sure to reveal the character of Christ. The Lord will be your efficiency, your strength, and your exceeding great reward if you will trust constantly in Him.[2]

AN INDIVIDUAL WORK

As ye have therefore received Christ Jesus the Lord, so walk ye in him: rooted and built up in him, and stablished in the faith, as ye have been taught, abounding therein with thanksgiving. Col. 2:6, 7.

If ever there was a time when those who claim to be Christians should be all that the name comprehends, it is now. Are we following Christ in very reality? . . . This is an individual work. We are to look earnestly to our own standing and accountability. . . .

Are those who know the truth for this time anchored in Bible doctrines? Are our weapons, "Thus saith the Lord," "It is written"? Is our anchor cast within the vail? Are we individually rooted and grounded in gospel truth so that we may be established, strengthened, and settled in the faith? Are we, as those who have the knowledge of the mysteries of God, those to whom God has committed the living oracles, loyal and true to our stewardship? Those who are truly converted will reveal, as missionaries for God, what the truth means to them in its transforming efficiency and sanctifying power.

If we are weighted with the treasures of eternal truth we shall proclaim to a world perishing in sin what it signifies to have the sanctifying, redeeming love of Christ in the soul. If we are verily and truly united in Christ, it is because truth has taken possession of the soul temple. . . .

The heart that has opened its doors to Jesus will love pure, cleansing, transforming truth, and will zealously contend for the faith once delivered to the saints. Let no man stop short of entire, unreserved surrender to God. Begin the work in the heart. Look away from the course of action pursued by others to Christ. You have a soul to save or a soul to lose, and this is too important a question to be regarded indifferently.

One of the most earnest prayers in the Inspired Word is, "Create in me a clean heart, O God" (Ps. 51:10); and from One who loved us and gave His life for us comes the great and important assurance, "A new heart also will I give you" (Eze. 36:26).[3]

PERFECTION THROUGH CHRIST'S MERITS

Be ye therefore perfect, even as your Father which is in heaven is perfect. Matt. 5:48.

Christ presents before us the highest perfection of Christian character, which throughout our lifetime we should aim to reach. . . . Concerning this perfection Paul writes: "Not as though I had already attained, either were already perfect: but I follow after. . . . I press toward the mark for the prize of the high calling of God in Christ Jesus" (Phil. 3:12-15). . . .

How can we reach the perfection specified by our Lord and Saviour Jesus Christ—our Great Teacher? Can we meet His requirement and attain to so lofty a standard? We can, else Christ would not have enjoined us to do so. He is our righteousness. In His humanity He has gone before us and wrought out for us perfection of character. We are to have the faith in Him that works by love and purifies the soul. Perfection of character is based upon that which Christ is to us. If we have constant dependence on the merits of our Saviour, and walk in His footsteps, we shall be like Him, pure and undefiled.

Our Saviour does not require impossibilities of any soul. He expects nothing of His disciples that He is not willing to give them grace and strength to perform. He would not call upon them to be perfect if He had not at His command every perfection of grace to bestow on the ones upon whom He would confer so high and holy a privilege. He has assured us that He is more willing to give the Holy Spirit to them that ask Him than parents are to give good gifts to their children.

Our work is to strive to attain in our sphere of action the perfection that Christ in His life on the earth attained in every phase of character. He is our example. In all things we are to strive to honor God in character. In falling day by day so far short of the divine requirements, we are endangering our soul's salvation. We need to understand and appreciate the privilege with which Christ invests us, and to show our determination to reach the highest standard. We are to be wholly dependent on the power that He has promised to give us.[4]

THE SCIENCE OF HOLINESS

To the end he may stablish your hearts unblameable in holiness before God, even our Father, at the coming of our Lord Jesus Christ with all his saints. 1 Thess. 3:13.

The ethics inculcated by the gospel acknowledge no standard but the perfection of God's mind, God's will. God requires from His creatures conformity to His will. Imperfection of character is sin, and sin is the transgression of the law. All righteous attributes of character dwell in God as a perfect, harmonious whole. Every one who receives Christ as his personal Saviour is privileged to possess these attributes. This is the science of holiness. . . .

The glory of God is His character. . . . This character was revealed in the life of Christ. That He might by His own example condemn sin in the flesh, He took upon Himself the likeness of sinful flesh. Constantly He beheld the character of God; constantly He revealed this character to the world. Christ desires His followers to reveal in their lives this same character.[5]

Before the world, God is developing us as living witnesses to what men and women may become through the grace of Christ. We are enjoined to strive for perfection of character. The divine Teacher says, "Be ye therefore perfect, even as your Father which is in heaven is perfect" (Matt. 5:48). Would Christ tantalize us by requiring of us an impossibility? Never, never! What an honor He confers upon us in urging us to be holy in our sphere, as the Father is holy in His sphere He can enable us to do this, for He declares, "All power is given unto me in heaven and in earth" (Matt. 28:18). This unlimited power it is our privilege to claim. . . .

God works with those who properly represent His character. Through them His will is done on earth as it is done in heaven. . . .

It is our lifework to be reaching forward to the perfection of Christian character, striving constantly for conformity to God's will. Day by day we are to press upward, ever upward, until of us it can be said, "Ye are complete in him" (Col. 2:10).[6]

ABIDING IN CHRIST

Abide in me, and I in you. As the branch cannot bear fruit of itself, except it abide in the vine; no more can ye, except ye abide in me. John 15:4.

"Abide in me" are words of great significance. Abiding in Christ means a living, earnest, refreshing faith that works by love and purifies the soul. It means a constant receiving of the spirit of Christ, a life of unreserved surrender to His service. Where this union exists, good works will appear. The life of the vine will manifest itself in fragrant fruit on the branches. The continual supply of the grace of Christ will bless you and make you a blessing, till you can say with Paul, "I am crucified with Christ: nevertheless I live; yet not I, but Christ liveth in me" (Gal. 2:20).

The sacred union with Christ will unite the brethren in the most endearing bonds of Christian fellowship. Their hearts will be touched with divine compassion one for another. . . . Coldness, variance, strife, are entirely out of place among the disciples of Christ. They have accepted the one faith. They have joined to serve the one Lord, to endure in the same warfare, to strive for the same object, and to triumph in the same cause. They have been bought with the same precious blood, and have gone forth to preach the same message of salvation. . . .

Those who are constantly drawing strength from Christ will possess His spirit. They will not be careless in word or deportment. An abiding sense of how much their salvation has cost in the sacrifice of the beloved Son of God will rest upon their souls. Like a fresh and vivid transaction the scenes of Calvary will present themselves to their minds and their hearts will be subdued and made tender by this wonderful manifestation of the love of Christ to them. They will look upon others as the purchase of His precious blood, and those who are united with Him will seem noble and elevated and sacred because of this connection. The death of Christ on Calvary should lead us to estimate souls as He did. His love has magnified the value of every man, woman, and child.[7]

GENUINE FRUIT BEARING

I am the vine, ye are the branches: He that abideth in me, and I in him, the same bringeth forth much fruit: for without me ye can do nothing. John 15:5.

Said Christ, "I am the true vine, and my Father is the husbandman." "I am the vine, ye are the branches." "Every branch in me that beareth not fruit he taketh away: and every branch that beareth fruit, he purgeth it, that it may bring forth more fruit" (John 15:1, 5, 2). That unpruned branch may have looked good to human eyes but the eye of One who never slumbers nor sleeps leaves it not alone to die of discouragement. The Husbandman pruneth it, that it may produce fruit unto life eternal. . . .

Whenever professed Christians are constantly flaunting their leaves of profession before the eyes of others, there is no real fruit to the glory of God. Their religious life and experience seem satisfactory to themselves. They have exaggerated emotions, effusive expressions of fervor, and highest exaltations. Their religion consists largely in feeling and excitement. There is very little in their own souls that corresponds to their profession of faith. Self is their ideal of perfection. They value more the outward impression they make upon others than the inner life which is hidden with Christ in God.

Let everyone who would reveal Christ by being a doer of His Word, become rooted in Christ Jesus, rooted and grounded in the truth. Put away all self-assertion. Let living and acting the lessons of Christ Jesus speak of your perfect obedience to Jesus Christ. . . .

The formation of the character must go on day by day, hour by hour. The inward working of the Holy Spirit is revealed outwardly in the appearance of fruit, ripening and perfecting to the glory of God. The inward life speaks in the outward action, in the producing of rich fruit. This is showing forth the praises of Him who hath called them out of darkness into His marvelous light. If the Lord Jesus is formed within, the hope of glory, the life will be rich in good works, corresponding with the truth which they profess to believe.[8]

GLORIOUS POSSIBILITIES BEFORE US

Let this mind be in you, which was also in Christ Jesus. Phil. 2:5.

How glorious are the possibilities set before the fallen race! Through His Son, God has revealed the excellency to which man is capable of attaining. Through the merits of Christ man is lifted from his depraved state, purified, and made more precious than the golden wedge of Ophir. It is possible for him to become a companion of the angels in glory, and to reflect the image of Jesus Christ. . . . Yet how seldom he realizes to what heights he could attain if he would allow God to direct his every step!

God permits every human being to exercise his individuality. He desires no one to submerge his mind in the mind of a fellow mortal. Those who desire to be transformed in mind and character are not to look to men, but to the divine Example. God gives the invitation, "Let *this mind* be in you, which was also in Christ Jesus." By conversion and transformation men are to receive the mind of Christ. Everyone is to stand before God with an individual faith, an individual experience, knowing for himself that Christ is formed within, the hope of glory. . . .

As our example we have One who is all and in all, the Chiefest among ten thousand, One whose excellency is beyond comparison. He graciously adapted His life for universal imitation. United in Christ were wealth and poverty; majesty and abasement; unlimited power, and meekness and lowliness, which in every soul who receives Him will be reflected. . . .

O that we might more fully appreciate the honor Christ confers upon us! By wearing His yoke and learning of Him, we become like Him in aspiration, in meekness and lowliness, in fragrance of character, and unite with Him in ascribing praise and honor and glory to God as supreme. Those who live up to their high privileges in this life will receive an eternal reward in the life to come. If faithful we shall join the heavenly musicians in singing with sweet accord songs of praise to God and to the Lamb.[9]

LIMITLESS HEIGHTS TO REACH

Wherefore gird up the loins of your mind, be sober, and hope to the end for the grace that is to be brought unto you at the revelation of Jesus Christ. 1 Peter 1:13.

"Gird up the loins of your mind," says the apostle; then control your thoughts, not allowing them to have full scope. The thoughts may be guarded and controlled by your own determined efforts. Think right thoughts and you will perform right actions. You have, then, to guard the affections, not letting them go out and fasten upon improper objects. Jesus has purchased you with His own life; you belong to Him, therefore He is to be consulted in all things as to how the powers of your mind and the affections of your heart shall be employed. . . .

Every wrong tendency may be, through the grace of Christ, repressed, not in a languid, irresolute manner, but with firmness of purpose, with high resolves to make Christ the pattern. Let your love go out for those things that Jesus loved, and be withheld from those things that will give no strength to right impulses. With determined energy seek to learn, and to improve the character every day. You must have firmness of purpose to take yourself in hand and be what you know God would be pleased to have you.[10]

Thoughts of God and of heaven are ennobling. There is no limit to the height you may reach, for it will be like swimming in waters where there is no bottom. . . . There is nothing belittling in the pure religion of Christ. The gospel received will bow down the loftiness of human understanding and lay the haughtiness of man low, that God alone may be exalted. But in this it does not dwarf the intellect and cripple the energies. . . . True religion unfolds and calls out the mental energies. Conviction and repentance of sin, renunciation of self, and trust in the merits of the blood of Christ cannot be experienced without the individual being made more thoughtful, more intellectual, than he was before. No one will become mentally imbecile by having his attention directed to God. Connection with God is connection with all true wisdom.[11]

THE PRECIOUSNESS OF CHRIST

His mouth is most sweet: yea, he is altogether lovely. S. of Sol. 5:16.

We should bring the attractiveness of Christ into our Christian service. The soft beams of the Sun of Righteousness should shine into our hearts, that we may be pleasant and cheerful and have a strong and blessed influence on all around us. The truth of Jesus Christ does not tend to gloom and sadness. . . . We must look away from the disagreeable to Jesus. We must love Him more, obtain more of His attractive beauty and grace of character, and cease the contemplation of others' mistakes and errors. We should remember that our own ways are not faultless. We make mistakes again and again. . . . No one is perfect but Jesus. Think of Him and be charmed away from yourself, and from every disagreeable thing, for by beholding our defects faith is weakened. God and His promises are lost from sight. . . .

O what deep, rich experiences we might gain if we were devoting all our God-given ability to seeking knowledge and spiritual strength from God! . . . How little we really know of sweet communion with God. How little we know the mysteries of the future life. We may know far more than we do know if all our powers are sanctified to discern the character of Christ.

There are heights for us to reach, depths of experience to sound, if we are to be the light of the world. . . . Let the mind expand, that you may take in the heavenly beauties of the blessed promises. Only believe in Jesus and learn in the school of the greatest Teacher the world ever knew, and His grace will act mightily upon the human intellect and heart. His teaching will give clearness to the mental vision. It will give compass to the thoughts; the soul hunger will be filled. The heart will be softened and subdued and filled with glowing love, that neither discouragement, despondency, affliction, or trial can quench. God will open to the mind's eye His preciousness and His fullness. Then let us love and labor. I point you to Christ, the Rock of Ages.[12]

INFLUENCE OF OUR WORDS

And whatsoever ye do in word or deed, do all in the name of the Lord Jesus, giving thanks to God and the Father by him. Col. 3:17.

Men are greatly under the influence of their own words. You are not conscious how much you are affected by your words. You accustom yourself to speak in a certain way, and your thoughts and actions follow your words. One accustoms himself to assert certain things in regard to himself, and at last he comes to believe them. Our thoughts produce our words and our words react upon our thoughts. If a man forms the habit of using sacred words reverently, he will form the custom of carefulness of speech, knowing that there is a Witness to every word uttered. When the feelings become excited and the speech is exaggerated, the mode of speaking is always extreme. It acts and reacts upon ourselves.

The Word declares, "By thy words thou shalt be justified, and by thy words thou shalt be condemned" (Matt. 12:37). If our words act upon ourselves they act more powerfully upon others. There is great mischief done by words spoken. God alone knows and measures the result of a careless, exaggerated mode of speaking. There is much swearing done in spirit. . . .

You are reproducing your own character in others. You may express many things that will create in other minds a course of thought which will lead them into false paths. God may spare you to outlive your exasperated feelings and come to have sensible thoughts. You may outlive your doubts, and through repentance toward God and faith in Jesus Christ escape from the snare of the fowler. You may pass into the sunshine of faith, but oh, you may never be conscious . . . that these words are doing their mischievous work in the soil of the hearts of others, and poisoning it. Here is a harvest some must reap. . . .

Raise the standard for Christ Jesus and have all your words select, seasoned with salt. Cultivate true dignity. . . . Let your words feel the influence of the converting power of God. Let wholesome words be spoken.[13]

A HOLY LISTENER

There is not a word in my tongue, but, lo, O Lord, thou knowest it altogether. Ps. 139:4.

Every hour of the day we should realize that the Lord is near, that He sees all we do, and hears every word we utter. . . . Cheap, earthly, unchristian words may be represented as "strange fire," and with this God can have nothing to do. The loud, boisterous laugh is a denial of God in the soul, for it reveals that the truth is not ruling in the heart. . . . By our vain words and unchristian example we dishonor God, and imperil not only our own souls but also the souls of those with whom we associate.

The example which Christ has given to the world forbids all levity and cheapness, and if the life is made fragrant by the grace of God, these elements will not appear. A genuine cheerfulness, an uplifting influence, will flow forth from all who love God and keep His commandments. And this carries with it a convincing, converting power. "Work out your own salvation with fear and trembling" (Phil. 2:12), says the apostle. Why with fear and trembling? Lest you shall in any way misrepresent your holy faith by lightness, by trifling, by jesting or joking, and thus give others the impression that the truth which you profess has no sanctifying influence upon the character.[14]

As followers of Christ we should make our words such as to be a help and an encouragement to one another in the Christian life. Far more than we do, we need to speak of the precious chapters in our experience. We should speak of the mercy and loving-kindness of God, of the matchless depths of the Saviour's love. Our words should be words of praise and thanksgiving. If the mind and heart are full of the love of God, this will be revealed in the conversation. . . . Great thoughts, noble aspirations, clear perceptions of truth, unselfish purposes, yearnings for piety and holiness, will bear fruit in words that reveal the character of the heart treasure. When Christ is thus revealed in our speech, it will have power in winning souls to Him.[15]

OUR EXAMPLE IN SELF-CONTROL

Who did no sin, neither was guile found in his mouth: who, when he was reviled, reviled not again; when he suffered, he threatened not; but committed himself to him that judgeth righteously. 1 Peter 2:22, 23.

The highest evidence of nobility in a Christian is self-control. We should copy the example of Jesus, for when He was reviled, He reviled not again, but "committed himself to him that judgeth righteously." Our Redeemer met insult and mockery with uncomplaining silence. All the cruel taunts of the murderous throng who exulted in His humiliation and trial in the judgment hall could not bring from Him one look or word of resentment or impatience. He was the Majesty of heaven, and in His pure breast there dwelt no room for the spirit of retaliation, but only for pity and love.[16]

There seems to be a mist before the eyes of many, for they fail to discern spiritual things, and do not recognize the workings of Satan to entrap their souls. Christians are not to be the slaves of passion; they are to be controlled by the Spirit of God. But many become the sport of the enemy, because when temptation comes, they do not rest in Jesus, but worry themselves out of His arms. . . . We make failures in our little, daily difficulties, and allow them to irritate and vex us; we fall under them, and so make stumbling blocks for ourselves and others. But blessings of the greatest importance are to result from the patient endurance of these daily vexations, for we are to gain strength to bear greater difficulties. . . .

O that we might control our words and actions! . . . What harm is wrought in the family circle by the utterance of impatient words, for the impatient utterance of one leads another to retort in the same spirit and manner. Then come words of retaliation, words of self-justification, and it is by such words that a heavy, galling yoke is manufactured for your neck, for all these bitter words will come back in a baleful harvest to your soul. . . . How much better to have the oil of grace in the heart, to be able to pass by all provocation, and bear all things with Christlike meekness and forbearance.[17]

DIGNITY WITHOUT PRIDE

*My lips shall not speak wickedness, nor my tongue utter deceit. . . .
My righteousness I hold fast, and will not let it go: my heart shall not
reproach me so long as I live. Job 27:4-6.*

We should preserve the strictest chastity in thought, and word,
and deportment. Let us remember that God sets our secret sins in the
light of His countenance. There are thoughts and feelings suggested
and aroused by Satan that annoy even the best of men, but if they
are not cherished, if they are repulsed as hateful, the soul is not contaminated with guilt, and no other is defiled by their influence. O that
we each might become a savor of life unto life to those around us!

There is great need of a deeper appreciation of the holy truth of
God. If all had a realization of the solemnity and weight of the message, many sins that are now carelessly committed would cease from
among us. Is there not too often the common thought and communication mingled with the sacred themes of truth? Wherever this is done,
the standard is lowered. Your example leads others to regard the truth
lightly, and this is one of the greatest sins in the sight of God.

It is the privilege of everyone to so live that God will approve
and bless him. You may be hourly in communion with Heaven; it is
not the will of your heavenly Father that you should ever be under
condemnation and darkness. It is not pleasing to God that you
should demerit yourself. You should cultivate self-respect by living
so that you will be approved by your own conscience, and before
men and angels.

It is not an evidence of true humility that you go with your head
bowed down and your heart filled with thoughts of self. It is your
privilege to go to Jesus and be cleansed, and to stand before the law
without shame and remorse. "There is therefore now no condemnation to them which are in Christ Jesus, who walk not after the flesh,
but after the Spirit" (Rom. 8:1). While we should not think of ourselves more highly than we ought, the Word of God does not condemn a proper self-respect. As sons and daughters of God we
should have a conscious dignity of character, in which pride and
self-importance have no part.[18]

CHEERFULNESS WITH SOBRIETY

Hear; for I will speak of excellent things; and the opening of my lips shall be right things. Prov. 8:6.

*I ask that the Holy Spirit shall control my thoughts through the day. I plead for wisdom in judgment, clearness of brain, and understanding, that I may see the treasures in the Word of God and bring out the precious truth in the simplest language. Thus did the greatest Teacher the world ever knew.

I feel more and more impressed with the greatness of the subject of the Lord's soon appearing in the clouds of heaven, with power and great glory. This faith moves me greatly to observe due solemnity at all times and in all places, but while I enjoin upon myself and others to be sober, they are not to cherish sadness and gloom. . . .

While we are not to be gloomy, but cheerful and happy, there is to be no silliness, but a sobriety in harmony with our faith. Words and actions form character. Therefore our words should be clean, pure, simple, yet elevated. The gift of speech is a valuable talent, and the Lord has no pleasure in hearing low, cheap, degrading nonsense which tastes strongly of vice and revelry. No Christian should condescend to imitate and catch such habits from another. . . . These evil, silly words are discordant notes and contribute to the happiness of no one. They are a detriment to spirituality. The Word of God forbids them.

"A good man out of the good treasure of the heart bringeth forth good things: and an evil man out of the evil treasure bringeth forth evil things. But I say unto you, That every idle word that men shall speak, they shall give account thereof in the day of judgment. For by thy words thou shalt be justified, and by thy words thou shalt be condemned" (Matt. 12:35-37).

"And Jesus knowing their thoughts said, Wherefore think ye evil in your hearts?" (Matt. 9:4). Jesus reads the hearts and minds and thoughts. . . . There is a Witness present, tracing every word spoken and every act performed, good or evil.[19]

---

*Early morning diary entry, July 12, 1897.

"WITH JOY UNSPEAKABLE"

Whom having not seen, ye love; in whom, though now ye see him not, yet believing, ye rejoice with joy unspeakable and full of glory. 1 Peter 1:8.

He [Christ] says, "If ye keep my commandments, ye shall abide in my love; even as I have kept my Father's commandments, and abide in his love. These things have I spoken unto you, that my joy might remain in you, and that your joy might be full" (John 15:10, 11). In Him there is joy that is not uncertain and unsatisfying. If the light that flows from Jesus has come to you, and you are reflecting it upon others, you show that you have joy that is pure, elevating, and ennobling. Why should not the religion of Christ be represented as it really is, as full of attractiveness and power? Why should we not present before the world the loveliness of Christ? Why do we not show that we have a living Saviour, one who can walk with us in the darkness as well as in the light, and that we can trust in Him? . . .

But minds that are occupied with frivolous reading, with exciting stories, or with seeking after amusement, do not dwell upon Christ, and cannot rejoice in the fullness of His love. The mind that finds pleasure in foolish thoughts and trifling conversation is as destitute of the joy of Christ as were the hills of Gilboa of dew or rain. . . . We need to be constantly filling the mind with Christ, and emptying it of selfishness and sin.[20]

The life in which the fear of the Lord is cherished will not be a life of sadness and gloom. It is the absence of Christ that makes the countenance sad and the life a pilgrimage of sighs. . . . But Christ dwelling in the soul is a wellspring of joy. For all who receive Him, the keynote of the Word of God is "rejoicing."

Why should not our joy be full—full, lacking nothing? We have the assurance that Jesus is our Saviour, and that we may freely partake of the rich provision He has made for us. . . . It is our privilege to seek constantly the joy of His presence. He desires us to be cheerful and to be filled with praise to His name. He wants us to carry light in our countenances and joy in our hearts.[21]

142

UNDER GOD'S GUARDIANSHIP

Behold, he that keepeth Israel shall neither slumber nor sleep. The Lord is thy keeper. the Lord is thy shade upon thy right hand . . . The Lord shall preserve thee from all evil: he shall preserve thy soul. Ps. 121:4-7.

July 16, 1897. I awakened this morning at three o'clock and lifted my heart in prayer and thanksgiving to God for His watchful care over the household. I pray the Lord to take us all under His guardianship today and make His face to shine upon us. I pray most earnestly that He will honor our humble dwelling with His abiding presence in our home. We may every individual in the family have the converting power of God daily upon heart and character.

The religion of Christ in the heart is the wellspring of life. It is the living water that Christ will give to every thirsting soul that asks Him. There are many who keep religion in practice far from the soul temple, and their faith is not in Jesus Christ. . . . The heavenly Guest should be invited to occupy the throne of the soul, to control every impulse of the mind, and to bring even the thoughts into subjection to Jesus Christ. . . .

July 26, 1897. I render thanks unto my heavenly Father for His blessing, after seeking the Lord in prayer. I go to my heavenly Father as a child in need goes to his temporal earthly father. We know that God must be interested in us, as the earthly parent is interested in his child, but to a much larger degree. I place myself as His child, and in simple faith ask for the small favors as I would ask for larger gifts, believing the Lord hears the simple, contrite prayer.

I keep saying in my heart, He loves me, He wants my love, and He wants me to be happy. "No good thing will he withhold from them that walk uprightly." "For the Lord God is a sun and shield: the Lord will give grace and glory." "O Lord of hosts, blessed is the man that trusteth in thee" (Ps. 84:11, 12).

I will appropriate His promises to myself, and will be glad in the Lord and ever praise His holy name.[22]

---

*Early morning diary entries.

THE VOICE OF NATURE

And God saw every thing that he had made, and, behold, it was very good. Gen. 1:31.

God does not design that we shall take no pleasure in the things of His creation. . . . He watches with a Father's joy the delight of His children in the beautiful things around them. While on earth the Redeemer of the world sought to make His lessons of instruction plain and simple, that all might comprehend them; and can we be surprised that He should choose the open air as His sanctuary, that He should desire to be surrounded by the works of His creation? . . . The things which His own hand had made He took as His lesson book. He saw in them more than finite minds could comprehend.

The birds, caroling forth their songs without a care, the flowers of the valley glowing in their beauty, the lily that reposed in its purity on the bosom of the lake, the lofty trees, the cultivated land, the waving grain, the barren soil, the tree that bore no fruit, the everlasting hills, the bubbling stream, the setting sun tinting and gilding the heavens—all these He employed to impress His hearers with divine truth. He connected the work of God's finger in the heavens and upon the earth with the Word of life. From these He drew His lessons of spiritual instruction. He would pluck the lilies, the flowers of the valley, and place them in the hands of the little children, as instructors to proclaim the truth of His Word. . . .

The beauties of nature have a tongue that speaks to us without ceasing. The open heart can be impressed with the love and glory of God as seen in the works of His hand. The listening ear can hear and understand the communications of God through the things of nature. There is a lesson in the sunbeam and in the various objects of nature that God has presented to our view. The green fields, the lofty trees, the buds and flowers, the passing cloud, the falling rain, the babbling brook, the sun, moon, and stars in the heavens—all invite our attention and meditation, and bid us become acquainted with Him who made them all.[23]

TOKENS OF GOD'S LOVE EVERYWHERE

For thus saith the Lord that created the heavens; God himself that formed the earth and made it; he hath established it, he created it not in vain, he formed it to be inhabited: I am the Lord; and there is none else. Isa. 45:18.

Through the goodness of God we have been surrounded with innumerable blessings. There are tokens of His love on every hand. Nature seems to be rejoicing before us. The beautiful things in heaven and earth express the love and favor of the Lord of hosts toward the inhabitants of the world. The sunshine and the rain fall on the evil and the good. The hills and seas and plains are all speaking eloquently to the soul of man of the Creator's love. It is God who brings the bud to bloom, the flower to fruit, and it is He who supplies our daily needs. Not a sparrow falls to the ground without the Father's notice. Our minds should go up in gratitude and adoration to the Giver of every good and perfect gift.

We should teach our children to consider the works of God. They should be instructed of His love and the provision He has made for their salvation. Lead them to give their young hearts as a grateful offering, fragrant with love, to Him who has died for them. Point out the attractive loveliness of the earth, and tell them of the world that is to come that shall never know the blight of sin and death, where the face of nature will no more wear the shadow of the curse. Lead their young minds to contemplate the glories of the reward that awaits the children of God. Cultivate their imaginative powers by picturing the splendor of the new earth and the city of God; and when they are charmed with the prospect, tell them it will be more glorious than their brightest imagination can portray. . . .

The poet and the naturalist have many things to say about nature, but it is the Christian who enjoys the beauty of the earth with the highest appreciation, because he recognizes his Father's handiwork and perceives His love in flower and shrub and tree. No one can fully appreciate the significance of hill and vale, river and sea, who does not look upon them as an expression of the love of God to man.[24]

EVIDENCES OF GOD'S GREATNESS

For thou, Lord, hast made me glad through thy work: I will triumph in the works of thy hands. O Lord, how great are thy works and thy thoughts are very deep. Ps. 92:4, 5.

The scenery through which we passed* was altogether too majestic, too awfully grand, to give anything like a description that can compare to the scenery as it really is. The battlements of rocks—the timeworn rocky walls that have stood since the Flood, washed with the mountain torrents—stand out smooth as if polished, while rocks diverse from these in shape are seen in regular layers, as if art had fashioned them. Here . . . we viewed the most interesting, grand scenery that our eyes ever looked upon. The rocks ascend higher and still higher from the earth, and growing from these rocks are beautiful, dark-colored pines intermingled with the lighter and most beautiful living green of the maple and beech. . . . Such wild grandeur, such solemn scenery, carries one back to the period when the waters rose to the highest points of land, and the unbelieving antediluvians perished for their great wickedness in the waters of the Flood.

As we look upon . . . the rocks of every conceivable shape, we say, "How wonderful, O Lord, are thy works in all the earth." The softening, subduing touches penciled by the great Master Artist in the beautiful arrangement of dress of dark and living green, this beautiful combination of colors to cover the rugged, time-seamed rocks! Then the deep gorges, the noisy, fast-rushing streams, and the grand mountains covered with forest trees in their beautiful summer robes!

The view is grand in the extreme, and presents to the senses such high and holy and strong and sacred ideas of God our Maker. And then the thought that we may call Him Father! . . . If anyone can look upon this scenery without being impressed with the greatness and majesty of God, his heart must indeed be unimpressible. I do so long for a closer connection with God. This God of majesty and might may be our Father, our Friend, our hope and crown of rejoicing.[25]

---

*Ellen White is here describing a carriage journey in Switzerland.

ON THE PREPARATION DAY

Remember the sabbath day, to keep it holy. Ex. 20:8.

Friday, Feb. 21, 1896, This day is preparation day. We would come up to the Sabbath with our work closed up in proper shape and not dragging into the Sabbath. We must commence in the morning to look after every piece of clothing if we have neglected to do this through the week, that our garments may be neat and orderly and comely to appear in the place where God's people assemble to worship Him. . . . Entering upon new business should be avoided, if possible, but endeavor to close up the things already started that are half accomplished. Prepare everything connected with the household matters so that there shall be freedom from worries, and the mind, be prepared to rest and to meditate upon heavenly things.

There needs to be much more close investigation of the week past. Review it and see if, as a branch of the living Vine, you have drawn nourishment from the parent Vine to bear much fruit to the glory of God. If there has been feverish excitement, if hasty words have been spoken, if passion has been revealed, these have surely been the working on Satan's side of the question. Clear the heart by confession. Sincerely make everything right before the Sabbath. Examine your own selves, whether ye be in the faith. We need to guard our own souls constantly, lest we make a great profession but, like the flourishing fig tree spreading its branches in pretentious foliage, reveal no precious fruit. Christ is hungering to see and receive fruit. Leaves of profession without fruit are to Christ just as worthless as those of the fig tree which He cursed. . . .

The humble dependence upon God, the faith that takes Him at His word and trusts Him at all times and under all circumstances, is the wearing of the yoke of Christ. The Christian brings all his passions under control to God. Then if the thoughts are brought into captivity to Jesus Christ, there is a healthful growth in beauty and grace of character.[26]

---

*Diary entry.

THROUGH NATURE TO NATURE'S GOD

But as it is written, Eye hath not seen, nor ear heard, neither have entered into the heart of man, the things which God hath prepared for them that love him. 1 Cor. 2:9.

If our hearts were softened and subdued with the love of God they would be open to discern His mercy and loving-kindness, as expressed to us in every shrub and in the profusion of blooming flowers which meet our eye in God's world. The delicate leaf, the spires of grass, every lofty tree, is an expression of the love of God to His children. They tell us that God is a lover of the beautiful. He speaks to us from nature's book, that He delights in the perfection of beauty of character. He would have us look up through nature to nature's God, and would have our hearts drawn out in love and affection to Him as we view His created works. . . .

God designs that the scenes of nature should influence the children of God to delight in the pure, simple, quiet beauty with which our Father adorns our earthly home. Jesus tells us that the mightiest king that ever swayed a scepter could not compare in gorgeous array to the simple flowers that God has clothed with loveliness. . . .

We must be preparing for the white robe of character, in order that we may pass within the pearly gates of the city of God to a heaven of bliss. Revelation presents the scene—fountains of living waters, rivers that are as clear as crystal proceeding out of the throne of God and the Lamb, trees of living green growing on either side of this river of life. . . .

We have in the glorious things of nature a mere shadow of the original which we shall see in their full loveliness in the Paradise of God. Let us learn the precious lesson which God designed we should. He who careth for the simple flowers in their season, will He not much more care for you whom He has created in His own image? Look upon these things of beauty. God prepares and clothes them with a robe of loveliness, and yet they perish in a day. All these earthly, temporal beauties are to be appreciated as the voice of God speaking to us of the treasures and glories of the unseen and the eternal.[27]

HONORING GOD IN THE HOME

Let the word of Christ dwell in you richly in all wisdom; teaching and admonishing one another in psalms and hymns and spiritual songs, singing with grace in your hearts to the Lord. Col. 3:16.

This is what we need in our households. There is in it no fault-finding, no harshness; but peace, and joy, and rest in the Lord. . . . God calls for loving service. He calls upon parents to speak lovingly and tenderly to their children. Let them see that you think they help you. Give them responsibilities to bear, small ones at first, and larger ones as they grow older. Never, never, let them hear you say of them, "They hinder me more than they help me." . . .

How many there are who forget that the home is a school in which children are trained to work either for Christ or Satan. Fathers and mothers, remember that every word you speak in the hearing of your children has an influence upon them, an influence either for good or for ill. Remember that if you find fault with one another you are educating your children to find fault.

With your children around you, bow before the Father in heaven. Ask Him for help to guard the trust He has given you. Let your petitions be short and earnest. Say, "Heavenly Father, I want my children to be saved. Grant me the aid of Thy Spirit that I may so train them that they may be counted worthy to inherit eternal life." Train your children to offer their simple words of prayer. Tell them that God delights to have them call upon Him.

We can subdue our children only as we subdue ourselves. But there are so many parents who have brought with them into the home life their hereditary and cultivated tendencies to wrong. They have not left their childishness behind. They scold their children for things which should never be noticed. Parents, never scold your children. Deal firmly but kindly with them. Keep them busy. Make them feel that they are a part of the family firm, that they can help mother and father. Thank them for what they do for you.

Let your home be a place where God is loved and honored.[28]

IN GOD'S WORKSHOP

Ye also, as lively stones, are built up a spiritual house, an holy priesthood, to offer up spiritual sacrifices, acceptable to God by Jesus Christ. 1 Peter 2:5.

The Word of God has served as a mighty cleaver to separate the children of God from the world. As they are taken out of the quarry of the world they are as rough stones, unfit for a place in the glorious temple of God. But they are brought into the Lord's workshop, to be hewed and squared and polished, that they may become precious, accepted stones. This work of preparation for the heavenly temple is going on continually during probationary time. We are naturally inclined to desire our own way and will, but when the transforming grace of Christ takes hold upon our hearts the inquiry of our souls is, Lord, what wilt thou have me to do? When the Spirit of God works within us, we are led to will and to do of the Lord's good pleasure, and there is obedience in heart and action. . . .

Christians are to be God's noblemen, who will never grovel in bondage to the great adversary of souls, but will bind themselves to God, catching inspiration from Him whom they love, who is high and lifted up. The soul that loves God rises above the fog of doubt; he gains a bright, broad, deep, living experience, and becomes meek and Christlike. His soul is committed to God, hid with Christ in God. He will be able to stand the test of neglect, of abuse and contempt, because his Saviour has suffered all this. He will not become fretful and discouraged when difficulties press him, because Jesus did not fail or become discouraged. Every true Christian will be strong, not in the strength and merit of his good works, but in the righteousness of Christ, which through faith is imputed unto him.[29]

We are to occupy some place in the Lord's spiritual temple, and the important question is not as to whether you are a large or a small stone, but whether you have submitted yourself to God that He may polish you and make you emit light for His glory. If we are in the Lord's temple we must emit light. Are we permitting the heavenly Builder to hew and square and polish us? Have we faith to rest in Him?[30]

GOD'S SPIRITUAL TEMPLE

In whom all the building fitly framed together groweth unto an holy temple in the Lord: in whom ye also are builded together for an habitation of God through the Spirit. Eph. 2:21, 22.

The gospel is designed for all, and it will bring together in church capacity men and women who are different in training, in character, and in disposition. Among these will be some who are naturally slack, who feel that order is pride, and that it is not necessary to be so particular. God will not come down to their low standard. . . .

The people of God have a high and holy calling. They are Christ's representatives. Paul addresses the church in Corinth as those who are "sanctified in Christ Jesus, called to be saints" (1 Cor. 1:2). . . .

If we have habits of speech and deportment that do not rightly represent the Christian religion we should at once set about the work of reform. As we represent Christ to the world, let us form such habits as will honor Him. Everywhere hidden from observation, agencies are at work to draw souls from Christ, and God would have still more powerful agencies at work among His people to attract souls to Christ.[31]

The Jewish Temple was built of hewn stones quarried out of the mountains, and every stone was fitted for its place in the Temple, hewed, polished, and tested, before it was brought to Jerusalem. And when all were brought to the ground, the building went together without the sound of an ax or hammer. This building represents God's spiritual temple, which is composed of material gathered out of every nation and tongue and people, of all grades, high and low, rich and poor, learned and ignorant. These are not dead substances, to be fitted by hammer and chisel. They are living stones quarried out from the world by the truth, and the great Master Builder, the Lord of the temple, is now hewing and polishing them and fitting them for their respective places in the spiritual temple. When completed, this temple will be perfect in all its parts, the admiration of angels and of men, for its builder and maker is God. Truly, those who are to compose this glorious building are "called to be saints."[32]

SOLDIERS OF CHRIST

By the word of truth, by the power of God, by the armour of righteousness on the right hand and on the left. 2 Cor. 6:7.

The church of Christ may be fitly compared to an army. The life of every soldier is one of toil, hardship, and danger. On every hand are vigilant foes, led on by the prince of the powers of darkness, who never slumbers and never deserts his post. Whenever a Christian is off his guard, this powerful adversary makes a sudden and violent attack. Unless the members of the church are active and vigilant, they will be overcome by his devices.

What if half the soldiers in an army were idling or asleep when ordered to be on duty; the result would be defeat, captivity, or death. Should any escape from the hands of the enemy, would they be thought worthy of a reward? No; they would speedily receive the sentence of death. And is the church of Christ careless or unfaithful, far more important consequences are involved. A sleeping army of Christian soldiers—what could be more terrible! . . .

The Master calls for gospel workers. Who will respond? All who enter the army are not to be generals, captains, sergeants, or even corporals. All have not the care and responsibility of leaders. There is hard work of other kinds to be done. Some must dig trenches and build fortifications, some are to stand as sentinels, some to carry messages. While there are but few officers, it requires many soldiers to form the rank and file of the army, yet its success depends upon the fidelity of every soldier. . . .

There is earnest work to be done by us individually if we would fight the good fight of faith. Eternal interests are at stake. We must put on the whole armor of righteousness, we must resist the devil, and we have the sure promise that he will be put to flight. The church is to conduct an aggressive warfare, to make conquests for Christ, to rescue souls from the power of the enemy. God and holy angels are engaged in this warfare. Let us please Him who has called us to be soldiers.[33]

THE PROOF OF OUR DISCIPLE

By this shall all men know that ye are my disciples, if ye have love one to another. John 13:35.

There is nothing that can so weaken the influence of the church as the lack of love. . . . The people of the world are looking to us to see what our faith is doing for our characters and lives. They are watching to see if it is having a sanctifying effect on our hearts, if we are becoming changed into the likeness of Christ. They are ready to discover every defect in our lives, every inconsistency in our actions. Let us give them no occasion to reproach our faith.

It is not the opposition of the world that will most endanger us; it is the evil cherished right in our midst that works our most grievous disaster. It is the unconsecrated lives of halfhearted professors that retard the work of the truth and bring darkness upon the church of God.

There is no surer way of weakening ourselves in spiritual things than to be envious, suspicious of one another, full of faultfinding and evil surmising. . . .

When you are associated together, be guarded in you words. . . . If the love of the truth is in your heart you will talk of the truth. You will talk of the blessed hope that you have in Jesus. If you have love in your heart you will seek to establish and build up your brother in the most holy faith. If a word is dropped that is detrimental to the character of your friend or brother, do not encourage this evil speaking. It is the work of the enemy. Kindly remind the speaker that the Word of God forbids that kind of conversation. We are to empty the heart of everything that defiles the soul temple, that Christ may dwell within. Our Redeemer has told us how we may reveal Him to the world. If we cherish His spirit, if we manifest His love to others, if we guard one another's interests, if we are kind, patient, forbearing, the world will have an evidence by the fruits we bear that we are the children of God. It is the unity in the church that enables it to exert a conscious influence upon unbelievers and worldlings.[34]

COME WHERE THE LIGHT SHINES

Not forsaking the assembling of ourselves together, as the manner of some is; but exhorting one another: and so much the more, as ye see the day approaching. Heb. 10:25.

It is no small matter for a family in an unbelieving community to stand as representatives for Jesus, keeping God's law. We are required to be living epistles, known and read of all men. This position involves fearful responsibilities. In order to live in the light we must come where the light shines. It is not well for the people of God to lose the privilege of associating with those of like faith with themselves, for the truth loses its importance in their minds. . . . They are not strengthened by the words of the living preacher. . . .

The faith of most Christians will waver if they constantly neglect to meet together for conference and prayer. If it were impossible for them to enjoy such religious privileges, then God would send light direct from heaven by His angels, to animate, to cheer, and to bless His scattered people. But He does not propose to work a miracle to sustain the faith of His children. They are required to love the truth enough to make some effort to secure the privileges and blessings vouchsafed them of God. . . .

"Then they that feared the Lord spake often one to another: and the Lord hearkened, and heard it, and a book of remembrance was written before him for them that feared the Lord, and that thought upon his name. And they shall be mine, saith the Lord of hosts, in that day when I make up my jewels; and I will spare them, as a man spareth his own son that serveth him" (Mal. 3:16, 17).

It will pay, then, to improve the privileges within our reach, and even at some sacrifice to assemble with those who fear God and speak for Him. For He is represented as hearkening to those testimonies, while angels write them in a book. God will remember those who have met together and thought upon His name. . . . They will be as precious jewels in His sight when His wrath shall fall on the shelterless head of the sinner.[35]

A LIFE OF STRENGTH

I must work the works of him that sent me, while it is day: the night cometh, when no man can work. John 9:4.

The Christian life does not consist merely in the exercise of meekness, patience, humility, and kindness. One may possess these precious and amiable traits and yet be nerveless and spiritless, and almost useless when the work goes hard. Such persons lack the positiveness and energy, the solidity and strength of character, which would enable them to resist evil, and would make them a power in the cause of God.

Jesus was our example in all things, and He was an earnest and constant worker. He commenced His life of usefulness in childhood. At the age of twelve He was "about his Father's business." Between the ages of twelve and thirty, before entering upon His public ministry, He led a life of active industry. In His ministry Jesus was never idle. Said He, "I must work the works of him that sent me. . . ." The suffering who came to Him were not turned away unrelieved. He was acquainted with each heart and knew how to minister to its needs. Loving words fell from His lips to comfort, encourage, and bless, and the great principles of the kingdom of heaven were set before the multitudes in words so simple as to be understood by all.

Jesus was a silent and unselfish worker. He did not seek fame, riches, or applause, neither did He consult His own ease and pleasure. . . . He did not shirk care and responsibility, as many do who profess to be His followers. . . .

The claims of Christ upon our service are new every day. However complete may have been our consecration at conversion, it will avail us nothing unless it be renewed daily, but a consecration that embraces the actual present is fresh, genuine, and acceptable to God. We have not weeks and months to lay at His feet; tomorrow is not ours, for we have not yet received it, but today we may work for Jesus. Today we may lay our plans and purposes before Him for His inspection and approval. . . . This is God's day, and you are His hired servant.[36]

IMITATING CHRIST

Wherefore, holy brethren, partakers of the heavenly calling, consider the Apostle and High Priest of our profession, Christ Jesus; who was faithful to him that appointed him. Heb. 3:1, 2.

In giving to men an example of what they should be and do, Jesus, the world's Redeemer, did not have a smooth path to travel. . . . Jesus had been the commander of heaven, yet on earth He was as one that serveth. Uncomplainingly He endured privations, and lived the life of a poor man. He did not indulge in the luxuries that many who claim to be His followers surround themselves with; He studied not at all His pleasure, ease, or convenience. He was a man of sorrows and acquainted with grief. His whole life was one of self-denial, expressing the prayer, "Not my will, but thine, O God, be done."

Christ is our pattern, and those who follow Christ will not walk in darkness, for they will not seek their own pleasure. To glorify God will be the continual aim of their life. Christ represented the character of God to the world. The Lord Jesus so conducted His life that men were compelled to acknowledge that He had done all things well. The world's Redeemer was the light of the world, for His character was without fault. Though He was the only begotten Son of God, and the heir of all things in heaven and earth, He did not leave an example of indolence and self-indulgence. . . .

Christ never flattered anyone. He never deceived or defrauded, never changed His course of straightforward uprightness to obtain favor or applause. He ever expressed the truth. The law of kindness was in His lips, and there was no guile in His mouth. Let the human agent compare his life with the life of Christ, and through the grace which Jesus imparts to those who make Him their personal Saviour, reach the standard of righteousness. Let him imitate the example of Him who lived out the law of Jehovah, who said, "I have kept my Father's commandments" (John 15:10). Those who follow Christ will be continually looking into the perfect law of liberty, and through the grace given them by Christ, will fashion the character according to the divine requirements.[37]

GRACE AN EDUCATOR

I thank my God always on your behalf, for the grace of God which is given you by Jesus Christ; . . . who shall also confirm you unto the end, that ye may be blameless in the day of our Lord Jesus Christ. 1 Cor. 1:4-8.

In this world we have temporal duties to perform, and in the performance of these duties we are forming characters that will either stand the test of the judgment or be weighed in the balances and found wanting. We may do the smallest duties nobly, firmly, faithfully, as if seeing the whole heavenly host looking upon us. Take a lesson from the gardener. If he wishes a plant to grow he cultivates and trims it; he gives water, he digs about its roots, plants it where the sunshine will fall upon it, and day by day he works about it; and not by violent efforts, but by acts constantly repeated, he trains the shrub until its form is perfect and its bloom is full.

The grace of our Lord Jesus Christ works upon the heart and mind as an educator. The continued influence of His Spirit upon the soul trains and molds and fashions the character after the divine model. Let the youth bear in mind that a repetition of acts, forms habit, and habit, character. . . . Is the love of Christ a living, active agent in your soul, correcting, reforming, refining you, and purifying you from your wrong practices? There is need of cultivating every grace that Jesus through His suffering and death has brought within your reach. You are to manifest the grace that has been so richly provided for you, in the small as well as in the large concerns of life. . . . Great truths can be brought into little things, and religion can be carried into the little as well as into the large concerns of life.

The commandments of God are exceeding broad, and the Lord is not pleased to have His children disorderly, to have their lives marred by defects and their religious experience crippled, their growth in grace dwarfed, because they persist in cherishing hereditary and cultivated deficiencies in wrong habits that will be imitated by others and thus be perpetuated. If the grace of Christ cannot remedy these defects, what then constitutes transformation of character?[38]

A NEW SONG IN OUR HEARTS

And he hath put a new song in my mouth, even praise unto our God: many shall see it, and fear, and shall trust in the Lord. Ps. 40:3.

He who believes in Christ becomes one with Christ, to show forth the glory of God, for God hath put a new song into his mouth, even praise unto the Lord. He daily desires to know more of Christ, that he may become more like Him. He discerns spiritual things and enjoys contemplation of Christ, and by beholding Him he is changed, imperceptibly to himself, into the image of Christ. . . . He does not place his dependence for acceptance with God upon what he can do, but relies wholly upon the merits of Christ's righteousness. Yet he knows that he cannot be slothful and be a child of God. He searches the Scriptures that testify to him of Christ, that present before him the perfect Pattern. . . .

Precious truth is unfolded to his mind, and he receives it into the inner sanctuary of the soul. The attractions of the world become tame to him, for the glory and value of eternity are opened before him. He can say with the apostle, "Now we have received, not the spirit of the world, but the spirit which is of God" (1 Cor. 2:12). . . .

He who has a genuine experience in the things of God will not be indifferent to those who are in darkness, but will inquire, What would Jesus say to these poor needy souls? He will seek to let his light shine forth. He will pray for wisdom, grace, and tact, that he may know how to speak a word in season to him who is weary. In place of engaging in trifling conversation, in jesting and joking, he will as a faithful steward of the grace of God, make the most of his opportunity, and the seed sown will spring up and bear fruit unto life eternal. The treasure of truth is in his heart, and he brings forth good things. The wellspring of life is in his soul, and the living waters flow forth. . . .

Is this your experience? Are you growing up into Christ, your living head? . . . O that the youth may consider the life of Christ, and copy the Pattern![1]

NO STANDING STILL

To them that have obtained like precious faith with us through the righteousness of God and our Saviour Jesus Christ: grace and peace be multiplied unto you through the knowledge of God, and of Jesus our Lord. 2 Peter 1:1, 2.

What a grand theme this is for contemplation—the righteousness of God and our Saviour Jesus Christ! Contemplating Christ and His righteousness leaves no room for self-righteousness, for the glorifying of self. In this chapter there is no standstill. There is continual advancement in every stage in the knowledge of Christ. Through the knowledge of Christ is life eternal. In His prayer Jesus says, "This is life eternal, that they might know thee the only true God, and Jesus Christ, whom thou hast sent" (John 17:3). In God we are to glory. . . . "But of him are ye in Christ Jesus, who of God is made unto us wisdom, and righteousness, and sanctification, and redemption: that, according as it is written, He that glorieth, let him glory in the Lord" (1 Cor. 1:30, 31). . . .

We have been called to the knowledge of Christ, and that is to the knowledge of glory and virtue. It is a knowledge of the perfection of the divine character, manifested to us in Jesus Christ, that opens up to us communion with God. It is by the great and precious promises that we are to become partakers of the divine nature, having escaped the corruption that is in the world through lust.

What possibilities are opened up to the youth who lay hold of the divine assurances of God's Word! Scarcely can the human mind comprehend what is the breadth and depth and height of the spiritual attainments that can be reached by becoming partakers of the divine nature. The human agent who yields obedience to God, who becomes a partaker of the divine nature, finds pleasure in keeping the commandments of God, for he is one with God; he holds as vital a relation with God as does the Son to the Father.[2]

What privileges and blessings are granted to those who have obtained like precious faith with the disciples of Christ! Nothing is withheld from them.[3]

ADDING AND MULTIPLYING

According as his divine power hath given unto us all things that pertain unto life and godliness, through the knowledge of him that hath called us to glory and virtue. 2 Peter 1:3.

We may attain unto glory and virtue, though weak, sinful mortals, by learning daily lessons, in the school of Christ, by becoming conformed to the divine image, by manifesting His excellence of character, by adding grace to grace, by climbing round by round the ladder heavenward, by becoming complete in the Beloved. As we shall work upon the plan of addition, by faith adding grace to grace, God will work upon the plan of multiplication, and multiply grace and peace unto us. . . .

If our youth would take heed to the rules laid down in this chapter and practice them, what an influence they would exert on the side of right! . . . No longer would the law which they have transgressed be a yoke of bondage, but it would be the law of liberty, the freedom of sonship. Having repented toward God, having exercised faith in Christ, they have experienced forgiveness, and esteem the law of God above gold, yea, above fine gold.

Jesus is the sin bearer. He takes away our sins, and makes us partakers of His holiness. O what tender, pitying love dwells in the heart of Christ toward the purchase of His blood! He is able to save unto the uttermost all who come unto God by Him. There is power in these precious promises, and we should cooperate with the working of Christ, devoting all our God-given talents to the service of the Master, that the Holy Spirit may work through us to the glory and honor of Christ.

Students should have a growing, expanding idea of what it means to be a Christian. To be a Christian means to be a learner in the school of Christ. It means the connecting of soul, mind, and body with divine wisdom. When this union exists between the soul and God, we are taught of God, who gives wisdom and knowledge. His Spirit imparts thoughts that are clear and holy, and gives the knowledge that lives through eternal ages. Those who are consecrated, diligent, . . . fervent in spirit, serving the Lord, will reap an eternal reward.[4]

WHEN YOU ARE GROWING

But grow in grace, and in the knowledge of our Lord and Saviour Jesus Christ. To him be glory both now and for ever. Amen. 2 Peter 3:18.

It is the privilege of the young, as they grow in Jesus, to grow in spiritual grace and knowledge. We may know more and more of Jesus through an interested searching of the Scriptures and then following the ways of truth and righteousness therein revealed. Those who are ever growing in grace will be steadfast in the faith, and moving forward. There should be an earnest desire in the heart of every youth who has purposed to be a disciple of Jesus Christ to reach the highest Christian standard, to be a worker with Christ. If he makes it his aim to be of that number who shall be presented faultless before the throne of God he will be continually advancing. The only way to remain steadfast is to progress daily in divine life. Faith will increase if, when brought in conflict with doubts and obstacles, it overcomes them. . . . If you are growing in grace and the knowledge of Jesus Christ you will improve every privilege and opportunity to gain more knowledge of the life and character of Christ.

Faith in Jesus will grow as you become better acquainted with your Redeemer by dwelling upon His spotless life and His infinite love. . . . When you are growing in grace you will love to attend religious meetings, and you will gladly bear testimony of the love of Christ before the congregation. God, by His grace, can make the young man prudent, and He can give to the children knowledge and experience. They can grow in grace daily. . . . Set your aim in life high, as did Joseph and Daniel and Moses, and take into consideration the cost of the character building, and then build for time and for eternity. . . . In doing this work for yourself you are having an influence on many others. . . . How much strength a word of hope, courage, and determination in a right course will give one who is inclined to slide into habits that are demoralizing! The firm purpose you may possess in carrying out good principles will have an influence to balance souls in the right direction. There is no limit to the good you may do.[5]

REACHING THE STATURE OF CHRIST

Till we all come in the unity of the faith, and of the knowledge of the Son of God, unto a perfect man, unto the measure of the stature of the fulness of Christ. Eph. 4:13.

The tremendous issues of eternity demand of us something more than an imaginary religion. A stately form of worship and high devotional ceremonies do not constitute a light to the world, and yet truth that is looked upon and admired in the same way as a beautiful picture or lovely flower, and not brought into the inner sanctuary of the soul, is thought by many to be all that is required in a worshiper. . . .

We shall be saved eternally when we enter in through the gates into the city. Then we may rejoice that we are saved, eternally saved. But until then we need to heed the injunction of the apostle, and to "fear, lest, a promise being left us of entering into his rest, any of us should seem to come short of it" (Heb. 4:1). Having a knowledge of Canaan, singing the songs of Canaan, rejoicing in the prospect of entering into Canaan, did not bring the children of Israel into the vineyards and olive groves of the Promised Land. They could make it theirs in truth only by occupation, by complying with the conditions, by exercising living faith in God, by appropriating His promises to themselves. . . .

Christ is the author and finisher of our faith, and when we yield to His hand we shall steadily grow in grace and in the knowledge of our Lord and Saviour. We shall make progress until we reach the full stature of men and women in Christ. Faith works by love, and purifies the soul, expelling the love of sin that leads to rebellion against, and transgression of, the law of God. . . . Through the agency of the Holy Spirit the character is transformed and the mind and will of the human agent are brought into perfect conformity to the divine will, and this is conformity to the divine standard of righteousness. To those who are thus transformed Christ will say, "Blessed are they that do his commandments, that they may have right to the tree of life, and may enter in through the gates into the city" (Rev. 22:14).[6]

ARE *YOU* GROWING UP?

But speaking the truth in love, may grow up into him in all things, which is the head, even Christ. Eph. 4:15.

It is no real evidence that you are a Christian because your emotion is stirred, your spirit stirred by truth. The question is, Are you growing up into Christ, your living head? Is the grace of Christ manifested in your life? God gives His grace to men, that they may desire more of His grace. God's grace is ever working upon the human heart, and when it is received, the evidence of its reception will appear in the life and character of its recipient, for spiritual life will be seen developing from within. The grace of Christ in the heart will always promote spiritual life, and spiritual advancement will be made. We each need a personal Saviour or we shall perish in our sins. Let the question be asked of our souls, Are we growing up into Christ, our living head? Am I gaining advanced knowledge of God, and of Jesus Christ whom He hath sent? We do not see the plants grow in the field, and yet we are assured that they do grow, and may we not know of our own spiritual strength and growth?[7]

When we are truly Christ's, our hearts will be full of meekness, gentleness, and kindness, because Jesus has forgiven our sins. As obedient children we shall receive and cherish the precepts He has given, and shall attend to the ordinances He has instituted. We shall be seeking constantly to obtain a knowledge of Him. His example will be our rule of life. Those who are Christ's disciples will take the work where He left it and carry it forward in His name. They will copy the words, the spirit, the practices, of none but Him. Their eye is upon the Captain of their salvation. His will is their law. And as they advance, they catch more and clearer views of His countenance, of His character, of His glory. They do not cling to self, but hold fast His Word. . . . They reduce their knowledge of His will to practice. They hear and do the things that Jesus teaches. . . . Such are entitled to all the promises of His Word. Becoming one with Christ, they do the will of God, and exhibit the riches of His grace.[8]

GROWTH AND FRUIT BEARING

That your love may abound yet more and more in knowledge and in all judgment; that ye may approve things that are excellent; that ye may be sincere and without offence till the day of Christ. Phil. 1:9, 10.

It is the Lord's desire that His followers shall grow in grace, that their love shall abound more and more, that they shall be filled with the fruits of righteousness. . . . Where there is life, there will be growth and fruit bearing; but unless we grow in grace, our spirituality will be dwarfed, sickly, fruitless. It is only by growing, by bearing fruit, that we can fulfill God's purpose for us. "Herein is my Father glorified," Christ said, "that ye bear much fruit" (John 15:8). In order to bear much fruit, we must make the most of our privileges. We must use every opportunity granted us for obtaining strength.

A pure, noble character, with all its grand possibilities, has been provided for every human being. But there are many who have not an earnest longing for such a character. They are not willing to part with the evil that they may have the good. Great opportunities are placed within their reach. But they neglect to grasp the blessings that would place them in harmony with God. They work at cross-purposes with the One who is seeking their good. They are dead branches, having no living union with the Vine. They cannot grow.

One of the divine plans for growth is impartation. The Christian is to gain strength by strengthening others. "He that watereth shall be watered also himself" (Prov. 11:25). This is not merely a promise; it is a divine law, a law by which God designs that the streams of benevolence, like the waters of the great deep, shall be kept in constant circulation, continually flowing back to their source. . . .

Christians, is Christ revealed in us? Are we doing all in our power to gain a body that is not easily enfeebled, a mind that looks beyond self to the cause and effect of every movement, that can wrestle with hard problems and conquer them, a will that is firm to resist evil and defend the right? Are we crucifying self? Are we growing up unto the full stature of men and women in Christ?[9]

MARKS OF TRUE SANCTIFICATION

And the very God of peace sanctify you wholly; and I pray God your whole spirit and soul and body be preserved blameless unto the coming of our Lord Jesus Christ. 1 Thess. 5:23.

The work of sanctification begins in the heart, and we must come into such a relation with God that Jesus can put His divine mold upon us. We must be emptied of self in order to give room to Jesus, but how many have their hearts so filled with idols that they have no room for the Redeemer of the world. The world holds the hearts of men in captivity. They center their thoughts and affections upon their business, their position, their family. They hold to their opinions and ways, and cherish them as idols in the soul. . . . We must be emptied of self. But this is not all that is required, for when we have renounced our idols, the vacuum must be supplied. . . .

As you empty the heart of self you must accept the righteousness of Christ. Lay hold of it by faith. . . . If you open the door of the heart, Jesus will supply the vacuum by the gift of His Spirit, and then you can be a living preacher in your home, in the church, and in the world. You can diffuse light, because the bright beams of the Sun of Righteousness are shining upon you. Your humble life, your holy conversation, your uprightness and integrity, will tell to all around that you are a child of God, an heir of heaven, that you are not making the world your dwelling place, but that you are a pilgrim and a stranger here, looking for a better country, even an heavenly. . . .

In order to keep the world in its proper subordination it is necessary to have more than a mere casual, nominal faith in Christ. Many might give assent to the fact that Jesus was the Son of God and yet fail to have saving faith. Jesus must be all in all to the soul. You must believe in Him as your personal and complete Saviour.[10]

True sanctification will be evidenced by a conscientious regard for all the commandments of God, by a careful improvement of every talent, by a circumspect conversation, by revealing in every act the meekness of Christ.[11]

JESUS OUR ALL

But of him are ye in Christ Jesus, who of God is made unto us wisdom, and righteousness, and sanctification, and redemption. 1 Cor. 1:30.

It is growth in knowledge of the character of Christ that sanctifies the soul. To discern and appreciate the wonderful work of the atonement transforms him who contemplates the plan of salvation. By beholding Christ he becomes changed into the same image, from glory to glory, as by the Spirit of the Lord. The beholding of Jesus becomes an ennobling, refining process. . . . The perfection of Christ's character is the Christian's inspiration. . . .

Christ should never be out of the mind. The angels said concerning Him, "Thou shalt call his name Jesus: for he shall save his people from their sins" (Matt. 1:21). Jesus, precious Saviour! assurance, helpfulness, security, and peace are all in Him. He is the dispeller of all our doubts, the earnest of all our hopes. How precious is the thought that we may indeed become partakers of the divine nature, whereby we may overcome as Christ overcame! Jesus is the fullness of our expectation. He is the melody of our songs, the shadow of a great rock in a weary land. He is living water to the thirsty soul. He is our refuge in the storm. He is our righteousness, our sanctification, our redemption.[12]

The power of Christ is to be the comfort, the hope, the crown of rejoicing, of everyone that follows Jesus in his conflict, in his struggles in life. He who truly follows the Lamb of God which taketh away the sin of the world, can shout as he advances, "This is the victory that overcometh the world, even our faith" (1 John 5:4).

What kind of faith is it that overcomes the world? It is that faith which makes Christ your own personal Saviour—that faith which, recognizing your helplessness, your utter inability to save yourself, takes hold of the Helper who is mighty to save, as your only hope. It is faith that will not be discouraged, that hears the voice of Christ saying, "Be of good cheer, I have overcome the world, and my divine strength is yours." . . . "Lo, I am with you alway."[13]

AN ABIDING MOTIVE

For the love of Christ constraineth us. 2 Cor. 5:14.

In every act of life Christians should seek to represent Christ—seek to make His service appear attractive. Let none make religion repulsive by groans and sighs and a relation of their trials, their self-denials, and sacrifices. Do not give the lie to your profession of faith by impatience, fretfulness, and repining. Let the graces of the Spirit be manifested in kindness, meekness, forbearance, cheerfulness, and love. Let it be seen that the love of Christ is an abiding motive; that your religion is not a dress to be put off and on to suit circumstances, but a principle—calm, steady, unwavering. Alas that pride, unbelief, and selfishness, like a foul cancer, are eating out vital godliness from the heart of many a professed Christian! When judged according to their works, how many will learn, too late, that their religion was but a glittering cheat, unacknowledged by Jesus Christ.

Love to Jesus will be seen, will be felt. It cannot be hidden. It exerts a wondrous power. It makes the timid bold, the slothful diligent, the ignorant wise. It makes the stammering tongue eloquent, and rouses the dormant intellect into new life and vigor. It makes the desponding hopeful, the gloomy joyous. Love to Christ will lead its possessor to accept responsibilities for His sake, and to bear them in His strength. Love to Christ will not be dismayed by tribulation, nor turned aside from duty by reproaches.[14]

Pure love is simple in its operations, and separate from every other principle of action. When combined with earthly motives and selfish interests, it ceases to be pure. God considers more with how much love we work, than the amount we do. Love is a heavenly attribute. The natural heart cannot originate it. This heavenly plant only flourishes where Christ reigns supreme. Where love exists, there is power and truth in the life. Love does good and nothing but good. Those who have love bear fruit unto holiness, and in the end everlasting life.[15]

FIRST THINGS FIRST

While we look not at the things which are seen, but at the things which are not seen: for the things which are seen are temporal; but the things which are not seen are eternal. 2 Cor. 4:18.

Satan has worked continually to eclipse the glories of the future world, and to attract the whole attention to the things of this life. He has striven so to arrange matters that our thought, our anxiety, our labor, might be so fully employed in temporal things that we should not see or realize the value of eternal realities. The world and its cares have too large a place, while Jesus and heavenly things have altogether too small a share in our thoughts and affections. We should conscientiously discharge all the duties of everyday life, but it is also essential that we should cultivate above everything else, holy affection for our Lord Jesus Christ.[16]

Views of heavenly things do not incapacitate men and women for the duties of this life, but rather render them more efficient and faithful. Although the grand realities of the eternal world seem to charm the mind, engross the attention, and enrapture the whole being, yet with spiritual enlightenment there comes a calm, heaven-born diligence that enables the Christian to take pleasure in the performance of the commonplace duties of life. . . .

The contemplation of the love of God manifested in the gift of His Son for the salvation of fallen men will stir the heart and arouse the powers of the soul as nothing else will. The work of redemption is a marvelous work; it is a mystery in the universe of God. But how indifferent are the objects of such matchless grace! . . .

If our senses had not been blunted by sin and by contemplation of the dark pictures that Satan is constantly presenting before us, a fervent and continuous flow of gratitude would go out from our hearts toward Him who daily loads us with benefits of which we are wholly undeserving. The everlasting song of the redeemed will be praise to Him who hath loved us and washed us from our sins in His own blood; and if we ever sing that song before the throne of God we must learn it here.[17]

FITTING UP FOR HEAVEN

*But now they desire a better country, that is, an heavenly:
wherefore God is not ashamed to be called their God: for he hath
prepared for them a city. Heb. 11:16.*

We profess to be pilgrims and strangers on earth, journeying to
a better country, even an heavenly. If we are indeed but sojourners
here, traveling to a land where none but the holy can dwell, we shall
make it our first business to become acquainted with that country;
we shall make diligent inquiry as to the preparation needed, the
manners and character which we must have in order to become cit-
izens there. Jesus, the King of that land, is pure and holy. He has
commanded His followers, "Be ye holy; for I am holy" (1 Peter 1:16).
If we are hereafter to associate with Christ and sinless angels we
must here obtain a fitness for such society.

This is our work—our all-important work. Every other consideration is of minor consequence. Our conversation, our deportment,
our every act, should be such as to convince our family, our neighbors, and the world that we expect soon to remove to a better country. . . . Those whose faith is daily confirmed and strengthened by
their works will become acquainted with self-denial in restricting appetite, controlling ambitious desires, bringing every thought and
feeling into harmony with the divine will. . . .

The land to which we are traveling is in every sense far more attractive than was the land of Canaan to the children of Israel. . . .
What stayed their progress just in sight of the goodly land? . . . It was
their own willful unbelief that turned them back. They were unwilling to risk anything upon the promises of God. . . . The history of
the children of Israel is written as a warning to us "upon whom the
ends of the world are come." We are standing, as it were, upon the
very borders of the heavenly Canaan. We may, if we will, look over
on the other side and behold the attractions of the goodly land. If
we have faith in the promises of God we shall show in conversation
and in deportment that we are not living for this world, but are making it our first business to prepare for that holy land.[18]

169

"STEDFAST UNTO THE END"

For we are made partakers of Christ, if we hold the beginning of our confidence stedfast unto the end. Heb. 3:14.

We must all exercise faith. I am praying to the Lord to give me strength and health and clearness of mind, and I believe He hears my prayers. We are exhorted to be sober and watch unto prayer, but this does not mean that we are to mourn and repine, like orphaned children. True, the struggle for continual advancement in the Christian life must be lifelong, but our advancement in the heavenly path may be hopeful. If we manifest an intense energy, proportionate to the object for which we are striving, even eternal life, we are made partakers of Christ and of all the rich graces He is willing and ready to give to those who by patient continuance in well doing seek for glory and honor and immortality. If we hold the beginning of our confidence steadfast unto the end we shall see the King in His glory.

I do not ask for smooth paths, but I do supplicate my heavenly Father for an increase of faith, that I may surmount every apparent difficulty. He is able and willing to give us the Comforter, but we must have firmness and decision, maintaining under all circumstances a pure, Christian integrity and confidence in our Lord and Saviour Jesus Christ. The exhortation comes to us, "Ye therefore, beloved, seeing ye know these things before, beware lest ye also, being led away with the error of the wicked, fall from your own stedfastness" (2 Peter 3:17).

Eternal interests are to be gained, even the salvation of our souls, and every day we are to watch and be sober. Yet we are to be cheerful, thanking the Lord for His blessings. We must have faith, living faith. God is our efficiency, the source of all power. His resources cannot be exhausted. We can have a daily, abundant supply. . . .

For everyone whose hands seem to be weakening and losing their hold, I have the word, Grasp the standard more firmly. Faith says, Go forward. You must not fail nor be discouraged. There is no weakness of faith in him who is constantly advancing.[19]

THE COMING OF THE COMFORTER

And I will pray the Father, and he shall give you another Comforter, that he may abide with you for ever; even the Spirit of truth; whom the world cannot receive, because it seeth him not, neither knoweth him: but ye know him; for he dwelleth with you, and shall be in you. John 14:16, 17.

Christ was about to depart to His home in the heavenly courts, but He assured His disciples that He would send them the Comforter, who would abide with them forever. To the guidance of this Comforter all may implicitly trust. He is the Spirit of truth; but this truth the world can neither see nor receive. . . .

Christ desired His disciples to understand that He would not leave them orphans. "I will not leave you comfortless," He declared: "I will come to you" (John 14:18, 19). . . . Precious, glorious assurance of eternal life! Even though He was to be absent, their relation to Him was to be that of a child to its parent. . . .

The words spoken to the disciples come to us through their words. The Comforter is ours as well as theirs, at all times and in all places, in all sorrows and in all affliction, when the outlook seems dark and the future perplexing and we feel helpless and alone. These are times when the Comforter will be sent in answer to the prayer of faith.

There is no comforter like Christ, so tender and so true. He is touched with the feeling of our infirmities. His Spirit speaks to the heart. Circumstances may separate us from our friends; the broad, restless ocean may roll between us and them. Though their sincere friendship may still exist, they may be unable to demonstrate it by doing for us that which would be gratefully received. But no circumstances, no distance, can separate us from the heavenly Comforter. Wherever we are, wherever we may go, He is always there, one given in Christ's place, to act in His stead. He is always at our right hand, to speak soothing, gentle words, to support, sustain, uphold, and cheer. The influence of the Holy Spirit is the life of Christ in the soul. This Spirit works in and through everyone who receives Christ. Those who know the indwelling of this Spirit reveal its fruit—love, joy, peace, long-suffering, gentleness, goodness, faith.[20]

OUR DIVINE CREDENTIALS

Holy Father, keep through thine own name those whom thou hast given me, that they may be one, as we are. John 17:11.

The unity, the harmony, that should exist among the disciples of Christ is described in these words: "That they may be one, as we are." But how many there are who draw off and seem to think that they have learned all they need to learn. . . . Those who choose to stand on the outskirts of the camp cannot know what is going on in the inner circle. They must come right into the inner courts, for as a people we must be united in faith and purpose. . . . It is through this unity that we are to convince the world of the mission of Christ, and bear our divine credentials to the world. . . .

"I in them, and thou in me, that they may be made perfect in one; and that the world may know that thou hast sent me, and hast loved them, as thou hast loved me" (John 17:23). Can we comprehend the meaning of these words? Can we take it in? Can we measure this love? The thought that God loves us as He loves His Son should bring us in gratitude and praise to Him. Provision has been made whereby God can love us as He loves His Son, and it is through our oneness with Christ and with each other. We must each come to the fountain and drink for ourselves. A thousand around us may take of the stream of salvation, but we shall not be refreshed unless we drink of the healing stream ourselves. We must see the beauty, the light of God's Word for ourselves, and kindle our taper at the divine altar, that we may go to the world, holding forth the Word of life as a bright, shining lamp. . . .

How precious are these words! "Father, I will that they also, whom thou hast given me, be with me where I am; that they may behold my glory" (verse 24). . . . Christ wills that we should behold His glory. Where? In the kingdom of heaven. He wills that we should be one with Him. What a thought! How willing it makes me to make any and every sacrifice for His sake! He is my love, my righteousness, my comfort, my crown of rejoicing, and He wills that we should behold His glory.[21]

ONENESS WITH CHRIST AND THE FATHER

That they all may be one; as thou, Father, art in me, and I in thee, that they also may be one in us: that the world may believe that thou hast sent me. John 17:21.

Let these words be oft repeated and let every soul train his ideas and spirit and action daily that he may fulfill this prayer of Jesus Christ. He does not request impossible things of His Father. He prays for the very things which must be in His disciples in relation to their oneness to each other and their unity and oneness with God and Jesus Christ. Anything short of this is not attaining to perfection of Christian character. The golden chain of love, binding the hearts of the believers in unity, in bonds of fellowship and love, and in oneness with Christ and the Father, makes the connection perfect, and bears to the world a testimony of the power of Christianity that cannot be controverted. . . .

Then will selfishness be uprooted and unfaithfulness will not exist. There will not be strife and divisions. There will not be stubbornness in anyone who is bound up with Christ. Not one will act out the stubborn independence of the wayward, impulsive child who drops the hand that is leading him and chooses to stumble on alone. . . .

"A new commandment I give unto you, That ye love one another; as I have loved you, that ye also love one another. By this shall all men know that ye are my disciples, if ye have love one to another" (John 13:34, 35). Satan understands the power of such a testimony as a witness to the world of what grace can do in transforming character. He is not pleased that such a light shall shine forth from those who claim to believe in Jesus Christ, and he will work every conceivable device to break this golden chain which links heart to heart of those who believe the truth and binds them up in close connection with the Father and the Son. . . .

We believe in Jesus Christ. We unite our souls to Christ. He says, "Ye have not chosen me, but I have chosen you, and ordained you, that ye should go and bring forth fruit. . . . These things I command you, that ye love one another" (John 15:16, 17).[22]

GOD'S MEASUREMENT OF MY CHARACTER

For we dare not make ourselves of the number, or compare ourselves with some that commend themselves: but they measuring themselves by themselves, and comparing themselves among themselves, are not wise. 2 Cor. 10:12.

Many measure themselves among themselves, and compare their lives with the lives of others. This should not be. No one but Christ is given us as an example. He is our true pattern, and each should strive to excel in imitating Him. . . .

To be a Christian is not merely to take the name of Christ, but to have the mind of Christ, to submit to the will of God in all things. Many who profess to be Christians have yet to learn this great lesson. Many know little of what it is to deny self for Christ's sake. They do not study how they can best glorify God and advance His cause. But it is self, self, how can it be gratified? Such religion is worthless. In the day of God those who possess it will be weighed in the balance and found wanting.[23]

What men may say, what their opinion of us may be, amounts to very little. The question that concerns us is, What is God's measurement of my character? . . . He who sustains another man in a wrong course of action is not on God's side, but on the enemy's. "So did not I," Nehemiah says, "because of the fear of God" (Neh. 5:15). Every soul is to gird himself for the spiritual conflict before us. The world's plans, the world's customs, the world's conniving, are not for us. We are to say, "So did not I, because of the fear of God." Selfishness, dishonesty, craftiness, are trying to intrude into hearts. Let us not give them room.

Nehemiah kept his eye single to the glory of God. . . . By the stability of his course of action he gave evidence that he was a brave Christian. His conscience was cleansed, refined, and ennobled by obedience to God. He refused to depart from Christian principles.

Upon all who believe in Christ is laid the obligation of walking worthy of the vocation wherewith they are called, to reveal the character of Christ. The cross will honor every Christian who honors it.[24]

HOLINESS A COMPANION OF HUMILITY

Likewise, ye younger, submit yourselves unto the elder. Yea, all of you be subject one to another, and be clothed with humility: for God resisteth the proud, and giveth grace to the humble. 1 Peter 5:5.

How many cling with tenacious grasp to their self-termed dignity, which is only self-esteem. These seek to honor themselves instead of waiting in humbleness of heart for Christ to honor them. In conversation more time is spent in talking of self than in exalting the riches of the grace of Christ. . . .

True holiness and humility are inseparable. The nearer the soul comes to God, the more completely is it humbled and subdued. When Job heard the voice of the Lord out of the whirlwind, he exclaimed, "I abhor myself, and repent in dust and ashes" (Job 42:6). It was when Isaiah saw the glory of the Lord and heard the cherubim crying, "Holy, holy, holy, is the Lord of hosts," that he cried out, "Woe is me! for I am undone" (Isa. 6:3, 5). Daniel, when visited by the holy messenger, says, "My comeliness was turned in me into corruption" (Dan. 10:8). Paul, after he was caught up into the third heaven and heard things that it was not lawful for a man to utter, speaks of himself as "less than the least of all saints" (Eph. 3:8). It was the beloved John, who leaned on Jesus' breast and beheld His glory, who fell as one dead before the angel. The more closely and continuously we behold our Saviour, the less shall we see to approve in ourselves.[25]

He who catches a glimpse of the matchless love of Christ counts all other things as loss, and looks upon Him as the chiefest among ten thousand and as the one altogether lovely. As seraphim and cherubim look upon Christ, they cover their faces with their wings. Their own perfection and beauty are not displayed in the presence and glory of their Lord. Then how improper it is for men to exalt themselves! Let them rather be clothed with humility, cease all strife for supremacy, and learn what it means to be meek and lowly of heart. He who contemplates God's glory and infinite love, will have humble views of himself, but by beholding the character of God, he will be changed into His divine image.[26]

WHY BE LIFTED UP?

Let nothing be done through strife or vainglory; but in lowliness of mind let each esteem other better than themselves. Look not every man on his own things, but every man also on the things of others. Phil. 2:3, 4.

There is nothing which will weaken the strength of a church like pride and passion. . . . Christ has given us an example of love and humility and has enjoined upon His followers to love one another as He has loved us. We must in lowliness of mind esteem others better than ourselves. We must be severe upon our own defects of character, be quick to discern our own errors and mistakes, and make less of the faults of others than of our own. We must feel a special interest in looking upon the things of others—not to covet them, not to find fault with them, not to remark upon them and present them in a false light, but to do strict justice in all things to our brethren and all with whom we have any dealings. A spirit to work plans for our own selfish interest so as to grasp a little gain, or to labor to show a superiority or rivalry, is an offense to God. The spirit of Christ will lead His followers to be concerned not only for their success and advantage, but to be equally interested for the success and advantage of their brethren. This will be loving our neighbor as ourselves. . . .

Jesus alone is to be exalted. Whatever may be the ability or the success of any one of us, it is not because we have manufactured these powers ourselves; they are the sacred trust given us of God, to be wisely employed in His service to His glory. All is the Lord's entrusted capital. Why, then, should we be lifted up? Why should we call attention to our own defective selves? What we do possess in talent and wisdom is received from the Source of wisdom, that we may glorify God. . . .

Pride of talent, pride of intellect, cannot exist in hearts that are hid with Christ in God. . . . Then let us humble ourselves, and adore Jesus, but never, never, exalt self in the least degree. . . . If the motive of all our life is to serve and honor Christ and bless humanity in the world, then the dreariest path of duty will become a bright way—a path cast up for the ransomed of the Lord to walk in.[27]

176

"TAKE HEED UNTO THYSELF"

Take heed unto thyself, and unto the doctrine; continue in them: for in doing this thou shalt both save thyself, and them that hear thee. 1 Tim. 4:16.

Some seem to think that there is a certain amount of virtue in expressing their dissatisfaction in whatever is being done by others. . . .

There was Judas; Christ permitted him to be a member of the church, notwithstanding his covetous, avaricious character. He had some traits that might have been used to the glory of God, but he did not try to overcome the defects in his character. Christ bore with him long and patiently. . . . He had the same lessons set before him that were given to the other apostles, which would have set him right had he made a right use of them, but he did not sustain a right relation to Heaven. Christ knew his true condition, and gave him an opportunity. He connected John with the church, not because John was above human frailties, but that He might bind him to His great heart of love. If John overcame his defects of character, he would stand as a light to the church. Peter, if he corrected his faults, would inherit the promises of God. And Jesus said to him, after His resurrection, notwithstanding that he had but a few days before denied Him, "Feed my sheep," and "Feed my lambs" (John 21:16, 15). He could trust Peter now, for he had obtained an experience in the things of God. . . .

John was constantly learning to copy the life of Jesus. He was learning in Christ's school. . . . Lesson after lesson Christ gave to His disciples, that they might know the will of the Father and shine as lights in the world. John and Peter were men whom God could trust, but Judas was not. They had received and heeded the lessons and gained the victory, but Judas had failed at every trial. He saw his faults, but instead of correcting them revenged himself by picking flaws in others around him. . . . Paul says to Timothy, "Take heed unto thyself"; that is, seek God first for thyself. Let us individually turn our attention to ourselves, diligently guard our own souls, and set a Christlike example before those whom we would criticize.[28]

REVEALING CHRIST IN CHARACTER

In all things shewing thyself a pattern of good works: in doctrine shewing uncorruptness, gravity, sincerity, sound speech, that cannot be condemned; that he that is of the contrary part may be ashamed, having no evil thing to say of you. Titus 2:7, 8.

Let not anyone be afraid of going to extremes while he is a close student of the Word, humbling the soul at every step. Christ must dwell in him by faith. He, their Exemplar, was self-possessed. He walked in humility. He had true dignity. He had patience. If we individually possess these traits . . . there will be no extremists.

Christ never erred in His judgment of men and of truth. He was never deceived by appearances. He never raised a question but what was clearly appropriate. He never gave an answer but what was fitting and right to the point. He silenced the voice of the cavilling, shrewd, and cunning priests by penetrating through the surface and reaching the heart, flashing light into their consciences, which annoyed them; but they would not yield to conviction. Christ never went to extremes, never lost self-control or the balance of mind under any excitement. He never violated the law of good taste and discernment when to speak and when to keep silent. Then if all who claim to see the precious golden rays of the light of the Sun of Righteousness will follow the example of Christ there will be no extremists. . . .

Let calmness and self-possession be cultivated and perseveringly maintained, for this was the character of Christ. . . . We hear no noisy protestations of faith, nor do we see tremendous bodily contortions and exercises in the Author of all truth.

Remember, in Him dwelt all the fullness of the Godhead bodily. If Christ is abiding in our hearts by faith, we shall, by beholding the manner of His life, seek to be like Jesus—pure, peaceable, and undefiled. We shall reveal Christ in our character. We will not only receive and absorb light but will also diffuse it. We will have more clear and distinct views of what Jesus is to us. The symmetry, loveliness, and benevolence that were in the life of Jesus Christ will be shining forth in our lives.[29]

TARES AMONG THE WHEAT

Let both grow together until the harvest: and in the time of harvest I will say to the reapers, Gather ye together first the tares, and bind them in bundles to burn them: but gather the wheat into my barn. Matt. 13:30.

In this world we shall become hopelessly perplexed (as the devil wants us to be) if we keep looking upon those things that are perplexing, for by dwelling upon them, and talking of them, we become discouraged. . . . We may create an unreal world in our own mind or picture an ideal church, where the temptations of Satan no longer prompt to evil, but perfection exists only in our imagination. The world is a fallen world, and the church is a place represented by a field in which grow tares and wheat. They are to grow together until the harvest. It is not our place to uproot the tares, according to human wisdom, lest under the suggestions of Satan the wheat may be rooted up under the supposition that it is tares. The wisdom that is from above will come to him who is meek and lowly in heart, and that wisdom will not lead him to destroy, but to build up the people of God. . . .

None need to err, none need to lose the golden moments of time in their short life history through seeking to weigh the imperfections of professed Christians. Not one of us has time to do this. If we know what is the manner of character Christians should develop, and yet see in others that which is inconsistent with this character, let us determine that we will firmly resist the enemy in his temptations to make us act in an inconsistent way, and say, "I will not make Christ ashamed of me. I will more earnestly study the character of Christ in whom there was no imperfection, no selfishness, no spot, no stain of evil, who lived not to please and glorify Himself, but to glorify God and save fallen humanity. I will not copy the defective characters of these inconsistent Christians; the mistakes that they have made shall not lead me to be like them. I will turn to the precious Saviour, that I may be like Him, follow the instruction of the Word of God, which says, 'Let this mind be in you, which was also in Christ Jesus'" (Phil. 2:5).[30]

AS WE ARE FORGIVEN

And forgive us our debts, as we forgive our debtors. Matt. 6:12.

It is most difficult, even for those who claim to be followers of Jesus, to forgive as Christ forgives us. The true spirit of forgiveness is so little practiced, and so many interpretations are placed upon Christ's requirement, that its force and beauty are lost sight of. We have very uncertain views of the great mercy and loving-kindness of God. He is full of compassion and forgiveness, and freely pardons when we truly repent and confess our sins. . . .

Peter, when brought to the test, sinned greatly. In denying the Master he had loved and served, he became a cowardly apostate. But his Lord did not cast him off; He freely forgave him. . . . Henceforth, remembering his own weakness and failures, he would be patient with his brethren in their mistakes and errors. Remembering the patient love of Christ toward him, affording him another opportunity to bring forth the fruit of good works, he would be more conciliatory toward erring ones. . . .

The Lord requires of us the same treatment toward His followers that we receive of Him. We are to exercise patience, to be kind even though they do not meet our expectations in every particular. . . . The last six commandments specify man's duty to man. Christ did not say, You may tolerate your neighbor, but, "Thou shalt love thy neighbour as thyself." . . .

The love of Jesus needs to be brought to bear upon our lives. It will have a softening, subduing influence upon our hearts and characters. It will prompt us to forgive our brethren even though they have done us injury. Divine love must flow from our hearts in gentle words and kindly actions to one another. The fruit of these good works will hang as rich clusters upon the vine of character. . . .

Rejoicing in Christ as your Saviour, pitiful, compassionate, and touched with the feeling of your infirmities, love and joy will be revealed in your daily life. If you love Him who died to redeem mankind You will love those for whom He died.[31]

HOW TO SETTLE YOUR TROUBLES

Moreover if thy brother shall trespass against thee, go and tell him his fault between thee and him alone: if he shall hear thee, thou hast gained thy brother. Matt. 18:15.

We should carefully consider what is our relation to God and to one another. We are continually sinning against God, but His mercy still follows us; in love He bears with our perversities, our neglect, our ingratitude, our disobedience. He never becomes impatient with us. We insult His mercy, grieve His Holy Spirit, and do Him dishonor before men and angels, and yet His compassions fail not. The thought of God's long-suffering to us should make us forbearing to one another. How patiently should we bear with the faults and errors of our brethren when we remember how great are our own failings in the sight of God. How can we pray to our heavenly Father, "Forgive us our debts, as we forgive our debtors" (Matt. 6:12) if we are . . . exacting in our treatment of others? . . .

If you think your brother has injured you, go to him in kindness and love, and you may come to an understanding and to reconciliation. . . . If you succeed in settling the trouble you have gained your brother without exposing his frailties, and the settlement between you has been the covering of a multitude of sins from the observation of others. . . .

It takes special watchfulness to keep the affections alive and our hearts in a condition where we shall be sensible of the good that exists in the hearts of others. If we do not watch on this point, Satan will put his jealousy into our souls; he will put his glasses before our eyes, that we may see the actions of our brethren in a distorted light. Instead of looking critically upon our brethren we should turn our eyes within, and be ready to discover the objectionable traits of our own character. As we have a proper realization of our own mistakes and failures, the mistakes of others will sink into insignificance.

Satan is an accuser of the brethren. He is on the watch for every error, no matter how small, that he may have something on which to found an accusation. Keep off from Satan's side.[32]

LOOK FOR THE GOOD

Finally, brethren, whatsoever things are true, whatsoever things are honest, whatsoever things are just, whatsoever things are pure, whatsoever things are lovely, whatsoever things are of good report; if there be any virtue, and if there be any praise, think on these things. Phil. 4:8.

We are a part of the great web of humanity. We become changed into the image of that upon which we dwell. Then how important to open our hearts to the things that are true and lovely and of good report. Let into the heart the light of the Sun of Righteousness. Do not cherish one root of bitterness.[33]

Christ was infinite in wisdom and yet He thought best to accept Judas, although He knew what were his imperfections of character. John was not perfect; Peter denied his Lord; and yet it was of men like these that the early Christian church was organized. Jesus accepted them that they might learn of Him what constitutes a perfect Christian character. The business of every Christian is to study the character of Christ. . . .

Judas alone did not respond to divine enlightenment. . . . He braced his soul to resist the influence of the truth; and while he practiced criticising and condemning others, he neglected his own soul, and cherished and strengthened his natural evil traits of character until he became so hardened that he could sell his Lord for thirty pieces of silver.

O let us encourage our souls to look to Jesus! . . .

It is not an uncommon thing to see imperfection in those who carry on God's work. . . . Would it not be more pleasing to God to take an impartial outlook, and see how many souls are serving God and glorifying and honoring Him with their talents of means and intellect? Would it not be better to consider the wonderful, miracle-working power of God in the transformation of poor degraded sinners . . . ? The most unfavorable matters . . . should not cause us to feel perplexed and discouraged. Everything that causes us to see the weakness of humanity is in the Lord's purpose to help us to look to Him, and in no case put our trust in man, or make flesh our arm.[34]

SHEEP AND WOLVES

But I say unto you, Love your enemies, bless them that curse you, do good to them that hate you, and pray for them which despitefully use you, and persecute you. Matt: 5:44.

In these last days, when iniquity shall abound and the love of many shall wax cold, God will have a people to glorify His name, and stand as reprovers of unrighteousness. They are to be a "peculiar people," who will be true to the law of God when the world shall seek to make void its precepts, and when the converting power of God works through His servants, the hosts of darkness will array themselves in bitter and determined opposition. . . .

Satan is at enmity with the truth, and he will instigate against its advocates every manner of warfare.[35]

We must have our lives so hid with Christ in God that when bitter speeches and scornful words and unkind looks meet us, we shall not permit our feelings to be stirred up against this class, but shall feel the deepest sympathy for them, because they know nothing about the precious Saviour whom we claim to know. We must remember that they are in the service of one who is the bitterest enemy of Jesus Christ, and that while all heaven is opened to the sons and daughters of God, they have no such privilege. You ought to feel that you are the happiest people upon the face of the whole earth. Notwithstanding, as Christ's representatives, you are as sheep in the midst of wolves, you have One with you who can help you under all circumstances, and you will not be devoured by these wolves if you keep close to Jesus. How careful you should be to represent Jesus in every word and action! You should feel when you arise in the morning, and when you go out upon the street, and when you come in, that Jesus loves you, that He is by your side, and that you must not cherish a thought that will grieve your Saviour. . . .

The evil angels may be all around you to press their darkness upon you, but the will of God is greater than their power. And if you do not in word or action, or in any way, make Christ ashamed of you, the sweet blessing and peace of God will be in your heart every day you live.[36]

A TIME TO CLOSE THE MIND

Speak not evil one of another, brethren. He that speaketh evil of his brother, and judgeth his brother, speaketh evil of the law, and judgeth the law: but if thou judge the law, thou art not a doer of the law, but a judge. James 4:11.

If Satan can employ professed believers to act as accusers of the brethren, he is greatly pleased, for those who do this are just as truly serving him as was Judas when he betrayed Christ, although they may be doing it ignorantly. . . .

Floating rumors are frequently the destroyers of unity among brethren. There are some who watch with open mind and ears to catch flying scandal. They gather up little incidents which may be trifling in themselves, but which are repeated and exaggerated until a man is made an offender for a word. Their motto seems to be, "Report, and we will report it."

These talebearers are doing the devil's work with surprising fidelity, little knowing how offensive their course is to God. If they would spend half the energy and zeal that is given to this unholy work in examining their own hearts, they would find so much to do to cleanse their souls from impurity that they would have no time or disposition to criticize their brethren, and they would not fall under the power of this temptation.

The door of the mind should be closed against "they say" or "I have heard." Why should we not, instead of allowing jealousy or evil surmising to come into our hearts, go to our brethren, and, after frankly but kindly setting before them the things we have heard detrimental to their character and influence, pray with and for them? . . .

Let us diligently cultivate the pure principles of the gospel of Christ, the religion, not of self-esteem, but of love, meekness, and lowliness of heart. Then we shall love our brethren and esteem them better than ourselves. Our minds will not dwell on the dark side of their character; we shall not feast on scandal and flying reports. But "whatsoever things are . . . of good report; if there be any virtue, and if there be any praise," we shall "think on these things" (Phil. 4:8).[37]

FRAGRANT WITH HEAVEN'S BLESSING

Who is a wise man and endued with knowledge among you? let him show out of a good conversation his works with meekness of wisdom. But if ye have bitter envying and strife in your hearts, glory not, and lie not against the truth. James 3:13, 14.

What is lying against the truth? It is claiming to believe the truth while the spirit, the words, the deportment, represent not Christ but Satan. To surmise evil, to be impatient and unforgiving, is lying against the truth, but love, patience, and long forbearance are in accordance with the principles of truth. Truth is ever pure, ever kind, breathing a heavenly fragrance unmingled with selfishness. . . .

To be unkind, to denounce others, to give expression to harsh, severe judgments, to entertain evil thoughts, is not the result of that wisdom which is from above. . . . The language of the Christian must be mild and circumspect, for his holy faith requires him to represent Christ to the world. All those who abide in Christ will manifest the kind, forgiving courtesy that characterized His life. Their works will be works of piety, equity, and purity. They will have the meekness of wisdom, and will exercise the gift of the grace of Jesus.[38]

"Let the peace of God rule in your hearts, . . . and be ye thankful. Let the word of Christ dwell in you richly in all wisdom; teaching and admonishing one another in psalms and hymns and spiritual songs, singing with grace in your hearts to the Lord" (Col. 3:15, 16). This was Christ's practice. He was often assailed by temptation, but in place of yielding or being provoked, He sang God's praises. With spiritual songs He stopped the fluent speech of those whom Satan was using to create strife. . . .

When those who love God are tempted, let them sing the praises of their Creator rather than speak words of accusing or faultfinding. The Lord will bless those who thus try to make peace. Trust in God. Be careful not to give the enemy any advantage by your unguarded words. Keep looking to Jesus. He is your strength. . . .

Be so considerate, so tender, so compassionate, that the atmosphere surrounding you will be fragrant with Heaven's blessing.[39]

THE GREATEST SERVICE

Be ye kind one to another, tenderhearted, forgiving one another, even as God for Christ's sake hath forgiven you. Eph. 4:32.

The greatest service we can render to the cause of God, and which will reflect steady beams of light upon the pathway of others, is to be patient, kind, steadfast as a rock to principle, God-fearing. This will constitute us the salt of the earth, the light of the world. We shall be often disappointed, for we shall not find perfection in those who are connected with us, and they will not see perfection in us. It is only by agonizing effort on our part that we shall become unselfish, humble, childlike, teachable, meek and lowly of heart, like our divine Lord. We must bring our hearts and minds up to a high point of education in spiritual and heavenly things.

This world is not heaven, but it is the workshop of God for the fitting up of His people for a pure and holy paradise. And while each one of us is to feel that he is a part of the great web of humanity, he must not expect that others in that web will be without a flaw any more than himself. Mistakes will be made, and if the erring are willing to be corrected, a valuable experience is gained, so that their defeat is turned to victory. You should consider that many of your own errors are not brought to light, and be careful not to make the mistakes and imperfection of others appear in their worst light, either to yourself or to others. No man is perfect, and unjust criticism indulged towards others is not wise or Christlike. . . .

We have a serious, solemn work to do for ourselves to cleanse our own souls from spot and stain if we will stand before the Son of man when He shall appear, acquitted of Him. We must be educators as well as reformers. To cut loose from everyone who errs and does not follow our own ideas is not doing as Christ is doing for us. We are all fallible, and we need pity, forbearance, kindly consideration, and sympathetic love for those with whom we are connected. We are all unworthy of the love and confidence of God.[40]

BUILDING UP ONE ANOTHER

We then that are strong ought to bear the infirmities of the weak, and not to please ourselves. Rom. 15:1.

God does not want us to place ourselves upon the judgment seat and judge each other. . . . When we see errors in others, let us remember that we have faults graver, perhaps, in the sight of God than the fault we condemn in our brother. Instead of publishing his defects, ask God to bless him and to help him to overcome his error. Christ will approve of this spirit and action, and will open the way for you to speak a word of wisdom that will impart strength and help to him who is weak in the faith.

The work of building one another up in the most holy faith is a blessed work, but the work of tearing down is a work full of bitterness and sorrow. Christ identifies Himself with His suffering children, for He says, "Inasmuch as ye have done it unto one of the least of these my brethren, ye have done it unto me" (Matt. 25:40). . . . Every heart has its own sorrows and disappointments, and we should seek to lighten one another's burdens by manifesting the love of Jesus to those around us. If our conversation were upon heaven and heavenly things, evil speaking would soon cease to have any attraction for us. . . .

Instead of finding fault with others, let us be critical with ourselves. The question with each one of us should be, Is my heart right before God? Will this course of action glorify my Father which is in heaven? If you have cherished a wrong spirit, let it be banished from the soul. It is your duty to eradicate from your heart everything that is of a defiling nature. Every root of bitterness should be plucked up, lest others be contaminated by its baleful influence. Do not allow one poisonous plant to remain in the soil of your heart. Root it out this very hour, and plant in its stead the plant of love. Let Jesus be enshrined in the soul. Christ is our example. He went about doing good. He lived to bless others. Love beautified and ennobled all His actions, and we are commanded to follow in His steps.[41]

THE HIGHEST LEARNING

For God, who commanded the light to shine out of darkness, hath shined in our hearts, to give the light of the knowledge of the glory of God in the face of Jesus Christ. 2 Cor. 4:6.

This knowledge—the knowledge of the glory of God—is the highest class of learning that mortals can obtain. And "we have this treasure in earthen vessels, that the excellency of the power may be of God, and not of us" (2 Cor. 4:7).

Human fallacies are abundant and specious. Unseen agencies are at work to make falsehood appear as truth; errors are clothed with a deceptive garb that men may be led to accept them as essential to higher education. And these fallacies will deceive many of our students unless they are thoroughly guarded, and unless they are led by the Spirit of God to take the grand and holy truths of the Word into their hearts and minds, accepting these as the principles underlying the higher education. No instruction can exceed in value the pure instruction of God, which comes for the enlightenment of all who will be enlightened. . . . There can be no education higher than that which was given by the Great Teacher.[1]

There is nothing more detrimental to the soul's interest, its purity, its true and holy conceptions of God and of sacred and eternal things than constantly giving heed to and exalting that which is not from God. It poisons the heart and degrades the understanding. Pure truth can be traced to its divine Source by its elevating, refining, sanctifying influence upon the character of the receiver.[2]

At this time when every conceivable thing is being brought in to confuse the people of God, let your spiritual eyesight be strengthened; let your faith in the Word of God be firm. Know for yourselves that the words and teachings of Christ, which are the words and teachings of Jehovah, contain the highest instruction it is possible for men to gain. When any would seek to confuse your minds, repeat to them the words of Christ, "No man can serve two masters" (Matt. 6:24). Let the Word of the Lord stand forth clearly and distinctly.[3]

GREATEST EDUCATOR OF ALL TIME

The people were astonished at his doctrine: for he taught them as one having authority, and not as the scribes. Matt. 7:28, 29.

The world's men of learning are not easily reached by the practical truths of God's Word. The reason is, they trust to human wisdom and pride themselves upon their intellectual superiority, and are unwilling to become humble learners in the school of Christ.

Our Saviour did not ignore learning or despise education, yet He chose unlearned fishermen for the work of the gospel because they had not been schooled in the false customs and traditions of the world. They were men of good natural ability and of a humble, teachable spirit, men whom He could educate for His great work. In the ordinary walks of life there is many a man patiently treading the round of daily toil, all unconscious that he possesses powers which if called into action would raise him to an equality with the world's most honored men. The touch of a skillful hand is needed to arouse and develop those dormant faculties. It was such men whom Jesus connected with Himself, and He gave them the advantages of three years' training under His own care. No course of study in the schools of the rabbis or the halls of philosophy could have equaled this in value. The Son of God was the greatest educator the world ever knew.

The learned lawyers, priests, and scribes scorned to be taught by Christ. They desired to teach Him, and frequently made the attempt, only to be defeated by the wisdom that laid bare their ignorance and rebuked their folly. . . . They knew that He had not learned in the schools of the prophets, and they could not discern the divine excellence of His character beneath the lowly disguise of the Man of Nazareth. But the words and deeds of the humble Teacher, recorded by the unlettered companions of His daily life, have exerted a living power upon the minds of men from that day to the present. Not merely the ignorant and humble, but men of education, intellect, and genius reverently exclaim, with the wondering and delighted listeners of old, "Never man spake like this man" (John 7:46).[4]

FACING THE LIGHT

Take heed therefore that the light which is in thee be not darkness. If thy whole body therefore be full of light, having no part dark, the whole shall be full of light, as when the bright shining of a candle doth give thee light. Luke 11:35, 36.

The moment the eye is turned from Jesus, darkness is seen, darkness is felt, for Jesus only is light and life and peace and assurance forever. "If therefore thine eye be single, thy whole body shall be full of light" (Matt. 6:22). . . . What is it to have a single eye? It is to have a disposition to look upon Christ, for by beholding we become changed from glory to glory, from character to character.

As we keep Christ in view, the bright rays of the Sun of Righteousness shine upon us and flood the chambers of the mind and heart and fill the soul temple with light. As the Light of the world shines upon us, we diffuse it to those around "as when the bright shining of a candle doth give . . . light." The soul that is stayed upon God commits to Christ all that perplexes, all that annoys, all that gives anxiety. The light of Christ shines in the soul in all goodness and peace, for in Him dwelleth all the fullness of the Godhead bodily. . . .

Those who behold Christ will never plead that their own will may be done, or that their old ways and habits may be left undisturbed. As they behold Jesus, His image becomes engraved on heart and soul, and in all their practices they reflect His example upon the world. Day by day the hands, the feet, the tongue, follow the dictates of the spiritual nature, and faith makes their path a path that grows brighter and brighter unto the perfect day. Everything that keeps us from attaining unto the likeness of Christ is working out for us eternal loss. Then let no one plead for a continuance of his own way. Let no one seek to excuse his deficiencies of character by saying, It is "my way." Cooperate with Jesus Christ and you will see that your own way is a way full of deficiency and fault, and that if it is not corrected it will cause you to put into your character building traits that will be as rotten timbers. . . . Let nothing of these defects of character be found in your building. Build on the rock Christ Jesus.[5]

OPENING THE MYSTERIES OF REDEMPTION

Then opened he their understanding, that they might understand the scriptures. Luke 24:45.

The Lord wants every one of us to have a deeper, richer experience in the knowledge of our Lord and Saviour Jesus Christ. He desires that we shall grow in knowledge—not earthward, but heavenward, upward to Christ our living Head. How high, how great, is this knowledge to be? To the full stature of men and women in Christ Jesus. We cannot grow too much, we cannot gather up too many of the precious rays of light that God sends us. . . .

We know falsehoods are coming in like a swift current, and that is just the reason why we want every ray of light that God has for us, that we may be able to stand amid the perils of the last days. . . .

O how Christ longs to open before us the mysteries of redemption! He longed to do this for His disciples when He was among them on earth, but they were not far enough advanced in spiritual knowledge to comprehend His words. He had to say to them, "I have yet many things to say unto you, but ye cannot bear them now" (John 16:12). O how much better could they have borne the terrible ordeal through which they had to pass at His trial and crucifixion if they had advanced and been able to bear the instruction of Christ! Shall we not let Jesus open our understanding? . . .

We are on the borders of the eternal world, and we must have a testimony with which all heaven shall be in harmony.[6]

The Lord is coming, and we must be ready! Every moment I want His grace—I want the robe of Christ's righteousness. We must humble our souls before God as never before, come low to the foot of the cross, and He will put a word in our mouths to speak for Him, even praise unto our God. He will teach us a strain from the song of the angels, even thanksgiving to our heavenly Father. We can do nothing of ourselves, but God wants to touch our lips with a living coal from off the altar. He wants to sanctify our tongues—to sanctify our whole being.[7]

OBJECT OF THE ORACLES

The entrance of thy words giveth light; it giveth understanding unto the simple. Ps. 119:130.

The light and understanding which God's Word imparts is not designed merely, or chiefly, to promote intellectual culture. For an object higher than any earthly or temporal good were the holy oracles committed unto men. We see therein revealed the great plan of human redemption, the means devised to free mankind from the power of Satan. We see Christ, the Captain of our salvation, meeting the prince of darkness in open battle, and single-handed, obtaining the victory in our behalf. We learn too that by this victory was opened to us a door of hope, a source of strength, and that we may, as faithful soldiers, fight our own battles with the wily foe, and conquer in the name of Jesus. The powers of darkness must be met by every soul. The young as well as the old will be assailed, and all should understand the nature of the great controversy between Christ and Satan, and should realize that it concerns themselves. . . .

It is not enough to have an intellectual knowledge of the truth. . . . There must be an entrance of the Word into the heart. It must be set home by the power of the Holy Spirit. The will must be brought into harmony with its requirements. Not only the intellect but the heart and conscience must concur in the acceptance of the truth.

The entrance of God's Word gives understanding to the simple— those who are untaught in the wisdom of the world. The Holy Spirit brings the saving truths of the Scriptures within the comprehension of all who desire to know and do the will of God. Uneducated minds are enabled to grasp the most sublime and soul-stirring themes that can engage the attention of men—themes that will be the study and the song of the redeemed through all eternity.

It is the knowledge which God's Word supplies, and which can be found nowhere else, that we need above every other. We want to know what to do in this our day to escape the snares of Satan and to win the crown of glory.[8]

WISDOM FROM THE FATHER OF LIGHT

For the Lord giveth wisdom: out of his mouth cometh knowledge and understanding. Prov. 2:6.

The great and essential knowledge is the knowledge of God and His Word. . . . The Christian will grow in grace just in proportion as he depends upon and appreciates the teaching of the Word of God, and habituates himself to meditate upon divine things. . . .

But let no one imagine that we would discourage education or put a low estimate upon the value of mental culture and discipline. God would have us students as long as we remain in this world, ever learning and bearing responsibility. . . . But no one should set himself as a critic to measure the usefulness and influence of his brother who has had few advantages in obtaining book knowledge. He may be rich in a rarer wisdom. He may have a practical education in the knowledge of the truth. Says the psalmist, "The entrance of thy words giveth light; it giveth understanding unto the simple" (Ps. 119:130). . . . The wisdom spoken of by the psalmist is that which is attained when the truth is opened to the mind and applied to the heart by the Spirit of God, when its principles are wrought into the character by a life of practical godliness. . . .

It is the Spirit of God that quickens the lifeless faculties of the soul to appreciate heavenly things, and attracts the affections toward God and the truth. Without the presence of Jesus in the heart, religious service is only dead, cold formalism. The longing desire for communion with God soon ceases when the Spirit of God is grieved from us, but when Christ is in us the hope of glory, we are constantly directed to think and act in reference to the glory of God. The questions will arise, "Will this do honor to Jesus? Will this be approved of by Him? Shall I be able to maintain my integrity if I enter into this arrangement?" God will be made the counselor of the soul, and we shall be led into safe paths, and the will of God will be made the supreme guide of our lives. This is heavenly wisdom, . . . and it makes the Christian, however humble, the light of the world.[9]

THE CHRISTIAN'S TEXTBOOK

Search the scriptures; for in them ye think ye have eternal life: and they are they which testify of me. John 5:39.

The admonition to "search the Scriptures" was never more appropriate than at the present time. This is an age of unrest, and the youth drink deeply of its spirit. Would that they could be made to realize the importance and the peril of the position they occupy! . . . Never were such momentous issues before any generation as await the one now coming upon the stage of action. Never were the youth of any age or country so earnestly observed by the angels of God as are the youth of today. All heaven is watching with intense interest for every indication of the characters they are forming—whether when brought to the test they will stand firmly for God and the right, or be swayed by worldly influences. . . .

God has a great work to be done in a short time. He has committed to the young, talents of intellect, time, and means, and He holds them responsible for the use they make of these good gifts. He calls upon them to come to the front, to resist the corrupting, bewitching influences of this fast age and to become qualified to labor in His cause. They cannot become fitted for usefulness without putting heart and energy into the work of preparation. . . .

It is a divine law that blessings come at some cost to the receiver. Those who would become wise in the sciences must study, and those who would become wise in regard to Bible truth, that they may impart that knowledge to others, must be diligent students of God's Holy Word. There is no other way; they must search the Scriptures diligently, interestedly, prayerfully. . . . And after all their research, there is beyond an infinity of wisdom, love, and power.

The Bible should ever be the Christian's textbook. Of all books it should be made the most attractive to the young. If they drink deep of its spirit they will be prepared to withstand the wiles of Satan and to resist the temptations of this infidel age.[10]

EXPLORING THE MINE OF TRUTH

For the prophecy came not in old time by the will of man: but holy men of God spake as they were moved by the Holy Ghost. 2 Peter 1:21.

Some have neglected the Bible under the erroneous impression that the indwelling of the Spirit was preferable to the study and guidance of the Scriptures. Such will be exposed to Satan's snares and fatal delusions. The Holy Spirit and the Word are in perfect harmony. The Holy Spirit inspired the Scriptures and always leads to the Scriptures. . . .

Everything in the religious world is to be tried by the Scriptures. "To the law and to the testimony: if they speak not according to this word, it is because there is no light in them" (Isa. 8:20). The claimed enlightenment of the Spirit within is to be tested and tried by the Word of God, which is the detector of the pure wheat. . . .

The mine of truth is to be explored interestedly, diligently. How often we find Christ applying the Old Testament Scriptures, expounding their truths, showing their spiritual character, clothing them with freshness and richness and beauty the people had never beheld before. . . . The truths our Saviour reveals in His exposition are capable of constant expansion and new and richer developments. While searching the Scriptures, the mind that is led by the Holy Spirit sees their Author, and by beholding is constantly brightening while looking at the Word, Thus the intellect aspiring to reach the standard of perfection becomes elevated to comprehend it. . . .

The truth of heavenly origin is represented as "treasure hid in a field; the which when a man hath found, he hideth, and for joy thereof goeth and selleth all that he hath, and buyeth that field" (Matt. 13:44) that he may work every part of it. In his persevering efforts he discovers concealed jewels and precious ore. He who labors wisely sinks the shaft deeper and deeper and discovers a rich and precious lode. He finds that the field of revelation is interlaced with golden veins of precious treasures and is indeed the storehouse of the unsearchable riches of Christ—light, truth, and life.[11]

A VOICE FROM GOD

These were more noble than those in Thessalonica, in that they received the word with all readiness of mind, and searched the scriptures daily, whether those things were so. Acts 17:11.

To some the Word of God is uninteresting. The reason is, they have so long indulged in the bewitching stories to be found in the literature of the present day that they have no relish for the reading of God's Word or for religious exercises. This reading disqualifies the mind to receive sound Bible principles and to work out practical godliness. . . .

When reading the Bible with humble, teachable heart, we are holding intercourse with God Himself. The thoughts expressed, the precepts specified, the doctrines revealed, are a voice from the God of heaven. The Bible will bear to be studied, and the mind, if not bewitched by Satan, will be attracted and charmed. . . . The light which beams through the Scriptures is light from the eternal throne flashed down to this earth. . . .

All who make the Word of God their guide in this life will act from principle. Those who are vacillating, vain, and extravagant in dress, who are gratifying the appetite and following the promptings of the natural heart, will, in obeying the teachings of God's Word, become balanced. They will devote themselves to duty with an energy that never falters, and they will rise from one degree of strength to another. Their characters will be beautiful and fragrant and devoid of selfishness. They will make their way and be acceptable anywhere among those who love truth and righteousness.[12]

The psalmist prayed, "Open thou mine eyes, that I may behold wondrous things out of thy law." The Lord heard him, for how full of assurance are the words, "How sweet are thy words unto my taste! yea, sweeter than honey to my mouth!" "More to be desired are they than gold, yea, than much fine gold: sweeter also than honey and the honeycomb." (Ps. 119:18, 103; 19:10.) And as the Lord heard and answered David, so He will hear and answer us, making our hearts full of gladness and rejoicing.[13]

BOOK OF THE AGES

For ever, O Lord, thy word is settled in heaven. Ps. 119:89.

The Word of God covers a period of history reaching from the Creation to the coming of the Son of man in the clouds of heaven. Yea, more, it carries the mind forward to the future life, and opens before it the glories of Paradise restored. Through all these centuries the truth of God has remained the same. That which was truth in the beginning is truth now. Although new and important truths appropriate for succeeding generations have been opened to the understanding, the present revealings do not contradict those of the past. Every new truth understood only makes more significant the old.[14]

Commencing with the Fall, down through the patriarchal and Jewish ages even to the present time, there has been a gradual unfolding of the purposes of God in the plan of redemption. Noah, Abraham, Isaac, Jacob, and Moses understood the gospel through Christ; they looked for the salvation of the race through man's substitute and surety. These holy men of old held communion with the Saviour who was to come to our world in human flesh, and some of them talked with Christ and heavenly angels face to face, as a man talks with his friend.[15]

As time has rolled on from Creation and the cross of Calvary, as prophecy has been and is still fulfilling, light and knowledge have greatly increased. . . . In the life and death of Christ, a light flashes back upon the past, giving significance to the whole Jewish economy, and making of the old and the new dispensations a complete whole. Nothing that God has ordained in the plan of redemption can be dispensed with. It is the working out of the divine will in the salvation of man.[16]

All the truths of revelation are of value to us, and in contemplating things of eternal interest, we shall gain true perceptions of the character of God. . . . The entire character will be elevated and transformed. The soul will be brought into harmony with Heaven.[17]

197

TRUE CHRISTIAN CULTURE

But God, who is rich in mercy, for his great love wherewith he loved us, even when we were dead in sins, hath quickened us together with Christ, . . . and hath raised us up together, and made us sit together in heavenly places in Christ Jesus. Eph. 2:4-6.

If you come into close relationship to Jesus Christ you see wondrous things out of His law that are not now seen. The softening, subduing influence of the Spirit of God upon human hearts and minds will make the true children of God to sit together in heavenly places in Christ Jesus. Christian culture will be carried on in every heart worked by the Holy Spirit. There will be a soft, subdued spirit in all those who are looking unto Jesus. The love of Jesus always leads to Christian courtesy, refinement of language, and purity of expression that testify the company we are with—that like Enoch we are walking with God. There is no storming, no harshness, but a sweet fragrance in speech and in spirit.

The Word is to be our study. Here is a mine of precious ore. Much of it has been glimpsed at, but there is the digging to be done to secure much more precious treasures. There have been many who have just rummaged over the surface in a most careless, slovenly manner, when others are searching more carefully and prayerfully and perseveringly, and hidden, inestimable treasures are found. . . .

Let it be seen that your life is hid with Christ in God. Let there be no hasty speech, no cheap words, no slang phrases. Let it be demonstrated that you are conscious of a Companion whom you honor, and that you will not make Him ashamed of you. Only think, we are representatives of Jesus Christ! Then represent His character in words, in deportment. . . . The converting power of God is needed every day to sanctify and fit vessels for the Master's use. O there are precious lessons in the Holy Book that we are yet to find and practice! Our conscience must recognize and revere a higher standard of Christianity. . . . You may be all light in the Lord. You may be increasing in efficiency, in purity, in the knowledge of God, if you keep meek and lowly of heart.[18]

TRUTHS THAT TRANSFORM

The word of God is quick, and powerful, and sharper than any two-edged sword, piercing even to the dividing asunder of soul and spirit, and of the joints and marrow, and is a discerner of the thoughts and intents of the heart. Heb. 4:12.

The truths of the Bible, treasured in the heart and mind and obeyed in the life, convince and convert the soul, transform the character, and comfort and uplift the heart. . . . The Word makes the proud humble, the perverse meek and contrite, the disobedient obedient. The sinful habits natural to man are interwoven with the daily practice. But the Word cuts away the fleshly lusts. It is a discerner of the thoughts and intents of the mind. It divides the joints and marrow, cutting away the lusts of the flesh, making men willing to suffer for their Lord.[19]

The service of Christ is a heavenly and holy and blessed thing. The Word is to be diligently searched, for the ministry of the Word discovers the imperfections in our characters and teaches us that the sanctification of the Spirit is a work of heavenly devising, presenting in Christ Jesus the true perfection that if maintained will become a perfect whole in behalf of every soul. We are educated in Bible lines to become complete in Christlikeness and to see His Father's face in Him who gave His own life for the saving of the soul.[20]

If you are an intelligent Christian you will maintain religious vitality and will not be deterred by difficulties. . . . You will work the works of God in gloom as well as in glory, in shade as well as in sunshine, in trial as well as in peace. The truth must be treasured up in your heart as well as incorporated in your being, so that no temptation and no argument can induce you to yield to Satan's suggestions or devices. The truth is precious. It has wrought important changes upon the life and upon the character, exerting a masterly influence over words, deportment, thoughts, and experience. The soul who appreciates the truth lives under its influence and senses the tremendous realities of eternal things. He lives not to himself, but to Jesus Christ who died for him. To him, God lives and is very cognizant of all his words and actions.[21]

TRUTH A DIVINE SENTINEL

Let no man despise thy youth; but be thou an example of the believers, in word, in conversation, in charity, in spirit, in faith, in purity. 1 Tim. 4:12.

I appeal to the youth. Consider your ways. . . .

No youth can withstand the temptations of Satan if the truth, with its purifying, uplifting power, is not abiding in the heart. Truth has a correcting influence upon the life. It is a divine sentinel, keeping watch in your souls and rousing to action against Satan's assaults. Under the divine influence of truth the mind will be strengthened, the intellect invigorated, and there will be a growing up in the knowledge of the only true God, and Jesus Christ whom He has sent. Do not tarnish the truth by indulging in habits and practices that are inconsistent with its holy character, but hold it as a treasure of highest value. . . .

The Lord desires you to understand the position you occupy as sons and daughters of the Most High, children of the Heavenly King. He desires you to live in close connection with Him. . . . Determine that you will be on the Lord's side. If you will stand under the blood-stained banner of Prince Emmanuel, faithfully doing His service, you need never yield to temptation, for One stands by your side who is able to keep you from falling. Every youth is granted a probation in which to form a character for the future, immortal life. Precious, golden moments these will be to you if you improve them according to the light God is permitting to shine upon you from His throne. . . .

Will the youth turn their faces heavenward? Will they open the chambers of the mind to the Sun of Righteousness? Will they throw open the door of the heart and welcome Jesus in? What beauty of character shone forth in the daily life of Christ! He is to be our pattern. There is a great work to be done in fashioning the character after the divine similitude. The grace of Christ must mold the entire being, and its triumph will not be complete until the heavenly universe shall witness habitual tenderness of feeling, Christlike love, and holy deeds in the deportment of the children of God.[22]

GOLDEN PROMISES

Thy words were found, and I did eat them; and thy word was unto me the joy and rejoicing of mine heart: for I am called by thy name, O Lord God of hosts. Jer. 15:16.

In the night season I was before a company,* talking with them upon faith, and trying to make them understand that they were far behind in this respect. . . . They had a deficient experience in the knowledge of God and their Redeemer. I was trying to show them that they must be able intelligently to voice the words of John, "Behold the Lamb of God, which taketh away the sin of the world" (John 1:29), that they must behold Him as their sin bearer.

Then the Word of God was opened before me in a most beautiful, striking light. Page after page was turned, and I read the gracious invitations and words of entreaty to seek God's glory and God's will, and all other things would be added. These invitations, promises, and assurances stood out as in golden letters. Why do you not grasp them? I said. Seek first to know God before any other thing. Search the Scriptures. Feed on the words of Christ, which are spirit and life, and your knowledge will enlarge and expand. Study your Bible. Study not the philosophy contained in many books, but study the philosophy of the Word of the living God. Other literature is of little consequence when compared with this. Do not crowd into your minds so many things that are cheap and unsatisfying. In the Word of God is spread before you the richest banquet. It is the Lord's table, abundantly provided, whereof you may eat and be satisfied.

The promises of God stood out clear and distinct, as though placed in letters of gold. Why, oh, why are they not appreciated! Why is not the heart filled with thanksgiving and praise? Why are your tongues so silent? . . . The talent of speech is misappropriated. Let the talent of choice words be given to God in thanksgiving and rejoicing, and this will glorify His name. Surrender self entirely to God. "Let the peace of God rule in your hearts . . . ;and be ye thankful" (Col. 3:15).[23]

---

*Ellen White is here describing a dream or night vision.

SPRINGS OF COMFORT

My soul shall be satisfied as with marrow and fatness; and my mouth shall praise thee with joyful lips. Ps. 63:5.

There is marrow and fatness for all who seek for truth as the miner seeks for gold. Who is it that God will instruct? Isaiah tells us: "Thus saith the high and lofty One that inhabiteth eternity, whose name is Holy; I dwell in the high and holy place, with him also that is of a contrite and humble spirit, to revive the spirit of the humble, and to revive the heart of the contrite ones" (Isa. 57:15)—those who see the evil of their unconverted characters, and repent, mourning over the life that has so poorly represented Christ. . . .

Gather the precious rays of light shining around you and focus them in one blaze upon the Word, and truths hidden from the casual reader will stand forth plainly and distinctly. All over the field of revelation are scattered grains of gold—the sayings of the wisdom of God. If you are wise you will gather up these precious grains of truth. Make the promises of God your own. Then when test and trial come, these promises will be to you glad springs of heavenly comfort. As you study the Word, it will become to you a wellspring of wisdom. Thus you eat the flesh and drink the blood of the Son of God.

Ask God to reveal light and truth to you by His Holy Spirit, that you may understand what you read in His Word. When, after the resurrection, Christ walked with the disciples to Emmaus, He opened their understanding that they might understand the Scriptures. The same divine Teacher will enlighten our understanding if we keep the windows of the heart opened heavenward and closed earthward. The office of the Holy Spirit is to bring all things to our remembrance and to guide us into all truth.

The Lord loves us, and we are to love Him with the whole heart. Ask Him to guide you into all truth. He will do this. He longs to do it. He is waiting for you to ask Him with true humility and a firm belief that He will hear and answer you.[24]

LOSS THAT IS GAIN

Yea doubtless, and I count all things but loss for the excellency of the knowledge of Christ Jesus my Lord: for whom I have suffered the loss of all things, and do count them but dung, that I may win Christ. Phil. 3:8.

What is God's will? What shall I do to glorify God? I am pledged to serve my Saviour with undivided affection. I count everything but dross that I may win Christ. Heaven, eternal life, is worth everything to me, and Christ has died that I might come into possession of the eternal weight of glory. . . .

We cannot afford to make any mistake where eternal interests are involved. To be indifferent to the claims of God upon us is most ungrateful. We cannot neglect this great salvation and be guiltless. An eternity of bliss has been purchased for every son and daughter of Adam, and all may have a clear title to the immortal inheritance, the eternal substance, if they will in probationary time prove their obedience to the commandments of God. All will be tested in this life. If they . . . by faith lay hold on the merits of Christ and serve God with all their hearts they will have a title to those mansions that Jesus has prepared for all that love Him. . . .

Let us love God supremely, allowing no influence to come between us and our God. We must give heed to the light which God has permitted to shine upon our pathway; we must show before all heaven that we appreciate every ray of light; we must reflect that light upon others. We are responsible to God for our influence. Even if we are compelled to stand apparently alone, we are not alone, for Christ is with us to encourage and strengthen and bless us. He is acquainted with every desire of your heart, with every purpose of your soul. He says, "I will not leave you comfortless: I will come to you" (John 14:18). Let us believe that God will do just as He has promised. . . .

We must not allow our minds to drift and come to no point. We know that the Lord is soon to come, and we must serve God from principle and be firm as a rock to follow in the path of obedience, because it is the only safe path.[25]

THE PERIL OF NEGLECT

Wherefore the rather, brethren, give diligence to make your calling and election sure: for if ye do these things, ye shall never fall. 2 Peter 1:10.

The world's Redeemer has said, "Search the scriptures" (John 5:39). In them is laid open the bounteous provisions for human necessities, and the strongest motives are set forth to influence to repentance and obedience. Here the seeker for truth may read, contemplate, and be stirred to the very depths of his being by that which a good and gracious God has done and is continually doing for him. He will be amazed that he should ever have treated with indifference the marvelous love and pardon proffered, for in redeeming man, God gave the greatest that He could offer. And if the objects of so great a love neglect salvation, there is nothing that Heaven can do more in their behalf. . . .

You need to study, to contemplate these great themes, lest you cherish indifference and become too hardened to yield to the conditions of the wonderful plan of salvation, and too proud to be humbled by a realization of your own fallen condition. . . .

The Lord enjoins upon children and youth to search for truth as for hidden treasure, and to be attracted and fascinated by that which unites the human with the divine. . . . Well may the apostle ask, "How shall we escape, if we neglect so great salvation?" (Heb. 2:3). . . .

The power of an angel could not make an atonement for our sins. The angelic nature united to the human could not be as costly, as elevated, as the law of God. It was the Son of God alone who could present an acceptable sacrifice. God Himself became man and bore all the wrath that sin had provoked. This problem—How could God be just and yet the justifier of sinners?—baffled all finite intelligence. A divine person alone could mediate between God and man. Human redemption is a theme which may well tax the faculties of the mind to the utmost. . . .

We cannot say to the youth or those of mature age, You have nothing to do yourself in this great work. We urge to constant effort. You must be diligent to make your calling and election sure.[26]

RICH DEPTHS OF KNOWLEDGE

If any man will do his will, he shall know of the doctrine, whether it be of God, or whether I speak of myself. John 7:17.

The more earnestly we apply our minds to the investigation of truth, the clearer will the evidences of truth appear, and the more closely we relate ourselves to the God of all wisdom, coming into communion with Him who has created all things, the richer will be our knowledge, the more fully shall we comprehend divine truth. God has graciously endowed men with intellectual powers, and these powers are to be wisely improved, that men may have ability to search into and understand rich depths of knowledge in the character, Word, and works of God. God will open the treasures of His love to the willing and obedient; he that willeth to do the will of God shall know of the doctrine.

By communion with God we become refined, broadened, and elevated. To him who desires the knowledge of divine things, God will open hidden wonders that are beyond the comprehension of those who are unenlightened by the Spirit of God. . . .

The great gift of salvation has been placed within our reach at an infinite cost to the Father and the Son. To neglect salvation is to neglect the knowledge of the Father and of the Son whom God hath sent. . . .

The greatness, the breadth, of the plan of salvation invests it with incomparable grandeur, but it can only be spiritually discerned, and it increases in greatness as we contemplate it. Looking to Jesus dying upon the cross, and knowing that it was our sin that placed the innocent Sufferer there, we are bowed down before Him in wonder and love.[27]

All who come to Christ for a clearer knowledge of the truth will receive it. He will unfold to them the mysteries of the kingdom of heaven, and these mysteries will be understood by the heart that longs to know the truth. A heavenly light will shine into the soul temple and will be revealed to others as the bright shining of a lamp on a dark path.[28]

HUMAN VERSUS DIVINE WISDOM

That your faith should not stand in the wisdom of men, but in the power of God. 1 Cor. 2:5.

The prevailing spirit of our times is that of infidelity and apostasy. The spirit manifested in the world is one of pride and self-exaltation. Men boast of illumination, which in reality is the blindest presumption, for they are in opposition to the plain Word of God. Many exalt human reason, idolize human wisdom, and set the opinions of men above the revealed wisdom of God. . . . Among the great mass of professed Christians the grievous character of the transgression of the law of God is not understood. They do not realize that salvation can be obtained only through the blood of Christ. . . .

In the eyes of men, vain philosophy and science, falsely so-called, are of more value than the Word of God. The sentiment prevails to a large extent that the divine Mediator is not essential to the salvation of man. A variety of theories advanced by the so-called worldly wise men for man's elevation are believed and trusted in more than is the truth of God as taught by Christ and His apostles.[29]

The Lord would have us individually search the Scriptures that we may become acquainted with the great plan of redemption and take in the grand subject as far as it is possible for the human mind, enlightened by the Spirit of God, to understand the purpose of God. He would have us comprehend something of His love in giving His Son to die that He might counteract evil, remove the defiling stains of sin from the workmanship of God, and reinstate the lost, elevating and ennobling the soul to its original purity through Christ's imputed righteousness. The only way in which the fallen race could be restored was through the gift of His Son, equal with Himself, possessing the attributes of God. . . .

God has endowed humanity with attributes whereby we may appreciate God, and though man has revolted from God and has endeavored to supply the place of God with other objects of worship, the true God alone can fill the wants of the soul.[30]

AUTHOR AND TEACHER OF TRUTH

To this end was I born, and for this cause came I into the world, that I should bear witness unto the truth. Every one that is of the truth heareth my voice. John 18:37.

Christ is the author of all truth. Every brilliant conception, every thought of wisdom, every capacity and talent of men, is the gift of Christ. He borrowed no new ideas from humanity, for He originated all. But when He came to earth He found the bright gems of truth which He had entrusted to man all buried up in superstition and tradition. Truths of most vital importance were placed in the framework of error, to serve the purpose of the arch deceiver. . . . But Christ swept away erroneous theories of every grade. No one save the world's Redeemer had power to present the truth in its primitive purity, divested of the error that Satan had accumulated to hide its heavenly beauty. . . . The work of Christ was to take the truth of which the people were in want, and separate it from error and present it free from the superstitions of the world, that the people might accept it on its own intrinsic and eternal merit. He dispersed the mists of doubt, that the truth might be revealed and shed distinct rays of light into the darkness of men's hearts.[31]

The truth came from His lips clothed in new and interesting representations that gave it the freshness of a new revelation. His voice was never pitched to an unnatural key, and His words came with an earnestness and assurance appropriate to their importance and the momentous consequences involved in their reception or rejection.[32]

He invited men to learn of Him, for He was a living representation of the law of God. He was the only one in human garb that could stand among a nation of witnesses, and looking round upon them, say, "Which of you convinceth me of sin?" (John 8:46). He knew that no man could point out any defect in His character or conduct. What power His spotless purity gave to His instructions, what force to His reproofs, what authority to His commands! . . . He proved Himself to be the way, the truth, and the life.[33]

CENTRAL THEME OF THE SCRIPTURES

And beginning at Moses and all the prophets, he expounded unto them in all the scriptures the things concerning himself. Luke 24:27.

There is one great central truth to be kept ever before the mind in the searching of the Scriptures—Christ and Him crucified. Every other truth is invested with influence and power corresponding to its relation to this theme. It is only in the light of the cross that we can discern the exalted character of the law of God. The soul palsied by sin can be endowed with life only through the work wrought out upon the cross by the Author of our salvation. The love of Christ constrains man to unite with Him in His labors and sacrifice. The revelation of divine love awakens in them a sense of their neglected obligation to be light bearers to the world, and inspires them with a missionary spirit. This truth enlightens the mind and sanctifies the soul. It will banish unbelief and inspire faith. . . . When Christ in His work of redemption is seen to be the great central truth of the system of truth, a new light is shed upon all the events of the past and the future. They are seen in a new relation, and possess a new and deeper significance.[34]

The Old Testament is as verily the gospel in types and shadows as the New Testament is in its unfolding power. The New Testament does not present a new religion; the Old Testament does not present a religion to be superseded by the New. The New Testament is only the advancement and unfolding of the Old. Abel was a believer in Christ and was as verily saved by His power as was Peter or Paul. Enoch was a representative of Christ as surely as was the beloved disciple John. . . . That God who walked with Enoch was our Lord and Saviour, Jesus Christ. He was the light of the world then, just as He is now.[35]

The truth for this time is broad in its outlines, far reaching, embracing many doctrines, but these doctrines are not detached items which mean little; they are united by golden threads, forming a complete whole, with Christ as the living center.[36]

A WILL OF YOUR OWN?

The discretion of a man deferreth his anger; and it is his glory to pass over a transgression. Prov. 19.11.

There are duties to the body and duties to the soul, and these every human agent must cooperate with God in seeking to perform. . . . Do not submit to receive a cheap mold. The young need sound common sense, for they are living for two worlds. . . .

Apply the truth to your own individual case. You have a soul to save or a soul to lose. Have a will of your own, but let it be subject to the will of God. Be determined that you will not become angry, that you will not become self-sufficient, that you will not be hasty and overbearing. If this is your weak point, guard that point as a man would guard a broken limb. Watch your spirit, and let not a hasty spirit conquer you. Be careful to examine the weak points in your character, knowing that the evils which exist may be overcome by steadfastly refusing to yield to your weakness. The evil of hasty, wicked, indulgence of temper makes any youth a madman. Keep sane. A soft answer turneth away wrath. Evil can and will grow . . . through repetition.

Do not underrate the importance of little things because they are little. By action and reaction these little defects accumulate and bind themselves together like rods of steel. That little action, that un-guarded word, repeated, becomes habit, . . . and habit constitutes character. . . .

Cultivate a kind, tender, sympathetic heart, and never call these attributes weakness, for they are the attributes of Christ. Be careful of your influence. Let it be of so pure and fragrant a character that you will never be ashamed to have it reproduced in others.

As drops of water make the river, so little things make up life. Life is a river, peaceful, calm, and enjoyable, or it is a troubled river, always casting up mire and dirt. In this life you may place yourself under the discipline of the Holy Spirit. Through the sanctification of the Spirit you will thus grow more and more like Christ.[37]

THE PLATFORM OF TRUTH

For the wisdom of this world is foolishness with God. For it is written, He taketh the wise in their own craftiness. And again, The Lord knoweth the thoughts of the wise, that they are vain. 1 Cor. 3:19, 20.

The Word of God is to be our guide. About the truths that this Word contains there is no guesswork. Let us not leave this unerring guide in order to seek for something new and strange. . . . There are many such doctrines that have not for their foundation, "It is written." They are but human suppositions. It was with the word "It is written" that Christ met every temptation of Satan in the wilderness, and armed with this weapon, He could say to the enemy, "Thus far shalt thou come, and no farther."

We cannot with safety accept the opinions of any man, however learned, unless they are in harmony with the words of the Great Teacher. The opinions of erring men will be presented for our acceptance, but God's Word is our authority, and we are never to accept human teaching without the most conclusive evidence that it agrees with the teaching of God's Word. We are to know that we do know that we are standing on the platform of eternal truth—the Word of the living God.[38]

Truth, precious truth from the Word of God is to be presented, both in public and in families. We have a message that is to prepare a people to stand amid the perils of the last days. . . . Truth will stand every test that is brought to bear upon it. It cannot be overthrown by the sophistries of Satan. The more it is assailed the more bright and clear it will shine out. As we see indications of the active, earnest efforts of the enemy, shall we not make determined efforts to give the message in clear, decided lines? Shall we not stand forth in the power and Spirit of God, and receive and impart lessons from the Great Teacher? . . . "O Lord, thou art my God; I will exalt thee, I will praise thy name; for thou hast done wonderful things; thy counsels of old are faithfulness and truth" (Isa. 25:1). . . . Let us anchor ourselves to the words of the Lord God of Israel.[39]

GOD'S APPOINTED SIGNATURE

And hallow my sabbaths; and they shall be a sign between me and you, that ye may know that I am the Lord your God. Eze. 20:20.

How shall we distinguish God's true servants from the false prophets who Christ said should arise to deceive many? There is only one test of character—the law of Jehovah.

The Israelites placed over their doors a signature of blood to show that they were God's property. So the children of God in this age will bear the signature God has appointed. They will place themselves in harmony with God's holy law. A mark is placed upon every one of God's people just as verily as a mark was placed over the doors of the Hebrew dwellings, to preserve the people from the general ruin. God declares, "I gave them my sabbaths, to be a sign between me and them" (Eze. 20:12). . . . There is no need for us to be deceived. . . .

Satanic agencies have made the earth a stage for horrors which no language can describe. War and bloodshed are carried on by nations claiming to be Christian. A disregard for the law of God has brought its sure result. The great conflict now being waged is not merely a strife of man against man. On one side stands the Prince of life, acting as man's substitute and surety; on the other, the prince of darkness, with the fallen angels under his command. . . .

There will be a sharp conflict between those who are loyal to God and those who cast scorn upon His law. The church has joined hands with the world. Reverence to God's law has been subverted. The religious leaders are teaching for doctrine the commandments of men. As it was in the days of Noah, so it is in this age of the world. But shall the prevalence of disloyalty and transgression cause those who have reverenced the law of God to have less respect for it, to unite with the powers of earth to make it void? The truly loyal will not be carried away by the current of evil. They will not throw scorn and contempt on that which God has set apart as holy. The test comes to everyone. There are only two sides. On which side are you?[40]

SAFETY IN THE "OLD PATHS"

Thus saith the Lord, Stand ye in the ways, and see, and ask for the old paths, where is the good way, and walk therein, and ye shall find rest for your souls. Jer. 6:16.

There is no safety anywhere. Satan has come down with great power and is working with all deceivableness of unrighteousness in them that perish. Those who do not follow in Christ's footsteps will find themselves following another leader. They have listened to strange voices until they cannot distinguish the voice of the True Shepherd. Little by little they ceased to heed the warnings, the reproofs, the instructions. Human wisdom came in, human imaginations were followed. Much reliance is placed upon human exertion and devices, and they imperceptibly go on until they are fully satisfied with their own wisdom, their own inventions, and are filled with their own doings.

Drink deep at the fountain of truth, and be a close student of the Word, for the Lord will take the words of truth and through the Holy Spirit imprint them on your heart that you may present the precious Word with simplicity and fervor. "Rejoice in the Lord alway: . . ." that Jesus is glad to receive you with all your imperfections, with all your weakness, and acknowledge you as His child. Therefore, trust Him. Adorn the doctrine of Christ our Saviour by a well-ordered life and a godly conversation. "Let your moderation be known unto all men. The Lord is at hand. Be careful for nothing"—that is, be not overanxious—"but in every thing by prayer and supplication with thanksgiving let your requests be made known unto God." What a privilege is this given to everyone to trust in Jesus and tell Him everything! "And the peace of God, which passeth all understanding, shall keep your hearts and minds through Christ Jesus" (Phil. 4:4-7).

Have faith in God. However stormy may be the times, looking unto Jesus who is the author and the finisher of your faith, you will be complete in Him. Abide in the old paths, whoever may turn back. Be rooted and grounded and built up in the most holy faith, a living epistle known and read of all men.[41]

THE GARDEN OF GOD

For all flesh is as grass, and all the glory of man as the flower of grass. The grass withereth, and the flower thereof falleth away: but the word of the Lord endureth for ever. 1 Peter 1:24, 25.

If our minds are open to the impressions of the Spirit of God, we may learn lessons from the simple and beautiful things of nature. I feel oppressed in the crowded cities where there is naught for the eyes to look upon but houses. The flowers are to us constant teachers. The shrubs and flowers gather to themselves the properties of earth and air which they appropriate to perfect the beautiful buds and blossoming flowers for our happiness, but they are God's preachers, and we are to consider the lessons which they teach us.

Just so has God given us the precious promises throughout His Word. The Scriptures are open to us as the garden of God, and their promises are as fragrant flowers blooming all over that garden. God especially calls our attention to the very ones that are appropriate for us. In these promises we may discern the character of God and read His love to us. They are the ground upon which our faith rests, the support and strength of our faith and hope, and through these we are to delight our souls in God and breathe in the fragrance of heaven. Through the precious promises He withdraws the veil from the future and gives us glimpses of the things which He has prepared for those who love Him. . . .

We should not regard them with carelessness or indifference. But as we would examine the precious flowers, . . . delighting our senses with their loveliness and fragrance, just so we should take the promises of God, one by one, and examine them closely on every side—take in their richness, and be soothed, comforted, encouraged, and strengthened by them. God has provided for all the comforts the soul needs. They are suited to the friendless, the poverty stricken, the wealthy, the sick, the bereaved—all may have their appropriate help if they will see and take hold upon these by faith. God scatters blessings all along our path to brighten the rugged way of life, and we want to be receiving all the comfort and tokens of God's love with grateful hearts.[42]

TO WHICH PARTY DO YOU BELONG?

Whosoever therefore shall confess me before men, him will I confess also before my Father which is in heaven. Matt. 10:32.

The truth, to be genuine in its influence on the human heart, must be acknowledged before the universe of heaven, before the worlds unfallen, and before men. Let no one entertain the idea that he may work out his own salvation or receive the smallest spiritual blessing which the gospel offers, by stealth. The Lord calls for open, manly confession. "Ye are my witnesses, saith the Lord" (Isa. 43:10). Nothing can be effectually gained in advancing in the knowledge of God and our Saviour Jesus Christ until the unbelieving one, longing after Christian excellence of character, shall become as God has intended—a spectacle unto the world, to angels, and to men, a city set on a hill that cannot be hid. . . .

When one places his feet on the solid rock Christ Jesus as his foundation, he receives an endowment of power from the Source of all knowledge, all wisdom, and spiritual efficiency, that all may know to which party he belongs—commandment keepers or commandment breakers. The banner of Prince Emmanuel that floats over his head will not fail to clear away all uncertainty and give all to understand that we keep the commandments of God and have the testimony of Jesus Christ. The love of Jesus Christ possesses a constraining power.[43]

When Jesus was asked the question, Art thou the Son of God? He knew that to answer in the affirmative would make His death certain; a denial would leave a stain upon His humanity. There was a time to be silent, and a time to speak. He had not spoken until plainly interrogated. In His lessons to His disciples He had declared: "Whosoever therefore shall confess me before men, him will I confess also before my Father which is in heaven." When challenged, Jesus did not deny His relationship with God. In that solemn moment His character was at stake and must be vindicated. He left on that occasion an example for man to follow under similar circumstances. He would teach him not to apostatize from his faith to escape suffering or even death.[44]

NONCOMMITTAL CHRISTIANS

Ye are the light of the world. A city that is set on an hill cannot be hid. Neither do men light a candle, and put it under a bushel, but on a candlestick; and it giveth light unto all that are in the house. Matt. 5:14,15.

Let no one feel inclined to hide his light. Those who hide their light so that the world may not distinguish between them and those who walk in darkness will soon lose all power to diffuse light. They are the ones who are represented by the five foolish virgins, and when the crisis comes, when the call is heard "Behold, the bridegroom cometh; go ye out to meet him" (Matt. 25:6), they will arouse at last to find that their lamps have gone out, that they have mixed with the elements of the world and have not provided themselves with the oil of grace. They were lulled to sleep by the cry of peace and safety, and did not keep their lamps trimmed and burning. Aroused to their darkness they plead for oil, but it is impossible for one Christian to impart character to another soul. Character is not transferable. Those who are ease-loving, world-loving, fashion-loving professors of Christianity will not go in to the marriage supper of the Lamb with those who are represented by the five wise virgins. When they solicit entrance they are told that the door is shut. Now is the time to impart light. . . .

It is not to be looked upon as a trifling matter to have the light of present truth, and yet to be noncommittal. It is no trifling thing to say by attitude and sentiment, even though that sentiment is not expressed in words, "My Lord delayeth his coming." The spirit and influence of the peace and safety sentiment is in our very midst, and the very atmosphere that surrounds the soul of many who profess to be believers in the soon coming of Christ is of a malarious character, calculated to soothe the very ones who would be stirred if we showed zeal and determination and stood at our post of duty to warn men of the speedy advent of our Lord. . . . We must speak forth the truth, we must let our light shine forth in clear, steady rays, lest some soul shall stumble and fall because our light is eclipsed.[45]

PASSING ON THE LIGHT

Let your light so shine before men, that they may see your good works, and glorify your Father which is in heaven. Matt. 5:16.

Those who have an experimental knowledge of the truth are under obligation to God to communicate the precious light. . . . Some will be convicted and will heed the words spoken to them in love and tenderness. They will acknowledge that the truth is the very thing they need to set them free from the slavery of sin and the bondage of worldly principles. There are opened before them themes of thought, fields for action, that they had never comprehended. In Jesus the Redeemer they discern infinite wisdom, infinite justice, infinite mercy—depths, heights, lengths and breadths of love which passeth knowledge. Beholding the perfection of Christ's character, contemplating His mission, His love, His grace, His truth, they are charmed; the great want of the soul is met, and they will say with the psalmist, "I shall be satisfied, when I awake, with thy likeness" (Ps. 17:15). The divine object of faith and love they see to be Jesus Christ. With them the love of the world, the worshiping of earthly treasures, have come to an end.

Such a soul appropriates the Word of God to himself. He sees that the miracles, the self-denial, the self-sacrifice of Christ, His being lifted up on the cross, were for him. The language of the heart will be, "He died for me. He triumphed in death that I should not perish but believe in Him as my personal Saviour, and have that life which measures with the life of God. In the riches of His grace I am possessed of treasures that are as enduring as eternity."

The world is no longer his study and his god. He hungers for a knowledge of the Word which contains for him treasures that are to be constantly sought and are constantly satisfying—an inexhaustible mine of precious things to be sought for in faith, to be appropriated and communicated to others. He has discovered the fountain of living waters, the wells of salvation, from which he may continually draw, and there will be no diminishing of the supply.[46]

LIGHT FOR THOSE WHO LOVE LIGHT

Light is sown for the righteous, and gladness for the upright in heart. Ps. 97:11.

Christ has left His Holy Spirit to be His representative in the world, to give celestial aid to every hungering, thirsting soul. . . . We are living in a most solemn period of this world's history, but light is shining for those who will walk in the light. . . .

There are many who have not had the light, and they are not judged guilty. They mourn because of their human ignorance. They find nothing satisfactory, and thirst for a knowledge of the only true God. They have an ideal of God in their minds and they desire to find Him. He has entrusted light to His people to give to all those who are praying for light. He has sent forth His streams of salvation to refresh those who are athirst for a knowledge of truth, virtue, and holiness. To such we should speak as did the apostle Paul to the Athenians, "Whom therefore ye ignorantly worship, him declare I unto you" (Acts 17:23). Heavenly inspiration has come to men, and they have been entrusted with gospel truth, and have thereby been weighted with a solemn responsibility to devote their God-given powers to making God known to man. Christ says, "And this is life eternal, that they might know thee the only true God, and Jesus Christ, whom thou hast sent" (John 17:3). . . .

Those who have the mind of Christ will "walk even as he walked." They will live out the law of God, will feed upon Christ, be partakers of the divine nature, and stand as living sentinels for truth. In integrity of heart they will voice the cry, "Come out from among them, and be ye separate, saith the Lord, and touch not the unclean thing; and I will receive you, and will be a Father unto you, and ye shall be my sons and daughters . . ." (2 Cor. 6:17, 18). . . .

God gives light to those who love light. He imparts truth to those who search for truth as for something of most precious value in order that they may impart light to those who are in the valley and the shadow of death.[47]

LET GOD MANAGE YOU

And let the beauty of the Lord our God be upon us. Ps. 90:17.

God wants you to let Him manage you, that you may be a lovable Christian. The Lord would have the natural and hereditary traits of character come under the pruning knife. Look steadfastly unto Jesus, that you may catch His spirit and cherish the qualities of Christlike character. Then it will be recognized by all who have any connection with you, that you have learned of Christ His meekness, His affection, His tenderness, His sympathy. Never rest satisfied until you possess a loving and lovable spirit. Your words may come from the good treasure of the heart to strengthen, help, bless, and win all around you. . . . Others catch your spirit. The seeds we sow will bear a harvest in goodness, patience, kindness, and love, or exactly the opposite. . . .

Many, many need melting over. Be sound in principle, true to God, but do not manifest one stern, ungenial phase of character. God does not want you to incur contempt by manifesting a disposition like a ball of putty, but He does want you to be in principle as sound as a rock, yet with a healthful mellowness. Like the Master, be full of grace and truth. Jesus was incorruptible, undefiled, yet in His life were mingled gentleness, meekness, benignity, sympathy, and love. The poorest were not afraid to approach Him; they did not fear a rebuff. What Christ was, every Christian should strive to be. In holiness and winsomeness of character He is our model. . . .

We should all learn of Christ what it means to be a Christian. Let us learn of Him how to combine firmness, justice, purity, and integrity with unselfish courtesy and kindly sympathy. Thus the character becomes lovable and attractive. The beauty of holiness will disarm scoffers. . . .

The heart must receive the divine current, and let it flow out in rich streams of mercy and grace to other hearts. All who would win souls to Christ must be winsome.[48]

SUBJECTS OF THE KING!

For the Lord is our judge, the Lord is our lawgiver, the Lord is our king; he will save us. Isa. 33:22.

This morning* my soul is filled with praise and thanksgiving to God from whom come all our mercies and blessings. The Lord is good, and His mercies endure forever. I will praise Him who is the light of my countenance and my God. He is the source of all efficiency and power. Why do we not praise Him by speaking words of hope and comfort to others? Why are our lips so silent? Speech is a gift of Heaven, and it should be used in sounding forth the praises of Him who hath called us out of darkness into His marvelous light. . . .

O how much good would be accomplished were God honored by all who profess to be Christians! . . . The Light of the world is shining upon men in richest blessing. Every provision has been made for the supplying of our temporal and spiritual needs. Yet how little thanksgiving the Giver receives! . . .

In receiving Christ as our Captain there must be a complete surrender of the human will to the divine will. The Lord can work out His will through those who have made this surrender, for they give prompt and cheerful obedience to His commands. God expects us to obey without questioning. We are to ask, "Lord, what wilt thou have me to do?" Then, though the command may be as stern and startling as that given to Abraham, we are to obey. Abraham's soul was rent asunder by the command, "Take now thy son, thine only son Isaac, whom thou lovest, and offer him for a sacrifice on one of the mountains which I will tell thee of" (Gen. 22:2). But he did not hesitate to obey.

All our activities, all our business arrangements, should be in perfect accord with the Lord's commands. The laws of God's kingdom must be obeyed by the subjects of that kingdom. Our zeal for the advancement of God's kingdom is to mark us as faithful subjects of the cross of Christ. God can trust as His representatives those who implicitly obey Him.[1]

*Early morning diary entry, Sept. 5, 1900.

IN THE MASTER'S STEAD

Moreover it is required in stewards, that a man be found faithful. 1 Cor. 4:2.

A steward identifies himself with his master. His master's interests become his. He has accepted the responsibilities of a steward and he must act in the master's stead, doing as the master would do if he were presiding over his own goods. The position is one of dignity, in that his master trusts him. If a steward in any wise acts selfishly and turns the advantages gained in trading with his lord's goods to his own advantage, he has perverted the trust reposed in him. The master can no longer look upon him as a servant to be trusted, one on whom he can depend.

Every Christian is a steward of God, entrusted with His goods. . . . Let all who claim to be Christians deal wisely with the Lord's goods. God is making an inventory of the money lent you and the spiritual advantages given you. Will you as stewards make careful inventory? Will you examine whether you are using economically all that God has placed in your charge, or whether you are wasting the Lord's goods by selfish outlay in order to make a display? Would that all that is spent needlessly were laid up as treasure in heaven![2]

However large the income or the possessions of any person, any family, or any institution, let all remember that they are only stewards, holding in trust the Lord's money. All profit, all pay, our time, our talents, our opportunities, are to be accounted for to Him who gives them all. . . .

God will encourage His faithful stewards who are ready to put all their energies and God-given endowments to the very best use. As all learn the lesson of faithfully rendering to God what is His due, He through His providence will enable some to bring princely offerings. He will enable others to make smaller offerings, and the small and the large gifts are acceptable to Him if given with an eye single to His glory.[3]

SUPPORT OF THE LORD'S PLAN

Bring ye all the tithes into the storehouse, that there may be meat in mine house, and prove me now herewith, saith the Lord of hosts, if I will not open you the windows of heaven, and pour you out a blessing, that there shall not be room enough to receive it. Mal. 3:10.

We are not to look upon the property we are handling as our own, with which we may do as we please. It is the Lord's, to be administered in accordance with His prescribed plans.[4]

God wants all His stewards to be exact in following divine arrangements. They are not to offset the Lord's plans with some deed of charity, some gift, or some offering, done or given when and how they, the human agents, shall see fit. God has made His plan known, and all who cooperate with Him will carry out His plan instead of daring to attempt to improve on it by their own arrangements. . . . God will honor them and work in their behalf, for we have His pledged word that He will open the windows of heaven and pour us out a blessing such as there will not be room enough to receive.

It is a very poor policy for men to seek to improve on Gods plan and invent a makeshift, averaging up their good impulses in this and that instance and offsetting them against all that is required by God. . . . We are to strike true and faithful figures in tithing, and then say to the Lord, I have done as Thou hast commanded me. If Thou wilt honor me by trusting me with Thy goods to trade upon, I will, by Thy grace, be a faithful steward, doing all in my power to bring meat to Thy house. . . .

Men who have large responsibilities are to be sure that they are not robbing God in any jots or tittles, when so much is involved, as is so plainly stated in Malachi. Here we are told that a blessing is given for a faithful disposition of the tithes, and a curse for the covetous retention of the money which should flow into the treasury. Then ought we not to be sure to work on the safe side, so dealing with God in handling the property lent us on trust that no shadow of reproach shall fall upon us? . . . I need not ask, Will not God bless those who are faithful? We have His pledged word.[5]

221

BEWARE OF SATAN'S SNARES

But they that will be rich fall into temptation and a snare, and into many foolish and hurtful lusts, which drown men in destruction and perdition. 1 Tim. 6:9.

Satan has nets and snares, like the snares of the fowler, all prepared to entrap souls. It is his studied purpose that men shall employ their God-given powers for selfish ends rather than yield them to glorify God. God would have men engage in a work that will bring them peace and joy and will render them eternal profits, but Satan wants us to concentrate our efforts for that which profiteth not, for things that perish with the using. . . .

The heart of man may be the abode of the Holy Spirit. The peace of Christ that passeth understanding may rest in your soul, and the transforming power of His grace may work in your life and fit you for the courts of glory. But if brain and nerve and muscle are all employed in the service of self, you are not making God and heaven the first consideration of your life. It is impossible to be weaving the graces of Christ into your character while you are putting all your energies on the side of the world. You may be successful in heaping up treasure on the earth for the glory of self, but "where your treasure is, there will your heart be also" (Matt. 6:21). Eternal considerations will be made of secondary importance. You may take part in the outward forms of worship, but your service will be an abomination to the God of heaven. . . .

If the eye is single, if it is directed heavenward, the light of heaven will fill the soul, and earthly things will appear insignificant and uninviting. The purpose of the heart will be changed, and the admonition of Jesus will be heeded. You will lay up your treasure in heaven. Your thoughts will be fixed upon the great reward of eternity. All your plans will be made in reference to the future, immortal life. You will be drawn toward your treasure. You will not study your worldly interest, but in all your pursuits the silent inquiry will be, "Lord, what wilt thou have me to do?" (Acts 9:6). Bible religion will be woven into your daily life.[6]

A SAFE PLACE FOR OUR TREASURES

Lay not up for yourselves treasures upon earth, where moth and rust doth corrupt, and where thieves break through and steal: but lay up for yourselves treasures in heaven, where neither moth nor rust doth corrupt, and where thieves do not break through nor steal: for where your treasure is, there will your heart be also. Matt. 6:19-21.

Mark these words of the Great Teacher, who spake as never man spake. He sets before you the course to pursue if you would serve your best interests in this life, and lay up for yourselves an eternal treasure. Lay not up for yourselves treasures upon earth. There is danger of losing all in the pursuit of worldly gain, for in the feverish eagerness for earthly treasure, higher interests are forgotten. . . .

If your thoughts, your plans, your purposes, are all directed toward the accumulation of the things of earth, your anxiety, your study, your interests, will all be centered upon the world. The heavenly attractions will lose their beauty. The glories of the eternal world will cease to have the force of reality to you. Your heart will be with your treasure, and every faculty of your mind will be so concentrated on the work you have chosen that you will not heed the warnings and entreaties of the Word and Spirit of God. You will have no time to devote to the study of the Scriptures and to earnest prayer that you may escape the snares of Satan.[7]

This work of transferring your possessions to the world above is worthy of all your best energies. It is of the highest importance, and involves your eternal interests. That which you bestow in the cause of God is not lost. All that is given for the salvation of souls and the glory of God is invested in the most successful enterprise in this life and in the life to come. Your talents of gold and silver, if given to the exchangers, are gaining continually in value, which will be registered to your account in the kingdom of heaven. You are to be the recipients of the eternal wealth that has increased in the hands of the exchangers. In giving to the work of God, you are laying up for yourselves treasures in heaven. All that you lay up above is secure from disaster and loss and is increasing to an eternal, and enduring, substance.[8]

GOD'S TREASURE HOUSE OF SUPPLIES

But my God shall supply all your need according to his riches in glory by Christ Jesus. Phil. 4:19.

The children of God are called upon to be representatives of Christ, showing forth the goodness and mercy of the Lord. If they but revealed His goodness from day to day, barriers would be raised around their souls against the temptations of the evil one. . . .

God knows our wants, and has provided for them. The Lord has a treasure house of supplies for His children, and can give them what they need under all circumstances. Then why do we not trust Him? He has made precious promises to His children on condition of faithful obedience to His precepts. There is not a burden but He can remove, no darkness but He can dispel, no weakness but He can change to power, no fears but He can calm, no worthy aspiration but He can guide and justify.

We are not to look at ourselves. The more we dwell upon our own imperfections, the less strength we shall have to overcome them. We are to render a cheerful service to God. It is the work of Satan to present the Lord as lacking in compassion and pity. . . . We fasten our minds upon the misrepresentations of Satan and dishonor God by mistrusting Him and by murmuring against Him. When we act like culprits under sentence of death we bear false witness against God. The Father gave His only begotten and well-beloved Son to die for us, and in so doing He placed great honor upon humanity, for in Christ the link that was broken through sin was reunited and man again connected with Heaven.

You who doubt the mercy of God, look at the Lamb of God, look at the Man of sorrows, who bore your grief and suffered for your sin. He is your friend. He died on the cross because He loved you. He is touched with the feeling of your infirmities and bears you up before the throne. In view of His unspeakable love should not hope, love, and gratitude be cherished in your heart? Should not gladness fill your service to God?[9]

A NEVER-FAILING REFUGE

Be careful for nothing; but in every thing by prayer and supplication with thanksgiving let your requests be made known unto God. Phil. 4:6.

It is not the will of God that His people should be weighed down with care. But our Lord does not deceive us. He does not say to us, "Do not fear; there are no dangers in your path." He knows there are trials and dangers, and He deals with us plainly. He does not propose to take His people out of a world of sin and evil, but He points them to a never-failing refuge. . . .

How can we remain in doubt, questioning whether Jesus loves us, sinful though we be and compassed with infirmities? He gave Himself for us that He might redeem us from all iniquity and purify unto Himself a peculiar people, zealous of good works. He came to our world in the humble guise of a man, that He might become acquainted with the griefs and temptations that beset man's pathway, and that He might know how to help the weary with His offer of rest and peace. But thousands upon thousands refuse His assistance and only cling more firmly to their burden of care. He comes to the afflicted, and offers to soothe their grief and heal their sorrow. . . . To the disappointed, the unbelieving, and the unhappy He offers contentment, while pointing to mansions that He is preparing for them. . . . Jesus, our precious Saviour, should be first in our thoughts and affections, and we should trust Him with entire confidence. . . .

As each day comes we must in the strength of Jesus meet its trials and temptations. If we fail one day we add to the burdens of the next, and have less strength. We should not cloud the future by our carelessness in the present, but by thoughtful and careful performance of today's duties be preparing to meet the emergencies of tomorrow.

We need to cultivate a spirit of cheerfulness. . . . Let us ever look on the bright side of life and be hopeful, full of love and good works, rejoicing in the Lord always. "Let the peace of God rule in your hearts," and "be ye thankful" (Col. 3:15).[10]

A PROGRESSIVE FAITH

But without faith it is impossible to please him: for he that cometh to God must believe that he is, and that he is a rewarder of them that diligently seek him. Heb. 11:6.

The time has come when we are to expect large blessings from the Lord. We must rise to a higher standard on the subject of faith. We have too little faith. The Word of God is our endorsement. We must take it, simply believing every word. With this assurance we may claim large things, and according to our faith it will be unto us. . . .

The work of faith means more than we think. It means genuine reliance upon the naked word of God. By our actions we are to show that we believe that God will do just as He has said. The wheels of nature and of providence are not appointed to roll backward nor to stand still. We must have an advancing, working faith, a faith that works by love and purifies the soul from every vestige of selfishness. It is not self, but God, that we must depend upon. We must not cherish unbelief. We must have that faith that takes God at His word. . . .

True faith consists in doing just what God has enjoined, not manufacturing things He has not enjoined. Justice, truth, mercy, are the fruit of faith. We need to walk in the light of God's law; then good works will be the fruit of our faith, the proceeds of a heart renewed every day. The tree must be made good before the fruit can be good. We must be wholly consecrated to God. Our will must be made right before the fruit can be good. We must have no fitful religion. "Whatsoever ye do, do all to the glory of God" (1 Cor. 10:31).

O what a field is opened before me! Our people must have the deep working of the Spirit of God every day. They must have a faith that works by love, a faith that emanates from God. There must not be a thread of selfishness drawn into the fabric. When our faith works by love, just such a love as Christ revealed in His life, it will be of a firm texture; it will be the fruit of a will subdued. But not until self dies can Christ live in us. Not until self dies can we possess a faith that works by love and purifies the soul.[11]

A DANGEROUS GUEST

And he said unto them, Why are ye so fearful? how is it that ye have no faith? Mark 4:40.

Why are we so weak in faith? . . . We are so faithless, so unbelieving, that the Lord cannot do for us those things which He longs to do. There are doubts in our minds that are very saddening and very difficult to dispel.

These doubts that bow down the soul we should each one bravely face, and tell the soul that we must conquer them at once. Make no delay, for there can be no peace where faith is lost. We need not express these doubts, for they may cause some poor soul to stumble. But examine them in the light of God's Word, then talk them over with Jesus with His Word of promise in your hand, and pray for their removal. Tell the Lord, "Lord, I believe; help thou mine unbelief" (Mark 9:24). Let not doubt be placed in a comfortable, easy chair. It is a dangerous guest when it is left to rankle in the mind and counteract faith. . . .

Genuine faith is life, and where there is life there is growth. The life which Jesus imparts cannot but grow more and more abundantly. A living faith means an increase of vigor, a confiding trust, by which the soul becomes a conquering power. He who drinks of the water of life which Jesus gives, possesses within himself a well of water springing up into everlasting life. Though it shall be cut off from all created springs, it is fed from the hidden fountain. It is a perpetual spring, in immediate communication with the inexhaustible fountain of life.

The Lord is dishonored when any who profess His name have an emptiness. This misrepresents God. Nothing but Christ manifested in spirit and life and character can reveal God to a world that knows Him not. The soul renewed in the knowledge of God and Jesus Christ whom He has sent, demonstrates its divine fullness in a living, growing experience—even the fullness of Him that filleth all things.[12]

CONQUERING OUR DOUBTS

O thou of little faith, wherefore didst thou doubt? Matt. 14:31.

"Wherefore didst thou doubt?" said Christ to the sinking Peter. The same question may be addressed to us. . . . The Lord has pledged Himself to give us strength to enable us to stand. As we search the Scriptures we find ground for confidence, provision for sufficiency. It is our privilege to say boldly, yet humbly, The Lord is my helper, therefore I shall not be moved from my steadfastness. My life is hid with Christ in God. Because He lives, I shall live also. Let us pledge ourselves before God and the angels of heaven that we will not dishonor God by speaking words of discouragement or unbelief. . . Close the door to distrust and open the door wide to faith. Invite into the soul temple the heavenly Guest.[13]

You may have your choice as to who shall rule your heart and control your mind. If you choose to open the door to the suggestions of the evil one, your mind will be filled with distrust and rebellious questioning. You may talk out your feelings, but every doubt you utter is a seed that will germinate and bear fruit in another's life, and it will be impossible to counteract the influence of your words. You may be able to recover from your season of temptation . . . , but others that have been swayed by your influence may not be able to escape from the unbelief you have suggested. How important it is that we speak to those around us only those things which will give spiritual strength and enlightenment![14]

It is our duty to encourage faith, to talk faith that we may have faith. If we talk doubt and encourage doubt we shall have abundant doubt, for Satan will help us in this kind of work. We need sanctified hearts and sanctified lips. We need to breathe in the rich, bracing atmosphere that comes from the heavenly Canaan. . . . Why should we fill the gallery of the mind with gloomy scenes of doubt? Why not let the bright beams of the Sun of Righteousness shine into the chambers of heart and mind, and dispel the shadows of unbelief? Turn to the Light, to Jesus the precious Saviour.[15]

THE FAITH GOD ACCEPTS

For as the body without the spirit is dead, so faith without works is dead also. James 2:26.

There are many in the Christian world who claim that all that is necessary to salvation is to have faith; works are nothing, faith is the only essential. But God's Word tells us that faith without works is dead, being alone. . . . Faith and works go hand in hand. . . . Works will never save us; it is the merit of Christ that will avail in our behalf. Through faith in Him, Christ will make all our imperfect efforts acceptable to God. The faith we are required to have is not a do-nothing faith; saving faith is that which works by love and purifies the soul. He who will lift up holy hands to God without wrath and doubting will walk intelligently in the way of God's commandments.

If we are to have pardon for our sins we must first have a realization of what sin is, that we may repent and bring forth fruits meet for repentance. We must have a solid foundation for our faith; it must be founded on the Word of God, and its results will be seen in obedience to God's expressed will. . . . Faith and works will keep us evenly balanced, and make us successful in the work of perfecting Christian character. . . . We are living in an important and interesting period of this earth's history. We need more faith than we have yet had; we need a firmer hold from above. Satan is working with all power to obtain the victory over us, for he knows that he has but a short time in which to work. . . .

There is no excuse for sin or for indolence. Jesus has led the way, and He wishes us to follow in His steps. He has suffered, He has sacrificed as none of us can, that He might bring salvation within our reach. We need not be discouraged. Jesus came to our world to bring divine power to man, that through His grace we might be transformed into His likeness. When it is in the heart to obey God, when efforts are put forth to this end, Jesus accepts this disposition and effort as man's best service, and He makes up for the deficiency with His own divine merit.[16]

CULTIVATING THE PLANT OF FAITH

And the apostles said unto the Lord, Increase our faith. Luke 17:5.

Faith should be cultivated. If it has become weak it is like a sickly plant that should be placed in the sunshine and carefully watered and tended. The Lord would have everyone who has had light and evidence cherish that light and walk in its brightness. God has blessed us with reasoning powers so that we may trace from cause to effect. If we would have light we must come to the light. We must individually lay hold on the hope set before us in the gospel. . . . How foolish it would be to go into a cellar, and mourn because we were in the dark. If we want light we must come up into a higher room. It is our privilege to come into the light, to come into the presence of God. . . .

We should grow daily in faith in order that we may grow up to the full measure of the spiritual stature in Christ Jesus. We should believe that God will answer our prayers, and not trust to feeling. We should say, My gloomy feelings are no evidence that God has not heard me. I do not want to give up on account of these sad emotions, for "faith is the substance of things hoped for, the evidence of things not seen" (Heb. 11:1). The rainbow of promise encircles the throne of God. I come to the throne, pointing to the sign of God's faithfulness, and cherish the faith that works by love and purifies the soul.

We are not to believe because we feel or see that God hears us. We are to trust to the promise of God. We are to go about our business believing that God will do just what He has said He would do, and that the blessings we have prayed for will come to us when we most need them. Every petition enters into the heart of God when we come believing. We have not faith enough. We should look upon our heavenly Father as more willing to help us than an earthly parent is to help his child. Why not trust Him?

"He that spared not his own Son, but delivered him up for us all, how shall he not with him also freely give us all things?" (Rom. 8:32).[17]

MUCH FAITH, MUCH PEACE

Oh how great is thy goodness, which thou hast laid up for them that fear thee; which thou hast wrought for them that trust in thee before the sons of men! Ps. 31:19.

The more our faith fastens to Christ in perfect trust, the more peace we shall have. Faith will grow by exercise. God's rule is, One day at a time. Day by day do the work for each day as if you are conscious that you are working in the sight of the angels, cherubim and seraphim, and God and Christ. You are "a spectacle unto the world, and to angels, and to men" (1 Cor. 4:9). "Give us this day our daily bread" (Matt. 6:11). "As thy days, so shall thy strength be" (Deut. 33:25). "Looking unto Jesus the author and finisher of our faith" (Heb. 12:2). Living thus, the Holy Spirit helps our memory, sanctifies every faculty, and keeps us reminded of our daily and hourly dependence upon our heavenly Father's care, . . . and unceasing love.

This is the childlike spirit Jesus declared His disciples must have in order to enter into the kingdom of heaven—trusting as a little child in God their heavenly Father. Then Satan's temptations are discerned and more easily resisted, for there is in the heart a constant drawing nigh to God. The feeling of self-sufficiency which works the ruin of so many souls does not have an atmosphere in which to flourish.

"Seek ye first the kingdom of God, and his righteousness; and all these things shall be added unto you" (Matt. 6:33). Here is a precious promise from One who means every word He says. Then why are we fearful, distrustful, and unbelieving? . . . Our time is the Lord's. Our talents are the Lord's. Then how can any individual feel that he can be independent, not subject to the Spirit of God—independent of God's will, independent of God's providences and plans? . . .

"Who is among you that feareth the Lord . . . ? let him trust in the name of the Lord, and stay upon his God" (Isa. 50:10). . . . We are not safe in following the imaginations of our own hearts. We cannot be independent. Our only safety is in dependence on God our Redeemer.[18]

231

FAITH SEES BEYOND THE DARKNESS

Trust in the Lord, and do good; so shalt thou dwell in the land, and verily thou shalt be fed. Ps. 37:3.

"Trust in the Lord." Each day has its burdens, its cares and perplexities, and when we meet, how ready we are to talk of our difficulties and trials. . . . Some are always fearing and borrowing trouble. Every day they are surrounded by the tokens of God's love, every day they are enjoying the bounties of His providence, but they overlook these present blessings. . . .

Why should we be ungrateful and distrustful? Jesus is our friend. All heaven is interested in our welfare, and our anxiety and fear grieve the Holy Spirit of God. We should not indulge in a solicitude which only frets and wears us but does not help us to bear trials. No place should be given to that distrust of God which leads us to make a preparation against future want the chief pursuit of life, as though our happiness consisted in these earthly things. . . .

You may be perplexed in business; your prospects may grow darker and darker and you may be threatened with loss. But do not become discouraged; cast your care upon God and remain calm and cheerful. Begin every day with earnest prayer, not omitting to offer praise and thanksgiving. Ask for wisdom to manage your affairs with discretion and thus prevent loss and disaster. Do all you can on your part to bring about favorable results. . . . When, relying upon your tried Helper, you have done all you can, accept the result cheerfully. It will not always be gain from the worldling's standpoint, but perhaps success might have been the worst thing for you. . . .

We want an eye single to the glory of God in all the affairs of life; we want a living faith that holds fast the promises of God no matter how dark the prospect. We are not to look at the things which are seen, and judge from the world's standpoint, and be ruled by the world's principles, but we are to look at the things which are unseen, eternal.[19]

TAKE TIME TO THINK

*Let us search and try our ways, and turn again to the Lord.
Let us lift up our heart with our hands unto God in the heavens.
Lam. 3:40, 41.*

I would appeal to the youth to consider their ways, to take time to
think, to weigh their actions. . . . Compassed with temptation as you
are, nothing will be sufficient as a safeguard against evil except the indwelling of Christ in your hearts through faith in His righteousness.
You must practice His virtues, making Him your daily pattern. . . .

Good character does not come by chance; it is formed by persevering, untiring effort. The youth should seek to make all that is possible of themselves, by improving every entrusted talent and
capability to the glory of God. The world's Redeemer says, "Without
me ye can do nothing" (John 15:5). Faith in Jesus Christ as your personal Saviour will give strength and solidity to your character. Those
who have faith in Christ will be sober-minded, ever remembering
that God's eye is upon them, that angels of God are watching to see
what manner of characters they will develop. . . .

Individually, probation is granted to you in order that you may
form characters for the future, immortal life. Precious, golden moments are given you that you may improve them according to the
light which the Lord has graciously permitted to shine upon you
from the throne of His glory. . . . Christ is the greatest teacher the
world ever knew. Where He abides in the heart by faith, His spirit
will become a vitalizing agent to purify and vivify the soul. . . .

The truth in the heart will surely have a correcting influence on
the character. Hold the truth as from God, as a treasure of the highest value, that must not be dimmed or tarnished by evil practices that
are wholly out of harmony with its holy character. Under the divine
influence of truth the mind will be strengthened, the intellect invigorated, and that which is useless will be discarded for that which is
pure and beneficial. Under the influence of truth the Christian character will develop through the knowledge of the only true God and
Jesus Christ whom He hath sent.[20]

A HOLY WATCHER

Neither is there any creature that is not manifest in his sight: but all things are naked and opened unto the eyes of him with whom we have to do. Heb. 4:13.

In every place, at every hour in the day, there is a holy Watcher who balances every account, whose eye takes in the whole situation, whether it is one of fidelity or one of disloyalty and deception.

We are never alone. We have a Companion whether we choose Him or not. Remember, young men and young women, that wherever you are, whatever you are doing, God is there. To your every word and action you have a witness—the holy, sin-hating God. Nothing that is said or done or thought can escape His infinite eye. Your words may not be heard by human ears, but they are heard by the Ruler of the universe. He reads the inward anger of the soul when the will is crossed. He hears the expression of profanity. In the deepest darkness and solitude He is there. No one can deceive God; none can escape from their accountability to Him.

"O Lord, thou hast searched me, and known me," writes the psalmist. "Thou knowest my downsitting and mine uprising, thou understandest my thought afar off. Thou compassest my path and my lying down, and art acquainted with all my ways. . . . If I say, Surely the darkness shall cover me; even the night shall be light about me. Yea, the darkness hideth not from thee; but the night shineth as the day: the darkness and the light are both alike to thee" (Ps. 139:1-12).

Day by day the record of your words, your actions, and your influence is being made in the books of heaven. This you must meet.[21]

All heaven is interested in our salvation. The angels of God are . . . marking the deeds of men. They record in the books of God's remembrance the words of faith, the acts of love, the humility of spirit, and in that day when every man's work shall be tried of what sort it is, the work of the humble follower of Christ will stand the test, and will receive the commendation of Heaven. "Then shall the righteous shine forth as the sun in the kingdom of their Father" (Matt. 13:43).[22]

THE MIGHTY DELIVERER

I have spread out my hands all the day unto a rebellious people, which walketh in a way that was not good, after their own thoughts. Isa. 65:2.

The Lord God through Christ holds out His hand all the day long in invitations to the needy. He will receive all. He welcomes all. He rejects none. It is His glory to pardon the chief of sinners. He will take the prey from the mighty, He will deliver the captive, He will pluck the brand from the burning. He will lower the golden chain of His mercy to the greatest depths of human wretchedness and guilt and lift up the debased soul contaminated with sin. But man must will to come, and cooperate in the work of saving his soul by availing himself of opportunities given him of God. The Lord forces no one. The spotless wedding robe of Christ's righteousness is prepared to clothe the sinner, but if he refuses it he must perish.[23]

The record of the past can be blotted out with His [Christ's] blood, the page made clean and white. "Come now, and let us reason together, saith the Lord: though your sins be as scarlet, they shall be as white as snow; though they be red like crimson, they shall be as wool" (Isa. 1:18). . . .

The words falling from the lips of Jesus, "Thy sins be forgiven thee" (Matt. 9:2), are worth everything to us. He saith, I have borne your sins in My own body on Calvary's cross. He sees your sorrows. His hand is laid upon the head of every contrite soul, and Jesus becomes our Advocate before the Father, and our Saviour. The lowly, contrite heart will make very much of forgiveness and pardon. . . .

We may repeat His tender compassion for us to others who are wandering in the mazes of sin. The grace of Christ revealed to us must be tenderly revealed to others. A great tenderness and compassion will fill the soul for human beings who are still under the control of Satan. Christ is to be multiplied in every man and woman who believes in Him, for they are to live over the life of Christ in blessing and enlightening and bringing hope and peace and joy to other hearts?[24]

THE SOWING TIME

Flee also youthful lusts: but follow righteousness, faith, charity, peace, with them that call on the Lord out of a pure heart. 2 Tim. 2:22.

I long to address the young men and women who are so willing to reach only cheap standards. O that the Lord might influence their minds to see what perfection of character is! O that they might know the faith that works by love and purifies the soul! We are living in days of peril. Christ alone can help us and give us the victory. Christ must be all in all to us; He must dwell in the heart; His life must circulate through us, as the blood circulates through the veins. His Spirit must be a vitalizing power.[25]

It is anything but wise, my young friends, to seek your own pleasure, to sow a crop of tares in foolish, sinful actions, which will not only lead others to do the same but will bring forth a bitter harvest for your own reaping. The Lord says: ". . . Whatsoever a man soweth, that shall he also reap. For he that soweth to his flesh shall of the flesh reap corruption; but he that soweth to the Spirit shall of the Spirit reap life everlasting" (Gal. 6:7, 8). Youth is the sowing time, and the words and deeds of the early life are like seeds that will germinate and produce a harvest after their kind. Then why not sow seeds of kindness, of love, of faith, of patience, of self-denial, and true benevolence, and keep all your passions under control? Such sowing will produce a harvest after its kind. Let every word and deed be a seed that will result in good fruit.

If you seek the help and grace of God, the Holy Spirit will take possession of mind and character and work in you that which you can work out with all safety to yourself, and with all benefit to others. . . . The atmosphere that surrounds your soul will be of a pure, healthful character.[26]

The Lord loves the youth. He sees in them great possibilities, and is ready to help them to reach a high standard if they will only realize the need of His help and lay a foundation of character that cannot be moved.[27]

UNDER GOD'S SEARCHING EYE

That ye put off concerning the former conversation the old man, which is corrupt according to the deceitful lusts; and be renewed in the spirit of your mind; and that ye put on the new man, which after God is created in righteousness and true holiness. Eph. 4:22-24.

Provision has been made whereby every soul that is struggling under sinful practices may be made free from sin. "Behold the Lamb of God, which taketh away the sin of the world" (John 1:29). The Christian is not to retain his sinful habits and cherish his defects of character, but he is to be renewed in the spirit of his mind after the divine similitude. Whatever may be the nature of your defects, the Spirit of the Lord will enable you to discern them, and grace will be given you whereby they may be overcome. Through the merits of the blood of Christ you may be a conqueror—yes, more than a conqueror. . . .

Ask the Lord to reveal to you yourself; place your life under His searching eye, and when He lays hold upon your case you will see that you have made grievous mistakes, and what you supposed was of little importance was offensive in the sight of Heaven. You will see that there is a decided need of thorough transformation of character. You will realize that you must put away the evil of your doings, and cooperate with God and heavenly angels who are sent to minister unto those who shall be heirs of salvation. . . .

Self must die. Every practice, every habit, that has a harmful tendency, however innocent it may be regarded by the world, must be battled with until overcome, that the human agent may perfect a character after the divine Pattern. . . .

The crooked ways, the perverse doings of those around us, are not to dim the luster of our piety or to lead us to conform our habits to, and assimilate our customs and practices with, the world's. Let the prayer go forth from the lips of those who claim to be the sons and daughters of God, "Search me, O God, and know my heart: try me, and know my thoughts: and see if there be any wicked way in me, and lead me in the way everlasting" (Ps. 139:23, 24).[28]

MERCY FOR THE REPENTANT

If we confess our sins, he is faithful and just to forgive us our sins, and to cleanse us from all unrighteousness. 1 John 1:9.

All are fallible, all make mistakes and fall into sin; but if the wrongdoer is willing to see his errors, as they are made plain by the convicting Spirit of God, and in humility of heart will confess them . . . , then he may be restored. . . .

The mansions that Jesus has gone to prepare for all who love Him will be peopled by those who are free from sin. But sins that are not confessed will never be forgiven; the name of him who thus rejects the grace of God will be blotted out of the book of life. The time is at hand when every secret thing shall be brought into judgment, and then there will be many confessions made that will astonish the world. The secrets of all hearts will be revealed. The confession of sin will be most public. The sad part of it is that confession then made will be too late to benefit the wrongdoer or to save others from deception. It only testifies that his condemnation is just. . . . You may now close the book of your remembrance in order to escape confessing your sins, but when the judgment shall sit and the books shall be opened, you cannot close them. The recording angel has testified that which is true. All that you have tried to conceal and forget is registered, and will be read to you when it is too late for wrongs to be righted. . . . Unless your sins are canceled, they will testify against you at *that day.*[29]

The prophet Daniel was drawing very near to God when he was seeking Him with confession and humiliation of soul. He did not try to excuse himself or his people, but acknowledged the full extent of their transgression. In their behalf he confessed sins of which he himself was not guilty, and besought the mercy of God, that he might bring his brethren to see their sins. . . .

To all who seek Him with true repentance God gives the assurance: "I have blotted out, as a thick cloud, thy transgressions, and, as a cloud, thy sins: return unto me; for I have redeemed thee" (Isa. 44:22).[30]

FROM DEFEAT TO VICTORY

Confess your faults one to another, and pray one for another, that ye may be healed. James 5:16.

All are liable to err, therefore the Word of God tells us plainly how to correct and heal these mistakes. None can say that he never makes a mistake, that he never sinned at all, but it is important to consider what disposition you make of these wrongs. The apostle Paul made grievous mistakes, all the time thinking that he was doing God service, but when the Spirit of the Lord set the matter before him in its true light, he confessed his wrongdoing, and afterward acknowledged the great mercy of God in forgiving his transgression. You also may have done wrong, thinking you were perfectly right, but when time reveals your error, then it is your duty to humble the heart and confess your sin. . . .

Whatever the character of your sin, confess it. If it is against God only, confess only to Him. If you have wronged or offended others, confess also to them, and the blessing of the Lord will rest upon you. In this way you die to self, and Christ is formed within. . . .

When, under the temptations of Satan, men fall into error, and their words and deportment are not Christlike, they may not realize their condition, because sin is deceptive and tends to deaden the moral perceptions. But through self-examination, searching of the Scriptures, and humble prayer, they will, by the aid of the Holy Spirit, be enabled to see their mistake. If they then confess their sins and turn from them, the tempter will not appear to them as an angel of light, but as a deceiver. . . .

Those who acknowledge reproof and correction as from God, and are thus enabled to see and correct their errors, are learning precious lessons, even from their mistakes. Their apparent defeat is turned into victory. They stand, trusting not to their own strength, but to the strength of God. They have earnestness, zeal, and affection, united with humility and regulated by the precepts of God's Word. . . . They walk not stumblingly, but safely, in a path where the light of heaven shines.[31]

A STRONG DEFENSE AGAINST TEMPTATION

For in that he himself hath suffered being tempted, he is able to succour them that are tempted. Heb. 2:18.

Our Redeemer perfectly understood the wants of humanity. He who condescended to take upon Himself man's nature was acquainted with man's weakness. Christ lived as our example. He was tempted in all points as we are, that He might know how to succor all who should be tempted. He has trodden the path of life before us and endured the severest tests in our behalf. He was a man of sorrows and acquainted with grief. . . .

Christ took upon Himself our infirmities, and in the weakness of humanity He needed to seek strength from His Father. He was often to be found in earnest prayer, in the grove, by the lakeside, and in the mountains. He has enjoined upon us to watch and pray. . . . Without a deep sense of our need of help from God there will be but little earnest, heartfelt prayer for divine aid. Our hearts are deceitful, our foes many and vigilant. If we neglect to fortify a single weak point in our character, Satan will assail us at that point with his temptations. He is constantly plotting the ruin of the soul, and he will take every advantage of our careless security.

Christ came to our world to engage in singlehanded combat with this enemy of man, and thus to wrest the race from Satan's grasp. In the accomplishment of this object He withheld not His own life. And now, in the strength that Christ will give, man must stand for himself, a faithful sentinel against the wily, plotting foe. Says the great apostle, "Walk circumspectly"—guard every avenue of the soul, look constantly to Jesus, the true and perfect Pattern, and seek to imitate His example, not in one or two points merely, but in all things. We shall then be prepared for any and every emergency. . . . He whose mind loves to dwell upon God has a strong defense. He will be quick to perceive the dangers that threaten his spiritual life, and a sense of danger will lead him to call upon God for help and protection.[32]

HOW TO GET RID OF GUILT

Who is a God like unto thee, that pardoneth iniquity, and passeth by the transgression of the remnant of his heritage? he retaineth not his anger for ever, because he delighteth in mercy. Micah 7:18.

I am glad indeed that our feelings are no evidence that we are not children of God. The enemy will tempt you to think that you have done things that have separated you from God, and that He no longer loves you, but our Lord loves us still. . . .

Look away from yourself to the perfection of Christ. We cannot manufacture a righteousness for ourselves. Christ has in His hands the pure robes of righteousness, and He will put them upon us. He will speak sweet words of forgiveness and promise. He presents to our thirsty souls fountains of living water whereby we may be refreshed. He bids us come unto Him with all our burdens, all our griefs, and He says we shall find rest. . . .

Jesus sees the guilt of the past, and speaks pardon, and we must not dishonor Him by doubting His love. This feeling of guiltiness must be laid at the foot of the cross of Calvary. The sense of sinfulness has poisoned the springs of life and of true happiness. Now Jesus says, "Lay it all on Me. I will take your sins; I will give you peace. Banish no longer your self-respect, for I have bought you with the price of My own blood. You are Mine. Your weakened will I will strengthen; your remorse for sin I will remove." Then turn your grateful heart, trembling with uncertainty, to Him and lay hold on the hope set before you. God accepts your broken, contrite heart, and extends to you free pardon. He offers to adopt you into His family, with His grace to help your weakness, and the dear Saviour will lead you on step by step, you placing your hand in His and letting Him guide you.

Search for the precious promises of God. If Satan thrusts threatenings before your mind, turn from them and cling to the promises, and let your soul be comforted by their brightness. The cloud is dark in itself, but when filled with the light it is turned to the brightness of gold, for the glory of God is upon it.[33]

241

UNDER THE DISCIPLINE OF GOD

Who can understand his errors? cleanse thou me from secret faults. Ps. 19:12.

We need to study the character of the motives that prompt us to action in the light of the law of God, in order that we may be made aware of our deficiencies. But while the human agent may see his sins, he is not to become discouraged, although he finds himself condemned by the precepts of righteousness. He is to see and to realize the sinfulness of sin, to repent, and to have faith in Christ as his personal Saviour.

It is never safe for us to feel that we are possessed of virtues, and that we may congratulate ourselves on our excellences of character and our present state of purity and piety. David often triumphed in God, and yet he dwelt much upon his own unworthiness and sinfulness. His conscience was not asleep or dead. "My sin," he cries, "is ever before me" (Ps. 51:3) . . . . As he saw the depths of deceit in his heart he was deeply disgusted with himself, and prayed that God would keep him back by His power from the presumptuous sins, and cleanse him from secret faults.

It is not safe for us to close our eyes and harden our conscience so that we shall not see or realize our sins. We need to cherish the instruction we have had in regard to the hateful character of sin, in order that we may truly confess and forsake our sins. "If we confess our sins, he is faithful and just to forgive us our sins, and to cleanse us from all unrighteousness" (1 John 1:9). Are you willing to be cleansed from all unrighteousness? . . .

If you are pressing forward and upward, seeking to attain new heights in education and in spiritual things, you will have discernment to understand that which is required of you. You will have the Holy Spirit to help all your infirmities. It is natural for the youth to love amusement . . . , but the natural inclinations must be overcome by putting the soul under discipline to God. . . . Walk not hesitatingly, but firmly in the strength and grace of Jesus Christ.[34]

THE SIN GOD CANNOT FORGIVE

Wherefore I say unto you, All manner of sin and blasphemy shall be forgiven unto men: but the blasphemy against the Holy Ghost shall not be forgiven unto men. Matt. 12:31.

"The blood of Jesus Christ his Son cleanseth us from all sin" (1 John 1:7). No matter how sinful a person has been, no matter what his position may be, if he will repent and believe, coming unto Christ and trusting Him as his personal Saviour, he may be saved unto the uttermost. . . .

I know the danger of those who refuse to walk in the light as God gives it. They bring upon themselves the terrible crisis of being left to follow their own ways, to do after their own judgment. The conscience becomes less and less impressible. The voice of God seems to become more and more distant, and the wrongdoer is left to his own infatuation. In stubbornness he resists every appeal, despises all counsel and advice, and turns from every provision made for his salvation. . . . The Spirit of God no longer exerts a restraining power over him, and the sentence is passed, "He is joined to idols; let him alone" (see Hosea 4:17). . . . This is the process through which the soul passes that rejects the working of the Holy Spirit. . . .

No one need look upon the sin against the Holy Ghost as something mysterious and indefinable. The sin against the Holy Ghost is the sin of persistent refusal to respond to the invitation to repent. If you refuse to believe in Jesus Christ as your personal Saviour . . . , you love the atmosphere that surrounded the first great apostate. You choose this atmosphere rather than the atmosphere that surrounds the Father and the Son, and God allows you to have your choice. But let no soul be discouraged by this presentation of the matter. Let no one who is striving to do the will of the Master be cast down.[35]

Come with your whole heart to Jesus. Repent of your sins, make confession to God, forsake all iniquity, and you may appropriate to yourself all His promises. "Look unto me, and be ye saved" (Isa. 45:22) is His gracious invitation.[36]

TRIFLING WITH GOD'S SPIRIT

And grieve not the holy Spirit of God, whereby ye are sealed unto the day of redemption. Eph. 4:30.

When the Lord presents evidence upon evidence and gives light upon light, why is it that souls hesitate to walk in the light? . . . By every hesitation and delay, we place ourselves where it is more and more difficult for us to accept the light of heaven, and at last it seems impossible to be impressed by admonitions and warnings. The sinner says, more and more easily, "Go thy way for this time; when I have a convenient season, I will call for thee" (Acts 24:25). . . .

The person who is drawn again and again by his Redeemer, and who slights the warnings given, yields not to his convictions to repent, and heeds not when he is exhorted to seek pardon and grace, is in a perilous position. Jesus is drawing him, the Spirit is exerting His power upon him, urging him to surrender his will to the will of God; and when this invitation is unheeded, the Spirit is grieved away. The sinner chooses to remain in sin and impenitence, although he has evidence to encourage his faith, and more evidence would do no good. . . . There is another drawing to which he is responding, and that is the drawing of Satan. He yields obedience to the powers of darkness. This course is fatal, and leaves the soul in obstinate impenitence. This is the blasphemy that is most general among men, and it works in a most subtle way, until the sinner feels no remorse of conscience, no repentance, and consequently has no pardon. . . .

Those who resist the Spirit of God think that they will repent at some future day when they get ready to take a decided step toward reformation, but repentance will then be beyond their power. According to the light and privileges given will be the darkness of those who refuse to walk in the light while they have the light. . . .

Never, never, feel at liberty to trifle with the opportunities granted to you. Study the will of God; do not study how you can avoid keeping the commandments of God, but study rather how you may keep them in sincerity and truth and truly serve Him whose property you are.[37]

HOW TO RESIST SATAN

Submit yourselves therefore to God. Resist the devil, and he will flee from you. James 4:7.

Our work is to "resist the devil," not harbor his doubts; and if we do this, the promise is "he will flee from you."

But the question is often asked, How can I resist Satan? There is only one way by which you can do this, and that is by faith, taking Christ as your helper and pleading with Him for strength. When Satan suggests doubt to your soul, when he tells you that you are too unworthy, too sinful, to realize the blessing of God, present Christ before him as your Advocate and Saviour. Tell him you know that you are a sinner, but that Jesus came to seek and save that which was lost. He came "not to call the righteous, but sinners to repentance" (Mark 2:17).

Repeat His promises: "Him that cometh to me I will in no wise cast out" (John 6:37). . . . "Let him take hold of my strength, that he may make peace with me; and he shall make peace with me" (Isa. 27:5). "Whatsoever ye shall ask in prayer, believing, ye shall receive" (Matt. 21:22). Be simplehearted enough to believe these promises of God. When Satan comes to you, and tells you that because you are unhappy, perplexed, and troubled you are not a child of God, do not become discouraged for one moment, but gird up the loins of your mind. Let your heart repose in God. He has promised that if you come to Him, you shall find rest to your soul; and if you have done this, rest assured that He will fulfill His word in you. . . .

Many pass long years in darkness and doubt because they do not feel as they desire. But feeling has nothing to do with faith. That faith which works by love and purifies the soul is not a matter of impulse. It ventures out upon the promises of God, firmly believing that what He has said, He is able also to perform. Our souls may be trained to believe, taught to rely upon the Word of God. That Word declares that "the just shall live by faith" (Rom. 1:17), not by feeling.[38]

DRAWING NIGH TO GOD

Draw nigh to God, and he will draw nigh to you. James 4:8.

We should seek to understand what it means to draw nigh to God. We are to come near to Him, not to stand a great way off, for in that case we shall not be able to feel the influence of His divine Spirit. Those who came into the presence of Christ, drawing nigh to Him, could more readily breathe in the atmosphere that surrounded Him, catch His spirit, and be impressed with His lessons. We are engaged in a serious, solemn work, and we should seek to be in that humble position, to have that teachable spirit, that the Lord can impress our hearts, and that we may feel His drawing power. We never draw nigh to God but that He is drawing us.[39]

God has angels whose whole work is to draw those who shall be heirs of salvation. Whenever one takes a step toward Jesus, Jesus is taking steps toward him. The angels' work is to keep back the powers of Satan.[40]

Those who are ever pressing a little closer to the world, and becoming more like them in feelings, in plans, in ideas, have left a space between them and the Saviour, and Satan has pressed his way into this space, and low, worldly tainted, selfish plans become interwoven with their experience.[41]

If we draw nigh to God, we shall draw nigh to one another. We cannot draw nigh to the same cross without coming into unity of spirit. Christ prayed that His disciples should be one as He and the Father are one. We should seek to be one in spirit and in understanding. We should seek to be one that God may be glorified in us as He was glorified in the Son, and God will love us as He loves His Son.[42]

God loves you. He does not wish to draw you nigh to Him to hurt you, oh, no; but to comfort you, to pour in the oil of rejoicing, to heal the wounds that sin has made, to bind up where Satan has bruised. He wants to give you the garments of praise for the spirit of heaviness.[43]

NO EXCUSE FOR FAILURE

We know that whosoever is born of God sinneth not; but he that is begotten of God keepeth himself, and that wicked one toucheth him not. 1 John 5:18.

Many fail to recognize the claims that God has upon them. They profess to be sons and daughters of God, but they do not behave as children of God. They argue that their evil habits and customs which they followed when they served under the black banner of the prince of darkness must be excused on the ground of their weakness, while they claim that "it is their way." . . . Their objectionable hereditary traits of character they choose to retain as idols.

When a soul is truly converted, old habits and natural evil besetments are done away in Christ Jesus and all things become new. Among those who profess to be servants of Christ an earnest purpose should be cultivated, such as Daniel manifested in the courts of Babylon. He knew that God was his strength and his shield, his front guard and his rear guard. Amid the corruptions that surrounded him in the courts of Babylon he kept himself free from those sights and sounds which would allure him and draw him into temptation. When his duties required that he be present at scenes of revelry, intemperance, and basest idolatry, he cultivated the habit of silent prayer, and thus he was kept by the power of God. To have the mind uplifted to God will be a benefit in all times and in all places. . . .

Let the soul cultivate the habit of contemplating the world's Redeemer. . . . Help has been laid upon One that is mighty. Jesus has given His life, that every soul might have abundant help in Him. . . .

Will you who read these words resolve that you will never again seek to excuse your defects of character by saying, "It is my way"? Let no one declare, "I cannot change my natural habits and tendencies." The truth must be admitted into the soul, and it will work the sanctification of the character. It will refine and elevate the life, and fit you for an entrance into the mansions which Jesus has gone to prepare for those who love Him.[44]

BATTLEFIELD OF THE SOUL

As for me, thou upholdest me in mine integrity, and settest me before thy face for ever. Ps. 41:12.

Some regard sin as altogether so light a matter that they have no defense against its indulgence or consequence. . . . With some . . . , religion is purely a thing of feeling. You will see a fair show of fervor and devotedness for a time, but soon a change comes. . . . They want a sip of the pleasure of excitement—the ballroom, the dance, and the show. . . .

If you suppose for a moment that God will treat sin lightly or make provisions or exemptions so that you can go on in committing sin, and the soul suffer no penalty for thus doing, it is a terrible delusion of Satan. Any willful violation of the righteous law of Jehovah exposes your soul to the full assaults of Satan. When you lose your conscious integrity your soul becomes a battlefield for Satan. You have doubts and fears enough to paralyze your energies and drive you to discouragement. The favor of God is gone. Some . . . have tried to supply its place and seek compensation for the loss of the Holy Spirit's witness that you are a child of God, in worldly excitement in the society of worldlings. In short, you have plunged deeper into sin. . . .

Remember that temptation is not sin. Remember that however trying the circumstances in which a man may be placed, nothing can really weaken his soul so long as he does not yield to temptation but maintains his own integrity. The interests most vital to you individually are in your own keeping. No one can damage them without your consent. All the satanic legions cannot injure you unless you open your soul to the arrows of Satan. As long as you are firm to do right, your ruin can never take place. If there is not pollution of mind in yourself, all the surrounding pollution cannot taint and defile you.

Eternal life is worth everything to us or it is worth nothing. Those only who put forth persevering effort and untiring zeal with intense desire proportionate to the object they are in pursuit of will gain that life that measures with the life of God.[45]

248

THE ONLY PATH OF SAFETY

And thine ears shall hear a word behind thee, saying, This is the way, walk ye in it, when ye turn to the right hand, and when ye turn to the left. Isa. 30:21.

I know that human beings suffer much because they step out of the path that God has chosen for them to follow. They walk in the sparks of the fire they have kindled themselves, and the sure result is affliction, unrest, and sorrow, which they might have avoided if they had submitted their will to God and had permitted Him to control their ways. God sees that it is necessary to oppose our will and our way and bring our human will into subjection.

Whatever path God chooses for us, whatever way He ordains for our feet, that is the only path of safety. We are daily to cherish a spirit of childlike submission, and pray that our eyes may be anointed with the heavenly eyesalve in order that we may discern the indications of the divine will, lest we become confused in our ideas, because our will seems to be all-controlling. With the eye of faith, with childlike submission as obedient children, we must look to God, to follow His guidance, and difficulties will clear away. The promise is, "I will instruct thee and teach thee . . . : I will guide thee with mine eye" (Ps. 32:8). . . .

If we come to God in a humble and teachable spirit, not with our plans all formed before we ask Him and shaped according to our own will, but in submission, in willingness to be taught, in faith, it is our privilege to claim the promise every hour of the day. We may distrust ourselves, and we need to guard against our own inclinations and strong tendencies lest we shall follow our mind and plans and think it is the way of the Lord. . . .

Our heavenly Father is our Ruler, and we must submit to His discipline. We are members of His family. He has a right to our service, and if one of the members of His family would persist in having his own way, persist in doing just that which he pleased, that spirit would bring about a disordered and perplexing state of things. We must not study to have our own way, but God's way and God's will.[46]

MY LORD AND I

Can two walk together, except they be agreed? Amos 3:3.

Enoch walked with God. He was of one mind with God. The prophet asks, "Can two walk together, except they be agreed?" If we are of one mind with God, our will will be swallowed up in God's will and we shall follow wherever God leads the way. As a loving child places his hand in that of his father, and walks with him in perfect trust whether it is dark or bright, so the sons and daughters of God are to walk with Jesus through joy or sorrow. . . .

The followers of Christ are to manifest to the world the characteristics of their Lord. They must not become careless or inattentive to their duty, or indifferent as to their influence, for they are to be representatives of Jesus in the earth. . . .

Those who do not walk in all faith and purity find the thought of coming into the presence of God a thought of terror. They do not love to think or speak of God. They say in heart and by their actions, "Depart from us, O God; we desire not the knowledge of thy ways." But through faith in Christ the true Christian knows the mind and will of God. He understands by a living experience something of the length and depth and breadth and height of the love of God that passeth knowledge.

The soul that loves God loves to draw strength from Him by constant communion with Him. When it becomes the habit of the soul to converse with God, the power of the evil one is broken, for Satan cannot abide near the soul that draws nigh unto God. If Christ is your companion, you will not cherish vain and impure thoughts; you will not indulge in trifling words that will grieve Him who has come to be the sanctifier of your soul. . . .

Those who are sanctified through the truth are living recommendations of its power, and representatives of their risen Lord. The religion of Christ will refine the taste, sanctify the judgment, elevate, purify, and ennoble the soul, making the Christian more and more fit for the society of the heavenly angels.[1]

LISTEN TO GOD'S VOICE

The steps of a good man are ordered by the Lord: and he delighteth in his way. Ps. 37:23.

Young men and young women will often be brought into positions where they are uncertain what to do. Their inclination leads them in one direction, and the Holy Spirit of God draws them in another direction. Satan presses his temptation upon them and urges them to follow the inclinations of the natural heart. But those who desire to be true to Christ will listen to the voice that says, "This is the way, walk ye in it" (Isa. 30:21). They will decide to take the course of the righteous, although it is more difficult to pursue, more painful to follow, than the way of their own heart. . . .

We need to receive divine wisdom in the daily concerns of life in order that we may display sound judgment and choose the safe path because it is the right one. He who acts upon his own judgment will follow the inclination of the natural heart, but he whose mind is opened to the Word of God will prayerfully consider every way of his feet, so that he may honor God and keep the way of the Lord. He will remember that even Christ pleased not himself, and he will consider it a great privilege to follow in His steps. He will take his perplexities to God in prayer and ask the guidance of Him whose property he is. He will realize that he belongs to God—soul, body, mind, and strength. . . .

Let every youth train himself in practical lines, to trust the Lord and not to follow his own ways. "Trust in the Lord with all thine heart; and lean not unto thine own understanding. In all thy ways acknowledge him, and he shall direct thy paths. Be not wise in thine own eyes: fear the Lord, and depart from evil. . . . Happy is the man that findeth wisdom, and the man that getteth understanding. . . . She is more precious than rubies: and all the things thou canst desire are not to be compared unto her. Length of days is in her right hand; and in her left hand riches and honour. Her ways are ways of pleasantness, and all her paths are peace" (Prov. 3:5-17).[2]

251

WATCH FOR GOD'S GUIDANCE

Behold, as the eyes of servants look unto the hand of their masters, and as the eyes of a maiden unto the hand of her mistress; so our eyes wait upon the Lord our God, until that he have mercy upon us. Ps. 123:2.

The children of God should cultivate a keen sensitiveness to sin. . . . It is one of Satan's most successful devices to lead men to the commission of little sins, to blind the mind to the danger of little indulgences, little digressions from the plainly stated requirements of God. Many who would shrink with horror from some great transgression are led to look upon sin in little matters as of trifling consequence. But these little sins eat out the life of godliness in the soul. . . .

God requires us to prove our loyalty to Him by unquestioning obedience. In deciding upon any course we should not ask merely whether we can see harm to result from it, but whether it is contrary to the will of God. We must learn to distrust self and to rely wholly upon God for guidance and support, for a knowledge of His will, and for strength to perform it. We must be much in communion with God. Prayer in secret, prayer while the hands are engaged in labor, prayer while walking by the way, prayer in the night season, the heart's desires ever ascending to God—this is our only safety. In this manner Enoch walked with God. In this manner our Exemplar obtained strength to tread the thorny path from Nazareth to Calvary.

Christ the sinless One, upon whom the Holy Spirit was bestowed without measure, constantly acknowledged His dependence upon God and sought fresh supplies from the Source of strength and wisdom. How much more should finite, erring man feel his need of help from God every hour and every moment. How carefully should he follow the leading Hand, how carefully treasure every word that has been given for his guidance and instruction! "As the eyes of servants look unto the hand of their masters, and as the eyes of a maiden unto the hand of her mistress," so should our eyes be upon the Lord our God. His commands should be received with implicit faith, and obeyed with cheerful exactness.[3]

THE MARCH TO VICTORY

But thanks be to God, which giveth us the victory through our Lord Jesus Christ. 1 Cor. 15:57.

Nothing can be more helpless, nothing can be more dependent, than the soul that feels its nothingness and relies wholly upon the merits of the blood of a crucified and risen Saviour. The Christian life is a life of warfare, of continual conflict. It is a battle and a march. But every act of obedience to Christ, every act of self-denial for His sake, every trial well endured, every victory gained over temptation, is a step in the march to the glory of final victory.

If we take Christ for our guide, He will lead us safely along the narrow way. The road may be rough and thorny; the ascent may be steep and dangerous; there may be pitfalls upon the right hand and upon the left; we may have to endure toil in our journey; when weary, when longing for rest, we may have to toil on; when faint, we may have to fight; when discouraged, we may be called upon to hope; but with Christ as our Guide we shall not lose the path to immortal life, we shall not fail to reach the desired haven at last.

Christ Himself has trod the rough pathway before us and has smoothed the path for our feet. The narrow path of holiness, the way cast up for the ransomed of the Lord to walk in, is illuminated by Him who is the light of the world. As we follow in His steps, His light will shine upon us, and as we reflect the light borrowed from the glory of Christ, the path will grow brighter and brighter unto the perfect day.

We may think it pleasant at first to follow pride and worldly ambition, but the end is pain and sorrow. Selfish plans may present flattering promises and hold out the hope of enjoyment, but we shall find that our happiness is poisoned and our life embittered by hopes that center in self. In following Christ we are safe, for He will not suffer the powers of darkness to hurt one hair of our heads. He will keep that which is committed to His trust, and we shall be more than conquerors through Him that loved us.[4]

THOSE FIRST DANGEROUS STEPS

Take heed, brethren, lest there be in any of you an evil heart of unbelief, in departing from the living God. Heb. 3:12.

When the Redeemer of the world walked among men, many who identified themselves with Him as His disciples afterward forsook Him and became His bitterest enemies. The Saviour tested their faith and developed the real characters of the most ardent believers by applying spiritual truths to their hearts. . . .

They must be Christlike, meek and lowly of heart, self-denying, self-sacrificing; they must walk in the narrow path trodden by the Man of Calvary if they would share in the gift of life and the glory of heaven. But the test was too great. They walked no more with Him. They could not hear the saying nor comprehend the nature of the truth He taught. . . .

The work of apostasy begins in some secret rebellion of the heart against the requirements of God's law. Unholy desires, unlawful ambitions, are cherished and indulged, and unbelief and darkness separate the soul from God. If we do not overcome these evils, they will overcome us. Men who have long been advancing in the path of truth will be tested with trial and temptation. Those who listen to the suggestions of Satan and swerve from their integrity begin the downward path, and some masterful temptation hastens them on in the way of apostasy, till their descent is marked and rapid. . . .

We need to be constantly on our guard, to watch and pray lest we enter into temptation. The indulgence of spiritual pride, of unholy desires, of evil thoughts, of anything that separates us from an intimate and sacred association with Jesus imperils our souls. . . . If the thought of apostasy is grievous to you, and you do not desire to become the enemies of the truth, the accusers of the brethren, then "abhor that which is evil; cleave to that which is good" (Rom. 12:9), and believe in Him who is "able to keep you from falling, and to present you faultless before the presence of his glory with exceeding joy" (Jude 24).[5]

THE DECEITFULNESS OF SIN

*But exhort one another daily, while it is called To day; lest any
of you be hardened through the deceitfulness of sin. Heb. 3:13.*

"The wages of sin is death" (Rom. 6:23). Sin, however small it may
be esteemed, can be persisted in only at the cost of eternal life. . . .

Adam and Eve persuaded themselves that in so small a matter as
eating of the forbidden fruit there could not result such terrible consequences as God had declared. But this small matter was sin, the
transgression of God's immutable and holy law, and it opened the
floodgates of death and untold woe upon our world. Age after age
there has gone up from our earth a continual cry of mourning, and
the whole creation groaneth and travaileth together in pain as a consequence of man's disobedience. Heaven itself has felt the effects of
his rebellion against God. Calvary stands as a memorial of the amazing sacrifice required as a propitiation for the transgression of the divine law. Let us not esteem sin as a trivial thing. Are not the hands
and feet and side of the Son of the infinite God to bear an eternal
testimony before the universe of its untold malignity and curse?

O that a right impression might be made upon the minds of
young and old in regard to the exceeding sinfulness of sin! . . .

God is not deceived by appearances of piety. He makes no mistake in His estimation of character. Men may be deceived by those
who are corrupt in heart, but God pierces all disguises and reads the
inner life. The moral worth of every soul is weighed in the balance
of the heavenly sanctuary. Shall not these solemn thoughts have an
influence upon us, that we may cease to do evil and learn to do well?
There is nothing gained by a life of sin but hopeless despair. . . .

Let faith lay hold on the promises of God. Jesus is mighty to save
His people from their sins. Light from Heaven has illumined our
pathway. Sin has been revealed to us by the Word and the Spirit of
truth, that we may not be found transgressors of the divine precepts,
and there is no opportunity to plead the excuse of ignorance. The
command is "Depart from iniquity" (2 Tim. 2:19).[6]

THE CONFLICT IS FOR US

To him that overcometh will I grant to sit with me in my throne, even as I also overcame, and am set down with my Father in his throne. Rev. 3:21.

These are the words of our substitute and surety. He who is the divine Head of the church, the mightiest of conquerors, would point His followers to His life, His toils, His self-denials, His struggles and sufferings, through contempt, through rejection, ridicule, scorn, insult, mockery, falsehood, up the path of Calvary to the scene of the crucifixion, that they might be encouraged to press on toward the mark for the prize and reward of the overcomer.[7]

The plan of salvation is not appreciated as it should be. It is not discerned or comprehended. It is made altogether a cheap affair, whereas to unite the human with the divine required an exertion of Omnipotence. . . . Christ, by clothing His divinity with humanity, elevates humanity in the scale of moral value to an infinite worth. But what a condescension on the part of God and on the part of His only begotten Son, who was equal with the Father! . . .

So great has been the spiritual blindness of men that they have sought to make of none effect the Word of God. They have declared by their traditions that the great plan of redemption was devised in order to abolish and make of none effect the law of God, when Calvary is the mighty argument that proves the immutability of the precepts of Jehovah. . . . The state of the character must be compared with the great moral standard of righteousness. There must be a searching out of the peculiar sins which have been offensive to God, which have dishonored His name and quenched the light of His Spirit and killed the first love from the soul. . . .

Victory is assured through faith and obedience. . . . The work of overcoming is not restricted to the age of the martyrs. The conflict is for us, in these days of subtle temptation to worldliness, to self-security, to indulgence of pride, covetousness, false doctrines, and immorality of life. . . . Shall we stand before the proving of God?[8]

TRUST IN TIME OF TRIAL

And we know that all things work together for good to them that love God, to them who are the called according to his purpose. Rom. 8:28.

The Christian's hope does not rest upon the sandy foundation of feeling. Those who act from principle will behold the glory of God beyond the shadows, and rest upon the sure word of promise. They will not be deterred from honoring God however dark the way may seem. Adversity and trial will only give them an opportunity to show the sincerity of their faith and love. When depression settles upon the soul, it is no evidence that God has changed. He is "the same yesterday, and to day, and for ever" (Heb. 13:8). You are sure of the favor of God when you are sensible of the beams of the Sun of Righteousness; but if the clouds sweep over your soul, you must not feel that you are forsaken. Your faith must pierce the gloom. . . . The riches of the grace of Christ must be kept before the mind. Treasure up the lessons that His love provides. Let your faith be like Job's, that you may declare, "Though he slay me, yet will I trust in him" (Job 13:15). Lay hold on the promises of your heavenly Father and remember His former dealing with you and with His servants, for "all things work together for good to them that love God."

The most trying experiences in the Christian's life may be the most blessed. The special providences of the dark hours may encourage the soul in future attacks of Satan, and equip the servant of God to stand in fiery trials. The trial of your faith is more precious than gold. You must have that abiding confidence in God that is not disturbed by the temptations and arguments of the deceiver. Take the Lord at His word. . . .

It is faith that familiarizes the soul with the existence and presence of God, and when we live with an eye single to His glory we discern more and more the beauty of His character. Our souls become strong in spiritual power, for we are breathing the atmosphere of heaven and realizing that God is at our right hand. . . . We should live as in the presence of the Infinite One.[9]

AND JESUS PRAYED

And it came to pass in those days, that he went out into a mountain to pray, and continued all night in prayer to God. Luke 6:12.

The Majesty of heaven, while engaged in His earthly ministry, was often in earnest prayer. Frequently He spent the entire night thus. His spirit was sorrowful as He felt the power of the darkness of this world, and He left the busy city and the noisy throng to seek a retired place for intercession with His Father. The Mount of Olives was the favorite resort of the Son of God. Frequently, after the multitude had left Him for the retirement of the night, He rested not, though weary with the labors of the day. . . . While the city was hushed in silence and His disciples had retired to obtain refreshment in sleep, His divine pleadings were ascending to His Father from the Mount of Olives, that His disciples might be kept from the evil influences which they would daily encounter in the world, and that His own soul might be strengthened and braced for the duties and trials of the coming day. All night, while His followers were sleeping, was their divine Teacher praying, while the dew and frost of night fell upon His bowed head. . . .

The example of Christ is left on record for His followers. Jesus was Himself a source of blessing and strength. He could heal the sick and raise the dead; He commanded even the tempests, and they obeyed Him; He was unsullied with corruption, a stranger to sin; yet He endured agony which required help and support from His Father, and He prayed often with strong crying and tears. He prayed for His disciples and for Himself, thus identifying Himself with the needs, the weaknesses, and the failings which are common to humanity. He was a mighty petitioner, not possessing the passions of our human, fallen natures, but compassed with like infirmities, tempted in all points even as we are. . . .

Christ, our Example, turned to His Father in these hours of distress. He came to earth that He might provide a way whereby we could find grace and strength to help in every time of need by following His example in frequent, earnest prayer.[10]

"COME YE YOURSELVES APART"

Wait on the Lord: be of good courage, and he shall strengthen thine heart: wait, I say, on the Lord. Ps. 27:14.

No other life was ever so crowded with labor and responsibility as was that of Jesus, yet how often He was found in prayer! How constant was His communion with God! . . . As one with us, a sharer in our needs and weaknesses, He was wholly dependent upon God, and in the secret place of prayer He sought divine strength that He might go forth braced for duty and trial. In a world of sin Jesus endured struggles and torture of soul. In communion with God He could unburden the sorrows that were crushing Him. . . .

In Christ the cry of humanity reached the Father of infinite pity. As a man He supplicated the throne of God till His humanity was charged with a heavenly current that should connect humanity with divinity. Through continual communion He received life from God, that He might impart life to the world. His experience is to be ours. "Come ye yourselves apart" (Mark 6:31), He bids us. If we would give heed to His Word we should be stronger and more useful. . . . If today we would take time to go to Jesus and tell Him our needs we should not be disappointed; He would be at our right hand to help us. . . .

In all who are under the training of God is to be revealed a life that is not in harmony with the world, its customs, or its practices, and everyone needs to have a personal experience in obtaining a knowledge of the will of God. We must individually hear Him speaking to the heart. When every other voice is hushed, and in quietness we wait before Him, the silence of the soul makes more distinct the voice of God. He bids us, "Be still, and know that I am God" (Ps. 46:10). Here alone can true rest be found. And this is the effectual preparation for all who labor for God. Amid the hurrying throng and the strain of life's intense activities, the soul that is thus refreshed will be surrounded with an atmosphere of light and peace. The life will breathe out fragrance and will reveal a divine power that will reach men's hearts.[11]

ACCEPTABLE PRAYER

And it came to pass, that, as he was praying in a certain place, when he ceased, one of his disciples said unto him, Lord, teach us to pray, as John also taught his disciples. Luke 11:1.

Jesus taught His disciples to pray, and He often urged upon them the necessity of prayer. He did not bid them to study books to learn a form of prayer. They were not to offer prayer to men, but to make their requests known to God. He taught them that the prayer which God accepts is the simple, earnest petition from a soul that feels its need. . . .

God invites us to come to Him with our burden of guilt and our heart sorrows. Sin fills us with fear of God. When we have sinned we try to hide ourselves from Him. But whatever our sin, God bids us come unto Him through Jesus Christ. It is only by taking our sins to God that we can be freed from them. Cain, under the rebuke of God, acknowledged his guilt in killing Abel, but he fled away from God, as if he could thus escape from his sin. Had he fled to God with his burden of guilt he would have been forgiven. The prodigal son, realizing his guilt and wretchedness, said, "I will arise and go to my father" (Luke 15:18). He confessed his sin and was taken back to his father's heart.

If we would offer acceptable prayer, there is a work to be done in confessing our sins to one another. If I have sinned against my neighbor in word or action I should make confession to him. If he has wronged me he should confess to me. So far as is possible the one who has wronged another is to make restitution. Then in contrition he is to confess the sin to God, whose law has been transgressed. In sinning against our brother, we sin against God, and we must seek pardon from Him. Whatever our sin, if we but repent and believe in the atoning blood of Christ we shall be pardoned. . . . We have only one channel of approach to God. Our prayers can come to Him through one name only—that of the Lord Jesus, our advocate.[12]

Christ is represented as stooping from His throne and bending earthward to send help to every needy soul who asks Him in faith.[13]

THE MODEL PRAYER

After this manner therefore pray ye: Our Father which art in heaven, Hallowed be thy name. Thy kingdom come. Thy will be done in earth, as it is in heaven. Give us this day our daily bread. And forgive us our debts, as we forgive our debtors. And lead us not into temptation, but deliver us from evil: For thine is the kingdom, and the power, and the glory, for ever. Amen. Matt. 6:9-13.

*This morning my prayer to the Lord is for His rich grace. I never choose to begin a day without receiving special evidence that the Lord Jesus is my Helper, and that I have the rich grace that it is my privilege to receive.

In my morning devotions I have regarded it my privilege to close my petition with the prayer that Christ taught to His disciples. There is so much that I really must have to meet the needs of my own case that I sometimes fear that I shall ask amiss; but when in sincerity I offer the model prayer that Christ gave to His disciples I cannot but feel that in these few words all my needs are comprehended. This I offer after I have presented my special private prayer. If with heart and mind and soul I repeat the Lord's prayer, then I can go forth in peace to my work, knowing that I have not asked amiss. . . .

The scribes and the Pharisees often offered their prayers in the market places and in the streets of the cities. Christ called them hypocrites. In every age men have prayed that they may be seen of men. . . . When Christ sees in His disciples errors that are liable to lead them astray, He always instructs them in the right way. He does not give an admonition without also giving an instructive lesson showing how to remedy the error. After instructing His disciples not to use vain repetitions in their prayers, in kindness and mercy He gave them a short sample prayer in order that they might know how to avoid imitating the prayers of the Pharisees. In giving this prayer, He knew that He was helping human infirmity by framing into words that which comprehends every human need. "We know not what we should pray for as we ought," but Christ's instruction to us is clear and definite.[14]

*Diary entry, Aug. 2, 1902.

WHAT IS GOD LIKE?

For the mountains shall depart, and the hills be removed; but my kindness shall not depart from thee, neither shall the covenant of my peace be removed, saith the Lord that hath mercy on thee. Isa. 54:10.

We are not to think of God only as a judge and to forget Him as our loving Father. Nothing can do our souls greater harm than this, for our whole spiritual life will be molded by our conceptions of God's character. . . .

Now let us improve the precious opportunities to become acquainted with our heavenly Father, who "so loved the world, that he gave his only begotten Son, that whosoever believeth in him should not perish. . . ." Wondrous love that God, the infinite God, has made it our privilege to approach Him by the name of *Father!* No earthly parent could plead more earnestly with an erring child than He who made us pleads with the transgressor. No human, loving interest has ever followed the impenitent with such tender invitations. . . .

His word is pledged. The mountains shall depart, and the hills be removed, but His kindness shall not depart from His people, neither shall the covenant of His peace be removed. His voice is heard, "I have loved thee with an everlasting love" (Jer. 31:3). "With everlasting kindness will I have mercy on thee" (Isa. 54:8). How amazing is this love, that God condescends to remove all cause for doubt and questioning from human fears and weakness and takes hold of the trembling hand reached up to Him in faith; and He helps us to trust Him by multiplied assurances and securities. He has made us a binding agreement upon condition of our obedience, and He comes to meet us in our own understanding of things. We think that a pledge or promise from our fellow men, if recorded, still needs a guarantee. Jesus has met all these peculiar fears, and He has confirmed His promise with an oath: "Wherein God, willing more abundantly to shew unto the heirs of promise the immutability of his counsel, confirmed it by an oath: . . ." What more could our Lord do to strengthen our faith in His promises?[15]

A TENDER, MERCIFUL FATHER

Like as a father pitieth his children, so the Lord pitieth them that fear him. Ps. 103:13.

Our God should be regarded as a tender, merciful father. The service of God should not be looked upon as a heart-saddening, distressing exercise. It should be a pleasure to worship the Lord and to take part in His work. As the people of God meditate upon the plan of salvation their hearts will be melted in love and gratitude. . . .

God would not have His children, for whom so great a salvation has been provided, act as though He were a hard, exacting taskmaster. He is their best friend, and when they worship Him, He expects to be with them to bless and comfort them and fill their hearts with joy and love. The Lord desires His children to take comfort in His service, and to find more pleasure than hardship in His work. The Lord desires that those who come to worship Him shall carry away with them precious thoughts of His care and love that they may be cheered in all the employments of daily life, that they may have grace to deal honestly and faithfully in all things. . . .

We dishonor God when we think of Him only as a judge ready to pass sentence upon us, and forget that He is a loving Father. The whole spiritual life is molded by our conceptions of God, and if we cherish erroneous views of His character, our souls will sustain injury. We should see in God one who yearns toward the children of men, longing to do them good. . . . All through the Scriptures, God is represented as one who calls, woos by His tender love, the hearts of His erring children. No earthly parent could be as patient with the faults and mistakes of their children as is God with those He seeks to save. No one could plead more tenderly with the transgressor. No human lips ever poured out more tender entreaty to the wanderer than does He. O shall we not love God, and show our love by humble obedience? Let us have a care for our thoughts, our experiences, our attitude toward God, for all His promises are but the breathings of unutterable love.[16]

263

THE TERMS OF OUR SALVATION

Whatsoever ye shall ask the Father in my name, he will give it you. Hitherto have ye asked nothing in my name: ask, and ye shall receive, that your joy may be full. John 16:23, 24.

The disciples of Christ who were with Him from day to day did not comprehend His mission. . . . They were unacquainted with His unlimited resources and power. Although they had witnessed His miracles they did not discern His relationship to the Father. Just before His death He said to them, "Hitherto have ye asked nothing in my name." In simple language Jesus explained to them that the secret of their success would be in asking the Father for strength and grace in His name. He would be present before the face of the Father to make request in their behalf. . . .

We need to become better acquainted with the terms upon which salvation will be ours, and better understand the relation which Christ sustains to us and to the Father. He has pledged Himself to honor His Son's name as we present it at the throne of grace. We should consider the great sacrifice that was made in our behalf to purchase for us the robe of righteousness woven in the loom of heaven. He has invited us to the wedding feast, and has provided for every one of us the wedding garment. The robe of righteousness has been purchased at infinite cost, and how daring is the insult to Heaven when one presents himself as a candidate for entrance at the wedding feast when wearing his own citizen's dress of self-righteousness! How greatly he dishonors God, openly showing contempt for the sacrifice made on Calvary! . . .

No one will taste of the marriage supper of the Lamb who has not on a wedding garment. But John writes, ". . . He that overcometh, the same shall be clothed in white raiment; and I will not blot out his name out of the book of life, but I will confess his name before my Father, and before his angels." Then, before it is eternally too late, let each one go to the heavenly Merchantman for the white raiment, the eyesalve, the gold tried in the fire, and the oil of heavenly grace.[17]

THE POWER OF JESUS' NAME

Let us therefore come boldly unto the throne of grace, that we may obtain mercy, and find grace to help in time of need. Heb. 4:16.

Christ is our pattern, the perfect and holy example that has been given us to follow. We can never equal the Pattern, but we may imitate and resemble it according to our ability. When we fall, all helpless, suffering in consequence of our realization of the sinfulness of sin; when we humble ourselves before God, afflicting our souls by true repentance and contrition; when we offer our fervent prayers to God in the name of Christ; we shall as surely be received by the Father as we sincerely make a complete surrender of our all to God. We should realize in our inmost soul that all our efforts in and of ourselves will be utterly worthless, for it is only in the name and strength of the Conqueror that we shall be overcomers.

If we believe in the power of Jesus' name, and present our petitions to God in His name, we shall never be turned away. . . . Our help cometh from God, who holds all things in His own hands. Our peace is in the assurance that His love is exercised toward us. If faith grasps this assurance, we have gained all; if we lose this assurance, all is lost. When we surrender all we have and are to God and are placed in trying and dangerous positions, coming in contact with Satan, we should remember that we shall have victory in meeting the enemy in the name and power of the Conqueror. Every angel would be commissioned to come to our rescue when we thus depend upon Christ rather than that we should be permitted to be overcome.

But we need not expect to get the victory without suffering, for Jesus suffered in conquering for us. While we suffer in His name, while we are called upon to deny appetite, and to withdraw ourselves from lovers of pleasure, we should not murmur, but should rather rejoice that we are privileged in a very small degree to be partakers with Christ of the trial, the sacrifice, the self-denial, and the suffering that our Lord endured on our behalf that we might obtain eternal salvation.[18]

I PRAY FOR GUIDANCE

They that wait upon the Lord shall renew their strength; they shall mount up with wings as eagles; they shall run, and not be weary; and they shall walk, and not faint. Isa. 40:31.

Friday, Feb. 14, 1896. I awake at half past two, and seek the Lord, as is my practice, for wisdom and grace, mingling my prayers with thanksgiving for His tender, loving compassion toward us. The words of Isaiah 40:28-31 seem appropriate and impressed upon my mind . . .

My prayer is, Help me, O my heavenly Father, to trust wholly in Thy wisdom and not to lean to my own understanding. Guide Thou my pen and direct my speech that I shall not sin against Thee with voice or pen. I must have grace. I plead, Teach me Thy truth, that I shall not err from Thy way. O my Lord, I am weakness itself, but Thou art strength, fortitude, and courage to Thy people if they will only diligently make Thee their trust. . . .

Sabbath, Feb. 15, 1896. The Lord is good and merciful. I want my gratitude offering constantly ascending to God. I long to have a deeper sense of His goodness and of His changeless love. I long daily for the waters of life. . . . I must continually have my strength in God. My dependence must not waver. No human agency must come between my soul and my God. The Lord is our only hope. In Him I trust, and He will *never, no never,* fail me. He hath hitherto helped me when under great discouragement. . . .

I will thank the Lord and praise His holy name. I will praise the Lord that in Him I can trust at all times. He is the health of my countenance and my strong tower into which I can run and be safe. He understands my necessities and He will give me the light of His countenance that I may reflect light upon others. I will not fail nor be discouraged. I look to Thee, my heavenly Father, to give strength and grace. . . . I will praise the Lord at all times and not wait for a happy flight of feeling. Then praise the Lord, for He is good, and His mercies will attend me morning, noon, and night. A happy flight of feeling is not evidence; His Word is my assurance.[19]

THE CHRISTIAN'S SAFEGUARD

Praying always with all prayer and supplication in the Spirit, and watching thereunto with all perseverance and supplication for all saints. Eph. 6:18.

There is a feverish love of pleasure at this time, a fearful increase of licentiousness, a contempt for all authority. Not only worldlings but professed Christians also are governed by inclination rather than duty. The words of Christ are sounding down through the ages, "Watch and pray" (Matt. 26:41).[20]

Watchfulness and vigilance are needed now as never before in the history of the race. The eye must be turned off from beholding vanity. Lawlessness, the prevailing spirit of the age, must be met with a decided rebuke. Let none feel that they are in no danger. As long as Satan lives, his efforts will be constant and untiring to make the world as wicked as before the Flood and as licentious as were the inhabitants of Sodom and Gomorrah. The prayer may well be offered daily by those who have the fear of God before them, that He will preserve their hearts from evil desires and strengthen their souls to resist temptation. Those who in their self-confidence feel no need of watchfulness and unceasing prayer are near some humiliating fall. All who do not feel the importance of resolutely guarding their affections will be captivated by those who practice their arts to ensnare and lead astray the unwary. Men may have a knowledge of divine things and an ability to fill an important place in the work of God, yet, unless they cherish a simple faith in their Redeemer they will be ensnared and overcome by the enemy.

It is because the duties of watchfulness and prayer have been so sadly neglected that there is so great a lack of moral power. This is why so many who have a form of godliness bring forth no corresponding works. A careless indifference, a carnal security concerning religious duties and eternal things, prevails to an alarming extent. The Word of God exhorts us to be found "praying always . . . , and watching thereunto with all perseverance. . . ." Here is the Christian's safeguard, his protection amid the perils that surround his pathway.[21]

QUIET REST IN GOD

Be merciful unto me, O God, be merciful unto me: for my soul trusteth in thee: yea, in the shadow of thy wings will I make my refuge, until these calamities be overpast. Ps. 57:1.

I am so sorry that men who want to be obedient to God put so much confidence in human sympathy and human help which disappoint so often. But God, the living God, is unchangeable. He is the same kind, tender, pitiful, loving Saviour today, yesterday, and forever. Satan is now working with all his might, and leaving no means untried to unsettle minds because they see men of long experience make mistakes. But Jesus is faultless. . . . Make God your entire trust. Pray, pray, pray, pray in faith. Then trust the keeping of your soul to God. He will keep that which is committed to Him against that day. . . . Walk humbly with God. The Lord sees every sorrow, every grief, every trial that besets the human soul, and He knows how to apply the balm. . . .

In God you can do valiantly. Tell it to the Lord in prayer, talk it to the Lord by the way. "Thee I seek; Thee I will follow; Thee I will serve. Under the shadow of Thy wings will I abide. Command me as Thou wilt; I will obey Thy voice." Yield always to the heavenly guidance. When trials come, possess your soul in patience. Wait on the Lord and have one purpose in view, to seek the eternal good of all those with whom you are connected, holding fast your integrity in the strength of your God. He will redeem His promise. Your bread shall be provided; your water shall be sure. This means not only temporal bread and water but the bread and water of eternal life.

Stand in God. Work under the sweet influence of His grace. The truth of God sanctifying the heart of the believer guides his life. We may stand firmly and assuredly. If you make the face of clay your dependence you lean on a reed that has oft broken in your hand and will break. Trust fully, unwaveringly, in God. He is the wonderful Counselor, the Mighty God, the everlasting Father, the Prince of Peace. We may keep the conscience unsullied and in peace and quiet rest in God.[22]

FEEBLE EFFORTS NOT ENOUGH

Hear my cry, O God; attend unto my prayer. From the end of the earth will I cry unto thee, when my heart is overwhelmed: lead me to the rock that is higher than I. Ps. 61:1, 2.

When we are burdened, when we are pressed with temptation, when the feelings and desires of the natural heart are contending for the victory, we should offer up fervent, importunate prayer to our heavenly Father in the name of Christ, and this will bring Jesus to our help, so that through His all-powerful and efficacious name we may gain the victory and banish Satan from our side. But we should not flatter ourselves that we are safe while we make but feeble efforts in our own behalf. . . . "Strive [agonize] to enter in at the strait gate" (Luke 13:24).

Our danger does not arise from the opposition of the world, but it is found in the liability of our being in friendship with the world and imitating the example of those who love not God or His truth. The loss of earthly things for the truth's sake, the suffering of great inconvenience for loyalty to principle, does not place us in danger of losing our faith and hope; but we are in danger of suffering loss because of being deceived and overcome by the temptations of Satan. Trials will work for our good if we receive and bear them without murmuring, and will tend to separate us from the love of the world and will lead us to trust more fully in God.

There is help for us only in God. We should not flatter ourselves that we have any strength or wisdom of our own, for our strength is weakness, our judgment foolishness. Christ conquered the foe in our behalf because He pitied our weakness and knew that we would be overcome and would perish if He did not come to our help. He clothed His divinity with humanity, and thus was qualified to reach man with His human arm while with His divine arm He grasped the throne of the Infinite. The merits of Christ elevate and ennoble humanity, and through the name and grace of Christ it is possible for man to overcome the degradation caused by the Fall, and through the exalted, divine nature of Christ to be linked to the Infinite.[23]

FERVENT, EFFECTUAL PRAYER

The effectual fervent prayer of a righteous man availeth much.
James 5:16.

The sincere, humble prayer of the true worshiper ascends to heaven, and Jesus mingles with our lowly petitions the holy incense of His own merit. Through His righteousness we are accepted. Christ makes our prayers wholly efficacious through the savor of His righteousness. In these days of peril we need men who will wrestle with God as did Jacob and who, like Jacob, will prevail. Thank God that the world's Redeemer promised that if He went away He would send the Holy Spirit as His representative. Let us pray and grasp the rich promises of God, and then praise God that in proportion to our earnest, humble supplications the Holy Spirit will be appointed to meet our needs. If we seek God with all our heart we shall find Him, and obtain the fulfillment of the promise.[24]

Let those who love the Lord and His truth unite by two's and three's to seek places of retirement and pray for God's blessing upon the minister, who can hardly find time to pray because he is constantly engaged attending to so many requests, sitting in councils, answering inquiries, giving advice, writing important letters. Let the fervent, effectual prayer of the righteous ascend to God that the word spoken may be a message of truth to reach the hearts of the hearers, and that souls may thereby be won to Christ.[25]

In order to be a Christian it is not necessary for a man to have great talents. An earnest prayer offered from a contrite heart by one who desires to do the Master's will is of more value in God's sight than is eloquence of speech. The human agent may have no voice in legislative councils, he may not be permitted to deliberate in senates or vote in parliaments, yet he has access to God. The King of kings bends low to listen to the prayer coming from a humble, contrite heart. God hears every prayer that is offered with the incense of faith. The weakest child of God may exert an influence in harmony with the councils of heaven.[26]

DANIEL'S EXAMPLE OF PRAYER AND CONFESSION

And I set my face unto the Lord God, to seek by prayer and supplications, with fasting, and sackcloth, and ashes: and I prayed unto the Lord my God, and made my confession. Dan. 9:3, 4.

Daniel's example of prayer and confession is given for our instruction and encouragement. . . . Daniel knew that the appointed time for Israel's captivity was nearly ended, but he did not feel that because God had promised to deliver them, they themselves had no part to act. With fasting and contrition he sought the Lord, confessing his own sins and the sins of the people. . . .

Daniel makes no plea on the ground of his own goodness, but he says: "O my God, incline thine ear, and hear; open thine eyes, and behold our desolations, and the city which is called by thy name: for we do not present our supplications before thee for our righteousnesses, but for thy great mercies" (Dan. 9:18). His intensity of desire makes him earnest and fervent. He continues: "O Lord, hear; O Lord, forgive; O Lord, hearken and do; defer not, for thine own sake, O my God: for thy city and thy people are called by thy name." . . .

What a prayer was that which came forth from the lips of Daniel! What humbling of soul it reveals! The warmth of heavenly fire was recognized in the words that were going upward to God. Heaven responded to that prayer by sending its messenger to Daniel. In this our day, prayers offered in like manner will prevail with God. "The effectual fervent prayer of a righteous man availeth much" (James 5:16). As in ancient times, when prayer was offered, fire descended from heaven and consumed the sacrifice upon the altar, so in answer to our prayers, the heavenly fire will come into our souls. The light and power of the Holy Spirit will be ours. . . . That God who heard Daniel's prayer will hear ours when we come to Him in contrition. Our necessities are as urgent, our difficulties are as great, and we need to have the same intensity of purpose, and in faith roll our burden upon the great Burden Bearer. There is need for hearts to be as deeply moved in our time as in the time when Daniel prayed.[27]

THE PRECIOUSNESS OF SECRET PRAYER

Trust in him at all times; ye people, pour out your heart before him: God is a refuge for us. Ps. 62:8.

A deep sense of our need and a great desire for the things for which we ask must characterize our prayers, else they will not be heard. But we are not to become weary and cease our petitions because the answer is not immediately received. "The kingdom of heaven suffereth violence, and the violent take it by force" (Matt. 11:12). The violence here meant is a holy earnestness, such as Jacob manifested. We need not try to work ourselves up into an intense feeling, but calmly, persistently, we are to press our petitions at the throne of grace. Our work is to humble our souls before God, confessing our sins, and in faith drawing nigh unto God. . . . It is the design of God to reveal Himself in His providence and in His grace. The object of our prayers must be the glory of God, not the glorification of ourselves. . . .

God has honored us by showing how greatly He values us. We are bought with a price, even the precious blood of the Son of God. When His heritage shall conscientiously follow the Word of the Lord, His blessing will rest upon them in answer to their prayers. "Therefore also now, saith the Lord, turn ye even to me with all your heart, and with fasting, and with weeping, and with mourning: and rend your heart, and not your garments, and turn unto the Lord your God: for he is gracious and merciful, slow to anger, and of great kindness" (Joel 2:12, 13).[28]

In secret prayer the soul should be laid bare to the inspecting eye of God. . . . How precious is secret prayer—the soul communing with God! Secret prayer is to be heard only by the prayer-hearing God. No curious ear is to receive the burden of petitions. Calmly, yet fervently, the soul is to reach out after God; and sweet and abiding will be the influence emanating from Him who sees in secret, whose ear is open to the prayer arising from the heart. He who in simple faith holds communion with God will gather to himself divine rays of light to strengthen and sustain him in the conflict with Satan.[29]

PRAISE, LIKE CLEAR-FLOWING STREAMS

It is a good thing to give thanks unto the Lord, and to sing praises unto thy name, O most High: to shew forth thy lovingkindness in the morning, and thy faithfulness every night. Ps. 92:1, 2.

When the truth is appreciated, . . . we have a sense of the great mercy and loving-kindness of God. While we review not the dark chapters in our experience to complain, but the manifestations of His great mercy and unfailing love and power revealed in our deliverance, we will praise far more than complain. We will talk of the loving faithfulness of God, as the true, tender, compassionate Shepherd of His flock, which He has declared none shall pluck out of His hand. The language of the heart will not be selfish murmuring and repining, but praise, like clear-flowing streams, will come from God's truly believing ones. . . .

The Lord is full of resources. He has no lack of facilities. It is because of our lack of faith, our earthliness, our cheap talk, our unbelief, that dark shadows gather about us. . . .

The temple of God is opened in heaven, and the threshold is flushed with the glory that is for every church that will love God and keep His commandments. We need to study, to meditate, and to pray. Then we shall have spiritual eyesight to discern the inner courts of the celestial temple. We shall catch the themes of song and thanksgiving of the heavenly choir round about the throne. When Zion shall arise and shine, her light will be most penetrating, and precious songs of praise and thanksgiving will be heard in the assembly of the saints. Murmurings, complainings, and lamentations over little disappointments and difficulties will be lost sight of. As we apply the golden eyesalve we shall see the glories beyond. Faith will cut through the hellish shadow of Satan, and we shall see our Advocate offering up the incense of His own merits in our behalf. . . .

Let us take up the praise of God here below. Let us unite with the heavenly company above. Then we shall represent the truth as it is—a power to all who believe.[30]

A JUBILEE FOR JESUS?

And my tongue shall speak of thy righteousness and of thy praise all the day long. Ps. 35:28.

While I was in England, one day there was a great parade in the streets. It was the Queen's Jubilee. Everyone was talking about it. The shop windows were filled with her pictures, and all were extolling the queen of England. Could we have taken from the shop windows the pictures of the queen and the signs of her glory, and placed instead expressions of the glory and majesty of Jesus, would not the people have regarded us as religious fanatics? They would have thought that we were carrying religion too far. . . . But did not our Master lay aside His royal robes, His crown of glory? Did He not clothe His divinity with humanity, and come to our world to die man's sacrifice? Why should we not talk about it? Why should we not dwell on His matchless love?

O that our tongues might lose their paralysis, that we might speak forth His praise! O that the spiritual torpor which has come upon the souls of men might be removed, that we might discern the glory of God in the face of Jesus Christ! We are to be the representatives of our Lord upon earth. . . . He can communicate heaven's light through you to those who sit in darkness. You that have claimed to know the Lord, you who profess to have tasted and seen that the Lord is good, reveal it to those around you. Show forth the praises of Him who has called you out of darkness into His marvelous light. If men can make so much ado over the Queen's Jubilee, if they can manifest so much enthusiasm over a finite being, can we not speak to the glory of the Prince of Life, who is so soon to come in majesty to take His weary, worn followers to Himself; to unlock the prison bars of death, and set the captives free; to give His loved ones who sleep, a glorious immortality? Why cannot Christ be introduced into our conversation? We are almost home. Let us speak courage to the weary soldiers of the cross. . . . Let us tell the pilgrims and strangers of earth that we shall soon reach a better country, even a heavenly.[31]

SUFFERING FOR THE TRUTH'S SAKE

Remember the word that I said unto you, The servant is not greater than his lord. If they have persecuted me, they will also persecute you. John 15:20.

What will the human agent do to have the privilege of cooperating with God? Will he forsake all that he has rather than forsake Christ? . . . Will he suffer persecution for the truth's sake? Reproach and persecution have separated many souls from heaven, but never a soul from the love of Christ. Never yet did persecution drive the soul who was indeed a lover of Jesus Christ away from Him. The love of Jesus in the soul is all-absorbing, for that great love wherewith God hath loved us, revealed in giving Christ to us, is beyond a parallel. "God so loved the world, that he gave his only begotten Son." . . .

If we can bear persecution for His dear name's sake, His love becomes a ruling power in our hearts, for we have the assurance that nothing can separate us from the love of Christ. Never is the tempest-tried soul more dearly loved by his Saviour than when he is suffering reproach for the truth's sake. When for the truth's sake the believer stands at the bar of unrighteous tribunals, Christ stands by his side. All the reproaches that fall upon the human believer fall upon Christ in the person of His saints. "I will love him," said Christ, "and will manifest myself to him" (John 14:21). Christ is condemned over again in the person of His believing disciples. When for the truth's sake the believer is incarcerated in prison walls, Christ manifests Himself to him and ravishes his heart with His love. When he suffers death for the sake of Christ, Christ says to him, They may kill the body, but they cannot hurt the soul. "Be of good cheer; I have overcome the world" (John 16:33).[32]

The apostle says to us, ". . . If ye be reproached for the name of Christ, happy are ye; for the spirit of glory and of God resteth upon you: on their part he is evil spoken of, but on your part he is glorified." Ask yourself, "Is my Redeemer thus magnified in me before the universe of heaven, before the satanic agencies, and before the world?"[33]

STRENGTH THROUGH TRIAL

For thou, O God, hast proved us: thou hast tried us, as silver is tried. Ps. 66:10.

Untried character is not reliable. We are to be tried by temptation in order that we may learn to seek wisdom from God and to flee to the stronghold in time of trouble. He alone will be successful in resisting temptation who finds help and grace from God. Individually we stand as did our first parents—face to face with manifold temptations that solicit mind and heart. All heaven is watching with intense interest to see whether we will look unto Jesus and submit ourselves to His will, or whether in the temptation we shall follow the inclinations of the natural heart and the solicitations of the evil one.[34]

Let those who are perplexed with temptation go to God in prayer. . . . Persevere in prayer and watch thereunto without doubting, and the Holy Spirit will work in the human agent, bringing heart and mind into subjection to right principles.[35]

Those who through faith are kept by the power of God learn good and precious things. They experience the peace of Christ which passeth understanding. In resisting temptation you refuse to be confederate with Satan, and place yourselves under the banner of Jesus Christ. In the sight of heavenly intelligences you develop yourself as a conqueror. It is made manifest that you are a son of God. . . .

You represent Christ in true goodness of character, and understand what these words signify: "And the Word was made flesh, and dwelt among us, (and we beheld his glory, the glory as of the only begotten of the Father,) full of grace and truth. . . . And of his fulness have all we received, and grace for grace" (John 1:14-16). You receive grace, you develop grace; and as you reveal grace in your words, in your spirit and actions, God pours upon you a larger measure of grace. In proportion as you surrender yourselves to the working of the Holy Spirit you are supplied with heavenly grace. You are molded and fashioned a vessel unto honor, and become a channel through which God makes manifest His grace to the world.[36]

THE GLORIOUS FRUITS OF TRIAL

That the trial of your faith, being much more precious than of gold that perisheth, though it be tried with fire, might be found unto praise and honour and glory at the appearing of Jesus Christ. 1 Peter 1:7.

Let us believe in Jesus, trusting Him implicitly, although we may be tried as by fire. . . . We may love Christ more and increase our capacity for loving Him by contemplating and talking of His love. Cultivate the habit of talking with the Saviour when alone, when walking and working. Let gratitude and thanksgiving ascend to God because Jesus loves you and you love Jesus. . . .

The Lord Jesus gave Himself a sacrifice for us. He knows us and He knows just what we need. Trial lasts only for a season. Encourage your heart in faith. We must not look on trial as punishment. Christ is the sin bearer. He is our Redeemer, and He desires to purify us from all dross. He means to make us partakers of the divine nature, developing in us the peaceable fruits of righteousness. The very fact that we are called upon to endure trials proves that the Lord Jesus sees in us something very precious that He would have developed. If He saw nothing in us whereby we might glorify His name He would not spend time refining us. We do not take special pains to prune brambles. Christ does not cast valueless stones into His furnace. It is precious ore that He tests. He sees that the refining process will bring out the reflection of His own image. Be trustful, be hopeful, be strong in the Lord and in the power of His might. He loves you. Hear His words: "As many as I love, I rebuke and chasten" (Rev. 3:19). He has not passed you by as unworthy of a trial.

What is the result of this refining process? That ye may "be found unto praise and honour and glory at the appearing of Jesus Christ." O how precious to the soul is one word of commendation that comes from the Redeemer's lips! We may not understand all now, but the day is coming when we shall be more than satisfied, when we shall see as we are seen, and realize that trial has wrought out for us a far more exceeding and eternal weight of glory.[37]

WHY THESE AFFLICTIONS?

It is good for me that I have been afflicted; that I might learn thy statutes. Ps. 119:71.

We must not think when we are afflicted that the anger of the Lord is upon us. God brings us into trials in order that we may be drawn near to Him. The psalmist says, "Many are the afflictions of the righteous: but the Lord delivereth him out of them all" (Ps. 34:19). He does not desire us to be under a cloud. . . . He does not desire us to go in anguish of spirit. We are not to look at the thorns and the thistles in our experience. We are to go into the garden of God's Word and pluck the lilies and roses and the fragrant pinks of His promises. Those who look upon the difficulties in their experience will talk doubt and discouragement, for they do not behold Jesus, the Lamb of God, who taketh away the sins of the world.

We should keep our minds upon the love, the mercy, and the graciousness of our God. . . . It is no sign that Jesus has ceased to love us because we experience doubts and discouragements. Affliction comes to us in the providence of God in order that we may see that Christ is our helper, that in Him is love and consolation. We may receive grace whereby we may be overcomers and inherit the life that measures with the life of God. We must have such an experience that when affliction comes upon us we shall not depart from the faith. . . .

By the hand of faith grasp the promises of God and be upon vantage ground. Then you will be where Satan cannot come near and say, "God cannot help you, because you have sinned and you cannot claim the promises." The adversary desires to have us think that the way to life is so difficult that it will be impossible to reach the bliss of heaven. But God has placed us in circumstances where the very best of our natures may be developed and the highest faculties may be exercised. If we cultivate the good, the objectionable tendencies will not gain the supremacy, and at last we shall be accounted worthy to join the family above. If we desire to be saints above we must be saints upon the earth.[38]

BRING YOUR TROUBLES TO GOD

My brethren, count it all joy when ye fall into divers temptations; knowing this, that the trying of your faith worketh patience. But let patience have her perfect work, that ye may be perfect and entire, wanting nothing. James 1:2-4.

The Word does not say that we are to count it all joy when we fall under temptation, but when we fall into temptation. It is not necessary to fall under temptation, for temptation comes upon us for the trying of our faith. And the trying of our faith worketh patience, not fretfulness and murmuring. If we put our trust in Jesus, He will keep us at all times, and will be our strength and shield. We are to learn valuable lessons from our trials. Paul says, "We glory in tribulations also: knowing that tribulation worketh patience; and patience, experience; and experience, hope . . ." (Rom. 5:3-5).

Many seem to think that it is impossible not to fall under temptation, that they have no power to overcome, and they sin against God with their lips, talking discouragement and doubt instead of faith and courage. Christ was tempted in all points like as we are, yet without sin. He said, "The prince of this world cometh, and hath nothing in me" (John 14:30). What does this mean? It means that the prince of evil could find no vantage ground in Christ for his temptation. And so it may be with us. . . .

When we talk discouragement and gloom Satan listens with fiendish joy, for it pleases him to know that he has brought us into his bondage. Satan cannot read our thoughts, but he can see our actions, hear our words, and from his long knowledge of the human family he can shape his temptations to take advantage of our weak points of character. And how often do we let him into the secret of how he may obtain the victory over us![39]

We must learn to come to God in any and every emergency, as a child would come to its parents. . . . Don't go to others with your trials and temptations; God alone can help you. If you fulfill the conditions of God's promises, the promises will be fulfilled to you. . . . You will have an anchor to the soul both sure and steadfast.[40]

279

ADDRESSED TO ME PERSONALLY

I am poor and needy; yet the Lord thinketh upon me: thou art my help and my deliverer; make no tarrying, O my God. Ps. 40:17.

Do not let your great need discourage you. The Saviour of sinners, the Friend of the friendless, with compassion infinitely greater than that of a tender mother for a loved and afflicted child, is inviting, "Look unto me, and be ye saved" (Isa. 45:22). "He was wounded for our transgressions, he was bruised for our iniquities: the chastisement of our peace was upon him; and with his stripes we are healed" (Isa. 53:5). . . .

There is danger of not making Christ's teachings a personal matter, of not receiving them as though they were addressed to us personally. In His words of instruction Jesus means me. I may appropriate to myself His merits, His death, His cleansing blood, as fully as though there were not another sinner in the world for whom Christ died. . . .

There are toils and conflicts and self-denials for us all. Not one will escape them. We must tread the path where Jesus leads the way. It may be in tears, in trials, in bereavements, in sorrow for sins, or in seeking for the mastery over depraved desires, unbalanced characters, and unholy tempers. It requires earnest effort to present ourselves a living sacrifice, holy and acceptable to God. It takes the entire being. There is no chamber of the mind where Satan can hold sway and carry out his devices. Self must be crucified. Consecration, submission, and sacrifices must be made that will seem like taking the very lifeblood from the heart.[1]

Will it make you sad to be buffeted, despised, derided, maligned of the world? It ought not, for Jesus told us just how it would be. If the world hate you, He says, "ye know that it hated me before it hated you" (John 15:18). The apostle Paul, the great hero of faith, testifies: "For I reckon that the sufferings of this present time are not worthy to be compared with the glory which shall be revealed in us" (Rom. 8:18). "For our light affliction, which is but for a moment, worketh for us a far more exceeding and eternal weight of glory" (2 Cor. 4:17).[2]

WORKING THE HEART'S SOIL

Sow to yourselves in righteousness, reap in mercy; break up your fallow ground: for it is time to seek the Lord, till he come and rain righteousness upon you. Hosea 10:12.

Let every church member consider the breaking up of the fallow ground, the careful cleansing of the soil, and the depositing and harrowing of the seed, which is the laborious work of the husbandman. It is a rough and searching process. The harrowing of the seed is not always pleasant to the receiver, and sometimes disabling to him because he does not sense the virtue of the Word and become submissive under the tilling process in spiritual life. The sins committed require the sincere repentance that needeth not to be repented of, but when the hard soil is broken up and the stubborn clods are broken to pieces then the precious seed can be sown and harrowed into the soil. This represents the severe discipline of God. Often rebellion is manifested and the discipline of God must continue until the determined will is broken and the end is gained.

In things spiritual as well as natural this work must be done. Often severity is needed to bring in the spiritual harvest. It is God's great law that without the proper sowing of seed and the tillage there will be no harvest in sheaves. An experience is lacking. Divine blessings wait only for human spiritual working of the soil of the heart and the industry to care for the soil while the Lord is sowing His seed.

As a man soweth he shall also reap. All who study the Word with full purpose to cleanse away from the life all sin, and who search the Scriptures to learn what is truth, will welcome the truth of the Word as a Thus saith the Lord. They will repent under the sharp reproofs of Bible truth. . . . If a man sow true repentance he will reap the reward of sound good works. If he continues in the faith he reaps peace. If he becomes sanctified and cleansed from his appetite for cheapness and folly he shall . . . reap righteousness and perfect love. . . . A continuance in the well doing in overcoming makes him a daily victor because he keeps the mark of Christ's perfection ever before him.[3]

SPIRITUAL MUSCLE AND SINEW

Blessed is the man that endureth temptation: for when he is tried, he shall receive the crown of life, which the Lord hath promised to them that love him. James 1:12.

In seasons of temptation we seem to lose sight of the fact that God tests us that our faith may be tried and be found unto praise and honor and glory at the appearing of Jesus. The Lord places us in different positions to develop us. If we have defects of character of which we are not aware, He gives us discipline that will bring those defects to our knowledge, that we may overcome them. It is His providence that brings us into varying circumstances. In each new position, we meet a different class of temptations. How many times when we are placed in some trying situation we think, "This is a wonderful mistake. How I wish I had stayed where I was before." But why is it that you are not satisfied? It is because your circumstances have served to bring new defects in your character to your notice, but nothing is revealed but that which was in you. . . .

It is coming in contact with difficulties that will give you spiritual muscle and sinew. You will become strong in Christ if you endure the testing process and the proving of God. . . . Remember when trials come that you are a spectacle to angels and to men, and that every time you fail to bear the proving of the Lord you are lessening your spiritual strength. You should hold your peace from complaining, and take your burden to Jesus, and lay your whole soul open before Him. Do not carry it to a third person. Do not lay your burden upon humanity. Say, 'I will not gratify the enemy by murmuring. I will lay my care at the feet of Jesus. I will tell it to Him in faith." If you do this you will receive help from above; you will realize the fulfillment of the promise, "He is on my right hand that I should not be moved" (see Ps. 16:8).[4]

God's Word declares, "Many shall be purified, and made white, and tried" (Dan. 12:10). Only he who endures the trial will receive the crown of life.[5]

"MY GRACE IS SUFFICIENT FOR THEE"

And he said unto me, My grace is sufficient for thee: for my strength is made perfect in weakness. Most gladly therefore will I rather glory in my infirmities, that the power of Christ may rest upon me. 2 Cor. 12:9.

Through all my sickness the last eight months,* I have had during my sleepless hours the most precious contemplations of the love of God to man, expressed in the wonderful sacrifice made to save him from ruin. I loved to repeat the name of Jesus; how full of sweetness, light, and love it is! Looking upon the cross, at the humiliations and sufferings endured in bearing our sins, that His righteousness might be imputed to us, softens the heart and fills the soul with His love. . . .

When pain has seemed to be almost unbearable, I have looked to Jesus and prayed most earnestly, and He has been beside me, and the darkness has passed away and all has seemed light. The very air seemed like precious fragrance. How glorious seemed the truth! How uplifting! I could rest in the love of Jesus. Pain was still my portion, but the promise, "My grace is sufficient for thee," was enough to give me comfort. The sharpest pains seemed to be converted into peace and rest. For hours in the night season I have had sweet communion with God. My mind seemed to be illuminated. I had no disposition to murmur or complain.

Jesus was the spring of my hope and my joy and courage. Heaven has seemed to be very near, and Christ the great Physician, my restorer, the remedy of all sickness. In Him all fullness dwells. Jesus is music to my ears, and although drinking the cup of suffering, the water of life was presented to me to quench my thirst. Christ is our righteousness, our sanctification, our redemption. Through these months of suffering I have had such precious views of the goodness of Jesus that I want them never to become dim. I believe now that my sickness in this strange country is a part of God's plan. . . . How urgently my soul pleads for the heavenly endowment. Of myself I can do nothing. The power and the glory is all of God.[6]

---

*Written during Ellen White's long illness in Australia.

THE LORD IS MY HELPER

He hath said, I will never leave thee, nor forsake thee. So that we may boldly say, The Lord is my helper, and I will not fear what man shall do unto me. Heb. 13:5, 6.

We must fight every day, every hour, the good fight of faith. You will meet with many trials, but if you bear them patiently they will refine and purify, ennoble and elevate you spiritually. . . . Very great troubles are coming upon the world, and the powers of Satan are stirring with intensity the powers from beneath to work suffering, disaster, and ruin. His work is to create all the misery upon human beings that is possible. The earth is the scene of his action, but he is held in check. He can go no farther than the Lord permits.

O how gracious is our Lord! "I will never leave thee, nor forsake thee" (Heb. 13:5). "I have graven thee upon the palms of my hands" (Isa. 49:16). . . . "I will not leave you comfortless" (John 14:18). The Holy Spirit is to be given for the asking. Only think of it, He is more willing to give the Holy Spirit to them that ask Him than parents are to give good gifts unto their children. Then let us rejoice, let us be glad. Let us not look at the hellish work of the powers of darkness until hope and courage shall fail. Jesus lives, and we must let our faith pierce the blackness . . . and rest in the light, rejoice in the light of the Sun of Righteousness.

Jesus lives to make intercession for us. While the blackness and darkness are closing about the world, our lives are only secure as they are hid with Christ in God. Precious Saviour! In Him alone are our hopes of eternal life to be centered. We will then talk faith, talk hope, talk courage, and diffuse light on every side. "Ye are," saith Christ, "the light of the world. A city . . . set on an hill. . . . Let your light so shine before men, that they may . . . glorify your Father which is in heaven" (Matt. 5:14-16). Faith must pierce the darkest cloud. Simple, earnest trust in God will glorify His name, and in that trust you may be all light in the Lord. Praise the Lord. Praise Him, and glorify God for His matchless love.[7]

FEELINGS NO EVIDENCE OF REJECTION

The Lord is nigh unto all them that call upon him, to all that call upon him in truth. He will fulfil the desire of them that fear him: he also will hear their cry, and will save them. Ps. 145:18, 19.

I would call your attention to the precious promises in the Word of God. All who are children of God have not the same powers, the same temperaments, the same confidence and boldness. I am glad indeed that our feelings are no evidence that we are not children of God. The enemy will tempt you to think that you have done things that have separated you from God and that He no longer loves you, but our Lord loves us still, and we may know by the words He has placed on record for just such cases as yours. "If any man sin, we have an advocate with the Father, Jesus Christ the righteous" (1 John 2:1). "If we confess our sins, he is faithful and just to forgive us our sins, and to cleanse us from *all unrighteousness"* (1 John 1:9). . . .

God loves you; and the precious Saviour, who gave Himself for you, will not thrust you from Him because you are tempted and in your weakness may have been overcome. He loves you still.

Peter denied his Lord in the hour of trial, but Jesus did not forsake His poor disciple. Although Peter hated himself, the Lord loved him, and after His resurrection He called him by name and sent him a loving message. O what a kind, loving, compassionate Saviour we have! And He loves us though we err.

Now do not worry yourself out of the arms of the dear Saviour, but rest trustingly in faith. He loves you; He cares for you. He is blessing you and will give you His peace and grace. He is saying to you, "Thy sins be forgiven thee." You may be depressed with bodily infirmities, but that is not evidence that the Lord is not working in your behalf every day. He will pardon you, and that abundantly. Gather to your soul the sweet promises of God. Jesus is our constant, unfailing friend, and He wants you to trust in Him. . . . Look away from yourself to the perfection of Christ.[8]

"I HAVE PRAYED FOR THEE"

I have prayed for thee, that thy faith fail not. Luke 22:32.

To every Christian comes the word that was addressed to Peter, "Satan hath desired to have you, that he may sift you as wheat: but I have prayed for thee, that thy faith fail not" (Luke 22:31, 32). Thank God we are not left alone. This is our safety. Satan can never touch with eternal disaster one whom Christ has prepared for temptation by His previous intercession, for grace is provided in Christ for every soul, and a way of escape has been made, so that no one need fall under the power of the enemy.

Satan is preparing many and strong temptations with which to assail the people of God. He is represented as walking to and fro like a roaring lion, seeking for some unguarded soul whom he may be successful in deceiving through his subtlety, and may finally destroy. We are not safe without Christ for a single step. But what comfort is treasured for us in the words, "I have prayed for thee, that thy faith fail not"! Satan does not sift chaff; it is the wheat that he desires to have in his hands. Then let us take courage and pray at all times.

Christ offers our prayers to the Father, mingled with the merit of His sacrifice, and they come up before God as sweet incense. . . . Whenever you are tempted to sin remember that Christ's eye is upon you, and that Satan desires to have you that he may sift you as wheat. Remember to send your petitions heavenward, and see Jesus making intercession for you. Send up an earnest cry to God, "Lord, save me; I perish," and you will not be overcome; you will not enter into sin. Take your stand firmly on the words of Paul, and in the strength of Jesus say, "In all these things we are more than conquerors through him that loved us. For I am persuaded, that neither death, nor life, nor angels, nor principalities, nor powers, nor things present, nor things to come, nor height, nor depth, nor any other creature, shall be able to separate us from the love of God, which is in Christ Jesus our Lord" (Rom. 8:37-39).[9]

THE PRICE OF PERFECTION

For it became him, for whom are all things, and by whom are all things, in bringing many sons unto glory, to make the captain of their salvation perfect through sufferings. Heb. 2:10.

Christ's invitation to us all is a call to a life of peace and rest—a life of liberty and love, and to a rich inheritance in the future immortal life. . . . We need not be alarmed if this path of liberty is laid through conflicts and sufferings. The liberty we shall enjoy will be the more valuable because we made sacrifices to obtain it. The peace which passeth knowledge will cost us battles with the powers of darkness, struggles severe against selfishness and inward sins. . . .

We cannot appreciate our Redeemer in the highest sense until we can see Him by the eye of faith reaching to the very depths of human wretchedness, taking upon Himself the nature of man, the capacity to suffer, and by suffering putting forth His divine power to save and lift sinners up to companionship with Himself. O why have we so little sense of sin? Why so little penitence? It is because we do not come nearer the cross of Christ. Conscience becomes hardened through the deceitfulness of sin, because we remain away from Christ. Consider the Captain of our salvation. He suffered shame for us that we might not suffer everlasting shame and contempt. He suffered on the cross, that mercy might be granted to fallen man. God's justice is preserved, and guilty man is pardoned. Jesus dies that the sinner might live. Shame is borne by the Son of the Highest for the sake of poor sinners, that they might be ransomed and crowned with eternal glory. . . .

We must hide self in Jesus Christ, and let Him appear in our conversation and character as the One altogether lovely, and the chief among ten thousand. Our lives, our deportment, will testify how highly we prize Christ and the salvation He has wrought out for us at such a cost to Himself. While we look constantly to Him whom our sins have pierced and our sorrows have burdened, we shall acquire strength to be like Him. We shall bind ourselves in willing, happy, captivity to Jesus Christ.[10]

LIVING OUT GOD'S LAW

Neither knoweth any man the Father, save the Son, and he to whomsoever the Son will reveal him. Matt. 11:27.

Jesus came to represent the character of God in living out the holy law of Jehovah. In every lesson He gave to His disciples and to the people He sought to define clearly its principles. By personal obedience to the law He invested the common duties of life with a holy significance. He lived a man among men. . . . He lived among the people, He shared their poverty and their griefs. He dignified life in all its details by keeping before men the glory of God, and by subordinating everything to the will of His Father. His life was characterized by supreme love to God, and fervent love to His fellow men. . . .

His life from its beginning to its close, was one of self-denial and self-sacrifice. Upon the cross of Calvary He made the great sacrifice of Himself in behalf of all men, that the whole world might have salvation if they would. Christ was hid in God, and God stood revealed to the world in the character of His Son. . . .

Love for a lost world was manifested every day, in every act of His life. Those who are imbued by His Spirit will work in the same lines as those in which Christ worked. In Christ the light and love of God were manifested in human nature. No human being has ever possessed so sensitive a nature as did the sinless, holy One of God, who stood as head and representative of what humanity may become through the imparting of the divine nature. To those who believe in Christ as their personal Saviour, He imputes His merit and imparts His power. To those who come to Him with their burden of grief, disappointments, and trials, He will give rest and peace. It is through the grace of Christ that the soul sees his need of repentance toward God . . . , and is led to look to Christ by faith, realizing that His merit is efficacious to save to the uttermost all who come unto God by Him. . . . Let us open our hearts to receive the love which it is so essential that we should cultivate in order that we may fulfill the commandments of God.[11]

GOD'S LAW CHANGELESS AND ETERNAL

Think not that I am come to destroy the law, or the prophets: I am not come to destroy, but to fulfil. For verily I say unto you, Till heaven and earth pass, one jot or one tittle shall in no wise pass from the law, till all be fulfilled. Matt. 5:17, 18.

If Satan's work had succeeded in heaven the law of God would have been changed, but this could not be, for His law was a transcript of His character and as unchangeable as His character. If any change was possible in the law of God it would have been made then and there and saved the rebellion in heaven. But as it was not altered to meet the request of Satan, he . . . lost his high and holy position in the heavenly courts.

After his fall he worked upon the minds of Adam and Eve and seduced them from their loyalty. . . . Now if the law of God could have been changed and altered to meet man in his fallen condition, then Adam would have been pardoned and retained his home in Eden; but the penalty of transgression was death, and Christ became man's substitute and surety. Then was the time, could the law of God have been changed, to have made this change and retained Christ in the heavenly courts, that the immense sacrifice made to save a fallen race might have been avoided. But no, the law of God was changeless in its character and therefore Christ gave Himself a sacrifice in behalf of fallen man, and Adam lost Eden and was placed with all his posterity upon probation.

Had the law of God been changed in one precept since the expulsion of Satan from heaven, he would have gained on earth after his fall that which he could not gain in heaven before his fall. He would have received all that he asked for. We know that he did not. . . . The law . . . remains unalterable as the throne of God, and the salvation of every soul is determined by obedience or disobedience. . . . Jesus, by the law of sympathetic love, bore our sins, took our punishment, and drank the cup of the wrath of God apportioned to the transgressor. . . . He bore the cross of self-denial and self-sacrifice for us, that we might have life, eternal life. Will we bear the cross for Jesus?[12]

THE TEST OF OUR ACTIONS

Commit thy works unto the Lord, and thy thoughts shall be established. Prov. 16:3.

Let us feel thankful that we have the privilege of committing our works to God. We are to remember that we are not pieces of inanimate mechanism, but intelligent beings, able to choose the right and refuse the wrong, with a clear conscience and a pure purpose. We are to aim at consistency in all our works.

We are to commit our way to the Lord, testing it by His searching laws. "Commit thy way unto the Lord; trust also in him; and he shall bring it to pass" (Ps. 37:5). We cannot commit our way to God if we are working out deeds of injustice. "If I regard iniquity in my heart," the psalmist declares, "the Lord will not hear me" (Ps. 66:18). When we commit our way to the Lord we are to search the heart through and through, casting out all evil, that Christ may fill it with His righteousness. We are to seek the Lord in prayer, putting at the beginning of our petitions repentance for sin. . . .

God's law is the test of our actions. His eye sees every act, searches every chamber of the mind, detecting all lurking self-deception and all hypocrisy. All things are naked and open to the sight of Him with whom we have to do. But He will receive all who come to Him with contrite hearts and a true purpose to forsake every wrong. . . .

In all our business transactions, in every word and deed, we are to maintain a pure purpose and a clear conscience. We are to commit our works to God and then leave them in His hands. Our work is to be done in the strictest integrity. Nothing is to be cherished that we cannot carry into the heavenly courts. As we labor let us ask God's help, realizing that this is the only thing that can keep our work free from selfishness. . . . Look upward with intense sincerity, for you need constant draughts of the refreshing air of heaven. We need to live in constant communion with our heavenly Father. . . . Perform your duties as if in the sight of a holy God.[13]

HAPPINESS IN OBEDIENCE

Giving thanks unto the Father, which hath made us meet to be partakers of the inheritance of the saints in light: who hath delivered us from the power of darkness, and hath translated us into the kingdom of his dear Son. Col. 1:12, 13.

Our future eternal happiness depends upon having our humanity, with all its capabilities and powers, brought into obedience to God and placed under the control of Divinity. Many have no faith in Jesus Christ. They say, "It was easy for Christ to obey the will of His Father, for He was divine." But His Word declares He was "in all points tempted like as we are" (Heb. 4:15). He was tempted according to and in proportion to His elevation of mind, but He would not weaken or cripple His divine power by yielding to temptation. In His life on earth Christ was a representative of what humanity may be through the privileges and opportunities granted them in Him. . . .

When Satan tempted our first parents . . . he tried to flatter them into believing that they should be raised above the sphere of humanity. But Christ, by the example He has set before us, encourages the members of the human family to be men, obeying the Word of God within the sphere of their humanity. He Himself became a man—not a bond-slave to Satan to work out his attributes, but a man in moral power, obedient to the law of God, which is a transcript of His character. Those who would rebel against subjection to a wise and good law emanating from God are slaves to an apostate power.

Jesus became a man that He might mediate between man and God, . . . that He might restore to man the original mind which he lost in Eden through Satan's alluring temptation. . . . Disobedience is not in accordance with the nature which God gave to man in Eden.

Through the moral power Christ has brought to man, we may give thanks unto God who hath made us meet for the inheritance with the saints in light. Through Jesus Christ every man may overcome in his own behalf and on his own account, standing in his own individuality of character.[14]

POWER FOR OBEDIENCE

If ye keep my commandments, ye shall abide in my love; even as I have kept my Father's commandments, and abide in his love. John 15:10.

Some who claim to believe in Jesus Christ as their Saviour have said, "No one can keep the law." On this point the words of Christ are decisive. He states, "I have kept my Father's commandments." And He is our example in all things. . . .

In the Sermon on the Mount Christ plainly declared His mission. "Think not," He said, "that I am come to destroy the law, or the prophets: I am not come to destroy, but to fulfil" (Matt. 5:17). He came to carry out literally every specification concerning which the prophets had borne testimony. He who existed with the Father before the creation of the world, Himself gave the prophecies recorded by holy men—the prophecies that He came afterward to fulfill. . . .

Christ's position with His Father is one of equality. This enabled Him to become a sin offering for transgressors. He was fully sufficient to magnify the law and make it honorable. . . . He separated the precepts of Jehovah from the maxims and traditions of men. He held up the Ten Commandments as an expression of truth in all its purity. . . .

Christ came to the world to counteract Satan's falsehood that God had made a law which men could not keep. Taking humanity upon Himself, He came to this earth, and by a life of obedience showed that God has not made a law that man cannot keep. He showed that it is possible for man perfectly to obey the law. Those who accept Christ as their Saviour, becoming partakers of His divine nature, are enabled to follow His example, living in obedience to every precept of the law. Through the merits of Christ, man is to show by his obedience that he could be trusted in heaven, that he would not rebel.

Christ possessed the same nature that man possesses. He was tempted in all points like as man is tempted. The same power by which He obeyed is at man's command.[15]

EVIDENCE OF OUR ALLEGIANCE

If ye love me, keep my commandments. John 14:15.

Let this point be fully settled in every mind: If we accept Christ as a Redeemer we must accept Him as a Ruler. We cannot have the assurance, the perfect, confiding trust in Christ as our Saviour, until we acknowledge Him and are obedient to His commandments. Thus we evidence our allegiance to God. We have then the genuine ring in our faith. It works by love. Speak it from your heart: "Lord, I believe Thou hast died to redeem my soul. If Thou hast placed such a value upon my soul as to give Thy life for mine, I give my life and all its possibilities in all my weakness into Thy keeping." The will must be brought into *complete harmony* with the will of God.[16]

Today the invitation is given: "Come unto me, all ye that labour and are heavy laden, and I will give you rest. Take my yoke upon you, and learn of me; for I am meek and lowly in heart: and ye shall find rest unto your souls" (Matt. 11:28, 29). Christ has rest for all who will wear His yoke and learn His meekness and lowliness of heart. Here we are taught restraint and obedience, and in this we shall find rest. Thank God that in humility and obedience we shall find just that which we all need so much—the rest that is found in faith and confidence and perfect trust. We must not manufacture an oppressive yoke for our necks. Let us take the yoke of Christ and in entire obedience draw with Him. . . .

"If ye keep my commandments, ye shall abide in my love; even as I have kept my Father's commandments, and abide in his love" (John 15:10). This is the yoke which Christ invites us to wear—the yoke of obedience. Can we not say, "Lord, I take Thee at Thy word; I receive Thy promise. I come to Thee because I need Thee as a personal Saviour. I must have an abiding Christ. I am dependent on Thee. Thou art mine." Christ says, "He that hath my commandments, and keepeth them"—not in pretense, but with the whole mind, heart, soul, and strength—"he it is that loveth me" (John 14:21). This is the true test of character. We must be doers of the Word.[17]

WONDERFUL SIMPLICITY OF THE LAW

The law of the Lord is perfect, converting the soul: the testimony of the Lord is sure, making wise the simple. Ps. 19:7.

How wonderful in its simplicity, its comprehensiveness and perfection, is the law of Jehovah! In the purposes and dealings of God there are mysteries which the finite mind is unable to comprehend. . . .

But there is no mystery in the law of God. The feeblest intellect can grasp these rules to regulate the life and form the character after the divine Model. If the children of men would to the best of their ability obey this law, they would gain strength of intellect and power of discernment to comprehend still more of God's purposes and plans. . . .

The infinite sacrifice which Christ has made to magnify and exalt the law testifies that not one jot or tittle of that law will relinquish its claims upon the transgressor. Christ came to pay the debt which the sinner had incurred by transgression and by His own example to teach man how to keep the law of God. Said Christ, "I have kept my Father's commandments" (John 15:10). . . . It is inconceivable how so many, professing to be servants of God, can set aside His law and teach sinners that they are not amenable to its precepts. What a fatal delusion! . . .

We are living in a land of bondage and of death. Multitudes are enslaved by sinful customs and evil habits, and their fetters are difficult to break. Iniquity, like a flood, is deluging the earth. Crimes almost too fearful to be even mentioned are of daily occurrence. Shall we say that all this is because men live in obedience to the will of God, or is it because ministers and people hold and teach that its precepts have no binding force?[18]

"God so loved the world, that he gave his only begotten Son" that the lost might be reclaimed. . . . He who has tasted and found that the Lord is good cannot bear the thought of following in the path of transgression. It is pain to him to violate the law of that God who has so loved him.[19]

GOD'S MORAL LOOKING GLASS

But whoso looketh into the perfect law of liberty, and continueth therein, he being not a forgetful hearer, but a doer of the work, this man shall be blessed in his deed. James 1:25.

At Düsseldorf we changed cars,* and were obliged to wait two hours in the depot. Here we had an opportunity to study human nature. The ladies came in, changed their outer wraps, and then surveyed themselves on every side, to see that their dress was faultless. Then extra touches of powder must be put upon their faces. Long they lingered before the mirror in order to arrange their outward apparel to their satisfaction for the purpose of appearing their best when looked upon by human eyes. I thought of the law of God, the great moral looking glass into which the sinner is to look to discover the defects of his character. If all would study the law of God—the moral standard of character—as diligently and critically as many do their outward appearance by means of the looking glass, with a purpose to correct and reform every defect of character, what transformations would most assuredly take place in them. "For if any be a hearer of the word, and not a doer, he is like unto a man beholding his natural face in a glass: for he beholdeth himself, and goeth his way, and straightway forgetteth what manner of man he was" (James 1:23, 24). . . .

There are many who view themselves as defective in character when they look into God's moral mirror, His law, but they have heard so much of "All you have to do is to believe" . . . that after venturing to look into the mirror they straightway go from it retaining all their defects, with the words on their lips, "Jesus has done it all." These are represented by the figure that James has marked out—the man beholding himself and going away and forgetting what manner of man he was. . . . Faith and works are the two oars that must be used to urge the bark against the current of worldliness, pride, and vanity; and if these are not used, the boat will drift with the current downward to perdition. God help us to take care of the inward adorning, to set the heart in order as carefully as we arrange the outward apparel.[20]

---

*Written during a journey in Europe.

PRIVILEGES OF THE OBEDIENT

Ye are my friends, if ye do whatsoever I command you. John 15:14.

Those who live in close fellowship with Christ will be promoted by Him to positions of trust. The servant who does the best he can for his Master is admitted to familiar intercourse with the One whose commands he loves to obey. In the faithful discharge of duty we may become one with Christ, for those who are obeying God's commands may speak to Him freely. The one who talks most familiarly with his divine leader has the most exalted conception of His greatness and is the most obedient to His commands.

"If ye abide in me, and my words abide in you, ye shall ask what ye will, and it shall be done unto you. . . . Ye are my friends, if ye do whatsoever I command you. Henceforth I call you not servants; for the servant knoweth not what his lord doeth; but I have called you friends; for all things that I have heard of my Father I have made known unto you." . . .

The character of the one who comes to God in faith will bear witness that the Saviour has entered into his life, directing all, pervading all. Such a one is continually asking, "Is this Thy will and way, O my Saviour?" Constantly he looks to Jesus, the Author and Finisher of his faith. He consults the will of his divine Friend in reference to all his actions, for he knows that in this confidence is his strength. He has made it a habit to lift up the heart to God in every perplexity. . . .

He who accepts God as his sovereign must take the oath of allegiance to Him. He must put on the Christian uniform and bear aloft the banner that shows to whose army he belongs. He must make an open avowal of his allegiance to Christ. Concealment is impossible. Christ's impress must appear in the life in sanctified works.

"I am the Lord your God, which have separated you from other people. . . . Ye shall be holy unto me: for I the Lord am holy, and have severed you from other people, that ye should be mine" (Lev. 20:24-26). . . . "This people have I formed for myself; they shall shew forth my praise" (Isa. 43:21).[21]

THE MOTIVE FOR OBEDIENCE

For this is the love of God, that we keep his commandments: and his commandments are not grievous. 1 John 5:3.

It is the keeping of the commandments of God that honors and glorifies Him in His chosen. Wherefore every soul to whom God has given reasoning faculties is under obligation to God to search the Word and ascertain all that is enjoined upon us as God's purchased possession. We should seek to understand all that the Word requires of us. . . . We cannot show greater honor to our God, whose we are by creation and redemption, than to give evidence to the beings of heaven, to the worlds unfallen, and to fallen men, that we diligently hearken unto all His commandments, which are the laws that govern His kingdom.

We need to study diligently that we may gain a knowledge of the laws of God. How can we be obedient subjects if we fail to understand the laws that govern the kingdom of God? Then open your Bibles and search for everything that will enlighten you in regard to the precepts of God; and when you discern a Thus saith the Lord, ask not the opinion of men, but whatever the cost to yourself, obey cheerfully. Then the blessing of God will rest upon you. . . .

Often ask prayerfully, "Lord, what wilt thou have me to do? Am I in any way disregarding the divine precepts? Am I in any way placing my influence on the enemy's side? Am I showing a careless disregard of God's commandments? Am I willing to yoke up with Christ, to lift the burdens, and to be a colaborer with Him? Am I studying out possible excuses for neglecting obedience to a Thus saith the Lord? Am I risking the consequences of neglect to obey the clearly revealed precepts of Jehovah because I am not willing to come out from the world and be separate? Shall the fear of man have a greater influence over me than the fear of God?"

Surrender yourself to God, saying, "'Here, Lord, I give myself away; 'tis all that I can do.' I will not be found in disobedience to Thy law, for that would place me in the enemy's ranks."[22]

FOUNDATION OF GOD'S GOVERNMENT

Love worketh no ill to his neighbour: therefore love is the fulfilling of the law. Rom. 13:10.

The question of deepest interest to each one should be, Am I meeting the requirements of the law of God? That law is holy, just, and good, and God would have us daily compare our actions with this, His great standard of righteousness. Only by a close examination of self in the light of God's Word can we discover our deviations from His holy rule of right. . . .

Love is the principle that underlies God's government in heaven and on earth, and this love must be interwoven in the life of the Christian. The love of Christ is not a fitful love; it is deep, and broad, and full. Its possessor will not say, "I will love only those who love me." The heart that is influenced by this holy principle will be carried above everything of a selfish nature.

Even among professing Christians there are persons who are always on the watch for something at which to take offense. If their friends are absorbed in matters that require their attention and have no time to devote to them, they feel slighted and injured. . . . Their lives are like the gorgeous flowers which possess no fragrance. Much to be preferred is the simple, unpretending blossom that blesses with its sweet odor those who come in contact with it.

Instead of finding fault with others, these persons should seek to become lovely by putting on Christ. . . . The character of Christ is the standard which the Christian is to keep before him. His aim should be to possess those graces that were exemplified in the life of Christ in humanity. . . .

The religion of Jesus Christ is not merely to prepare us for the future immortal life; it is to enable us to live the Christ life here on earth. Jesus is not only our pattern, He is also our friend and our guide, and by taking hold of His strong arm and partaking of His Spirit, we may walk "even as he walked."[23]

GOD'S LAW IN THE HEART

For this is the covenant that I will make with the house of Israel after those days, saith the Lord; I will put my laws into their mind, and write them in their hearts: and I will be to them a God, and they shall be to me a people. Heb. 8:10.

The blessings of the new covenant are grounded purely on mercy in forgiving unrighteousness and sins. The Lord specifies, I will do thus and thus unto all who turn to Me, forsaking the evil and choosing the good. "I will be merciful to their unrighteousness, and their sins and their iniquities will I remember no more" (Heb. 8:12). All who humble their hearts, confessing their sins, will find mercy and grace and assurance.

Has God, in showing mercy to the sinner, ceased to be just? Has He dishonored His holy law, and will He henceforth pass over the violation of it? God is true. He changes not. The conditions of salvation are ever the same. Life, eternal life, is for all who will obey God's law. Perfect obedience, revealed in thought, word, and deed, is as essential now as when the lawyer asked Christ, "What shall I do to inherit eternal life?" Jesus said to him, "What is written in the law? how readest thou? . . . this do, and thou shalt live" (Luke 10:25-28).

Under the new covenant the conditions by which eternal life may be gained are the same as under the old—perfect obedience. Under the old covenant there were many offences of a daring, presumptuous character for which there was no atonement specified by law. In the new and better covenant Christ has fulfilled the law for the transgressors of law if they receive Him by faith as a personal Saviour. . . . Mercy and forgiveness are the reward of all who come to Christ trusting in His merits to take away their sins. In the better covenant we are cleansed from sin by the blood of Christ. . . . The sinner is helpless to atone for one sin. The power is in Christ's free gift, a promise appreciated by those only who are sensible of their sins and who forsake their sins and cast their helpless souls upon Christ, the sin-pardoning Saviour. He will put into their hearts His perfect law, which is "holy, and just, and good" (Rom. 7:12), the law of God's own nature.[24]

THE TRUE STANDARD OF CHARACTER

To the law and to the testimony: if they speak not according to this word, it is because there is no light in them. Isa. 8:20.

There is divine grace for all who will accept it, yet there is something for us to do. . . . There is a work for us to do to fit ourselves for the society of angels. We must be like Jesus, free from the defilement of sin. He was all that He requires us to be; He was a perfect pattern for childhood, for youth, for manhood. We must study the Pattern more closely.

Jesus was the Majesty of heaven, yet He condescended to take little children in His arms and bless them. He whom angels adore listened with tenderest love to their lisping, prattling praise. We must be like Him in noble dignity, while our hearts are softened and subdued by the divine love that dwelt in the heart of Christ. . . .

We have a work to do to fashion the character after the divine Model. All wrong habits must be given up. The impure must become pure in heart, the selfish man must put away his selfishness, the proud man must get rid of his pride, the self-sufficient man must overcome his self-confidence and realize that he is nothing without Christ. . . .

We need to be anchored in Christ, rooted and grounded in the faith. Satan works through agents. He selects those who have not been drinking of the living waters, whose souls are athirst for something new and strange, and who are ever ready to drink at any fountain that may present itself. Voices will be heard, saying, "Lo, here is Christ," or "Lo there," but we must believe them not. We have unmistakable evidence of the voice of the True Shepherd, and He is calling upon us to follow Him. He says, "I have kept my Father's commandments." He leads His sheep in the path of humble obedience to the law of God, but He never encourages them in the transgression of that law. . . .

None need be deceived. The law of God is as sacred as His throne, and by it every man who cometh into the world is to be judged. There is no other standard by which to test character.[25]

THE GAME OF LIFE

Watch ye, stand fast in the faith, quit you like men, be strong.
1 Cor. 16:13.

The truth of God obeyed, the living by every word of God, is alone sufficient to make any of us stand in these evil times. Satan is playing the game of life for the soul. . . .

There are opportunities and advantages which are within the reach of all to strengthen the moral and spiritual powers. The mind can be expanded and ennobled and should be made to dwell upon heavenly things. . . . Unless it flows in a heavenward direction it becomes an easy prey to the temptation of Satan to engage in worldly projects and enterprises that have no special connection with God. And all zeal and devotion and restless energy and feverish desire are brought into this work, and the devil stands by and laughs to see human effort wrestling so perseveringly for an object that it will never gain, which eludes its grasp. . . . Schemes and projects which Satan invents ensnare the soul, and poor, deceived human beings go on blindfolded to their own ruin. . . .

There is one safeguard against Satan's deceptions and snares, that is the truth as it is in Jesus. The truth planted in the heart, nourished by watchfulness and prayer, nourished by the grace of Christ, will give us discernment. The truth must abide in the heart, be felt in its power in spite of all the alluring enchantments of Satan, and your experience and mine must be that the truth can purify, guide, and bless the soul. . . .

The enemy is on the track of every one of us, and if we would resist temptations which assail us from without and from within, we need to make sure we are on the Lord's side, that His truth is in our hearts, that it keeps watch in our souls, ready to sound an alarm and summon us to action against every enemy. Without this defense amid unseen foes we shall be like the willow bending to the blast, driven of the wind and tossed. But if Christ abides in the soul we may be strong in the Lord and in the power of His might.[26]

FILLED WITH HIS FULLNESS

And to know the love of Christ, which passeth knowledge, that ye might be filled with all the fulness of God. Eph. 3:19.

There are many who think that it is impossible to escape from the power of sin, but the promise is that we may be filled with all the fullness of God. We aim too low. The mark is much higher. Our minds need expansion, that we may comprehend the significance of the provision of God. We are to reflect the highest attributes of the character of God. We should be thankful that we are not to be left to ourselves. The law of God is the exalted standard to which we are to attain. . . . We are not to walk according to our own ideas . . . , but we are to follow in the footsteps of Christ.[27]

The work of overcoming is in our hands, but we are not to overcome in our own name or strength, for of ourselves we cannot keep the commandments of God. The Spirit of God must help our infirmities. Christ has become our sacrifice and surety. He has become sin for us that we might become the righteousness of God in Him. Through faith in His name He imputes unto us His righteousness, and it becomes a living principle in our life. . . . Christ imputes to us His sinless character and presents us to the Father in His own purity.[28]

We cannot provide a robe of righteousness for ourselves, for the prophet says, "All our righteousnesses are as filthy rags" (Isa. 64:6). There is nothing in us from which we can clothe the soul so that its nakedness shall not appear. We are to receive the robe of righteousness woven in the loom of heaven, even the spotless robe of Christ's righteousness. We are to say, "He died for me. He bore my soul's disgrace, that in His name I might be an overcomer and be exalted to His throne."[29]

It is the privilege of the children of God to be filled with all the fullness of God. "Now unto him that is able to do exceeding abundantly above all that we ask or think, according to the power that worketh in us, unto him be glory in the church by Christ Jesus throughout all ages, world without end" (Eph. 3:20, 21).[30]

DISTINCT AND SEPARATE WAYS

Enter ye in at the strait gate: for wide is the gate, and broad is the way, that leadeth to destruction, and many there be which go in thereat: because strait is the gate, and narrow is the way, which leadeth unto life, and few there be that find it. Matt. 7:13, 14.

These roads are distinct, separate, extending in opposite directions. One leads to eternal death, the other to eternal life. One is broad and smooth, the other narrow and rugged. So the parties that travel them are opposite in character, in life, in dress, and in conversation. Those who travel in the narrow way are talking of the happiness they will have at the end of the journey. . . . They do not dress like the company in the broad road, nor talk like them, nor act like them. A pattern has been given them. A Man of sorrows and acquainted with grief opened that road for them and traveled it Himself. His followers see His footprints and are comforted and cheered. He went through safely; so can they, if they follow in His steps.

In the broad road all are occupied with their persons, their dress, and the pleasures in the way. They indulge freely in mirth and revelry, and think not of their journey's end, of the certain ruin at the termination of the path. Every day they approach nearer their destruction, yet they madly rush on faster and faster. . . . When it is too late they see that they have gained nothing substantial. They have grasped at shadows and lost eternal life. . . .

A form of godliness will not save any. All must have a deep and living experience. This alone will save them in the time of trouble before us. Then their work will be tried, of what sort it is. If it is gold, silver, and precious stones, they will be hid as in the secret of the Lord's pavilion. But if their work is wood, hay, stubble, nothing can shield them from the fierceness of Jehovah's wrath. . . .

Those who are willing to make any and every sacrifice for eternal life will have it, and it will be worth suffering for, worth crucifying self for, and sacrificing every idol for. The far more exceeding and eternal weight of glory outweighs every earthly treasure and eclipses every earthly attraction.[31]

THE CHALLENGE OF THE DIFFICULT

Strive to enter in at the strait gate: for many, I say unto you, will seek to enter in, and shall not be able. Luke 13:24.

A strait gate means a gate difficult to enter. By this illustration Christ showed how hard it is for men and women to leave the world and the attractions it holds, and heartily and lovingly obey the commandments of God. The wide gate is easy to enter. Entrance through it does not call for the restrictions which are painful to the human heart. Self-denial and self-sacrifice are not seen in the broad way. There depraved appetite and natural inclinations find abundant room. There may be seen self-indulgence, pride, envy, evil surmisings, love of money, self-exaltation.[32]

Said Christ, "Strive"—agonize—"to enter in. . . ." We must feel our continual dependence upon God and the great weakness of our own wisdom and our own judgment and strength, and then depend wholly upon Him who has conquered the foe in our behalf, because He pitied our weakness and knew we should be overcome and perish if He did not come to our help. . . . Think not that by any easy or common effort you can win the eternal reward. You have a wily foe upon your track. "To him that overcometh will I grant to sit with me in my throne, even as I also overcame, and am set down with my Father in his throne" (Rev. 3:21). Here is the battle to overcome as Christ has overcome. His life of temptation, of trial, of toil and conflict, is before us for us to imitate. We may make efforts in our own strength, but not succeed. But when we fall all helpless and suffering and needy upon the Rock of Christ, feeling in our inmost soul that our victory depends upon His merits, that all our efforts of themselves without the special help of the great Conqueror will be without avail, then Christ would send every angel out of glory to rescue us from the power of the enemy rather than that we should fall.[33]

We need to see that the way is narrow, and the gate strait. But as we pass through the strait gate, the wideness is without limit.[34]

A MARKED DISTINCTION

I pray not that thou shouldest take them out of the world, but that thou shouldest keep them from the evil. John 17:15.

Christians are to stand out distinct from the world as God's standard bearers, showing in their lives the influence of the transforming grace of Christ. They are raised up together to sit with Christ in heavenly places that they may reveal to the world, to angels, and to men an enduring representation of the eternal world. They are to hold forth the Word of life, warning men of the binding claims of God's law. God wants His servants to be of a high order. He wants them to obey laws of a higher order than the laws of the world— laws which are the transcript of His character.

God's work is supreme. He calls for all the powers of the intellect, all the spiritual endowments. They are to be consecrated to Him and to the service of humanity. He calls for workers who are partakers of the divine nature. Those who really believe in Jesus will be colaborers with Him, showing to the unfallen worlds and to the fallen world a character which is after the divine similitude. They are to show that they have a higher, holier order of enjoyment than the world can bestow. God will bestow the power of the Holy Spirit upon all who will cooperate with Him in the cultivation of all their endowments and talents, that they may stand on vantage ground. . . .

Christ's followers are to seek to improve the moral tone of the world, under the influence of the impartation of the Spirit of God. They are not to come down to the world's level, thinking that by doing this they will uplift it. In words, in dress, in spirit, in everything, there is to be a marked distinction between Christians and worldlings. This distinction has a convincing influence upon worldlings. They see that the sons and daughters of the Lord do separate themselves from the world, and that the Lord binds them up with Himself. . . . "And God hath both raised up the Lord, and will also raise up us by his own power" (1 Cor. 6:14). Who is willing to be raised to the highest level?[35]

CHRIST'S REPRESENTATIVES IN THE WORLD

They are not of the world, even as I am not of the world. Sanctify them through thy truth: thy word is truth. John 17:16, 17.

Jesus . . . says, "I sanctify myself, that they also may be sanctified through the truth" (John 17:19). "Thy word is truth." We need, then, to become familiar with the Word of God, to study and to practice it in life. . . . We deny Jesus Christ as the One who taketh away the sins of the world if we do not, after accepting the truth, reveal to the world the sanctifying effects of the truth on our own characters. If we are not better men and women, if we are not more kindhearted, more pitiful, more courteous, more full of tenderness and love, if we do not manifest to others the love that led Jesus to the world on His mission of mercy, we are not witnesses to the world of the power of Jesus Christ.

Jesus lived not to please Himself. He gave Himself as a living, consuming sacrifice for the good of others. He came to elevate, to ennoble, to make happy all with whom He came in contact. Those who receive Christ will drop out all that is uncourteous, harsh, and rough, and will reveal the pleasantness, the kindness, that dwelt in Jesus, because Christ abides in the heart by faith. Christ was the light that shineth in darkness, and His followers are also to be the light of the world. They are to kindle their taper from the divine altar. The character that is sanctified through the truth adds the perfect polish.

Christ is our model, but unless we behold Him, unless we contemplate His character, we shall not reflect His character in our practical life. He was meek and lowly in heart. He never did a rude action, never spoke a discourteous word. The Lord is not pleased with our blunt, hard, unsympathetic ways toward others. All this selfishness must be purged away from our characters, and we must wear the yoke of Christ. Then we . . . shall be fitting up for the society of heavenly angels. We are to be in the world but not of the world. We are to be a representation of Jesus Christ. As the Lord of life and glory came to our world to represent the Father, so we are to go to the world to represent Jesus.[36]

WHERE ARE YOU PITCHING YOUR TENT?

If ye then be risen with Christ, seek those things which are above, where Christ sitteth on the right hand of God. Set your affection on things above, not on things on the earth. Col. 3:1, 2.

Many who should be setting their tents nearer to the land of Canaan are pitching their camp nearer to Egypt. They are not living in the light of the Sun of Righteousness. Many attend places of amusement to gratify the taste, but no spiritual strength is gained by so doing, and you will find yourself on the losing side. To encourage the love of amusement is to discourage the love of religious exercises, for the heart becomes so crowded with trifling, with what is pleasing to the natural heart, that there is no room for Jesus. . . .

It requires the faith that works by love and purifies the soul to meet the mind of God. There are those who believe in Christ; they do not think Him an impostor; they believe the Bible to be a revelation of His divine character. They admire its holy doctrines, and revere the name, the only name given under heaven whereby men can be saved, and yet, with all this knowledge, they may be as truly ignorant of the grace of God as the veriest sinner. They have not opened the heart to let Jesus in.[37]

What shall I say for the benefit of the youth? Will you open your hearts to Jesus, that His love, His mercy, may fill the chambers of your soul, that you may sing and make melody in your hearts unto God? O if all your affections were given unto Jesus, you would learn the language and the songs of Canaan!

In the worldling you expect to see lightness, trifling, vanity, immorality, jesting, and joking, but let it not so much as be named among you who are risen with Christ. . . . We must now elevate our thoughts and come to learn in the school of the Master.[38]

As we near the close of time, the current of evil will set more and more decidedly toward perdition. We can be safe only as we hold firmly to the hand of Jesus, constantly looking to the Author and Finisher of our faith. He is our mighty Helper.[39]

WHO HAS OUR FRIENDSHIP?

Know ye not that the friendship of the world is enmity with God? whosoever therefore will be a friend of the world is the enemy of God. James 4:4.

The Scriptures furnish abundant evidence that it is safer to be joined to the Lord and lose the favor and friendship of the world, than to look to the world for favor and support and forget our dependence upon God. . . .

The Lord Himself has established a separating wall between the things of the world and the things which He has chosen out of the world and sanctified to Himself. The world will not acknowledge this distinction. . . . But God has made this separation, and He will have it exist. In both the Old and the New Testaments the Lord has positively enjoined upon His people to be distinct from the world, in spirit, in pursuits, in practice; to be a holy nation, a peculiar people, that they may show forth the praises of Him who hath called them out of darkness into His marvelous light. The east is not farther from the west than are the children of light, in customs, practices, and spirit, from the children of darkness. This distinction will be more marked, more decided, as we near the close of time. . . .

There is an element called love which would teach us to praise and flatter our associates and not to faithfully tell them of their dangers and warn and counsel them for their good. This love is not Heaven-born. Our words and actions should be serious and earnest, especially before those who are neglecting their soul's salvation. . . . If we unite with them in lightness, trifling, pleasure seeking, or in any pursuit which will banish seriousness from the mind, we are constantly saying to them by our example, "Peace, peace; be not disturbed. You have no cause for alarm." This is saying to the sinner, "It shall be well with thee."[40]

If we profess to be sons and daughters of God we should pursue such a course toward the unbelieving that our souls will be clear of their blood when we meet them in the great day of final reckoning.[41]

GOD OR MAMMON?

No man can serve two masters: for either he will hate the one, and love the other; or else he will hold to the one, and despise the other. Ye cannot serve God and mammon. Matt. 6:24.

You have, as an individual, a soul to save or to lose. And although Noah, Job, and Daniel were in the land they could save but their own souls through their righteousness. If you consider this it will help you to realize that you must be in earnest to apply your mind and all your powers day by day to secure profitable results.

The worshipers of the world make mammon their god, and everything else is subordinate to this worship. Should not the Christian keep in subordination the love of pleasure, the love of everything that is contrary to the interests of Jesus Christ? Precious time has not been given to be wasted on that which is less than nothing, and vanity. In thus doing we are cheating ourselves out of present peace in this life, and eternal happiness in the life to come. . . .

Do not make a low standard your aim; aim high. Never be found at any time working on the side of the great adversary of souls, who is seeking to counteract the workings of the Spirit of God. Walk not hesitatingly but firmly in the strength and grace of Jesus Christ. . . . You are the property of Christ both by creation and redemption, and the glory of God is involved in your individual success. . . .

You are a spectacle unto the world, to angels, and to men. Be brave in God. Put on the whole armor of God and let your unbelieving father* see that your life is not spoiled because you stand loyal and true to all the commandments of God as a Seventh-day Adventist. You can be, and God requires you to be, a decided witness for Him. . . . Do not work at all on Satan's side of the question. Probationary time is precious. Make the most of the golden moments, putting to use the talents God has given, that you may accumulate something for the Master and be a blessing to all around you. Let the heavenly angels look down with joy upon you because you are loyal and true to Jesus Christ.[42]

---

*From a letter to a youth whose father was an unbeliever.

THE CONDITION OF SONSHIP

Wherefore come out from among them, and be ye separate, saith the Lord, and touch not the unclean thing; and I will receive you, and will be a Father unto you, and ye shall be my sons and daughters, saith the Lord Almighty. 2 Cor. 6:17, 18.

Do you desire to become the sons and daughters of the Most High? Here is stated the condition of this great privilege. Come out, be separate, touch not the unclean. You cannot keep the fellowship of the world, participate in its pleasures, identify yourself with its interests, and still be the sons of God. Says John, "The world knoweth us not, because it knew him not" (1 John 3:1). But shall we let the desire for the favor of our Lord's enemies weigh against our accepting the conditions of salvation? . . .

There are great things expected from the sons and daughters of God. I look upon the youth of today, and my heart yearns over them. What possibilities are open before them! If they sincerely seek to learn of Christ, He will give them wisdom, as He gave wisdom to Daniel. . . . Let the youth try to appreciate the privilege that may be theirs, to be directed by the unerring wisdom of God. . . .

It is thought a great honor to be invited into the presence of a king of this earth. But let us consider the amazing privilege that is proffered to us. If we obey the requirements of God we may become the sons and daughters of the King of the universe. Through a crucified and risen Saviour we may be filled with the fruits of righteousness, and be fitted to shine in the courts of the King of kings through unending ages. The world does not know the exaltation of the sons and daughters of the Most High. Those around them do not see that the humble, self-denying spirit, the patient meekness of heart, has any extraordinary value. They did not know or appreciate Christ. . . . They could not understand Him; and the greater our likeness to the divine character of our Lord, the more we shall be misunderstood by the world. The more we come into fellowship with Christ and heaven, the less will be our fellowship with the world, for we are not of the world.[43]

SHUN THE WORLD'S PLEASURES

Love not the world, neither the things that are in the world. If any man love the world, the love of the Father is not in him. 1 John 2:15.

The true Christian will not desire to enter any place of amusement or engage in any diversion upon which he cannot ask the blessing of God. He will not be found at the theater, the billiard hall, or the bowling saloon. He will not unite with the gay waltzers, or indulge in any other bewitching pleasure that will banish Christ from the mind.

To those who plead for these diversions, we answer, We cannot indulge in them in the name of Jesus of Nazareth. . . . Go in imagination to Gethsemane and behold the anguish which Christ endured for us. See the world's Redeemer wrestling in superhuman agony, the sins of the whole world upon His soul. Hear His prayer, borne upon the sympathizing breeze, "O my Father, if it be possible, let this cup pass from me: nevertheless not as I will, but as thou wilt" (Matt. 26:39). The hour of darkness has come. Christ has entered the shadow of His cross. Alone He must drink the bitter cup. Of all earth's children whom He has blessed and comforted there is not one to console Him in this dreadful hour. He is betrayed into the hands of a murderous mob. Faint and weary, He is dragged from one tribunal to another. . . . He who knew not the taint of sin pours out His life as a malefactor upon Calvary. This history should stir every soul to its depths. It was to save us that the Son of God became a man of sorrows and acquainted with grief. . . . Let a sense of the infinite sacrifice made for our redemption be ever with you, and the ballroom will lose its attractions.

Not only did Christ die as our sacrifice, but He lived as our example. In His human nature He stands, complete, perfect, spotless. To be a Christian is to be Christlike. Our entire being—soul, body, and spirit—must be purified, ennobled, sanctified, until we shall reflect His image and imitate His example. . . . We need not fear to engage in any pursuit or pleasure that will aid us in this work. But it is our duty to shun everything that would divert our attention or lessen our zeal.[1]

311

THE ADORNING THAT NEVER FADES

Whose adorning let it not be that outward adorning of plaiting the hair, and of wearing of gold, or of putting on of apparel; but let it be the hidden man of the heart, in that which is not corruptible, even the ornament of a meek and quiet spirit, which is in the sight of God of great price. 1 Peter 3:3, 4.

The charms that consist only in the outward apparel are shallow and changeable; no dependence can be placed upon them. The adorning which Christ enjoins upon His followers will never fade. . . .

If half the time spent by the youth in making themselves attractive in outward appearance were given to soul culture, to the inward adorning, what a difference would be seen in their deportment, words, and actions! Those who are truly seeking to follow Christ will have conscientious scruples in regard to the dress they wear; they will strive to meet the requirements . . . so plainly given by the Lord.[2]

Many dress like the world to have an influence. They spend hours that are worse than thrown away, in studying this or that fashion to decorate the poor, mortal body. But here they make a sad and fatal mistake. If they would have a saving influence, if they would have their lives tell in favor of the truth, let them imitate the humble Pattern. Let them show their faith by righteous works, and make the distinction broad between themselves and the world. The words, the dress, and the actions should tell for God. Then a holy influence will be shed upon all, and all will take knowledge of them, that they have been with Jesus. Unbelievers will see that faith in Christ's coming affects the character. . . .

The external appearance is an index to the heart. When hearts are affected by the truth there will be a death to the world, and those who are dead to the world will not be moved by the laugh, the jeer, and the scorn of unbelievers. They will feel an anxious desire to be like their Master, separate from the world. They will not imitate its fashions or customs. The noble object will be ever before them, to glorify God and gain the immortal inheritance, and in comparison with this everything of an earthly nature will sink into insignificance.[3]

DAILY SELF-DENIAL

I beseech you therefore, brethren, by the mercies of God, that ye present your bodies a living sacrifice, holy, acceptable unto God, which is your reasonable service. Rom. 12:1.

Why will not the youth learn a lesson from the case of Adam? His failure in not bearing the slight test of God was followed by a terrible retribution. And yet Satan has such power to bewitch the mind that with this beacon of warning before us many will talk of liberality and not being so particular in regard to God's requirements. . . .

It is a very small offering, at best, that we can make to our heavenly Father. In view of our accountability to God, we are all under the strongest obligation to bring our appetites and passions under the control of the intelligent will. Taste has done more to pervert the understanding and becloud the spiritual sky than everything else beside. Satan benumbs the intellect of many through indulgence of appetite, and then he makes these intemperate ones special objects of temptation, to go still farther from the path of obedience and holiness. Those who have been entrusted with valuable talents will miss eternal life unless they shall see the necessity of daily self-denial, of what it means to be an overcomer. . . .

There is not, with many, . . . one half the vigor there might be, because of ailments brought on through indulgence of appetite and debasing habits. What clearness of perception the youth might have if they would adhere strictly to the laws of health, as did Daniel and his three companions! What freedom from pain, and with how much greater ease could they perform their duties! How much greater would be their spiritual fervor! And how much more good, by precept and example, would they do to others! . . .

God is able to make all grace abound toward you. We have no right to claim the promises of God till we comply with the conditions revealed in His Word. "Come out from among them, and be ye separate, saith the Lord, and touch not the unclean thing; and I will receive you" (2 Cor. 6:17). Will you do it?[4]

313

THE BATTLE AGAINST INTEMPERANCE

Wine is a mocker, strong drink is raging: and whosoever is deceived thereby is not wise. Prov. 20:1.

We as Christians should stand firmly in defense of temperance. There is no class of persons capable of accomplishing more and effecting the object more readily than the God-fearing Bible youth. In this age the young men of our cities should unite in a firm, decided army to set their faces as a flint against every form of selfish, health-destroying indulgence. What a power they might be for good! How many they might save from becoming demoralized because they visit the halls and gardens fitted up with music and every attraction to allure the youth! Intemperance and licentiousness and profanity are sisters. Let every God-fearing youth gird on the armor and press to the front. Put your names on every pledge. . . . Let no feeble, weak excuse be offered to refuse to put your name to the temperance pledge. . . .

Through intemperate appetite Adam and Eve lost Eden. If we gain the Paradise of God we must be temperate in all things. Shall any blush with shame to refuse the wine cup or the foaming mug of beer? Instead of this being a dishonorable work, they are doing service to God in the matter of refusing to indulge appetite, resisting temptation. Angels are looking upon both tempter and tempted. While sin is unmanly, indulgence of appetite is weak, cowardly, and debasing; the denial of appetite, honorable. The highest intelligences of heaven watch the conflict going on between the tempter and the tempted. And if the tempted turn away from temptation and in the strength of Jesus conquer, then angels rejoice, and Satan has lost in the conflict. . . . All who understand the great conflict of Christ upon the point of appetite in the wilderness of temptation will never lend one iota of their influence to brace up intemperance.

Jesus endured the painful fast in our behalf and conquered Satan in every temptation, thus making it possible for man to conquer in his own behalf, and on his own account, through the strength brought to him by this mighty victory gained as man's substitute and surety.[5]

THE CHRISTIAN RACE

Know ye not that they which run in a race run all, but one receiveth the prize? So run, that ye may obtain. And every man that striveth for the mastery is temperate in all things. Now they do it to obtain a corruptible crown; but we an incorruptible. 1 Cor. 9:24, 25.

Here Paul makes a sharp contrast, to put to shame the feeble efforts of professed Christians who plead for their selfish indulgences, and refuse to place themselves by self-denial and strictly temperate habits in a position that they will make a success of overcoming. All who entered the list in the public games were animated and excited by the hope of a prize if they were successful. In like manner a prize is held out before the Christian, the reward of faithfulness to the end of the race. . . . All ran in the race, but only one received the prize. The other strugglers for the perishable laurel wreath, however thorough their preparation, however earnest and determined their efforts, were doomed to failure. It is not so with the Christian race. . . . The weakest saint as well as the strongest may obtain the crown of immortal glory if he is thoroughly in earnest and will submit to privation and loss for Christ's sake. . . .

If we create unnatural appetites and indulge them in any degree we violate nature's laws, and enfeebled physical, mental, and moral conditions will result. We are hence unfitted for that persevering, energetic, and hopeful effort which we might have made had we been true to nature's laws. If we injure a single organ of the body we rob God of the service we might render to Him.[6]

The apostle calls our attention to the care and diligence which were required to secure the victory in these ancient games. He exhorts all who start in the Christian race to give all diligence to make success certain, while he presents before them for their encouragement the crown of glory which the righteous judge will award to all who are faithful to the end of the race. . . . This crown is not a perishable chaplet of flowers, but the glorious crown of everlasting life, which awaits all who, having completed the Christian race, love the appearing of our Lord.[7]

AN EXAMPLE OF THE BELIEVERS

For the grace of God that bringeth salvation hath appeared to all men, teaching us that, denying ungodliness and worldly lusts, we should live soberly, righteously, and godly, in this present world. Titus 2:11, 12.

There is a great work for us to do if we would inherit eternal life. We are to deny ungodliness and worldly lusts, and live a life of righteousness. . . . There is no salvation for us except in Jesus, for it is through faith in Him that we receive power to become the sons of God. But it is not merely a passing faith, it is faith that works the works of Christ. . . . Living faith makes itself manifest by exhibiting a spirit of sacrifice and devotion toward the cause of God. Those who possess it stand under the banner of Prince Emmanuel and wage a successful warfare against the powers of darkness. They stand ready to do whatsoever their Captain commands. Each one is exhorted to be "an example of the believers, in word, in conversation, in charity, in spirit, in faith, in purity" (1 Tim. 4:12), for we are to "live soberly, righteously, and godly" in this present evil world, representing the character of Christ, and manifesting His spirit. . . .

Those who are connected with Jesus are in union with the Maker and Upholder of all things. They have a power that the world cannot give nor take away. But while great and exalted privileges are given to them, they are not simply to rejoice in their blessings. As stewards of the manifold grace of God they are to become a blessing to others. They are entrusted with great truth, and "unto whomsoever much is given, of him shall be much required" (Luke 12:48). There are weighty responsibilities resting upon all who have received the message for this time. They are to exert an influence that will draw others to the light of God's Word. . . . We are our brother's keeper. . . .

If we are true believers in Jesus we shall be gathering rays from glory, and we shall shed light on the darkened pathway of those around us. We shall reveal the gracious character of our Redeemer, and many will be drawn by our influence to "behold the Lamb of God, which taketh away the sin of the world" (John 1:29).[8]

GOD'S PECULIAR PEOPLE

Who gave himself for us, that he might redeem us from all iniquity, and purify unto himself a peculiar people, zealous of good works. Titus 2:14.

That which more especially distinguishes God's people from the popular religious bodies is not their profession alone, but their exemplary character and their principles of unselfish love. The powerful and purifying influence of the Spirit of God upon the heart, carried out in words and works, separates them from the world, and designates them as God's peculiar people. The character and disposition of Christ's followers will be like the Master. He is the pattern, the holy and perfect example given for Christians to imitate. . . .

The self-denial, humility, and temperance required of the righteous . . . are . . . in contrast with the extravagant, health-destroying habits of the people who live in this degenerate age. God has shown that health reform is as closely connected with the third angel's message as the hand is united to the body. And there is nowhere to be found so great a cause of physical and moral degeneracy as a neglect of this important subject. . . . Whoever violates moral obligations in the matter of eating and dressing prepares the way to violate the claims of God in regard to eternal interests. Our bodies are not our own. God has claims upon us to take care of the habitation He has given us, that we may present our bodies to Him a living sacrifice, holy and acceptable. Our bodies belong to Him who made them, and we are in duty bound to become intelligent in regard to the best means of preserving from decay the habitation He has given us. If we enfeeble the body by self-gratification, by indulging the appetite, and by dressing in accordance with health-destroying fashions, in order to be in harmony with the world, we become enemies of God. . . .

God requires of us according to the grace He has bestowed upon us. . . . In order for us to meet our responsibilities we must stand on that elevated ground that the order and advancement of holy, sacred truth has prepared for us.[9]

DARE TO BE DIFFERENT!

That ye may be blameless and harmless, the sons of God, without rebuke, in the midst of a crooked and perverse nation, among whom ye shine as lights in the world. Phil. 2:15.

Let everyone, for Christ's sake and for his own soul's sake, shun conformity to the world, to its customs, vanities, and fashions. Beware of human commandments that will obscure the holy commandments of God. The pleasure lover is ever unsatisfied, and continually desires to seek again the excitement of the ballroom, the theater, or the party of pleasure. The time God has granted us in which to prepare for eternity is spent by thousands in poring over fictitious stories. God-given intellect is perverted, the Word of God is neglected, the mind and soul are robbed of moral power needed for wrestling against faults and errors, habits and practices, that disqualify the soul for the enjoyment of Christ's presence. . . .

Let the question be asked seriously and with intense interest, "How is it with my soul? Am I by my habits and practices working against my Redeemer?" Inquire, "Do I bring glory to Christ? Do I show to a disobedient and crooked generation that I choose to suffer reproach for the sake of Jesus?" . . . Will the professed followers of Christ aim high, and reach the standard of holiness? Better be a worldling than a common, cheap, professed Christian. Dare to come out from the world and be separate. Dare to be singular because you love Jesus better than the world, and righteousness with persecution better than disobedience with worldly prosperity. Holy and entire obedience through dependence upon the Lord Jesus Christ will strengthen the soul to be steadfast in the faith and hope of the gospel.

Jesus says, "Without me ye can do nothing" (John 15:5). Union with Christ is our only means for overcoming sin. Living in Christ, adhering to Christ, supported by Christ, drawing nourishment from Christ, we bear fruit after the similitude of Christ. We live and move in Him; we are one with Him and one with the Father. The name of Christ is glorified in the believing child of God. This is Bible religion.[10]

PRIVILEGES WITHOUT LIMIT

Blessed is the man that walketh not in the counsel of the ungodly, nor standeth in the way of sinners, nor sitteth in the seat of the scornful. Ps. 1:1.

Those who have the blessing of the Lord are highly favored. . . . Be sure, then, that you do not choose the ungodly as your companions, for they will influence you to do those very things that will displease God and deprive you of His blessing. . . .

When any open their minds and hearts to those who would advise them to do wrong in any way, then they are walking in the counsel of the ungodly. . . . They are standing in the way of sinners, . . . and in the next step they will find themselves sitting in the seat of the scornful unconcerned. . . . The message of mercy, of love, of peace, is scorned, and those who associate with this class will become like them, despisers of God's mercy. It is surprising to see how far the influence of one ungodly youth may extend, what a power he becomes in the hands of Satan for evil, how much his counsels are heeded, how much sorrow and sadness and grief he can bring. . . .

The privileges granted to the children of God are without limit— to be connected with Jesus Christ, who throughout the universe of heaven and worlds that have not fallen is adored by every heart, and His praises sung by every tongue; to be children of God, to bear His name, to become a member of the royal family; to be ranged under the banner of Prince Emmanuel, the King of kings and Lord of lords. His word is obeyed by the highest intelligences. . . .

The lowliest service done for Jesus is the greatest honor mortals can enjoy. Angels, pure and holy, obey His word; and shall we be deceived and deluded into the service of Satan? Shall we refuse obedience to His requirements? Shall it not be said of us individually, "But his delight is in the law of the Lord; and in his law doth he meditate day and night. And he shall be like a tree planted by the rivers of water, that bringeth forth his fruit in his season; his leaf also shall not wither; and whatsoever he doeth shall prosper."[11]

A HAPPY WALK WITH JESUS

And Enoch walked with God: and he was not; for God took him. Gen. 5:24.

Enoch lived in a corrupt age, when moral power was very weak. Pollution was teeming all around him, yet he walked with God. He educated his mind to devotion—to think on things that were pure and holy; and his conversation was upon holy and divine things. He was made a companion of God. He walked with Him, and received His counsel. He had to contend with the same temptations that we do. The society surrounding him was no more friendly to righteousness than is the society surrounding us at the present time. The atmosphere he breathed was tainted with sin and corruption, the same as ours, yet he was unsullied with the prevailing sins of the age in which he lived. And so may we remain as pure and uncorrupted as did the faithful Enoch.[12]

We are living in an age when wickedness prevails. The perils of the last days thicken around us, and because iniquity abounds the love of many waxes cold. . . . The shortness of time is urged as an incentive for us to seek righteousness and to make Christ our friend. This is not the great motive. It savors of selfishness. Is it necessary that the terrors of the day of God be held before us to compel us through fear to right action? This ought not to be. Jesus is attractive. He is full of love, mercy, and compassion. He proposes to be our friend, to walk with us through all the rough pathways of life. He says to you, I am the Lord thy God; walk with Me, and I will fill thy path with light. Jesus, the Majesty of heaven, proposes to elevate to companionship with Himself those who come to Him with their burdens, their weaknesses, and their cares. He will make them His dear children, and finally give them an inheritance of more value than the empires of kings, a crown of glory richer than has ever decked the brow of the most exalted earthly monarch. . . .

It is our privilege to have a calm, close, happy walk with Jesus every day we live.[13]

COUNT THE COST

For whosoever will save his life shall lose it; but whosoever shall lose his life for my sake and the gospel's, the same shall save it. For what shall it profit a man, if he shall gain the whole world, and lose his own soul? Or what shall a man give in exchange for his soul? Mark 8:35-37.

The Lord Jesus . . . lifts up His voice to break the spell of infatuation upon human minds and asks the momentous question, "What shall it profit a man, if he shall gain the whole world, and lose his own soul?" . . .

Disease and death are in our world, and how little we know when our individual probation shall end. . . . How many, if now called to render up their accounts, would do it with grief, regret, and remorse that their God-given probationary time was so fully employed in self-serving! The eternal interests of the soul have been fearfully neglected for unimportant affairs. The mind is kept busy, just as Satan designs it shall be, with selfish interests and nothing of any consequence, and time may be passing into eternity without a fitting up for heaven at all.

What can be compared with the loss of a human soul? It is a question which every soul must determine for himself—whether to gain the treasures of eternal life or to lose all because of his neglect to make God and His righteousness his first and only business. Jesus, the world's Redeemer, . . . looks with grief upon the large number of those who profess to be Christians who are not serving Him but themselves. They scarcely think of eternal realities, notwithstanding He calls their attention to the rich reward awaiting the faithful who will serve Him with their undivided affections. He brings eternal realities within the range of their vision. He bids them to count the cost now of being an obedient and faithful follower of Christ, and says, "Ye cannot serve God and mammon" (Matt. 6:24).

He would have every individual sense his responsibility to so use his precious time here in this world that it will be fruitful daily in good works. This is the only worthy aim of every living mortal— to employ his God-given faculties with endless results in view.[14]

CAST OUT EVERY IDOL

Then saith Jesus unto him, Get thee hence, Satan: for it is written, Thou shalt worship the Lord thy God, and him only shalt thou serve. Matt. 4:10.

"Thou shalt have no other gods before me" (Ex. 20:3). . . . It is not alone in denying the existence of God or in bowing down to idols of wood and stone that this first commandment is broken. By many who profess to be followers of Christ, its principles are infringed, but the Lord of heaven does not acknowledge those as His children who are cherishing in their hearts anything that takes the place which God alone should hold. With many the gratification of appetite holds sway, while with others dress and love of the world are given the first place in the heart. . . .

God has given us many things in this life upon which to bestow our affections, but when we carry to excess that which in itself is lawful we become idolaters. . . . Anything that separates our affections from God and lessens our interest in eternal things is an idol. Those who use the precious time given them by God—time that has been purchased at an infinite cost—in embellishing their homes for display, in following the fashions and customs of the world, are not only robbing their own souls of spiritual food, but are failing to give God His due. The time thus spent in the gratification of selfish desires might be employed in obtaining a knowledge of the Word of God, in cultivating our talents, that we might render intelligent service to our Creator. . . . God will not share a divided heart. If the world absorbs our attention, He cannot reign supreme. If this diminishes our devotion for God, it is idolatry in His eyes. . . .

"God is a Spirit: and they that worship him must worship him in spirit and in truth" (John 4:24). When our hearts are tuned to praise our Maker, not only in psalms and hymns and spiritual songs but also in our lives, we shall live in communion with Heaven. . . . There will be gratitude in the heart and in the home, in private as well as in public devotion. This constitutes the true worship of God.[15]

THREADS IN THE WEB OF HUMANITY

For the Son of man is as a man taking a far journey, who left his house, and gave authority to his servants, and to every man his work, and commanded the porter to watch. Mark 13:34.

When God commanded the tabernacle to be built in the wilderness, each man's work was assigned him. . . . In setting up and taking down the tabernacle, in moving from place to place in the wilderness, the position each was to occupy was plainly specified.

Christ was the invisible General of that company of more than a million people, and there were no haphazard, disorderly movements made. Order, dispatch, and exactitude were required of each one at the post of duty assigned him. This is an important lesson to the church and to every man whom God has chosen to act a part in His great work. No one is required to do another's work. Each is to do the work assigned him with exactness and integrity. The management of that great church in their journeyings in the wilderness symbolizes the management of the church till the close of earth's history, till we come into possession of the heavenly Canaan. . . .

The Lord has need of all kinds of skillful workmen. "And he gave some, apostles; and some, prophets; and some, evangelists; and some, pastors and teachers; for the perfecting of the saints, for the work of the ministry, for the edifying of the body of Christ" (Eph. 4:11, 12). . . . Each worker in every branch of work in the Lord's vineyard must have a head and a heart sanctified through the truth to enable him to see not merely the part of the work which is under his supervision, but its relation to the great whole. When the workers are consecrated to God they will reveal the love of God for their brethren who work under the unseen, divine Master Worker. "We are labourers together with God" (1 Cor. 3:9). . . .

We are all part of the great web of humanity, thread packed against thread to bring out the pattern of the fabric and make it a complete whole. . . . Be God's thread to work out His design. You can never handle yourself.[16]

TRADING ON GOD'S GIFTS

And unto one he gave five talents, to another two, and to another one; to every man according to his several ability; and straightway took his journey. Matt. 25:15.

The parable of the talents . . . has a personal and individual application to every man, woman, and child possessed of the powers of reason. Your obligation and responsibility are in proportion to the talents God has bestowed upon you. . . .

When the master of the house called his servants, he gave to every man *his* work. The whole family of God are included in the responsibility of using their Lord's goods. Every individual, from the lowliest and most obscure to the greatest and most exalted, is a moral agent endowed with abilities for which he is accountable to God. . . . The spiritual, mental, and physical ability, the influence, station, possessions, affections, sympathies, all are precious talents to be used in the cause of the Master. . . .

Let the businessman do his business in a way that will glorify his Master because of his fidelity. Let him carry his religion into everything that is done, and reveal to men the Spirit of Christ. Let the mechanic be a diligent and faithful representative of Him who toiled in the lowly walks of life in the cities of Judea. Let every one who names the name of Christ so work, that man by seeing his good works may be led to glorify his Creator and Redeemer. . . .

Those who have been blessed with superior talents should not depreciate the value of the services of those who are less gifted than themselves. The smallest trust is a trust from God. The one talent, through diligent use with the blessing of God, will be doubled, and the two used in the service of Christ will be increased to four; and thus the humblest instrument may grow in power and usefulness. The earnest purpose, the self-denying efforts, are all seen, appreciated, and accepted by the God of heaven. . . . God alone can estimate the worth of their service and see the far-reaching influence of him who works for the glory of his Maker.[17]

THE RELIGION OF LITTLE THINGS

*His lord said unto him, Well done, good and faithful servant;
thou hast been faithful over a few things, I will make thee ruler over
many things: enter thou into the joy of thy lord. Matt. 25:23.*

Said Christ, "He that is faithful in that which is least is faithful
also in much" (Luke 16:10). In the little matters some do not think it
necessary to be so very exact, but this is the deception of Satan.

Selfishness is at the root of all unfairness and all lack of fidelity.
. . . There is with many of the youth who profess to believe the truth
a vanity, pride, profligacy, and carelessness that are making them
reckless and disqualifying them for a noble and elevated life here,
and unfitting them for the future life hereafter. . . . There is not with
all a careful improvement of the time for which they are paid. Those
who fritter away their time or fail to put it to the best use are robbing God. Some . . . have a very favorable opinion of those who are
careless, reckless of money and reckless of time, but God regards all
these things in their true character—frauds which He will avenge.

Time, talents, and skill are to be brought into use and put to the
very best account. . . . Let everyone be true to principle, as if the
eye of the Infinite was upon him. You may, young men and
women, make of yourselves what you will, by the grace of God
combined with earnest efforts and determined will to resist inclination to indulgence. . . .

Christ gave to man a perfect example, but those who move out
on what they call a liberal plan, and become careless in the little
matters, will soon show a wide deviation from Christ's example, the
only true pattern. Young men and women, will you study more
closely and prayerfully the life of Christ and make that life your cri-
terion, your standard?[18]

Practical religion must be carried into the lowly duties of daily life.
And in the performance of these duties you are forming characters
that will stand the test of the judgment. Then, in whatever position
you may be placed, whatever your duties may be, do them nobly and
faithfully, realizing that all heaven is beholding your work.[19]

A DAY OF RECKONING

For unto every one that hath shall be given, and he shall have abundance: but from him that hath not shall be taken away even that which he hath. Matt. 25:29.

If talents are well improved, increased talents are the result. "Unto every one that hath shall be given." . . . If Heaven's bestowed gifts are not appreciated and improved as God's intrusted capital—if they are buried in worldliness, in selfishness—these powers capable of blessing humanity decrease, and because the God of heaven is not sought after and glorified as the source of all these precious endowments, He is dishonored, and He cuts off the supply. In order to increase, to grow in the knowledge of our Lord and Saviour Jesus Christ, we must put to use by human effort our physical and intellectual powers.[20]

Those who hoard up their talents to rust, unemployed, unimproved, must not think that such action in any way relieves them from responsibility, for God holds us responsible for the good we might do if we took up the yoke with Christ, lifting His burdens, learning more of His meekness and lowliness of heart day by day. The interest continues to accumulate on buried talents, and instead of decreasing our responsibility the burying of our talent only increases and intensifies it.

Let the human agent consider the solemn fact that the day of reckoning is just before us, and that we are daily deciding what our eternal destiny shall be. The Master examines every individual case, dealing personally with the talents entrusted by Him. O solemn day of reckoning; that day which will bring paleness to many faces; that day in which the words shall be spoken to many, "Thou art weighed in the balances, and found wanting"! It will be an awful thing to be found "wanting" when the book of accounts is opened in that great day. . . . Upon the decisions reached in that day depends the future, eternal interest of every soul. We shall have unspeakable joy, or unutterable woe and misery. . . . O how Jesus will love to recompense every true worker! Every faithfully performed duty will receive His blessing. It is then that He pronounces the benediction, "Well done."[21]

PUTTING OUR GIFTS TO WORK

But every man hath his proper gift of God, one after this manner, and another after that. 1 Cor. 7:7.

God gives more than money to His stewards. Your talent of imparting is a gift. What are you communicating of the gifts of God, in your words, in your tender sympathy? . . . The knowledge of truth is a talent. There are many souls in darkness that might be enlightened by true, faithful words from you. There are hearts that are hungering for sympathy, perishing away from God. Your sympathy may help them. The Lord has need of your words, dictated by His Holy Spirit. . . .

The first work for all Christians to do is to search the Scriptures with most earnest prayer, that they may have that faith that works by love and purifies the soul from every thread of selfishness. If the truth is received into the heart, it works like good leaven, until every power is brought into subjection to the will of God. Then you can no more help shining than can the sun. . . .

All natural gifts are to be sanctified as precious endowments. They are to be consecrated to God, that they may minister for the Master. All social advantages are talents. They are not to be devoted to self-pleasing, amusement, or self-gratification. . . . The gift of correct example is a great thing. But many gather about the soul an atmosphere that is malarious. . . .

The gifts of speech, of knowledge, of sympathy and love, communicate a knowledge of Christ. All these gifts are to be converted to God. The Lord stands in need of them, He calls for them. All are to act a part in preparing their own souls and the souls of others to rededicate their talents to God. Every soul, every gift, is to be laid under contribution to God. All are to cooperate with God in the work of saving souls. The talents you possess are given you of God to make you efficient colaborers with Christ. There are hearts hungering for sympathy, perishing for the help and assistance God has given you to give to them.[22]

INSTRUMENTS OF RIGHTEOUSNESS

Neither yield ye your members as instruments of unrighteousness unto sin: but yield yourselves unto God, as those that are alive from the dead, and your members as instruments of righteousness unto God. Rom. 6:13.

The Lord has given you talents to use, and in using these talents as He intended they should be used, you will have increased aptitude and wisdom and clear spiritual eyesight to understand His work. Your mind and eyes must watch for His appearing, your ears open to hear the faintest whisperings of His voice. Your knees He has made; use them in kneeling in prayer. He is your strength. By faith take hold of the Unseen. Let your feet be shod with the preparation of the gospel for running obediently in the way of His commandments. Your tongue and voice are a talent given you of God to tell the story of His life, of His lessons, of His death, of His resurrection, of His ascension. Your bodily strength is to be devoted to the Master in fighting the good fight of faith on the battlefield, overcoming His enemies with "It is written." Your sympathies and energies belong to God. Use them to glorify your Redeemer. . . .

Cultivate the thought that you are not alone. All your steps are watched by the Lord. You are encompassed with vigilant angels. . . . As the angels ministered unto Jacob, so certainly will they minister unto all of the Lord's humble, contrite ones. . . .

Reach up, higher and still higher, taking hold of one line of faith after another. Walk and work in love to God and the poor oppressed ones, and the Lord will be your helper. "Verily, verily, I say unto you, Hereafter ye shall see heaven open, and the angels of God ascending and descending upon the Son of man" (John 1:51). Jesus the precious Saviour, the Son of the living God, is the ladder uniting the celestial world with the terrestrial. His divinity lays hold of the throne of God. His humanity touches the earth. His human arm encircles the entire human race. Through Jesus Christ the angelic ministrations in love, in comfort, in reproof, in light, reach us. O thank the Lord, for He is good, and His mercies endure forever![23]

FOR THE MASTER'S USE

But in a great house there are not only vessels of gold and of silver, but also of wood and of earth; and some to honour, and some to dishonour. If a man therefore purge himself from these, he shall be a vessel unto honour, sanctified, and meet for the master's use, and prepared unto every good work. 2 Tim. 2:20, 21.

The Master has given to every man his work. He has given to every man according to his ability, and his trust is in proportion to his capacity. . . .

Let none mourn that they have not larger talents to use for the Master. . . . Go to work with steady patience and do your very best, irrespective of what others are doing. "Every one of us shall give account of himself to God" (Rom. 14:12). Let not your thought or your words be, "O that I had a larger work! O that I were in this or that position!" Do your duty where you are. Make the best investments possible with your entrusted gift in the very place where your work will count the most before God. . . . Be not envious of the talents of others, for that will not increase your ability to do a good or a great work. Use your gift in meekness, in humility, in trusting faith, and wait till the day of reckoning, and you will have no cause for grief or shame. . . .

Do not aspire to do some great service when the duty of today has not been done with fidelity. Take up the commonplace care, trade on the humble talent with a solemn sense of your responsibility for the right use of every power, every thought, that God has given you. God asks no less of the lowliest than of the most exalted; each must do his appointed work with cheerful alacrity, according to the measure of the gift of Christ. . . . The church of God is made up of persons of different abilities. Like vessels of various dimensions, we are placed in the house of the Lord; but it is not expected that the smaller vessels will contain all that the larger ones will hold. All that is required is that the vessel shall be full and hold according to its ability. If you perform faithfully the duties in your path you will be an acceptable servant, an honored vessel![24]

329

WORK WHERE YOU ARE

And said unto them; Go ye also into the vineyard, and whatsoever is right I will give you. And they went their way. Matt. 20:4.

There must be those who will come into the harvest field and who will be workers without expecting their wages in this world. In the next world they will be abundantly rewarded. There are men and women who have been letting their talents rust with inaction, . . . who could do a most precious work and grow in grace and capability to work by doing their best in accepting the work just where they are. They can single out individuals—their neighbors—and give them personal labor. . . .

The Lord will investigate the use we have made of the talents He has entrusted to us. He has paid the wages of His own blood and His own self-denial and sacrifice and sufferings, to secure the willing service of every soul as a laborer together with God. If only all felt their accountability to God wisely to employ the gifts in talents entrusted, what a revenue would be brought to God through Jesus Christ! The one talent may and will increase by use. The supposed lowliest gift, the humblest service, may reach minds and influence hearts that those who possess larger talents could not touch.

Now, now, now is our most favorable time to work. Individual visitation is of great value. In love for Jesus Christ and love for human souls the truth is to be carried to every family, talked of by every fireside that it is possible for you to find access to. . . . Bear in mind that the Holy Spirit is the worker. The human agent working for God is not alone. . . .

Labor in perseverance, in tenderness, compassion, prayerfulness, and love will do more than sermons. The Lord Jesus, in giving His life for the saving of the world from the curse of sin, intended greater things than our eyes have yet witnessed. The Holy Spirit is waiting for channels through whom to work. . . . Satan will not always triumph. The Spirit of God will be poured out upon the church just as soon as the vessels are prepared to receive it.[25]

"FAITHFUL IN THAT WHICH IS LEAST"

*He that is faithful in that which is least is faithful also in much:
and he that is unjust in the least is unjust also in much. Luke 16:10.*

The active service of God is directly connected with the ordinary
duties of life, even its humblest occupations. We are to serve God
just where He puts us. He is to place us individually, and not we
ourselves. Perhaps service in the home life is the place we are to occupy for a time, if not always. Then a preparation for that work
should be obtained, that we may do our best in service for the Lord.

The Lord is testing and proving us to see what sort of timbers, or
attributes, we are bringing into the character building. If we are listless
and indifferent, negligent and careless, in the small, everyday duties we
shall never be fitted for any other service for God. . . . He that is unfaithful in that which is least would certainly repeat this unfaithfulness
if placed in higher positions of trust and given larger responsibilities.
. . . The service of God will be done in a haphazard manner. . . .

The importance of little things is underrated just because they
are small, but the influence of the little things for good or evil is
great. They supply much of the actual discipline of life for every
human being. They are part of the training of the soul in the sanctification of all our entrusted talents to God. Faithfulness in the little
things in the line of duty makes the worker in God's service reflect
more and more the likeness of Christ.

Our Saviour is a Saviour for the perfection of the whole man. He
is not the God of part of the being only. The grace of Christ works
to the disciplining of the whole human fabric. He made all. He has
redeemed all. He has made the mind, the strength, the body as well
as the soul, partaker of the divine nature, and all is His purchased
possession. He must be served with the whole mind, heart, soul, and
strength. Then the Lord will be glorified in His saints in even the
common, temporal things with which they are connected. Holiness
unto the Lord will be the inscription placed upon them.[26]

331

NO ROOM FOR SHIRKERS

Curse ye Meroz, said the angel of the Lord, curse ye bitterly the inhabitants thereof; because they came not to the help of the Lord, to the help of the Lord against the mighty. Judges 5:23.

Shall not this be the time when all who are in connection with God shall come to the front and show their colors? Shall it be seen that men and women step back and show no interest, no zeal, no earnest effort when help is needed? When the car drags heavily, then is the time for everyone to push, put shoulders to the wheels, and not stand back giving orders, or accusing the ones who are trying to push the load, or criticizing everything they do, because it is not done in their way and after their ideas. . . . Let everyone do his level best to move the load with might and strength. . . .

If the Lord should treat us as some who claim to be Christians treat one another, we should have a sore, hard time. If He should look upon the selfish, the erring, or crooked ones as they look upon one another and deal with one another, what would become of us? But I am glad the Lord is not man. He bears with our crooked ways, our selfishness, our separation from Him, our defects of character, and seeks to inform us, sending message after message of mercy, encouragement, warning, reproof, and correction, to bring us into a right position before Him, that we may have His love, His care, His blessing, abiding upon us. . . .

We have each a work to do for the Master. Will we do this work, will we labor with unselfish, self-sacrificing interest to build up His cause, to advance His work? I am determined to do the will of God, to make straight paths for my feet, lest the lame be turned out of the way. There are halting, lame ones enough. . . . God forbid that any of those who have had a knowledge of, and an experience in, the workings of God should themselves be halting, and need to be carried. Let them come up to help; let them become spiritually strong by doing the will of our heavenly Father, and then they can help the halting, lame ones. . . .

May we work intelligently, heartily, with decision and positiveness, that we may be blessed and may bless others.[27]

SERVE THE LORD HEARTILY

And whatsoever ye do, do it heartily, as to the Lord, and not unto men, knowing that of the Lord ye shall receive the reward of the inheritance: for ye serve the Lord Christ. Col. 3:23, 24.

The Lord requires the physical strength, and you can reveal your love for Him by the right use of your physical powers, doing the very work which needs to be done. There is no respect of persons with God. . . .

There is science in the humblest kind of work, and if all would thus regard it, they would see nobility in labor. Heart and soul are to be put into work of any kind; then there is cheerfulness and efficiency. In agricultural and mechanical occupations, men may give evidence to God that they appreciate His gift in the physical powers, and the mental faculties as well. Let the educated ability be employed devising improved methods of work. This is just what the Lord wants. There is honor in any class of work that is essential to be done. . . .

"Thou shalt love the Lord thy God with all thy heart, and with all thy soul, and with all thy mind, and with all thy strength" (Mark 12:30). God desires the love that is expressed in heart service, in soul service, in the service of the physical powers. We are not to be dwarfed in any kind of service for God. Whatever He has lent us is to be used intelligently for Him. . . . There is need of intelligence and educated ability to devise the best methods in farming, in building, and in every other department, that the worker may not labor in vain. . . .

It is the duty of every worker not merely to give his strength but his mind and intellect to that which he undertakes to do. . . . You can choose to become stereotyped in a wrong course of action because you have not the determination to take yourselves in hand and reform, or you may cultivate your powers to do the very best kind of service, and then you will find yourselves in demand anywhere and everywhere. You will be appreciated for all that you are worth. "Whatsoever thy hand findeth to do, do it with thy might" (Eccl. 9:10). "Not slothful in business; fervent in spirit; serving the Lord" (Rom. 12:11).[28]

"BEAR YE ONE ANOTHER'S BURDENS"

If a brother or sister be naked, and destitute of daily food, and one of you say unto them, Depart in peace, be ye warmed and filled; notwithstanding ye give them not those things which are needful to the body; what doth it profit? James 2:15, 16.

Any neglect of duty to the needy and to the afflicted is a neglect of duty to Christ in the person of His saints. When the cases of all come in review before God, the question What did they profess? is never asked, but, What have they done? Have they been doers of the Word? Have they lived for themselves? or have they been exercised in works of benevolence, in deeds of kindness, in love preferring others before themselves, and denying themselves that they might bless others? If the record shows that this has been their life, that their characters have been marked with tenderness, self-denial, and benevolence, they will receive the blessed assurance and benediction from Christ, "Well done." . . .

Our spiritual strength and blessing will be proportionate to the labor of love and good works which we perform. The injunction of the apostle is, "Bear ye one another's burdens, and so fulfil the law of Christ" (Gal. 6:2). Keeping the commandments of God requires of us good works, self-denial, self-sacrifice, and devotion for the good of others, not that our good works alone can save us, but that we surely cannot be saved without good works. After we have done all that we are capable of doing we are then to say, We have done no more than our duty, and at best are unprofitable servants, unworthy of the smallest favor from God. Christ must be our righteousness. . . .

All around us there are those who have soul hunger and who long for love expressed in words and deeds. Friendly sympathy and real feelings of tender interest for others would bring to our souls blessings that we have never yet experienced, and would bring us into close relation to our Redeemer, whose advent to the world was for the purpose of doing good, and whose life we are to copy. What are we doing for Christ?[29]

SWEET MUSIC IN HEAVEN

Verily I say unto you, Inasmuch as ye have done it unto one of
the least of these my brethren, ye have done it unto me. Matt. 25:40.

Christ says to His redeemed people, "Come, ye blessed of my
Father, inherit the kingdom prepared for you from the foundation of
the world: for I was an hungred, and ye gave me meat: I was thirsty,
and ye gave me drink: I was a stranger, and ye took me in: naked,
and ye clothed me: I was sick, and ye visited me: I was in prison,
and ye came unto me" (Matt. 25:34-36). . . .

Prayers, exhortation, and talk are cheap fruits, which are frequently
tied on, but fruits that are manifested in good works, in caring for the
needy, the fatherless, and widows, are genuine fruits, and grow naturally upon a good tree. . . . When hearts sympathize with hearts burdened with discouragement and grief, when the hand dispenses to the
needy, when the naked are clothed, the stranger made welcome to a
seat at your fireside and to a place in your heart, angels are coming
very near, and an answering strain is responded to in heaven. Every
act, every deed of justice and mercy and benevolence, makes sweet
music ring in heaven. The Father from His throne beholds and numbers them with His most precious treasures. "And they shall be mine,
saith the Lord of hosts, when I make up my jewels." . . .

Our heavenly Father lays blessings disguised in our pathway,
which some will not touch for fear they will detract from their enjoyment. Angels are waiting to see if we embrace opportunities
within our reach of doing good—waiting to see if we will bless others, that they in turn may bless us. The Lord Himself has made us to
differ—some poor, some rich, some afflicted—that all may have an
opportunity to develop a character. The poor are purposely permitted of God to be thus, that we might be tested and proved, and develop what is in our hearts.[30]

Every merciful act done to the needy, the suffering, is counted
as though it were done to Jesus Himself. When you succor the poor,
sympathize with the afflicted and oppressed, and befriend the or-
phan, you bring yourselves into a closer relationship to Jesus.[31]

CHANNELS OF LIGHT AND BLESSING

Now when they saw the boldness of Peter and John, and perceived that they were unlearned and ignorant men, they marvelled; and they took knowledge of them, that they had been with Jesus. Acts 4:13.

The world cannot see the beauty, the loveliness, goodness, and holiness of divine truth. And in order that men may understand it, there must be a channel through which it shall come to the world. The Saviour has constituted the church that channel. . . . Christ has revealed Himself to us that we may reveal Him to others. . . .

If those who claim to be Christians will heed the words of Christ, all who come in contact with them will acknowledge that they have been with Jesus and have learned of Him. . . .

Simple faith in the atoning blood can save my soul; and with John, I must call the attention of all to the Lamb of God which taketh away the sin of the world. Jesus has saved me, though I had nothing to present to Him, and could only say, "In my hand no price I bring, Simply to thy cross I cling." Never did a sinner seek the Saviour with the whole heart but that the Saviour was found of him. . . .

We may claim the blessed assurance, "I have blotted out, as a thick cloud, thy transgressions" (Isa. 44:22). Thy "sins, which are many, are forgiven" (Luke 7:47). O how precious, how refreshing, is the sunlight of God's love! The sinner may look upon his sin-stained life, and say, "Who is he that condemneth? It is Christ that died" (Rom. 8:34). "Where sin abounded, grace did much more abound" (Rom. 5:20). Christ the Restorer plants a new principle of life in the soul, and that plant grows and produces fruit. The grace of Christ purifies while it pardons, and fits men for a holy heaven. We are to grow in grace and in the knowledge of our Lord Jesus Christ until we reach the full stature of men and women in Christ. O that we might all reach the high standard which God has set before us, and no longer remain dwarfs in the religious life! What beams of light would be reflected to the world in good works if we should become light bearers such as God would have us![32]

REPEATING CHRIST'S INVITATION

And the Spirit and the bride say, Come. And let him that heareth say, Come. And let him that is athirst come. And whosoever will, let him take the water of life freely. Rev. 22:17.

Jesus says, ". . . And let him that heareth say, Come. . . ."

Those who are of a contrite heart will receive the message of heaven, and will voice the words of the angel. This is the work of all who have heard the divine invitation. Jesus said to the woman of Samaria what He says to us all, "If thou knewest the gift of God, and who it is that saith to thee, Give me to drink; thou wouldest have asked of him, and he would have given thee living water. . . . But the water that I shall give him shall be in him a well of water springing up into everlasting life" (John 4:10-14).

The words spoken by Jesus Christ are to be repeated by those who believe them. Those who have genuine faith will make it evident by working for souls who are in darkness. . . . They will speak words of warning, of entreaty, and will point out the snow waters of Lebanon to those who are seeking to quench their thirst from the low streams of the valleys of the world. God calls for those who stand as soldiers under His blood-stained banner to go to work. He will clothe His messengers with divine power so that they may reach those who are perishing.[33]

Christ has opened a fountain for the sinful, suffering world, and the voice of divine mercy is heard: "Come, all ye thirsting souls; come and drink." You may take of the water of life freely. Let him that heareth say, Come; and whosoever will, let him come. Let every soul, women as well as men, sound this message. Then the work will be carried to the waste places of the earth. The scripture will be fulfilled: In that day the Lord shall open fountains in the valleys, and "rivers in the desert," and "with joy shall ye draw water out of the wells of salvation" (Isa. 41:18; 43:19; 12:3).[34]

A chain of living witnesses is to carry the invitation to the world. Will you act your part in this great work?[35]

337

AN INEXHAUSTIBLE STOREHOUSE

To the acknowledgement of the mystery of God, and of the Father, and of Christ; in whom are hid all the treasures of wisdom and knowledge. Col. 2:2, 3.

Said Christ, "All things that the Father hath are mine." "I and my Father are one" (John 16:15; 10:30). "I appoint unto you a kingdom" (Luke 22:29). The Lord Jesus lays His hand upon the eternal throne of God with all the ease and assurance of one who rules and reigns, putting on His head the crown of deity. He sits at the right hand of God and receives supreme honor as God, the glory He had before the world was. He distributes His gifts to all who by faith shall claim them. . . .

We have an inexhaustible storehouse, an ocean of love in the God of our salvation. He has placed in the hands of Christ all the treasures of the heavenly resources and says, "All these are for man, in order to convince fallen, sinful man of My love, . . . and that for his happiness I am working and will work." The happiness of man is to know God and Jesus Christ whom He hath sent. It was to make this vast treasure house of all good available that the Word became flesh and dwelt among us. He sprinkled every gift with His own blood. . . . The gift to our world in sending Jesus is an exhibition of His grace which God Himself cannot surpass. . . . But one thing is impossible with God—the power of eclipsing the greatness of His gift in showing His love for fallen man. . . .

Had God the Father come to our world and dwelt among us, humbling Himself, veiling His glory, that humanity might look upon Him, the history that we have of the life of Christ would not have been changed. . . . In every act of Jesus, in every lesson of His instruction, we are to see and hear and recognize God. In sight, in hearing, in effect, it is the voice and movements of the Father.

But language seems to be so feeble! I refrain, and with John exclaim, "Behold, what manner of love the Father hath bestowed upon us, that we should be called the sons of God" (1 John 3:1).[36]

CHRIST IS OUR MESSAGE!

For I determined not to know any thing among you, save Jesus Christ, and him crucified. 1 Cor. 2.2.

The burden of our message should be the mission and life of Jesus Christ. Let there be a dwelling upon the humiliation, self-denial, meekness, and lowliness of Christ, that proud and selfish hearts may see the difference between themselves and the Pattern, and may be humbled. . . .

Describe, if human language can, the humiliation of the Son of God, and think not that you have reached the climax when you see Him exchanging the throne of light and glory which He had with the Father for humanity. He came forth from heaven to earth, and while on earth, He bore the curse of God as surety for the fallen race. He was not obliged to do this. He chose to bear the wrath of God, which man had incurred. . . . He chose to endure the cruel mockings, the deridings, the scourging, and the crucifixion. . . . "He . . . became obedient unto death," but the manner of His death was an astonishment to the universe, for it was even the death of the cross.

Christ was not insensible to ignominy and disgrace. He felt it all most bitterly. He felt it as much more deeply and acutely than we can feel suffering, as His nature was more exalted and pure and holy than that of the sinful race for whom He suffered. He was the Majesty of heaven, He was equal with the Father, He was the Commander of the hosts of angels, yet He died for man the death that was, above all others, clothed with ignominy and reproach. O that the haughty hearts of men might realize this! O that they might enter into the meaning of redemption and seek to learn the meekness and lowliness of Jesus! . . .

The gifts of Him who has all power in heaven and in earth are in store for the children of God. Gifts so precious that they come to us through the costly sacrifice of the Redeemer's blood, gifts that will satisfy the deepest craving of the heart, gifts lasting as eternity, will be received and enjoyed by all who will come to God as little children.[37]

FULLNESS OF THE GODHEAD

And every creature which is in heaven, and on the earth, and under the earth, and such as are in the sea, and all that are in them, heard I saying, Blessing, and honour, and glory, and power, be unto him that sitteth upon the throne, and unto the Lamb for ever and ever. Rev. 5:13.

On the isle of Patmos John saw the things which God desired him to give to the people. Here is a theme worthy of our contemplation. Here are large and comprehensive lessons, which all the angelic hosts are now seeking to communicate. Infinite wisdom, infinite love, infinite justice, infinite mercy—depths, heights, lengths, breadths! Numberless pens have been employed to represent the life and character and mediatorial work of Christ, and yet to every mind through whom the Holy Spirit works these themes are presented fresh and new, just in accordance with the mind and spirit of the human agent. The Lord Jesus promised that the Spirit He would send would recall His words to the minds of those prepared to receive them. After His resurrection He opened their understanding, that they might understand the Scriptures. Up to that time the disciples had not comprehended them, for the rubbish of rabbinical lore had hidden the truth from their view.

The truth, if received, is capable of constant expansion and new developments. It will increase in brightness as we behold it, and grow in height and depth as we aspire to grasp it. Thus it will elevate us to the standard of perfection, and give us faith and trust in God as our strength for the work before us. We need the truth as it is in Jesus. . . . As His representatives and witnesses we need to come to a full understanding of the saving truth which we must know by an experimental knowledge.

"In whom we have redemption through his blood, even the forgiveness of sins" (Col. 1:14). This is the great practical truth which must be stamped upon the soul. It is of the greatest importance that all should comprehend the greatness and power of the truth to those who receive it. "In him dwelleth all the fulness of the Godhead bodily" (Col. 2:9).[38]

340

EXALTING THE MAN OF CALVARY

And as Moses lifted up the serpent in the wilderness, even so must the Son of man be lifted up: that whosoever believeth in him should not perish, but have eternal life. John 3:14, 15.

I point you to the cross of Calvary. I ask you to consider the infinite sacrifice made in your behalf that through faith in Jesus Christ you may not perish but have everlasting life. . . . I point you to Jesus. You are safe in committing to Him the innermost working of your mind. The Lord Jesus hath purchased you with an infinite price. You may commit the keeping of your soul to Jesus. You may trust Him as your Counselor. . . . Constantly draw nigh unto God. He will help you.

O be sure you receive your illumination from the Source of all light. He is the great central Light of the universe of heaven and the great Light of the world. He will enlighten every man that cometh into the world. Reach no cheap, low standard. Cultivate the gentleness of Christ. Secure the highest attainments, and draw your inspiration from Jesus Christ. He is your Friend. You may always depend upon Him and find Him faithful and true. When you need His sympathy in your greatest perplexity, wounded and bruised, He will not pass you by on the other side. To Him you may come in the simplicity of children. To Him you may come with joy and rejoicing. With everything that is flattering to your hopes, every success which attends your labors in the Lord, look up to Jesus and lay every honor at His feet. Everything depends upon your walking in all humility of mind. Write the name of Christ upon your banner and never dishonor your colors.

All heaven was given to us in Christ Jesus. . . . O honor Jesus by giving to Him the heart's best and holiest services He has given His life for you. Who is He that hath done this? The only begotten Son of God, He that was One with the Father before the world was.

Lift up your banner, lift it up higher. Never, never let it trail in the dust of the earth. Exalt Jesus. Lift Him up, the Man of Calvary, higher and still higher.[1]

NOW IS THE TIME TO SHINE

Arise, shine; for thy light is come, and the glory of the Lord is risen upon thee. Isa. 60:1.

We need now to arise and shine, for our light has come, and the glory of the Lord has risen upon us. We have no time to talk of self, no time to become like the sensitive plant, that cannot be touched without shrinking. In Jesus Christ is our sufficiency. Will we talk faith? Will we talk of the glorious hope, of the full and abundant righteousness of Jesus Christ, provided for every soul? . . .

The whole heavenly universe is interested, and the love of God is exercised in behalf of His faithful, commandment-keeping people. It is God in whom we must trust. . . . God has the world in His hand. We have God on our side. All heaven is waiting and longing for our cooperation. The Lord is supreme. Why then should we fear? The Lord is almighty; why should we tremble? In the past God has delivered His people, and He will be our helper if we will arise in His strength and go forward.

The Bible and the Bible only is to be our refuge. God is in His Word. He shall see of the travail of his soul, and shall be satisfied. That is enough for us. "By his knowledge shall my righteous servant justify many; for he shall bear their iniquities" (Isa. 53:11). If the great and loving heart of God is satisfied with the result of His mission in the souls saved, let us rejoice. Let us work as we have never done before. Let us put self aside and lay hold of Jesus Christ by faith. Let us reveal Him to the world as the One altogether lovely and the chiefest among ten thousand.

"After this I beheld, and, lo, a great multitude, which no man could number, of all nations, and kindreds, and people, and tongues, stood before the throne, and before the Lamb, clothed with white robes, and palms in their hands; and cried with a loud voice, saying, Salvation to our God which sitteth upon the throne, and unto the Lamb" (Rev. 7:9, 10).[2]

LIGHT FOR A WORLD IN DARKNESS

For, behold, the darkness shall cover the earth, and gross darkness the people: but the Lord shall arise upon thee, and his glory shall be seen upon thee. And the Gentiles shall come to thy light, and kings to the brightness of thy rising. Isa. 60:2, 3.

Darkness covers the earth and gross darkness the people, and how ardently we should desire the presence of the divine Instructor to lead us in the way of truth and righteousness. God has already spoken to man at sundry times and in divers places and in various ways, yet the world's ignorance is increasing. We must speak with more pronounced utterances concerning the truth, that we may bring to man a knowledge of God. The distinction between Christians and worldlings must be more marked. The Bible must become a book of more prominence among us, and the attentive, diligent searcher by painstaking effort must search for the hidden treasure. The maxims of men, the dogmas of error, though advanced by those who profess to be interpreters of the Word of God, must be discarded, for they are calculated to cover up the truth. . . .

The Jews turned from the Lord Jesus, whom the prophets foretold as the coming Messiah, and they have not been able to see to the end of that which was abolished. In making void the law of God, in turning from the truth with aversion, the Christian world have turned from Christ, and have made manifest the fact that they were not accustomed to looking upon truth of heavenly origin. The darkness has become like a funeral pall, and it covers the whole earth. This is not the time to become weak and sickly in faith. This is no time to permit the world to convert the church of God. Let those who have light now arise and shine. . . .

Those who are waiting for the appearing of our Lord and Saviour Jesus Christ cannot mingle with those who are lovers of pleasures more than lovers of God, who are seeking amusement in games and pleasure parties. As faithful watchmen they must proclaim the warning, "The morning cometh, and also the night" (Isa. 21:12).[3]

PLEDGE OF DIVINE POWER

But ye shall receive power, after that the Holy Ghost is come upon you: and ye shall be witnesses unto me both in Jerusalem, and in all Judaea, and in Samaria, and unto the uttermost part of the earth. Acts 1:8.

On the day of Pentecost the Infinite One revealed Himself in power to the church. By His Holy Spirit He descended from the heights of heaven as a rushing mighty wind to the room in which the disciples were assembled. Words of penitence and confession of sin were mingled with songs of praise for sins forgiven. Words of thanksgiving and of prophecy were heard. All heaven was bending low to behold and adore the wisdom of matchless, incomprehensible love.

The apostles and disciples were lost in wonder, and exclaimed, "Herein is love!" They grasped the imparted gift. Their hearts were surcharged with a benevolence so full, so deep, so far-reaching, that it impelled them to go to the ends of the earth testifying, God forbid that we should glory, save in the cross of our Lord Jesus Christ. They were filled with an intense longing to add to the church such as should be saved. . . .

As the disciples went forth to proclaim the gospel, filled with the power of the Spirit, so God's servants are to go forth today. All around us are fields white unto the harvest. These fields are to be reaped. We are to take up the work, filled with an unselfish desire to give the message of mercy to those who are in the darkness of error and unbelief. God will move on the hearts of believers to carry forward His work to the regions beyond. . . .

The Lord God is bound by an eternal pledge to supply power and grace to every one who is sanctified through obedience to the truth. Jesus Christ, to whom is given all power in heaven and on earth, unites in sympathy with His instrumentalities—the earnest souls who day by day partake of the living bread "which cometh down from heaven" (John 6:33). The church on earth, united with the church in heaven, can accomplish all things.[4]

REVEALING CHRIST IN THE CRISIS

O God, thou art terrible out of thy holy places: the God of Israel is he that giveth strength and power unto his people. Blessed be God. Ps. 68:35.

It is time we were endowed with power from on high. Satan and all his confederacy of evil are working with untiring vigilance to oppose good. Never was there a stronger combination formed to neutralize the lessons and teachings of Christ and to sow the seeds of infidelity in regard to the inspiration of the Scriptures. . . .

Satan is moving with his power from beneath to inspire men to form alliances and confederacies of evil against light and against the Word of God. Infidelity, papacy, and semi-papacy are coming in close and powerful companionship with professed Christianity. The low views of inspiration, the exalting of human ideas from men called wise, are placing human talent above the divine wisdom and forms, and science so-called above the power of vital godliness. These are the signs of the last days. Let everyone who believes in Jesus Christ . . . use his talent of voice in exalting Jesus and presenting testimonies that will magnify, honor, and adore the Word of God. . . . The gospel makes itself known in its power in the consistent, holy, pure lives of those who are believers, hearers, and doers of the Word.

Do not give to the world the impression that Christ has proved to you without form and comeliness . . . and that there is no beauty in Him that you should desire Him. Reveal Christ as He is—the one "altogether lovely" and the "chiefest among ten thousand" (S. of Sol. 5:16, 10). O how His glory is dimmed by His professed followers because they are earthly-minded, disobedient, unthankful, and unholy! How shamefully is the Lord Jesus kept in the background! How is His mercy, His forbearance, His long-suffering, and His matchless love veiled, and His honor beclouded by the perversity of His professed followers! . . . Lift up Jesus. Talk of His love, tell of His power, and let self be lost behind the glory of His person and the mighty power of the cross of Calvary.[5]

FORTRESS OF THE SOUL

Finally, my brethren, be strong in the Lord, and in the power of his might. Eph. 6:10.

This has always been applicable to God's people in every age of the world, but how much more so to the remnant church who have to meet the constant and most powerful masterly workings of the power of darkness for this last time. The words of the apostle come sounding down the lines to this time: "Put on the whole armour of God, that ye may be able to stand against the wiles of the devil. For we wrestle not against flesh and blood, but against principalities, against powers, against the rulers of the darkness of this world, against spiritual wickedness in high places" (Eph. 6:11, 12).

These words inspired of God are appropriate for us. They apply in a special manner to those who are endeavoring to keep the commandments of God amidst a crooked and perverse nation among whom they shine as lights in the world. O how solemn, how fearfully solemn is this time for the youth among us who have had great light, . . . that their words, spirit, and character shall not be misleading to those with whom they associate. . . .

"Take unto you the whole armour of God" (verse 13). Make your guide the Word. "Take" it. The whole armor which is furnished you in the Scriptures is all prepared for you to take. Wherefore take unto you the whole armour of God, that ye may be able to withstand in the evil day, and having done all, to stand. Stand therefore, having your loins girt about with truth (verses 13, 14).

Fiction, spurious interpretations of the Scriptures, dishes of fables, are everywhere presented for your acceptance. But great discernment is needed that the girdle should be the golden chain of truth. "And having on the breastplate of righteousness"—not your own, but the righteousness of Christ. This is the fortress of the soul. We may, with Christ's righteousness going before us, withstand the moral darkness and penetrate the devices of the satanic agencies.[6]

BRIGHTER AND BRIGHTER STILL

But the path of the just is as the shining light, that shineth more and more unto the perfect day. Prov. 4:18.

The great error with churches in all ages has been to reach a certain point in their understanding of Bible truth and there stop. There they anchored. They ceased to "Go forward," as much as to say, "We have all-sufficient light. We need no more." . . .

The Lord loves His people, and would lead them step by step onward under the banner of truth, the third angel's message. . . . In these last days we have the benefit of the wisdom and experience of past ages. The men of God, saints and martyrs, have made confession of their faith, and the knowledge of their experience and their burning zeal for God is transmitted to the world in the living oracles. . . . This hereditary trust has been gathered up by faithful witnesses that the bright light shining upon them in the knowledge of God might enlighten those living in these last days; and while they appreciate this light, they will advance to greater light. . . .

The Source of all light still invites us to come and absorb its rays. Light is not placed where the followers of Christ cannot obtain its benefits. It is not cut off from the world so there is no more or increased light to shine in greater clearness and more abundantly upon all who have improved the light given of God.

God's people in these last days are not to choose darkness rather than light. They are to look for light, to expect light. . . . The light will continue to shine in brighter and still brighter rays, and reveal more and more distinctly the truth as it is in Jesus, that human hearts and human characters may be improved, and moral darkness—which Satan is working to bring over the people of God—may be dispelled. . . . As we near the close of time there will be needed a deeper and clearer discernment, a more firm knowledge of the Word of God, a living experience, and the holiness of heart and life which we must have to serve Him.[7]

HE IS COMING AGAIN!

And, behold, I come quickly; and my reward is with me, to give every man according as his work shall be. Rev. 22:12.

Was Christ a false prophet when He uttered these words? More than eighteen hundred years have passed since John heard this great truth, and the Lord has not yet come to reign. But shall we give up looking for His appearance? Shall we say, "My lord delayeth his coming"?[8]

"And Enoch also, the seventh from Adam, prophesied of these, saying, Behold, the Lord cometh with ten thousands of his saints" (Jude 14) . . . . The doctrine of Christ's coming was made known at this early date to the man who walked with God in continual communion. The godly character of this prophet is to represent the state of holiness to which the people of God must attain who expect to be translated to heaven. . . .

Shall we say we have been deceived in regard to the doctrine of Christ's near coming? . . . Shall we say that all our work to make ready a people prepared for His coming has been for nought? Never. . . . "Let us hold fast the profession of our faith without wavering; . . . and let us consider one another to provoke"—unto doubts and unbelief, and apostasy? No, but "unto love and to good works: not forsaking the assembling of ourselves together, . . . but exhorting one another: and so much the more, as ye see the day approaching" (Heb. 10:23-25).

We must have a knowledge of the Scriptures, that we may trace down the lines of prophecy and . . . see that the day is approaching, so that with increased zeal and effort we may exhort one another to faithfulness. . . . Give up our faith? lose our confidence? become impatient? No, no. We will not think of such a thing. . . . See how the specifications of the prophecies have been and are fulfilling. Let us lift up our heads and rejoice, for our redemption draweth nigh. It is nearer than when we first believed. Shall we not wait patiently, filled with courage and faith? Shall we not make ready a people to stand in the day of final reckoning?[9]

WHY THE LORD DELAYS

But, beloved, be not ignorant of this one thing, that one day is with the Lord as a thousand years, and a thousand years as one day. The Lord is not slack concerning his promise, as some men count slackness; but is longsuffering to us-ward, not willing that any should perish, but that all should come to repentance. 2 Peter 3:8, 9.

As I have labored since 1843 and 1844 I have felt so thankful that the Lord has permitted time to last to do more fully the missionary work that was needing to be done to warn our cities. O our wise heavenly Father made the infinite sacrifice of His only begotten Son! He gave Him to our world that the world might, through the merciful provisions made, accept the Word—Bible truth—and prepare for the great event of His coming. That which caused the believing church so much sorrow in their disappointment in the time of His coming has been a reason of thanksgiving for the delay. Now the angels of God are preparing the way for the truth to reach all nations.

There are thousands in the cities, in the byways and the highways, to hear the warning message. Are we awake? Do we understand there is a world to have the warning? The cities are all to be worked diligently. We must arouse and do a great work. There are many more to hear the last warning message to a perishing world. We have no time to delay, for Satan is doing his best to destroy souls.

I now praise God for His long and merciful forbearance. The message has been carried to many countries. It is a worldwide message. There is most diligent work to do to warn our cities. We have had opportunity to send the light to many thousands who have rejoiced in the truth and sacrificed their time and their means to build up the sanitariums and churches in all parts of America. Schools have been established and new fields are opening, many in new countries. The work at times has moved slowly. . . . It is for the need of the Holy Spirit that many more places are not hearing the last message of warning. . . . Angels are waiting to fit up converted men and women to do this work if they will consecrate their whole heart, mind, and soul to the work. We have no time to lose.[10]

THE REVELATION OF CHARACTER

And while they went to buy, the bridegroom came; and they that were ready went in with him to the marriage: and the door was shut. Matt. 25:10.

Let none follow the example of the foolish virgins and think that it will be safe to wait until the crisis comes before gaining a preparation of character to stand in that time. It will be too late to seek for the righteousness of Christ when the guests are called in and examined. Now is the time to put on the righteousness of Christ—the wedding garment that will fit you to enter into the marriage supper of the Lamb. In the parable, the foolish virgins are represented as begging for oil and failing to receive it at their request. This is symbolic of those who have not prepared themselves by developing a character to stand in a time of crisis. It is as if they should go to their neighbors and say, Give me your character or I shall be lost. Those that were wise could not impart their oil to the flickering lamps of the foolish virgins. Character is not transferable. It is not to be bought or sold; it is to be acquired. The Lord has given to every individual an opportunity to obtain a righteous character . . . , but He has not provided a way by which one human agent may impart to another the character which he has developed. . . .

The day is coming, and it is close upon us, when every phase of character will be revealed by special temptation. Those who remain true to principle, who exercise faith to the end, will be those who have proved true under test and trial during the previous hours of their probation, and have formed characters after the likeness of Christ. It will be those who have cultivated close acquaintance with Christ who, through His wisdom and grace, are partakers of the divine nature. But no human being can give to another, heart devotion and noble qualities of mind, and supply his deficiencies with moral power.[11]

Let no one put off the day of preparation, lest the call be made, "Go forth to meet the bridegroom," and you be found as were the foolish virgins, with no oil in your vessels with your lamps.[12]

WATCH! WATCH! WATCH!

Watch ye therefore: for ye know not when the master of the house cometh, at even, or at midnight, or at the cockcrowing, or in the morning: lest coming suddenly he find you sleeping. And what I say unto you I say unto all, Watch. Mark 13:35-37.

It is a time now when we cannot for a moment take the spiritual eye from Christ Jesus. His admonition to us is, "What I say unto you I say unto all, Watch." Is there one professed Christian who needs not the warning, and whose heart will not bear watching? The heart must be kept with all diligence, under constant watchfulness. . . .

Watch the stealthy approach of the enemy, watch against old habits and natural inclinations lest they exert themselves; force them back, and watch; force them back if need be a hundred times. Watch the thoughts, watch the plans, lest they become selfish and self-centered. Watch and pray, lest ye enter into temptation. Watch over the souls whom Christ has purchased with His own blood. Watch for opportunities to do them good.

Like Mary, we need to sit at the feet of Jesus to learn of Him, having chosen that better part which will never be taken from us. Like Martha we need to be ever abounding in the work of the Lord. The higher Christian attainments can be reached only by being much on our knees in sincere prayer. . . . One fiber of the root of selfishness remaining in the soul will spring up when least expected, and thereby will many be defiled.[13]

We are in an enemy's country. He who was cast out of heaven has come down with great power. With every conceivable artifice and device he is seeking to take souls captive. Unless we are constantly on guard we shall fall an easy prey to his unnumbered deceptions.

We are stewards, entrusted by our absent Lord with the care of His household and His interests, which He came to this world to serve. He has returned to heaven, leaving us in charge, and He expects us to watch and wait and prepare for His coming. Let us be faithful to our trust, lest coming suddenly He find us sleeping.[14]

STANDING FIRM IN DAYS OF PERIL

But the end of all things is at hand: be ye therefore sober, and watch unto prayer. 1 Peter 4:7.

The signs of the times tell us that the end of all things is at hand. Prophecies fulfilled have become facts of history, clearly defining our position. We are standing upon the verge of the eternal world. . . . Our Lord forewarned His people that iniquity would abound in the last days and would have a paralyzing influence upon true godliness. Wickedness is seen and heard and felt all around us. It seems to permeate the very atmosphere, and affects the faith and love of God's professed people. It is difficult to hold fast Christian integrity. The fact is, much which is current in our day as Christianity is indebted for its very existence to the absence of persecution. When the test of fiery trial comes, a great proportion of these who profess the faith will show that their religion was hollow formalism. . . .

The days in which we live are days of peril. Carelessness, levity, love of pleasure and selfish gratification, are seen in the lives of very many professed Christians. Is this the time for Seventh-day Adventists to lose their faith and grow cold and formal? God forbid! Shall we turn traitor at the very moment when God would be most glorified by our steadfast adherence to principle? Shall we turn from the heavenly attractions now, when we can almost see the glories on the other shore? We are living in the most important period of earth's history. By maintaining our allegiance to God, we may bear the noblest testimony for Christ and the truth.

The true Christian will cling to the promises of God more firmly now than ever before. His heart is where he has laid up his treasure— in heaven. When right principles are despised and forsaken, then the true and loyal will show their warmest zeal and deepest love; then they will stand most firmly for truth, unpopular though it be. . . .

The Lord is coming. . . . Let us be consistent; let our works correspond with our profession of faith.[15]

QUALIFICATIONS OF HEAVENLY CITIZENSHIP

Blessed are they that do his commandments, that they may have right to the tree of life, and may enter in through the gates into the city. Rev. 22:14.

"Whatsoever a man soweth, that shall he also reap" (Gal. 6:7). I want to sow for time and eternity. My heart hungers and thirsts after righteousness. I want my life hid in Christ Jesus, that my sowing shall bring me the right kind of a harvest. I feel deeply in regard to my own self, for every day, in words or in actions, I am sowing either tares or wheat. I want to sow for time or eternity. I have lived nearly the period of my allotted time, and what shall the harvest be? I want a quiet and unwavering trust in the Most High. I have experienced His protecting care in a remarkable manner when following the path of duty. I want to go down to the grave as a shock of corn fully ripe. I want no complaining in my heart; only gratitude should abide there. God's mercy and His loving-kindness are to be kept, not as a thing out of mind, but as something so precious as never to be forgotten. As eyewitnesses of His majesty we may exalt and praise His holy name. We are with Him in the holy mount.

Every moment of time is precious and weighty with eternal consequences. We are in a world of appearances which mock and deceive like the apples of Sodom. O how the Lord looks upon the double-dealing and the duplicity which is in our world! If we could not get a glimpse above and beyond the clouds to the bright beams of the Sun of Righteousness we might well be downcast, but Jesus lives. . . .

The discipline in the school of Christ will cause the church to lean upon the arm of her Beloved. The redeemed of the Lord shall at last come to Zion with songs and everlasting joy upon their heads, in victorious triumph. All the angelic hosts will rejoice over them with singing. But what are the qualifications of our citizenship? "Blessed are they that do his commandments, that they may have right to the tree of life, and may enter in through the gates into the city." [16]

CRISIS OF THE AGES

Alas! for that day is great, so that none is like it: it is even the time of Jacob's trouble; but he shall be saved out of it. Jer. 30:7.

The fulfilling of the signs of the times gives evidence that the day of the Lord is near at hand. . . . The crisis is stealing gradually upon us. The sun shines in the heavens, passing over its usual round, and the heavens still declare the glory of God. Men are still eating and drinking, planting and building, marrying and giving in marriage. Merchants are still buying and selling. . . . Pleasure lovers are still crowding to theaters, horse races, gambling hells. The highest excitement prevails, yet probation's hour is fast closing, and every case is about to be eternally decided. Satan sees that his time is short. He has set all his agents to work, that men may be deceived, deluded, occupied, and entranced until the day of probation shall be ended and the door of mercy be forever shut. . . .

The "time of trouble, such as never was" (Dan. 12:1) is soon to open upon us, and we shall need an experience which many are too indolent to obtain. . . . Now, while our great High Priest is making the atonement for us, we should seek to become perfect in Christ. Not even by a thought could our Saviour be brought to yield to the power of temptation. Satan finds in human hearts some point where he can gain a foothold; some sinful desire is cherished, by means of which his temptations assert their power. But Christ declared of Himself, "The prince of this world cometh, and hath nothing in me" (John 14:30). Satan could find nothing in the Son of God that would enable him to gain the victory. He had kept His Father's commandments, and there was no sin in Him that Satan could use to his advantage. This is the condition in which those must be found who shall stand in the time of trouble.

"Our God shall come, and shall not keep silence: . . . He shall call to the heavens from above, and to the earth, that he may judge his people. Gather my saints together unto me; those that have made a covenant with me by sacrifice" (Ps. 50:3-5).[17]

A SAFE HIDING PLACE

Because thou hast kept the word of my patience, I also will keep thee from the hour of temptation, which shall come upon all the world, to try them that dwell upon the earth. Rev. 3:10.

God keeps a reckoning with the nations. . . . In this age a more than common contempt is shown to God. Men have reached a point in insolence and disobedience which shows that their cup of iniquity is almost full. . . . The Spirit of God is being withdrawn from the earth. When the angel of mercy folds her wings and departs, Satan will do the evil deeds he has long wished to do. Storm and tempest, war and bloodshed—in these things he delights, and thus he gathers in his harvest. And so completely will men be deceived by him that they will declare that these calamities are the result of the desecration of the first day of the week. From the pulpits of the popular churches will be heard the statement that the world is being punished because Sunday is not honored as it should be. . . .

Satan will bring in pleasing fables to meet the minds of all who love not the truth. With angry zeal he will accuse commandment keepers. . . . Satan claims the world, but there is a little company who withstand his devices and contend earnestly for the faith once delivered to the saints. Satan sets himself to destroy this commandment-keeping company. But God is their tower of defense. He will raise up for them a standard against the enemy. He will be to them "as an hiding place from the wind," and "as the shadow of a great rock in a weary land" (Isa. 32:2). He will say to them, "Come, my people, enter thou into thy chambers, and shut thy doors about thee: hide thyself as it were for a little moment, until the indignation be overpast. For, behold, the Lord cometh out of his place to punish the inhabitants of the earth for their iniquity: the earth also shall disclose her blood, and shall no more cover her slain" (Isa. 26:20, 21). "And the ransomed of the Lord shall return, and come to Zion with songs and everlasting joy upon their heads: they shall obtain joy and gladness, and sorrow and sighing shall flee away" (Isa. 35:10).[18]

IT WILL NOT BE LONG

Come, my people, enter thou into thy chambers, and shut thy doors about thee: hide thyself as it were for a little moment, until the indignation be overpast. Isa. 26:20.

It will not be long until the gathering storm will burst upon the world that is so asleep in sin. . . . When the earth is reeling to and fro like a drunkard, when the heavens are shaking, and the great day of the Lord has come, who shall be able to stand? One object they behold in trembling agony from which they will try in vain to escape. "Behold, he cometh with clouds; and every eye shall see him" (Rev. 1:7). The unsaved utter wild imprecations to dumb nature—their god: "Mountains and rocks, 'Fall on us, and hide us from the face of him that sitteth on the throne'" (Rev. 6:16).

Creation is loyal to her God, and deaf to the frenzied call. That unrequited love is now turned to wrath. Sinners who would not let Jesus take away their sins are rushing from place to place in search of a hiding place, crying, The harvest is past, the summer is ended, and our souls are not saved! . . .

That Lamb whose wrath will be so terrible to the scorners of His grace will be grace and righteousness and love and blessing to all who have received Him. The pillar of cloud that was dark with terror and avenging wrath to the Egyptians, was to the people of God a pillar of fire for brightness. So will it be to the Lord's people in these last days. The light and glory of God to His commandment-keeping people are darkness to the unbelieving. They see that it is a fearful thing to fall into the hands of the living God. The arm, long stretched, strong to save all who come unto Him, is strong to execute His judgment upon all who would not come unto Him that they might have life. God grant that while mercy still lingers, while the voice of invitation is still heard, there will be a turning unto the Lord. The sure provision has been made to shelter every soul and shield those who have kept His commandments until the indignation be overpast.[19]

THE BEST SPECIFICATION WE CAN HAVE

Looking for that blessed hope, and the glorious appearing of the great God and our Saviour Jesus Christ. Titus 2:13.

We are Adventists. We are looking for the appearing of our Lord and Saviour Jesus Christ, and we love to think about it. We know in whom we have believed, and are not afraid to commit the keeping of our souls unto Him against that day. We are not at all humiliated by confessing ourselves to be Adventists. . . .

We believe the Sabbath of the fourth commandment because it is written plainly and is the foundation of our religious faith. Let none of us be ashamed of this. . . . We accept not the authority of men's councils, but we go further back, even to the councils of heaven. "For ever, O Lord, thy word is settled in heaven" (Ps. 119:89). We take a "Thus saith the Lord." Here we stand. A doctrine that has not a "Thus saith the Lord" may be accepted by the whole world, but that does not make it truth. . . . If we want to know the way to heaven we must study the Bible, not man-made theories or man's suppositions. . . . We are not at all ashamed of our faith, Seventh-day Adventism, for it is the very best specification we can have. We are waiting for the second coming of our Lord and Saviour Jesus Christ. Men may scoff and ridicule our faith, but this should not provoke or surprise us. All these demonstrations do not make the truth error, neither do they make error truth. We take our stand firmly and unmovably upon the platform of the Word of God. . . .

Eternal realities must be kept before the mind's eye, and the attractions of the world will appear as they are—altogether profitless. . . . We are pilgrims and strangers who are waiting, hoping, and praying for that blessed hope, the glorious appearing of our Lord and Saviour Jesus Christ. If we believe this and bring it into our practical life, what vigorous action would this faith and hope inspire; what fervent love one for another; what careful holy living for the glory of God; and . . . what distinct lines of demarcation would be evidenced between us and the world![20]

A CONSTANT READINESS

Therefore be ye also ready: for in such an hour as ye think not the Son of man cometh. Matt. 24:44.

We are incapable of looking into the future, which often causes us disquietude and unhappiness. But one of the greatest evidences we have of the loving-kindness of God is His concealment of the events of the morrow. Our ignorance of tomorrow makes us more vigilant and earnest today. We cannot see what is before us. Our best-laid plans sometimes seem to be unwise and faulty. We think, "If we only knew the future!" But God would have His children trust in Him and be ready to go where He shall lead them. We know not the precise time when our Lord shall be revealed in the clouds of heaven, but He has told us that our only safety is in a constant readiness—a position of watching and waiting. Whether we have one year before us, or five, or ten, we are to be faithful to our trust today. We are to perform each day's duties as faithfully as though that day were to be our last.

We are not doing the will of God if we wait in idleness. To every man He has given his work, and He expects each one to do his part with fidelity. . . . As never before, resistance must be made against sin—against the powers of darkness. The time demands energetic and determined activity on the part of those who believe present truth. They should teach the truth by both precept and example.

If the time seems long to wait for our Deliverer to come, if, bowed by affliction and worn with toil, we feel impatient for our commission to close, and to receive an honorable release from the warfare, let us remember—and let the remembrance check every murmur—that God leaves us on earth to encounter storms and conflicts, to perfect Christian character, to become better acquainted with God our Father and Christ our Elder Brother, and to do work for the Master in winning many souls to Christ, that with glad heart we may hear the words "Well done, good and faithful servant; . . . enter thou into the joy of thy lord" (Matt. 25:23).[21]

THE DAY OF FINAL SETTLEMENT

And I saw the dead, small and great, stand before God; and the books were opened: and another book was opened, which is the book of life: and the dead were judged out of those things which were written in the books, according to their works. Rev. 20:12.

The Scriptures declare, "God shall bring every work into judgment, with every secret thing, whether it be good, or whether it be evil" (Eccl. 12:14). There is not a shadow of doubt about this matter. . . . Sin may be concealed, denied, covered up from father, mother, wife, children, and associates. No one but the guilty actors may cherish the least suspicion of the wrong, but it is laid bare before the intelligences of heaven. The darkness of the darkest night, the secrecy of all deceptive arts, is not sufficient to veil one thought from the knowledge of the Eternal. . . .

The Lord beheld Adam and Eve as they took of the forbidden tree. In their guilt they fled from His presence and hid themselves, but God saw them; they could not cover their shame from His eyes. When Cain slew his brother, he thought to hide his crime by denial of his deed, but the Lord said, "The voice of thy brother's blood crieth unto me from the ground" (Gen. 4:10). . . .

All sin unrepented of and unconfessed will remain upon the books of record. It will not be blotted out, it will not go beforehand to judgment, to be canceled by the atoning blood of Jesus. The accumulated sins of every individual will be written with absolute accuracy, and the penetrating light of God's law will try every secret of darkness. In proportion to the light, to the opportunities, and the knowledge of God's claims upon them will be the condemnation of the rejecters of God's mercy.

The day of final settlements is just before us. . . .

The Bible presents the law of God as a perfect standard by which to shape the life and character. The only perfect example of obedience to its precepts is found in the Son of God, the Saviour of lost mankind. There is no stain of unrighteousness upon Him, and we are bidden to follow in His steps.[22]

FEAR NOT, CHILD OF GOD

And when I saw him, I fell at his feet as dead. And he laid his right hand upon me, saying unto me, Fear not; I am the first and the last: I am he that liveth, and was dead; and, behold, I am alive for evermore, Amen; and have the keys of hell and of death. Rev. 1:17, 18.

John, exiled upon the Isle of Patmos, . . . hears a voice saying, "I am Alpha and Omega, the first and the last" (Rev. 1:11). At the sound of the voice John falls down in astonishment as if dead. He is unable to bear the sight of the divine glory. But a hand raises John up, and the voice he remembers as the voice of his Master. He is strengthened and can endure to talk with the Lord Jesus.

So will it be with the remnant people of God who are scattered—some in the mountain fastnesses, some exiled, some pursued, some persecuted. When the voice of God is heard and the brightness of the glory is revealed, when the trial is over, the dross removed, they know they are in the presence of One who has redeemed them by His own blood. Just what Christ was to John in his exile He will be to His people who are made to feel the hand of oppression for the faith and testimony of Jesus Christ. . . . These were driven by the storm and tempest of persecution to the crevices of the rocks, but were hiding in the Rock of Ages; and in the fastnesses of the mountains, in the caves and dens of the earth, the Saviour reveals His presence and His glory. Yet a little while, and He that is to come will come and will not tarry. His eyes as a flame of fire penetrate into the fast-closed dungeons and hunt out the hidden ones, for their names are written in the Lamb's book of life. These eyes of the Saviour are above us, around us, noting every difficulty, discerning every danger; and there is no place where His eyes cannot penetrate, no sorrows and sufferings of His people where the sympathy of Christ does not reach. . . .

The child of God will be terror-stricken at the first sight of the majesty of Jesus Christ. He feels that he cannot live in His holy presence. But the word comes to him as to John, "Fear not." Jesus laid His right hand upon John; He raised him up from his prostrate position. So will He do unto His loyal, trusting ones.[23]

ROBED IN HIS PERFECTION

And now, little children, abide in him; that, when he shall appear, we may have confidence, and not be ashamed before him at his coming. 1 John 2:28.

Jesus came into the world to save sinners, not *in* their sins but *from* their sins, and to sanctify them through the truth; and in order that He may become a perfect Saviour to us, we must enter into union with Him by a personal act of faith. Christ has chosen us, we have chosen Him, and by this choice we become united to Him and are to live from henceforth, not unto ourselves, but unto Him who has died for us. But this union can only be preserved by constant watchfulness, lest we fall into temptation and make a different choice, for we are free always to take another master if we so desire. Union with Christ means an unfailing preference for Him in every act and thought. . . .

We are to consider ourselves as constituting the family of Christ, and we are to follow Him as dear children. Adopted into the household of God, shall we not honor our Father and our kindred? . . .

We must establish an unyielding enmity between our souls and our foe, but we must open our hearts to the power and influence of the Holy Spirit. We want Satan's darkness to be shut out and the light of Heaven to flow in. We want to become so sensitive to holy influences that the lightest whisper of Jesus will move our souls. . . . Then we shall delight to do the will of God, and Christ can own us before the Father and before the holy angels as those who abide in Him. . . .

But we shall not boast of our holiness. As we have clearer views of Christ's spotless and infinite purity we shall feel as did Daniel when he beheld the glory of the Lord and said, "My comeliness was turned in me into corruption" (Dan. 10:8). We cannot say, "I am sinless" till this vile body is changed and fashioned like unto His glorious body. But if we constantly seek to follow Jesus, the blessed hope is ours of standing before the throne of God without spot, or wrinkle, or any such thing, complete in Christ, robed in His righteousness and perfection.[24]

ON THE THRESHOLD OF ETERNITY

So when this corruptible shall have put on incorruption, and this mortal shall have put on immortality, then shall be brought to pass the saying that is written, Death is swallowed up in victory. 1 Cor. 15:54.

How precious to those who are losing their loved of this world are their faith and hope in the promises of God which open before them the future immortal life! Their hopes may fasten upon unseen realities of the future world. Christ has risen from the dead the first fruits. Hope and faith strengthen the soul to pass through the dark shadows of the tomb, in full faith of coming forth to immortal life in the morning of the resurrection. The Paradise of God, the home of the blessed! There all tears shall be wiped from off all faces! When Christ shall come the second time, to be "admired in all them that believe" (2 Thess. 1:10), death shall be swallowed up in victory, and there shall be no more sickness, no more sorrow, no more death! A rich promise is given to us: "Blessed are they that do his commandments, that they may have right to the tree of life, and may enter in through the gates into the city" (Rev. 22:14). Is not this promise rich and comforting to those who love God?[25]

The resurrection of Jesus was a sample of the final resurrection of all who sleep in Him. The risen body of the Saviour, His deportment, the accents of His speech, were all familiar to His followers. In like manner will those who sleep in Jesus rise again. We shall know our friends even as the disciples knew Jesus. Though they may have been deformed, diseased, or disfigured in this mortal life, yet in their resurrected and glorified body their individual identity will be perfectly preserved, and we shall recognize, in the face radiant with the light shining from the face of Jesus, the lineaments of those we love.[26]

The Life-giver will call up His purchased possession in the first resurrection, and until that triumphant hour, when the last trump shall sound and the vast army shall come forth to eternal victory, every sleeping saint will be kept in safety and will be guarded as a precious jewel, who is known to God by name.[27]

AN ABIDING PLACE FOR YOU

Let not your heart be troubled: ye believe in God, believe also in me. In my Father's house are many mansions: if it were not so, I would have told you. I go to prepare a place for you. And if I go and prepare a place for you, I will come again, and receive you unto myself; that where I am, there ye may be also. John 14:1-3.

When Christ lay in the tomb, His disciples called to mind these words. They pondered over them, and wept because they could not fathom the meaning of them. No faith and hope relieved the brokenhearted disciples. They could only repeat the words, "I will come again, and receive you unto myself. . . ."

Mansions are prepared for all who have subjected themselves in obedience to the divine law. And in order that the human family might have no excuse because of Satan's temptations, Christ became one with them. The only Being who was one with God lived the law in humanity, descended to the lowly life of a common laborer, and toiled at the carpenter's bench with His earthly parent. He lived the life which He requires of all who claim to be His children. Thus was cut off the powerful argument of Satan that God required of humanity a self-denial and subjection that He would not Himself render. . . .

Jesus asks no more of men than that they shall follow in His footsteps. He was the Majesty of heaven, the King of glory, but for our sakes He became poor that we through His poverty might be made rich. Almost His last words to us are, "Let not your heart be troubled: ye believe in God, believe also in me." In the place of being sorrowful, your hearts troubled, you should rejoice. I came into the world for your sakes. My time here is now accomplished. I shall henceforth be in heaven. For your sakes I have been an interested worker in the world. In the future I shall be engaged just as devotedly in a more important work in your behalf. I came into the world to redeem you. I go to prepare an abiding place for you in My Father's kingdom.[28]

What a comfort these words should be to us! Think of the work Christ is now doing in heaven—preparing mansions for His children. He wants us to prepare to dwell in these mansions.[29]

WE SHALL SEE HIS FACE

And they shall see his face; and his name shall be in their foreheads. Rev. 22:4.

We cannot now see the glory of God, but it is only by receiving Him here that we shall be able by and by to see Him face to face. God would have us keep our eyes fixed on Him, that we may lose sight of the things of this world. We have . . . no time for any of us to delay that preparation which will enable us to see the face of God. . . .

Only by looking to Jesus, the Lamb of God, and following in His steps, can you prepare to meet God. Follow Him, and you will one day walk the golden streets of the city of God. You will see Him who laid aside His royal garments and His kingly crown, and disguising Himself with humanity, came to our world and bore our sins, that He might lift us up and give us a revelation of His glory and majesty. We shall see Him face to face if we now give ourselves up to be molded and fashioned by Him and prepared for a place in the kingdom of God.

Those who consecrate their lives to the service of God will live with Him through the ceaseless ages of eternity. "God himself shall be with them, and be their God" (Rev. 21:3). . . .

Their minds were given to God in this world; they served Him with their heart and intellect, and now He can put His name in their foreheads. "And there shall be no night there; . . . for the Lord God giveth them light: and they shall reign for ever and ever" (Rev. 22:5). They do not go in as those that beg a place there, for Christ says to them, "Come, ye blessed of my Father, inherit the kingdom prepared for you from the foundation of the world" (Matt. 25:34). He takes them as His children, saying, Enter ye into the joy of your Lord. The crown of immortality is placed on the brow of the overcomers. They take their crowns and cast them at the feet of Jesus, and touching their golden harps, they fill all heaven with rich music in songs of praise to the Lamb. Then "they shall see his face; and his name shall be in their foreheads." [30]

MYSTERIES YET TO BE UNFOLDED

And to make all men see what is the fellowship of the mystery, which from the beginning of the world hath been hid in God, who created all things by Jesus Christ. Eph. 3:9.

Many have endeavored to define the mystery which Paul here mentions. But it embraces much, and our ideas in regard to the love, the goodness, and the compassion of God are strangely limited. Because our knowledge of spiritual things has become so dwarfed and enfeebled, we have not advanced from light to greater light. The Lord has not been able to open to our understanding many precious things. In view of the losses which we have sustained by our earthliness and commonness we have much to make us humble. . . .

Since the promise given in Eden, God has revealed His mysteries through His prophets. . . . But many mysteries yet remain unrevealed. How much that is acknowledged to be truth is mysterious and unexplainable to the human mind! How dark seem the dispensations of Providence! What necessity there is for implicit faith and trust in God's moral government! . . . "How unsearchable are his judgments, and his ways past finding out!" (Rom. 11:33).

We are not now sufficiently advanced in spiritual attainments to comprehend the mysteries of God. But when we shall compose the family of heaven, these mysteries will be unfolded before us. . . .

Then much will be revealed in explanation of matters upon which God now keeps silence because we have not gathered up and appreciated that which has been made known of the eternal mysteries. The ways of Providence will be made clear; the mysteries of grace through Christ will be unfolded. That which the mind cannot now grasp, which is hard to be understood, will be explained. We shall see order in that which has seemed unexplainable, wisdom in everything withheld, goodness and gracious mercy in everything imparted. Truth will be unfolded to the mind, free from obscurity, in a single line, and its brightness will be endurable. The heart will be made to sing for joy. Controversies will be forever ended, and all difficulties will be solved.[31]

TRIUMPH OF GOD'S LOVE

The Lord reigneth; let the earth rejoice; let the multitude of isles be glad thereof. Clouds and darkness are round about him: righteousness and judgment are the habitation of his throne. Ps. 97:1, 2.

The law of love is the foundation of God's government, and the service of love the only service acceptable to Heaven. God has granted freedom of will to all, endowed men with capacity to appreciate His character, and therefore with ability to love Him and to choose His service. So long as created beings worshiped God they were in harmony throughout the universe. While love to God was supreme, love to others abounded. As there was no transgression of the law, which is the transcript of God's character, no note of discord jarred the celestial harmonies.

But known unto God are all His works, and from eternal ages the covenant of grace (unmerited favor) existed in the mind of God. It is called the everlasting covenant, for the plan of salvation was not conceived after the fall of man, but it was that which was "kept in silence through times eternal, but now is manifested, and . . . made known unto all the nations . . ." (Rom. 16:25, 26, RV). . . .

Before Him who ruleth in the heavens the mysteries of the past and future are alike outspread, and God sees beyond the woe and darkness and ruin that sin has wrought, the outworking of His purpose of love and blessing. Though clouds and darkness are round about Him, yet righteousness and judgment are the foundation of His throne. . . . Through the plan of salvation a larger purpose is to be wrought out even than the salvation of man and the redemption of the earth. Through the revelation of the character of God in Christ, the beneficence of the divine government would be manifested before the universe, the charge of Satan refuted, the nature and result of sin made plain, and the perpetuity of the law fully demonstrated.[32]

Then the extermination of sin will vindicate God's love and establish His honor before a universe of beings who delight to do His will, and in whose heart is His law.[33]

THE FULFILLMENT OF GOD'S PURPOSE

To the intent that now unto the principalities and powers in heavenly places might be known by the church the manifold wisdom of God, according to the eternal purpose which he purposed in Christ Jesus our Lord. Eph. 3:10, 11.

We should consider that it was not merely to accomplish the redemption of man that Christ came to earth, it was not merely that the inhabitants of this little world might regard the law of God as it should be regarded, but it was to demonstrate to all the worlds that God's law is unchangeable and that the wages of sin is death.

There is a great deal more to this subject than we can take in at a glance. O that all might see the importance of carefully studying the Scriptures! Many seem to have the idea that this world and the heavenly mansions constitute the universe of God. Not so. The redeemed throng will range from world to world, and much of their time will be employed in searching out the mysteries of redemption. And throughout the whole stretch of eternity this subject will be continually opening to their minds. The privileges of those who overcome by the blood of the Lamb and the word of their testimony are beyond comprehension.

We have each to battle with the fallen foe. . . . Begin the warfare at once by gaining victories over self. Do not give place to the devil. . . . Throw all the weight of your influence on the side of Christ.

When you look at the cross of Calvary you cannot doubt God's love or His willingness to save. He has worlds upon worlds that give Him divine honor, and heaven and all the universe would have been just as happy if He had left this world to perish, but so great was His love for the fallen race that He gave His own dear Son to die that they might be redeemed from eternal death. As we see the care, the love, that God has for us, let us respond to it; let us give to Jesus all the powers of our being, fighting manfully the battles of the Lord. We cannot afford to lose our souls; we cannot afford to sin against God. Life, eternal life in the kingdom of glory, is worth everything.[34]

THE JOY SET BEFORE HIM

Who for the joy that was set before him endured the cross, despising the shame, and is set down at the right hand of the throne of God. Heb. 12:2.

The work of Christ upon earth was to seek and save that which was lost. Ever before Him He saw the result of His mission, although the baptism of blood must first be received, although the weight of sins of the world was to gather upon His innocent soul, although the shadow of an unspeakable woe was ever over Him. Yet for the joy that was set before Him, He endured the cross and despised the shame. He endured all this that sinful man might be saved, that he might be elevated and ennobled and have a place with Him upon His throne.[35]

Christ is the originator of divine truth. He knew the height and depth, length and breadth and fullness of the compassion of divine love, as no mortal man can know it. He knows the blessedness that sinners are refusing when they reject divine light, the horrors that will come upon the soul that refuses the truth of Heaven. . . . Christ alone knows what means the exceeding weight of glory which those who rebel against God refuse to receive. . . .

Men are contaminated with sin, and they cannot have an adequate conception of the heinous character of the evil which they cherish. Because of sin the Majesty of heaven was stricken, smitten of God, and afflicted. Voluntarily our divine Substitute bared His soul to the sword of justice, that we might not perish but have everlasting life. Said Christ: "I lay down my life, that I might take it again. No man taketh it from me, but I lay it down of myself" (John 10:17, 18). . . . No man of earth nor angel of heaven could have paid the penalty of sin. Jesus was the only one who could save rebellious man.[36]

The joy that was set before Jesus was that of seeing souls redeemed by the sacrifice of His glory, His honor, His riches, and His own life. The salvation of man was His joy. When all the redeemed shall be gathered into the kingdom of God, He will see of the travail of His soul and be satisfied.[37]

THE RESULTS OF CHRIST'S TRAVAIL

He shall see of the travail of his soul, and shall be satisfied: by his knowledge shall my righteous servant justify many; for he shall bear their iniquities. Isa. 53:11.

What sustained the Son of God during His life of toil and sacrifice? He saw the results of the travail of His soul, and was satisfied. Looking into eternity, He beheld the happiness of those who through His humiliation had received pardon and everlasting life. His ear caught the shout of the redeemed. He heard the ransomed ones singing the song of Moses and the Lamb.[38]

"God so loved the world, that he gave his only begotten Son, that whosoever believeth in him should not perish, but have everlasting life." During every moment of Christ's life in our world, God was repeating His gift. Christ, the sinless One, was making an infinite sacrifice for sinners, that they might be saved. He came as a man of sorrows and acquainted with grief, and those for whom He came looked upon Him as stricken, smitten of God, and afflicted. The cup of suffering was placed in His hand, as if He were the guilty one, and He drained it to the dregs. He bore the sin of the world to the bitter end. . . . No line can fathom, no measurement compute, the love revealed by the cross of Calvary. . . .

In every pang of anguish endured we behold the throes of paternal love. The Father Himself travailed in the greatness of His almighty love in behalf of a world perishing in sin. By the sacrifice that has been made, the gift of eternal life has been placed within the reach of every son and daughter of Adam.[39]

Christ's redeemed ones are His jewels, His precious and peculiar treasure. "They shall be as the stones of a crown"—"the riches of the glory of his inheritance in the saints" (Zech. 9:16; Eph. 1:18). In them "he shall see of the travail of his soul, and shall be satisfied." Christ looks upon His people in their purity and perfection as the reward of all His sufferings, His humiliation, and His love, and the supplement of His glory—Christ the great center, from whom radiates all glory.[40]

ETERNITY BEFORE US

They go from strength to strength, every one of them in Zion appeareth before God. Ps. 84:7.

All heaven has been looking with intense interest upon those who claim to be God's commandment-keeping people. Here are the people who ought to be able to claim all the rich promises of God, who ought to be going on from glory to glory and from strength to strength, who ought to be in a position to reflect glory to God in the works that they do. . . .

We have received the rich blessing of God, but we must not stop here. We are to catch more and more the divine rays of light from heaven. We are to stand just where we can receive the light and reflect it, in its glory, upon the pathway of others. . . .

We need to drink deeper and deeper of the fountain of life. . . . You may have a living testimony to bear: "Hear what the Lord has done for my soul." The Lord is ready to impart still greater blessings. He permitted all His goodness to pass before Moses. He proclaimed His character to him as a God full of mercy—long-suffering and gracious, forgiving iniquity, transgression, and sin. Moses was to represent this character to the people of Israel, and we are to do the same. We are to go forth to proclaim the goodness of God and to make plain His real character before the people. We are to reflect His glory. . . . Let us declare the character of God to the people as Moses did to Israel, both in spirit and life. We are to catch the light of His countenance, full of compassion and love, and reflect it to perishing souls.

I beseech you to keep reaching out after God, to keep drinking of the fountain of living water. You may be as a tree planted by the rivers of waters, whose leaf does not wither. You may be full of moisture, and may be able to refresh others, and to give them grace and comfort. I love Jesus now, and I want to know more and more of Him. I have only begun to know Him, but there is an eternity before us in which there will be revealings of His glory, and we shall become better and better acquainted with our divine Lord.[41]

HOME AT LAST!

Father, I will that they also, whom thou hast given me, be with me where I am. John 17:24.

The love of God is without measure, without comparison. It is infinite. . . . When we contemplate the dignity and glory of Christ we see how great was that love that prompted the sacrifice made upon the cross of Calvary for the redemption of a lost world. This theme will fill the saints with wonder and amazement through eternal ages, and why should we not meditate upon it here in this world? . . .

O the mystery of godliness—God manifest in the flesh! This mystery increases as we try to comprehend it. It is incomprehensible, and yet human beings will allow worldly, earthly things to intercept the faint view it is possible for mortals to have of Jesus and His matchless love. . . . How can we be enthusiastic over earthly, common things and not be stirred with this picture—the cross of Calvary, the love that is revealed in the death of God's dear Son . . . ?

All this humiliation and anguish were endured to bring back the wanderers, guilty and thankless, to the Father's house. O the home of the blest—I cannot afford to lose it! I shall, if saved in the kingdom of God, be constantly discerning new depths in the plan of salvation. All the redeemed saints will see and appreciate as never before the love of the Father and the Son, and songs of praise will burst forth from immortal tongues. He loved us, He gave His life for us. With glorified bodies, with enlarged capacities, with hearts made pure, with lips undefiled, we shall sing the riches of redeeming love. There will be no suffering ones in heaven, no skeptics whom we must labor to convince of the reality of eternal things, no prejudices to uproot, but all will be susceptible to that love which passeth knowledge. Rest, thank God, there is a rest for the people of God, where Jesus will lead the redeemed into green pastures, by the streams of living waters which make glad the city of our God. Then the prayer of Jesus to His Father will be answered: "I will that they also, whom thou hast given me, be with me where I am."[42]

KEY TO ABBREVIATIONS

AA	*Acts of the Apostles, The*	MM	*Medical Ministry*
1 BC	Ellen G. White Comments in *SDA Bible Commentary,* vol. 1 (2 BC, etc. for vols. 2-7)	MS	Ellen G. White Manuscript
		PP	*Patriarchs and Prophets*
		RH	*The Advent Review and Sabbath Herald*
BE	*Bible Echo*		
CM	*Colporteur Ministry*	1 SM	*Selected Messages,* Book 1
COL	*Christ's Object Lessons*	SR	*Story of Redemption, The*
CT	*Counsels to Parents, Teachers, and Students*	ST	*Signs of the Times*
		1T	*Testimonies for the Church,* vol. 1 (2 T, etc. for vols. 2-9)
DA	*Desire of Ages, The*		
GC	*Great Controversy, The*	YI	*Youth's Instructor*
Letter	Ellen G. White Letter		
MB	*Thoughts From the Mount of Blessings*		

SOURCE REFERENCES

JANUARY

1. RH March 15, 1892
2. MB 34, 35
3. RH March 15, 1892
4. RH Sept 25, 1883
5. *Ibid.*
6. YI March 22, 1900
7. RH June 4, 1889
8. *Ibid.*
9. *Ibid.*
10. PP 34
11. 1 SM 247, 248
12. Letter 119, 1895
13. SR 20, 21
14. RH Feb. 24, 1874
15. BE July 24, 1899
16. RH Feb. 24, 1874
17. 1 BC 1083
18. RH March 27, 1888
19. GC 492, 493
20. DA 21, 22
21. ST April 28, 1890
22. RH July 18, 1882
23. MS 31, 1911
24. ST Feb. 20, 1893
25. *Ibid.*
26. ST Feb. 13, 1893
27. *Ibid.*
28. YI July 29, 1897
29. Letter 11, 1892
30. YI March 1, 1900
31. ST April 1, 1875
32. RH Nov. 11, 1890
33. Letter 116, 1896
34. 1T 291
35. PP 411, 412
36. PP 413
37. 7 BC 904
38. 7 BC 924
39. 5 BC 1131
40. 7 BC 925
41. YI Nov. 21, 1895
42. YI May 25, 1909
43. YI Sept. 8, 1898
44. YI Dec. 5, 1895
45. YI Sept. 8, 1898
46. ST July 30, 1896
47. 5 BC 1118, 1119
48. ST July 30, 1896
49. 5 BC 1117, 1118
50. RH Jan. 21, 1873
51. 5 BC 1079
52. Letter 159, 1903
53. RH June 10, 1890
54. 5 BC 1082
55. RH Feb. 5, 1895
56. 7 BC 930
57. RH Nov. 8, 1887
58. YI Feb. 11, 1897
59. YI Jan. 21, 1897
60. RH May 11, 1897

FEBRUARY

1. RH Jan. 7, 1890
2. MS 77, 1899
3. RH Jan. 7, 1890
4. MS 22, 1898
5. RH March 30, 1897
6. Letter 96, 1895
7. MS 55, 1895
8. RH May 17, 1898
9. MS 35, 1895
10. MS 22, 1898
11. MM 19, 20
12. Letter 1a, 1894
13. Letter 202, 1901
14. Letter 119, 1893
15. MS 18, 1898
16. Letter 1a, 1894
17. RH April 17, 1888
18. RH May 18, 1897
19. Letter 20, 1895
20. Letter 46, 1898
21. Letter 117, 1903

22 MS 24, 1890
23 Letter 36, 1892
24 Letter 71, 1893
25 MS 8, 1900
26 MS 41, 1896
27 YI Aug. 22, 1895
28 YI April 26, 1894
29 YI Sept. 5, 1895
30 YI Sept. 27, 1894
31 RH Oct. 7, 1890
32 Letter 12a, 1893
33 MS 60, 1894
34 6 BC 1088
35 5 BC 1102, 1103
36 RH Aug. 2, 1881

MARCH
1 RH Dec. 20, 1892
2 MS 18, 1898
3 5 BC 1127, 1128
4 YI Dec. 16, 1897
5 YI Oct. 17, 1895
6 MS 153, 1898
7 5 BC 1113
8 1 SM 301-303
9 6 BC 1053
10 6 BC 1053, 1054
11 MS 128, 1897
12 RH March 17, 1903
13 ST Feb. 14, 1900
14 6 BC 1077, 1078
15 8T 177-179
16 YI Jan. 16, 1896
17 Letter 13, 1894
18 RH June 9, 1896
19 Letter 100, 1895
20 AA 552, 553
21 Letter 119, 1893
22 MS 62, 1902
23 RH Nov. 11, 1890
24 YI Sept. 5, 1895
25 YI Oct. 10, 1895
26 RH Sept. 22, 1891
27 Letter 109, 1901
28 RH Sept. 23, 1884
29 YI Jan. 10, 1895
30 Letter 83, 1898
31 Letter 66, 1898
32 YI Sept. 13, 1894
33 YI June 21, 1894
34 RH Oct. 25, 1881
35 RH May 5, 1891

36 Ibid.
37 RH Sept. 22, 1891
38 Letter 74, 1897
39 Letter 4, 1885
40 7 BC 943
41 RH March 10, 1891

APRIL
1 YI Sept. 16, 1897
2 YI July 29, 1897
3 RH March 5, 1889
4 1 SM 259, 260
5 COL 386
6 YI Aug. 16, 1894
7 RH March 2, 1886
8 YI July 18, 1901
9 PP 366, 367
10 1 SM 258, 259
11 RH July 19, 1892
12 RH May 24, 1892
13 CT 37
14 RH Nov. 17, 1885
15 YI Nov. 11, 1897
16 YI March 12, 1896
17 4 BC 1178
18 MS 17, 1893
19 YI Dec. 6, 1894
20 YI June 21, 1894
21 1 SM 389-392
22 YI Sept. 16, 1897
23 RH July 1, 1884
24 RH Feb. 14, 1888
25 Ibid.
26 Letter 102, 1901
27 Letter 5, 1889
28 RH March 6, 1888
29 Letter 119, 1895
30 Letter 102, 1899
31 Letter 1f, 1890
32 Letter 135, 1897
33 RH May 5, 1891
34 Ibid.
35 MS 20, 1897
36 YI Nov. 21, 1883
37 YI May 7, 1884
38 RH May 11, 1897
39 Ibid.
40 Ibid.
41 RH April 17, 1888
42 RH March 6, 1888
43 Letter 150, 1897
44 YI Sept. 19, 1895

MAY
1 MS 66, 1896
2 Letter 25, 1903
3 Letter 178, 1899
4 MS 148, 1902
5 ST Sept. 3, 1902
6 Ibid.
7 ST March 23, 1888
8 MS 62, 1896
9 ST Sept. 3, 1902
10 YI April 21, 1886
11 Letter 17, 1878
12 MS 24, 1892
13 Letter 124, 1893
14 YI July 14, 1898
15 COL 338
16 RH Feb. 24, 1891
17 RH May 19, 1891
18 RH March 27, 1888
19 MS 174, 1897
20 RH March 15, 1892
21 ST Aug. 11, 1909
22 MS 174, 1897
23 YI March 24, 1898
24 RH Feb. 14, 1888
25 MS 56, 1886
26 MS 62, 1896
27 MS 20, 1886
28 MS 39, 1901
29 RH Dec. 3, 1889
30 RH May 19, 1891
31 RH May 6, 1884
32 Ibid.
33 5 T 394, 395
34 RH June 5, 1888
35 RH Nov. 14, 1882
36 RH Jan. 6, 1885
37 YI Oct. 18, 1894
38 YI Sept. 7, 1893

JUNE
1 YI Dec. 22, 1892
2 YI Oct. 24, 1895
3 YI Oct. 31, 1895
4 Ibid.
5 YI Sept. 1, 1886
6 YI Feb. 17, 1898
7 RH May 24, 1892
8 RH Aug. 4, 1891
9 ST June 12, 1901
10 RH Feb. 23, 1892
11 7 BC 908

373

12 RH Aug. 26, 1890
13 *Ibid.*
14 RH Nov. 29, 1887
15 7 BC 952
16 RH Jan. 7, 1890
17 *Ibid.*
18 RH Nov. 29, 1881
19 Letter 119, 1896
20 RH Oct. 26, 1897
21 RH March 11, 1890
22 Letter 110, 1893
23 RH Sept. 4, 1883
24 Letter 406, 1906
25 RH Dec. 20, 1881
26 RH Feb. 25, 1896
27 RH Sept. 4, 1900
28 RH Aug. 18, 1885
29 MS 24, 1890
30 RH Aug. 8, 1893
31 RH Nov. 16, 1886
32 RH Feb. 24, 1891
33 RH Aug. 15, 1893
34 *Ibid.*
35 RH May 8, 1888
36 RH April 10, 1888
37 RH June 3, 1884
38 RH March 12, 1895
39 YI Sept. 12, 1901
40 Letter 30, 1888
41 RH June 5, 1888

JULY

1 Letter 98, 1909
2 Letter 12, 1890
3 Letter 98, 1909
4 RH Sept. 25, 1883
5 YI Sept. 14, 1893
6 RH March 4, 1890
7 *Ibid.*
8 RH Sept. 25, 1883
9 RH April 17, 1888
10 YI May 7, 1884
11 MS 62, 1893
12 MS 6, 1878
13 Letter 25, 1903
14 RH March 2, 1886
15 ST Feb. 21, 1911
16 RH March 2, 1886
17 ST Feb. 21, 1911
18 Letter 171, 1897
19 MS 42, 1901
20 Letter 291, 1903

21 MS 70, 1894
22 YI Aug. 3, 1899
23 Letter 47, 1898
24 Letter 25, 1903
25 MS 51a, 1893
26 YI Aug. 31, 1887
27 RH March 10, 1891
28 COL 36
29 RH Nov. 8, 1892
30 *Ibid.*
31 RH Jan. 7, 1890
32 *Ibid.*
33 *Ibid.*
34 MS 31, 1890
35 6T 392
36 2 SM 87
37 Letter 46, 1898
38 Letter 25, 1903
39 Letter 268, 1906
40 RH Feb. 6, 1900
41 Letter 147, 1896
42 RH Oct. 11, 1887
43 Letter 128, 1895
44 5 BC 1124
45 Letter 84, 1895
46 Letter 47, 1894
47 Letter 84, 1895
49 Letter 53, 1895

AUGUST

1 MS 96, 1900
2 RH Supplement, June 21, 1898
3 RH April 18, 1912
4 RH Supplement, June 21, 1898
5 *Ibid.*
6 RH Jan. 24, 1888
7 *Ibid.*
8 *Ibid.*
9 RH Jan. 14, 1890
10 RH Feb. 3, 1885
11 Letter 105, 1898
12 Letter 70, 1897
13 RH June 9, 1896
14 RH Feb. 11, 1890
15 Undated MS 23
16 ST June 16, 1890
17 Letter 97, 1895
18 MS 56, 1893
19 RH Feb. 3, 1885
20 YI Jan.18, 1894

21 YI May 26, 1898
22 RH Sept. 16, 1890
23 Letter 22, 1892
24 Letter 120, 1893
25 YI Oct. 31, 1895
26 YI Sept. 26, 1895
27 YI Jan. 18, 1894
28 YI June 7, 1894
29 RH Dec. 16, 1890
30 *Ibid.*
31 RH Dec. 16, 1890
32 RH Oct. 11, 1881
33 Letter 99, 1896
34 YI July 5, 1894
35 RH June 29, 1897
36 5T 634
37 RH June 29, 1897
38 YI July 8, 1897
39 RH March 4, 1890
40 7 BC 922
41 7 BC 949
42 RH March 4, 1890
43 *Ibid.*
44 YI June 7, 1894
45 MS 70 1894
46 Letter 6, 1894

SEPTEMBER

1 RH Dec. 3, 1889
2 YI Sept. 19, 1895
3 RH Nov. 8, 1887
4 RH Feb. 5, 1895
5 RH May 8, 1888
6 RH March 27, 1888
7 RH July 24, 1888
8 *Ibid.*
9 RH Jan. 24, 1888
10 RH May 19, 1885
11 DA 362, 363
12 RH Feb. 9, 1897
13 Letter 134, 1899
14 MS 146, 1902
15 RH April 5, 1887
16 RH Jan. 14, 1890
17 YI Jan. 30, 1896
18 RH Feb. 5, 1895
19 MS 62, 1896
20 RH Dec. 20, 1881
21 RH Oct. 11, 1881
22 Letter 126, 1895
23 RH Feb. 5, 1895
24 Letter 13, 1894

[25] RH July 24, 1883
[26] MS 56, 1902
[27] RH Feb. 9, 1897
[28] *Ibid.*
[29] YI Nov. 3, 1898
[30] Letter 138, 1897
[31] RH Feb. 11, 1890
[32] Letter 116, 1896
[33] Letter 82, 1895
[34] YI Sept. 26, 1895
[35] YI Sept. 19, 1895
[36] YI Sept. 26, 1895
[37] Letter 113, 1898
[38] Letter 97, 1895
[39] RH May 19, 1891
[40] *Ibid.*

OCTOBER
[1] RH July 22, 1884
[2] *Ibid.*
[3] Letter 291, 1903
[4] RH Aug. 6, 1889
[5] COL 155
[6] Letter 28, 1892
[7] Letter 133, 1894
[8] Letter 99, 1896
[9] YI Dec. 20, 1894
[10] RH Aug. 2, 1881
[11] YI Aug. 16, 1894
[12] Letter 110, 1896
[13] Letter 406, 1906
[14] Letter 121, 1897
[15] MS 48, 1893
[16] MS 24, 1890
[17] Letter 66, 1898
[18] RH Sept. 14, 1886
[19] RH Jan. 24, 1888
[20] RH Oct. 11, 1887
[21] MS 96, 1900
[22] Letter 82, 1895
[23] YI June 10, 1897
[24] Letter 276, 1904
[25] RH Nov. 17, 1885
[26] Letter 17, 1886
[27] RH July 12, 1892
[28] *Ibid.*
[29] RH July 19, 1892
[30] *Ibid.*
[31] RH Dec. 12, 1882

[32] MS 165, 1899
[33] Letter 1b, 1873
[34] Letter 138, 1897
[35] Letter 199, 1899
[36] Letter 60, 1894
[37] RH Oct. 7, 1890
[38] *Ibid.*
[39] *Ibid.*
[40] RH Jan. 8, 1884
[41] *Ibid.*
[42] Letter 71, 1893
[43] RH Feb. 28, 1888

NOVEMBER
[1] RH Feb. 28, 1882
[2] YI Nov. 5, 1896
[3] RH Sept. 9, 1884
[4] MS 6, 1878
[5] RH April 19, 1887
[6] RH Oct. 18, 1881
[7] *Ibid.*
[8] RH March 6, 1888
[9] RH May 18, 1886
[10] Letter 82, 1895
[11] YI Oct. 20, 1886
[12] RH Aug. 23, 1881
[13] RH Aug. 2, 1881
[14] MS 45, 1890
[15] YI Dec. 31, 1896
[16] Letter 86a, 1893
[17] RH May 1, 1888
[18] MS 6, 1878
[19] YI Jan. 28, 1897
[20] RH April 12, 1887
[21] MS 13, 1895
[22] RH Supplement June 21, 1898
[23] Letter 152, 1896
[24] RH May 1, 1888
[25] Letter 171, 1897
[26] YI April 14, 1898
[27] Letter 30, 1888
[28] 5 BC 1112
[29] RH July 13, 1886
[30] RH April 20, 1886
[31] *Ibid.*
[32] RH July 14, 1891
[33] Letter 84, 1895
[34] 6T 86

[35] CM 18
[36] Letter 83, 1895
[37] RH Sept. 11, 1888
[38] MS 153, 1898

DECEMBER
[1] Letter 147, 1896
[2] Letter 138, 1897
[3] Letter 84, 1895
[4] MS 62, 1902
[5] Letter 110, 1893
[6] Letter 60, 1893
[7] MS 37, 1890
[8] RH July 31, 1888
[9] *Ibid.*
[10] MS 62, 1896
[11] YI Jan. 16, 1896
[12] YI Jan. 30, 1896
[13] Letter 36, 1894
[14] Letter 5, 1903
[15] RH Nov. 29, 1881
[16] MS 7a, 1896
[17] RH March 14, 1912
[18] RH Sept. 17, 1901
[19] Letter 137, 1896
[20] MS 39, 1893
[21] RH Oct. 25, 1881
[22] RH March 27, 1888
[23] MS 56, 1886
[24] ST March 23, 1888
[25] RH Oct. 11, 1887
[26] 6 BC 1092
[27] 4 BC 1143
[28] Letter 121, 1897
[29] MS 28, 1901
[30] YI Aug. 20, 1896
[31] ST March 25, 1897
[32] ST Feb. 13, 1893
[33] DA 764
[34] RH March 9, 1886
[35] RH Dec. 20, 1892
[36] *Ibid.*
[37] 2T 686
[38] AA 601
[39] Letter 100, 1911
[40] RH Oct. 22, 1908
[41] RH Feb. 26, 1889
[42] Letter 27, 1890

SCRIPTURE INDEX

The following Scripture Index, while not exhaustive, includes not only the scriptures quoted by the author but many alluded to or related to the author's comments. The daily memory texts are printed in italic.

378